OXFORD REFERENCE

AN A–Z OF SAILING TERMS

Ian Dear is the author of a number of books about the history of yachting, including *America's Cup* (1980), *Fastnet* (1981), *The Champagne Mumm Book of Ocean Racing* (1985), *The Royal Yacht Squadron* (1985), and *The Great Days of Yachting* (1988).

Peter Kemp is the editor of *The Oxford Companion to Ships and the Sea*. A former Head of Naval Historical Branch, Ministry of Defence, he has published widely on naval, military, and yachting subjects.

AN
A–Z
OF
SAILING
TERMS

Edited by

IAN DEAR *and* **PETER KEMP**

Oxford   New York

OXFORD UNIVERSITY PRESS

Oxford University Press, Walton Street, Oxford OX2 6DP

Oxford New York Toronto
Delhi Bombay Calcutta Madras Karachi
Kuala Lumpur Singapore Hong Kong Tokyo
Nairobi Dar es Salaam Cape Town
Melbourne Auckland Madrid

and associated companies in
Berlin Ibadan

Oxford is a trade mark of Oxford University Press

The Oxford Companion to Ships and the Sea
© *Oxford University Press and P. K. Kemp 1976*
This compilation © *Ian Dear 1987*

First published 1987 as The Pocket Oxford Guide to
Sailing Terms
Reissued as An A–Z of Sailing Terms *1992*

British Library Cataloguing in Publication Data

Data available

Library of Congress Cataloging in Publication Data
Pocket Oxford guide to sailing terms.
An A–Z of sailing terms / edited by Ian Dear and Peter Kemp.
p. cm.
Reprint. Originally published as: The Pocket Oxford guide to
sailing terms. 1987.
Compiled from The Oxford companion to ships & the sea.
1. Sailing—Dictionaries. 2. Seamanship—Dictionaries. I. Dear,
Ian. II. Kemp, Peter Kemp. III. Oxford companion to ships & the
sea. IV. Title.
797.1'24'03—dc20 GV811.P63 1987 91-30595
ISBN 0-19-286147-6

3 5 7 9 10 8 6 4 2

Printed in Great Britain by
Biddles Ltd
Guildford and King's Lynn

Publishers Note

* Words are asterisked in the text when they or their close derivatives are the subject of a separate article which it may help the reader to refer to at that point. Cross-references to major topics of relevance are given in small capitals at the foot of many articles.

A

aback, used of the sails of a square-rigged ship when the *yards are trimmed to bring the wind to bear on their forward side. Sails are laid aback when this is done purposely to stop a ship's way through the water or to assist her in *tacking; they are taken aback when the ship is inadvertently brought to by an unexpected change of wind or by lack of attention by the helmsman.

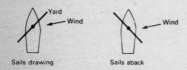

Sails drawing   Sails aback

abaft, towards the *stern of a ship, relative to some other object or position. Abaft the *beam, any *bearing or directions between the beam of a ship and her stern. See also AFT; but 'abaft' is always relative, e.g. abaft the mainmast (opposite to before); 'aft' is general (opposite to forward).

abeam, on a *bearing or direction at right angles to the fore-and-aft line of a ship. See also ABREAST.

aboard, in or on board a ship. The word is also widely used in other maritime meanings; thus for one ship to fall aboard another is for her to fall foul of another.

about, across the wind in relation to the *bow of a sailing vessel. Thus, when a ship *tacks across the wind to bring it from one side of the ship to the other, she is said to go about. **'Ready about'**, the order given in a sailing ship to tack across the wind, the

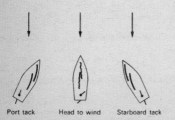

Port tack   Head to wind   Starboard tack

Three stages in going about

actual moment of the *helm being put down being signified by the order **'About ship'**. In yachts and smaller craft, this order is usually 'Lee-oh', indicating that the helm is being put down to leeward.

above-board, above the deck and therefore open and visible, which gave rise to the term used to denote open and fair dealing.

abox, an old sailing ship expression of the days of masts and *yards. To lay the head-yards abox in a square-rigged sailing vessel was to lay them *square to the foremast in order to *heave-to. This brought the ship more under command if it was subsequently required to *wear or to *stay the vessel. But to *brace abox is to brace the head-yards flat *aback to the wind, not square to the mast, in order to ensure that the wind acts on the sails so that the bows of the ship *cast the required way.

A-bracket, the triangular bracket, often also known as a sole-piece or sole-bracket, which extends from the hull of a steam or motor vessel to give support to the *propeller shafts where they extend beyond the hull.

abreast, the position of a ship in relation to another or to a recognizable mark or place, being directly opposite to the ship, mark, or place. Thus when a vessel is abreast, say, a *lightship, then the lightship is *abeam of her.

accommodation, an older term for a *cabin when fitted for the use of passengers. It is also the word used when referring to steps in a ship, and thus a flight of steps leading from deck to deck in a ship for convenience of access and egress is properly known as an accommodation ladder.

a-cockbill, orig. **a-cockbell,** a term used of an anchor when it hangs by its ring at the *cathead or from the *hawsehole ready for letting go. In the case of stockless anchors which are let go from the hawsehole, a few feet of cable are *veered so that the *shank hangs clear vertically.

Admiral's Cup, a perpetual challenge award established in 1957 by the Royal Ocean Racing Club, London, for biennial international team racing. The 'admiral' in the title was Sir Myles Wyatt, who in 1957 was 'admiral' of the Royal Ocean Racing Club.

adrift, floating at random, as of a boat or ship broken away from her moorings and at the mercy of wind and waves.

advantage, the term used to describe the method of *reeving a *tackle in order to gain the maximum increase in power. The power increase in a tackle is equal, if friction is disregarded, to the number of parts of the *fall at the moving block, and a tackle is rove to advantage when the hauling part of the fall leads from the moving block. Where a tackle is rigged so that the hauling part leads from the standing block, the power gained is less and the tackle is said to be rove to disadvantage. See also PURCHASE.

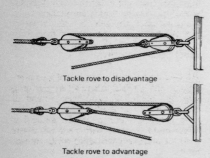

Tackle rove to disadvantage

Tackle rove to advantage

aerodynamics, a branch of the science of pneumatics which deals with air and other gases in motion and with their mechanical effects. In its maritime connection aerodynamics can be used to explain how a wind produces forward motion in a sailing vessel even though it blows from before the vessel's beam.

When a wind strikes a surface, its force can be resolved into two components, one acting at right angles to the surface and the other along the surface. If this surface is the sail of a boat, the component blowing along the sail can be disregarded, as it is providing no force on the sail, but the component at right angles to the sail does exert a force. That component can now similarly be resolved into two more components, not in relation to the angle of the sail but to the

fore and aft line of the boat. The larger of these two components exerts a force which tries to blow the boat directly to *leeward, and the smaller of them, blowing along the fore and aft line, is all that is left of the wind to drive the boat forward. It is at this point that the *keel of the boat, or the *centreboard in the case of *dinghies, comes into play. It provides a lateral grip on the water which offers considerable resistance to the larger component and very little resistance to the smaller, so that the boat moves forward and makes only a small amount of leeway.

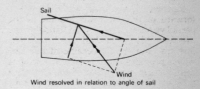

Wind resolved in relation to angle of sail

Part of wind resolved in relation to fore and aft line

Components of the wind

There is another element which gives forward movement to a sailing boat when the wind acts on her sail. In the resolution of forces described above, the sail has been considered as a flat surface on which the wind strikes at an angle. In fact a sail has a parabolic curve fore and aft, of which the steepest part of the curve is at the *luff. When an airstream meets a curve at an acute angle it creates a partial vacuum as it flows over the steepest part of the curve, and in a sailing boat this partial vacuum acts to pull her forward and reinforce the small component of the wind that is driving her forward.

The greater the speed of the airflow over the steepest part of the curve, the more effective the partial vacuum, and so modern sail design increases the speed of the airflow by creating a slot, or 'funnel', along the luff of the mainsail by setting a headsail forward of the mainsail. In cases where the *clew of the headsail overlaps the luff of the mainsail the wind is funnelled with even greater speed over the steepest part of the curve and so increases even more the partial vacuum.

When a sailing vessel is *close-hauled, with the wind blowing over the bow, she can thus move forward against the direction of the wind, first because of the small component of the wind which gives her forward motion, secondly because of the partial vacuum caused by the wind flowing over the curve at her luff which pulls her forward, and thirdly because of her keel which provides effective lateral resistance to the larger component of the wind and prevents her being blown down to leeward at right angles to her desired course.

afloat, the condition of a vessel when she is wholly supported by the water and clear of the ground. The word is also often used in a more general sense to mean at sea, or of life at sea.

aft, at or towards the stern or after part of a ship, as a word either of position or motion.

afterbody, that part of a ship's hull which lies *aft of the midship section. It embraces the whole of the after half of the hull from upper deck to *keel, and on the designed shape of the afterbody depends the *run of the ship.

afterguard, a term often used in yachting to denote the owner and his guests; in yacht racing, the helmsman and his advisers.

afterturn, the twist given to *rope, when the *strands are laid up to form it, in the opposite direction to the twist of the strands. See also FORETURN.

aground, of a ship, resting on the bottom. When put there purposely, a ship takes the ground, when by accident, she runs aground, or is *stranded.

ahead, a word (opposite to *astern) used in two senses at sea. Referring to direction, it means any distance directly in front of a ship on her current heading; referring to movement, it means the passage of a ship through the water in the direction in which her bows are pointing.

'ahoy!', the normal hail to a ship or boat to attract attention.

a-hull, or **lying a-hull,** the condition of a ship drifting under *bare poles with her *helm *a-lee, or hove-to (see HEAVE-TO) at sea under stress of weather. The term is also frequently applied to a ship which has been abandoned at sea.

airflow, see AERODYNAMICS.

Aldis lamp, a hand-held electric lamp fitted with a finger-operated mirror used for the sending of signals at sea.

a-lee, the position of the *helm when it has been pushed down to *leeward in order to tack a sailing vessel or to bring her bows up into the wind. **'Helm's a-lee'**, the response of the helmsman after putting the helm down on the order to *tack. When a vessel *heaves-to under storm canvas in rough weather, the helm is lashed a-lee so that the bows are continuously forced up towards the wind, in which position the vessel lies more easily.

all-a-taunt-o, the condition of a square-rigged sailing vessel where all the running rigging is hauled taut and *belayed and all her *yards are crossed on the masts, i.e. have not been sent down. In general it refers more to ships with very tall masts than to more rugged ships with shorter masts.

all in the wind, an expression used to describe the situation when a sailing vessel, while going about, is head to wind and all her sails are shivering.

all standing. A ship is said to be brought up all standing when she lets go her anchor with too much way on and so is brought suddenly to a stop as the anchor bites.

aloft, above, overhead, also anywhere about the upper *yards, *masts, and rigging of ships. **'Away aloft'**, the command for *topmen to take up their stations on the masts and yards. **'Gone aloft'**, a sailor's phrase for a seaman who has died.

alow, on or near the deck of a ship, the opposite of *aloft.

alternating light, a navigational light displayed by a *lighthouse, *lightship, or lighted *buoy in which two colours are shown alternately, with or without a period of darkness separating them. See CHARACTERISTICS.

altitude, from the Latin *altitudo*, height, the angle between the centre of a celestial body and the rational *horizon as measured from the centre of the earth. It is one of the three sides of the astronomical triangle, through the solution of which a position line can be plotted on a chart. In the case of altitudes of stars, most of which are infinitely distant, the observer's horizon can be accepted as the rational horizon without any loss of accuracy, but in an observation for navigational purposes of the sun or moon, which are both much closer to the earth, a correction, known as *semi-diameter, must be applied to the observed altitude to allow for the distance between the centre of the sun or moon and their lower limb, which is the point of observation, and for the distance between the observer's position on the earth's surface and the centre of the earth, which is the point from which the true altitude must be measured for astronomical calculations. See NAVIGATION, Celestial, and for illus. ZENITH DISTANCE.

America's **Cup,** a trophy, known at the time as the 'hundred guinea cup', originally presented by the Royal Yacht Squadron in 1851 for a yacht race round the Isle of Wight and won by the 170-ton *schooner *America* representing the New York Yacht Club against a competing British fleet of fifteen yachts. It was lodged in the keeping of the New York Yacht Club until won by *Australia II*, representing the Royal Perth Yacht Club, in 1983 by 4–3. The first challenge for the Cup was made in 1870 and there have been 27 in total.

Until the Second World War the matches were sailed between racing yachts of the largest class, including the *J-class. But between 1958 and 1987 it was mutually agreed to race in the International 12-m (39-ft) class (see International Metre Class Yacht), with the match being the best of seven races, and these took place about every four years. However, after 1987 this consensus broke down when a New

America's Cup—challenging yachts, owners, and defenders

1870	*Cambria*, sch., James Ashbury	*Magic*, sch.
1871	*Livonia*, sch., James Ashbury	*Columbia* and *Sappho*, schs.
1876	*Countess of Dufferin*, sch.	
	Royal Canadian Y.C. syndicate	*Madeleine*, sch.
1881	*Atalanta*, sl., Alex Cuthbert	*Mischief*, cut.
1885	*Genesta*, cut., Sir Richard Sutton	*Puritan*, cut.
1886	*Galatea*, cut., Lt. William Henn	*Mayflower*, cut.
1887	*Thistle*, cut., James Bell	*Volunteer*, cut.
1893	*Valkyrie II*, cut., Earl of Dunraven	*Vigilant*, cut.
1895	*Valkyrie III*, cut., Earl of Dunraven	*Defender*, cut.
1899	*Shamrock I*, cut., Sir Thomas Lipton	*Columbia*, cut.
1901	*Shamrock II*, cut., Sir Thomas Lipton	*Columbia*, cut.
1903	*Shamrock III*, cut., Sir Thomas Lipton	*Reliance*, cut.
1920	*Shamrock IV*, cut., Sir Thomas Lipton	*Resolute*, cut.
1930	*Shamrock V*, sl., Sir Thomas Lipton	*Enterprise*, cut.
1934	*Endeavour I*, sl., T.O.M. Sopwith	*Rainbow*, sl.
1937	*Endeavour II*, sl., T.O.M. Sopwith	*Ranger*, sl.
1958	*Sceptre*, 12-m, U.K. syndicate	*Columbia*, 12-m
1962	*Gretel*, 12-m, Australian syndicate	*Weatherly*, 12-m
1964	*Sovereign*, 12-m, U.K. syndicate	*Constellation*, 12-m
1967	*Dame Pattie*, 12-m, Australian syndicate	*Intrepid*, 12-m
1970	*Gretel II*, 12-m, Australian syndicate	*Intrepid*, 12-m
1974	*Southern Cross*, 12-m Australian syndicate	*Courageous*, 12-m
1977	*Australia*, 12-m Australian syndicate	*Courageous*, 12-m
1980	*Australia*, 12-m Australian syndicate	*Freedom*, 12-m
1983	*Australia II*, 12-m Australian syndicate	*Liberty*, 12-m
1987	*Stars and Stripes '87*, 12-m US syndicate	*Kookaburra IV*, 12-m
1988	*New Zealand*, N.Z. syndicate	*Stars and Stripes*, cat.

sch. = schooner   cut. = cutter   sl. = sloop   12-m = International 12-metre class
cat. = catamaran

Zealand syndicate challenged, as it was entitled to do under the original rules governing the Cup, in a radically designed monohull built to the maximum waterline length of 90 ft. The defending club answered the New Zealand challenge by being represented by a syndicate which built a *catamaran. This won the best-of-three match 2–0 with great ease but the New Zealand syndicate then challenged the legality of using a catamaran. The New York Supreme Court found in favour of the New Zealand syndicate but this was subsequently overturned and the US syndicate kept the Cup. While this legal wrangling was going on it was agreed in future to race in a new 75-ft class *sloop which is 57 ft on the waterline and sailed by a crew of 17. It is this new class which is being used in the 28th challenge taking place in San Diego at the time this book is published.

amidships, in the middle of the ship, whether longitudinally or laterally. It is more usually known as a *helm order, normally shortened to **midships**, to centre the helm in the line of the keel.

amplitude, the angle between the point at which the sun rises and sets and the true east and west points of the horizon.

anchor, a large and heavy instrument designed to hold a ship in any desired locality and prevent her from drifting at the mercy of wind, tide, or current. It is attached to the ship by a *cable, and digs itself into the sea bed to hold the ship fast.

A basic anchor, known as the fisherman's anchor, with two *flukes and the *stock at right-angles, remained the standard pattern of anchor for centuries, but in the early part of the 19th century a further improvement was made by curving the arms, which provided added strength in a period when welding was still an imperfect art. A persistent drawback to this type of anchor was the difficulty of stowage, but this was obviated later in the century by the invention of the Martin close-stowing anchor, in which the stock was in the same plane as the arms, which themselves canted about a pivot in the crown of the anchor and thus forced the flukes downwards into the sea bed to provide holding power. These anchors were stowed flat on an anchor-bed when not in use. It was a short step from the close-stowing to the stockless anchor, which had the advantages of

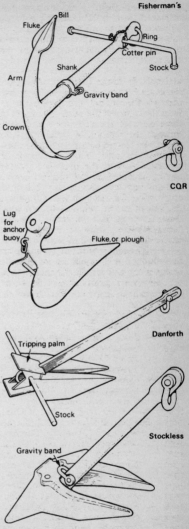

Four types of anchor

making anchor-beds unnecessary, of simplicity in working with a resulting saving of time and labour, and still greater ease of stowage.

For smaller craft, such as yachts, a further development of the stockless anchor has resulted in simpler and more efficient designs, such as the *CQR, or ploughshare (known in the USA as a plow anchor) and mushroom anchors and others similar in operation. While for their small size they provide better and more secure holding even than the stockless, they are unsuitable for sea-going ships of any size, since, when built large enough for this purpose, they present unacceptable problems of efficient stowage on board. But they are frequently used in cases where permanent anchoring is required, as in the case of *lightships, oil rigs at sea, and *moorings.

The most modern development is an anchor with particularly deep flukes which pivot round a stock at the bottom of the shank. For big ships it is the Meon anchor, and for small vessels the *Danforth. This development combines the advantages of both main types of anchor, as although it has a stock to turn the flukes into the ground, it can still be stowed in the *hawsepipe like a stockless anchor.
Efficiency factors of the different types of anchor have been worked out but are apt to be misleading as so much depends on the type of ground in which the anchor beds itself. In terms of resistance to drag, the CQR anchor is generally recognized as best, with the Danforth and Meon coming a close second. Least efficient is the fisherman's anchor.

To anchor, to let go the anchor. See also A-COCKBILL, APEAK, A-TRIP, A-WEIGH, BACK, to, BOWER ANCHOR, CATHEAD, DRAG, FISH, KEDGE, SEA ANCHOR, SHEET ANCHOR, SHOE, WEIGH.

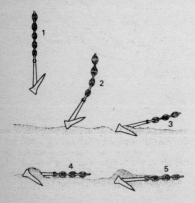

Stockless anchor digging in

anchorage, an area off the coast where the ground is suitable for ships to lie to an anchor, giving a good and secure holding. These areas are marked on a chart with the symbol of an anchor.

anchor buoy, a buoy used to mark the position of a ship's anchor when it is on the bottom. With small anchors, such as those of yachts, the buoy rope is usually attached to the *crown of the anchor with a turn round one of the *flukes so that it can be used to weigh the anchor if the flukes are caught in rocks or stones.

anchor light, another name for a *riding light.

anchor warp, the name given to a hawser or rope when it is attached to an anchor and used as a temporary *cable.

anemometer, an instrument for measuring the velocity of the wind. It consists of a number of wind-driven cups connected to a vertical spindle which, as it rotates, moves a pointer on a scale marked in *knots or miles an hour.

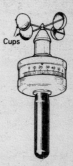

Cups

Hand-held anemometer of the wind-cup type

angle of cut, in navigation, the smaller angle at which two position lines on a chart intersect. The reliability of a *fix obtained by intersecting position lines depends on the angle of cut. When fixing a ship's position by cross bearings of two marks, the prudent navigator aims to select marks whose bearings differ by not less than about 30°, recognizing that the nearer is the difference of bearings to 90°, and other factors being equal, the more reliable will be the resulting fix. See also NAVIGATION.

answering pendant, a red and white vertically striped *pendant hoisted when answering a flag signal at sea to indicate that it has been understood. Until the signal has been fully understood, the answering pendant is hoisted at the dip, i.e., only half way up the signal *halyards. The same pendant is used both in the naval signal code and in the *International Code of Signals for merchant ships.

anticyclone, an area of high barometric pressure around which the wind circulates in a clockwise direction in the northern hemisphere and anti-clockwise in the southern. Anticyclones are always fairweather systems, usually slow moving, and with the strength of the wind never more than moderate.

antifouling paint, a composition which includes poisons, usually based on copper or mercury, applied to the bottoms and sides, below the waterline, of all vessels to inhibit the growth of weed and barnacles and, in the case of wooden vessels, attack by worm such as the teredo. The paint forms a toxic solution in the water immediately around the vessel and is so mixed that the release of the poisons is gradual, lasting as long as the paint itself.

apeak, the position of the *anchor when the bows of a ship have been drawn directly above it during weighing, just before it is broken out of the ground.

apostles, the two large *bollards, fixed to the main deck near the bows in the larger square-rigged sailing vessels, around which hawsers or anchor cables were *belayed.

apparent wind, the direction of the wind as it appears to those on board a sailing vessel. It differs from the true wind in speed and direction by an amount which can be worked out by a vector diagram: the vessel's speed through the water being represented by one leg of a triangle of which the true wind and the apparent wind form the other two sides. The difference between the apparent and true wind is most pronounced when the true wind blows from directly *abeam, and is reduced as the vessel sails closer to, or further off, the true wind. It disappears completely with the wind from dead astern. It is to the apparent wind, not the true wind, that a sailing vessel trims her sails. In the diagram the

strength of the wind has been taken as 12 knots and the speed of the vessel as four knots.

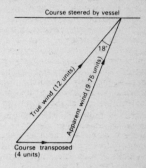

True and apparent wind

apron, a strengthening timber behind the lower part of the *stem and above the foremost end of the *keel of a wooden boat.

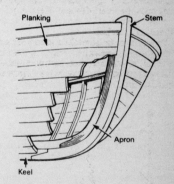

Apron

arm, to, place tallow in the cavity and over the base of the lead when taking a *sounding by *lead line, in order to discover the nature of the bottom (sand, shingle, mud, rock, etc.) by what adheres to the tallow when the lead strikes bottom.

artificial horizon, an aid to taking an astronomical sight with a *sextant when the sea horizon is obscured through haze, fog, or darkness. See also NAVIGATION.

aspect ratio, the ratio between the length of the *luff and the *foot of a yacht's mainsail.

Whereas in the early days of the so-called Bermudian or Marconi mainsails the aspect ratio used to be as low as 2:1, in modern class racing yachts the luff-to-foot length ratio is generally between 3.5:1 and 4:1. Such a high aspect ratio means a tall and narrow sail which is like a glider's wing set up on end. It is highly efficient in sailing very close to the wind as there is negligible twist in the surface of the sail from foot to head, whereas the older broader mainsails suffered from a pronounced sag to *leeward. To make up for the loss of driving power of these small modern mainsails, very large headsails, often of more than twice the area of the mainsail, must be carried under certain conditions.

astern, backwards, behind. It is a word employed in two senses in maritime use; in movement, that of a ship going backwards; in direction, directly behind a ship. See, e.g. AHEAD, and for illus. see RELATIVE BEARINGS.

astronomical navigation, see NAVIGATION.

athwart, a direction across the line of a ship's *course. **Athwart-hawse,** the position of a ship or other vessel driven by wind or tide across the stem of another. **Athwartships,** from one side of the ship to the other. **Athwart the tide,** the position of a ship held by the force of the wind lying across the direction of the tide when at anchor. See also WIND-RODE.

a-trip. An anchor is said to be a-trip at the moment of *weighing when it is broken out of the ground by the pull of the *cable. In square-rigged ships topsails are a-trip when they are hoisted to their full extent and ready for sheeting home (see SHEET), and *yards are a-trip when they are *swayed up and their stops cut ready for crossing. A topmast or topgallant mast is a-trip when the *fid is loosened ready for it to be struck, or lowered.

aurora, a display of atmospheric lights visible in high latitudes, *Borealis* in northern latitudes and *Australis* in southern. They are caused by electrical discharges in the atmosphere, and when the displays are particularly bright, and movement of the light rapid, are almost invariably accompanied by severe electrical storms.

auxiliary, the name by which an engine is known when fitted for occasional use in a sailing yacht.

avast, the order in any seamanship operation to stop or hold.

awash, almost submerged, as when seas wash over a wreck or shoal, or when a ship lies so low in the water that the seas wash over her. A falling *tide which exposes a rock or bank which is submerged at high water makes it awash.

a-weigh, or **aweigh,** the situation of the *anchor at the moment it is broken out of the ground when being weighed. See also A-TRIP. When the anchor is a-weigh the ship is no longer secured to the ground and will drift unless under sail or power. See also UNDER WAY.

awning, a canvas canopy spread over a deck for protection from the sun.

azimuth, from the Arabic *as sumat,* way or direction, a navigational term used to indicate the *bearing of a celestial body. Its navigational definition is the measure of the arc of the *horizon that lies between the elevated pole (north in northern hemisphere, south in southern) and the point where the celestial *great circle passing through the celestial body cuts the horizon. It can be measured by a ship's compass or, more usually, obtained from tables in the *Nautical Almanac.* It is a vital factor in fixing a ship's position by astronomical navigation since it is along the azimuth of the celestial body that the *intercept obtained from an observation is laid off on a chart to obtain a position line. Azimuths are also frequently used as a means of checking the *deviation of a magnetic compass, the difference between the compass azimuth and the true azimuth as obtained from the *Nautical Almanac* giving the compass deviation for the course on which the ship is sailing. See also NAVIGATION.

B

back, to. (1) The wind is said to back when it changes contrary to its normal pattern. In the northern hemisphere, north of the trade wind belt, the wind usually changes clockwise—from north through east, south, and west. When the change is anti-clockwise, the wind is backing. In southern latitudes, the reverse is the general pattern of the winds, but still anti-clockwise. When the wind backs in either hemisphere it is generally taken as a sign that it will freshen. **(2)** To back a square sail, to *brace the *yards so that the wind presses on the forward side of the sail to take the way off the ship. See also ABACK. **(3)** To back water is to push on the oars when rowing a boat, instead of pulling on them, in order to bring the boat to a stop. **(4)** To back an *anchor, the operation of laying out a smaller anchor, usually a *kedge or stream anchor, ahead of the *bower anchor in order to provide additional holding power and to prevent the bower from *coming home.

back a strand, to, in order to make a *long splice, to fill the *score vacated when unlaying a strand with one of the opposite strands.

backboard, a board across the *stern-sheets of a boat just aft of the seats to form a support for passengers or for the helmsman if the boat is under sail.

back splice, a method of finishing off the end of a rope to prevent the strands unravelling by forming a *crown knot with the strands and then tucking them back two or three times each.

backstay, a part of the standing *rigging of a sailing vessel to support the strain on all upper masts. In full-rigged sailing ships, backstays extend from all mast-heads above the lower mast and are brought back to both sides of the ship and set up with *deadeyes and *lanyards to the backstay or chain plates. Their main purpose is to provide additional support to the *shrouds when the wind is abaft the beam. In particularly heavy winds an additional backstay, known as a *preventer, is frequently rigged temporarily. In smaller sailing boats and yachts the backstays are usually known as *runners or running backstays, and the *lee one is generally slacked off to allow further movement forward of the *boom in order to present a squarer aspect of the sail to the wind. In *Bermuda-rigged yachts where the boom is short enough to swing across inside the stern when *tacking or *gybing, the normal two runners are replaced by a single backstay or pair of fixed backstays led from the masthead to the yacht's *taffrail or *quarters. For illus. see RIGGING.

baggywrinkle, sometimes written as **bag-o'-wrinkle,** a home-made substance to prevent chafe on sails from the *lifts, *stays, and *crosstrees during long periods of sailing. It is made by stretching two lengths of *marline at a convenient working height and cutting old *manila rope into lengths of about four inches which are then *stranded. These strands are laid across the two lengths of marline, the ends bent over and brought up between the two lengths, pulled tight, and pushed up against other pieces similarly worked, to provide a long length of bushy material. This is then cut into suitable lengths and *served round wire and spars wherever there is a danger of the sails chafing.

Back splice

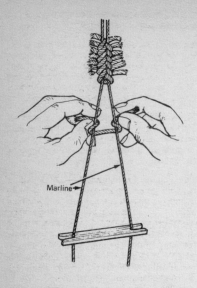

Baggywrinkle in the making

bail, to, empty out the water from a boat or small vessel. The term implies that this is done by hand, not by mechanical means. Originally a boat was bailed out with a bail, an old term used to describe a small bucket, but the modern word is bailer, generally in the form of a scoop with a handle so that water in a boat can be thrown out more rapidly than with a bucket.

balance, to, reduce canvas on a *lateen sail by lowering the *yard and rolling part of the *peak of the sail on to the yard, securing it to the yard about one-fifth of the way down. A **balance-reef** was a reefband which crossed a sail diagonally.

bald-headed, used of a square-rigged ship without her *royals set or a fore-and-aft rigged vessel without her topmasts. **Bald-headed schooner,** see RAM SCHOONER.

ballast, additional weight carried in a ship to give her stability and/or to provide a satisfactory trim fore and aft. In very small vessels the ballast is usually in the form of pigs of soft iron which are stowed as low as possible on the *floors.

Most racing and cruising yachts carry ballast externally in the shape of lead or cast iron formed into a *keel. Cruising yachts, however, may carry some ballast internally, in addition to the ballast keel, because by distributing the ballast, instead of concentrating it in a ballast keel, designers can obtain advantages such as an easier motion in a seaway.

bare boat charter, sometimes known as **bare hull** or **bare pole charter,** one in which a ship is chartered without her crew and with a minimum of restrictions as to her employment by the charterer.

bare poles, the condition of a ship when, in a severe storm, all her canvas has had to be taken in because of the fierceness of the wind.

barge, a large flat-bottomed coastal trading vessel having a large *spritsail and jib-headed topsail, a fore *staysail, and a very small *mizen; occasionally a jib is set on the *bowsprit. They are fitted with *leeboards in place of a keel so that they can operate without difficulty in shoal water. The absence of a keel permits them to operate effectively in shallow water and to remain upright when they are grounded. Normally the mast, which is *stepped on deck, is held in a *lutchet, a type of *tabernacle, so that it can be lowered to deck level when passing under bridges, etc. This type of barge is normally only found in the River Thames and on the south-east coast of England, and is used for the coastal transport of freight. A dumb barge is the hull of a barge, without means of self-propulsion, used for the carriage of cargo from ship to shore or vice versa in tow of a tug. It is more properly called a lighter.

barque, or **bark,** a sailing vessel with three masts, square-rigged on the fore and main and fore-and-aft rigged on the *mizen. See illus. of rigs, under RIG. Until the mid- 19th century, barques were relatively small sailing ships, but later were built up to about 3,000 tons, particularly for the grain and nitrate trade to South American ports round Cape Horn. Four-masted and even five-masted barques were later built for this trade, ranging up to about 5,000 tons. See also JACKASS-BARQUE. Barques are now obsolete as trading vessels, though there may be one or two small ones still used for inter-island trade in the Pacific, but several of the larger ones are still retained in commission as sail training ships, while others have been preserved in many countries as museum ships and examples of the great days of sail. In the USA the term is always bark, never barque.

barquentine, occasionally **barkenteen**, a vessel resembling a *barque but square-rigged on the foremast only, main and *mizen being fore-and-aft rigged. See illus. of rigs, under RIG.

batten down, to, secure the openings in the *deck and sides of a vessel when heavy weather is forecast.

batten, a thin wooden or plastic strip which fits into a long, narrow pocket in the *leech of a *Bermuda mainsail in racing and cruising yachts to hold the leech out when sailing. The name is also given to the long, thin strips of bamboo which are inserted in *lateen sails to hold the form of the sail. These bamboo battens are also particularly used in the sails of *junks in Far Eastern waters.

bawley, a small coastal fishing vessel, *cutter-rigged with short mast and top-mast, peculiar to Rochester and Whit-stable, Kent, and to Leigh-on-Sea and Harwich, Essex, within the Thames Estu-ary area. They set a *loose-footed main-sail on a very long *gaff, a *topsail and a *staysail. They are now obsolescent, having been driven out of use by motorized fishing vessels, though one or two still exist as conversions to local cruising craft.

beacon, (1) a stake or other erection sur-mounted by a distinctive topmark erected over a shoal or sandbank as an aid to navigation. In many coastal estuaries with-out important shipping the low water level is marked by local beacons, often in the form of withies, as a guide to fishing craft and yachts. **(2)** A prominent erection on shore which indicates a safe line of ap-proach to a harbour or a safe passage clear of an obstruction.

beam, (1) the transverse measurement of a ship in her widest part. It is also a term used in indicating direction in relation to a ship (see ABEAM), thus '**before the beam**', the arc of a semicircle extended to the horizon from one beam of the ship around the bows to the other beam; '**abaft the beam**', the similar semicircle extending round the stern of the ship. For illus. see RELATIVE BEARINGS. **(2)** One of the transverse members of a ship's frame on which the decks are laid. In vessels constructed of

wood they are supported on the ship's sides by right-angled timbers known as *knees.

beam ends. A ship is 'on her beam ends' when she has heeled over to such an extent that her deck-beams are nearly vertical and there is no righting moment left to bring her back to the normal upright position. See also METACENTRIC HEIGHT.

bean-cod, the English name of a small Portuguese vessel used for inshore and estuary fishing. They spread a very large *lateen sail extending the whole length of the vessel.

bear, to, used to express the direction of an object from the observer's position, usually in terms of a *compass, e.g., the land bears NE. by N. **To bear up**, in a sailing vessel, to sail closer to the wind; **to bear down**, to approach another ship from to windward; **to bear in with**, or **to bear off from**, to approach nearer or to stand farther off, usually in connection with the land. See also BEARING.

bearing, the horizontal angle between the direction of true north or south and that of the object of which the bearing is being taken. When the bearing is taken by a magnetic *compass, which is subject to *variation and *deviation, it has to be corrected by these before the true bearing is obtained.

beat, to, sail to windward by a series of alternate *tacks across the wind.

Beaufort scale, a scale, from 0 to 12, which indicates the force of the wind. 0 is flat calm with a mirror smooth sea, while 12 is hurricane force winds above 65 *knots where the air is filled with spray and visibility seriously affected.

becalm, to, blanket a ship by cutting off the wind, either by the proximity of the shore or by another ship. A ship motionless through the absence of wind is said to be becalmed.

becket, (1) a short length of rope whose ends have been spliced together to form a circle. **(2)** A short length of rope with an eye splice in one end and a stopper knot in the other used to hold various articles. **(3)** A short rope with an eye splice in each end used to hold the foot of a *sprit against the mast. **(4)** The eye at the base of a *block for making fast the standing end of a *fall.

becue, to, when using an anchor on rocky ground, to make a rope fast to the *flukes of the anchor and then lead it to the ring, where it is secured by a light *seizing. If the flukes are caught in the rocks, a sharp jerk will break the seizing and the anchor will then *come home easily, being hoisted from the flukes.

bee, a ring or hoop of metal. **Bees of the *bowsprit,** pieces of hard wood bolted to the outer end of the bowsprit of a sailing vessel through which are rove (see REEVE) the fore-topmast *stays before they are brought in to the bows and secured.

bee block, one of the wooden swells on each side of the after end of a *smack's or *yacht's *boom; they have sheaves through which to lead the *leech *reef *pendants or reefing *tackle.

belay, to, make fast a rope by taking turns with it round a cleat or belaying pin. In general terms it refers only to the smaller ropes in a ship, particularly the running *rigging in sailing vessels, as larger ropes and cables are bitted, or brought to the *bitts, rather than belayed round them. 'Belay' is also the general order to stop or cease.

belaying pin, a short length of wood, iron, or brass set up in a convenient place in the ship around which the running rigging can be secured or belayed.

bell buoy, a *can, conical, or spherical buoy, normally unlighted, on which is mounted a bell with four clappers, hung inside an iron cage, which is rung by the motion of the sea and serves as a warning to shipping of shoal waters.

bell rope, a short length of rope spliced into the eye of the clapper by which the ship's bell is struck. Traditionally the bell rope is finished with a double *wall knot *crowned on its end, though why this should be so is obscure except perhaps that it is a neat knot which fits well into the palm of the hand.

bellum, the long canoe-shaped boat of the Shatt-al-Arab and adjacent waters in Iraq. They are paddled or poled, according to the depth of water, the larger ones being capable of carrying from fifteen to twenty-five men.

belly band, a strip of canvas sometimes sewn midway between the lower *reef-points and the *foot of a square sail to strengthen it.

bend, (1) the generic maritime name for a *knot which is used to join two ropes or *hawsers together or to attach a rope or *cable to an object. In strict maritime meaning, a knot is one which entails unravelling the strands of a rope and tucking them over and under each other, such as in a stopper knot (*turk's Head, *Matthew Walker, etc.) and is akin to a *splice in this respect. Bends, which are also known as *hitches, have a variety of different forms (*reef, *bowline, *clove hitch, etc.) designed to perform a particular function on board ship. **(2)** In sailing vessels, the chock of the *bowsprit.

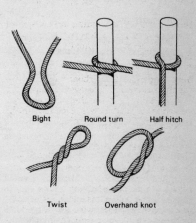

Bight   Round turn   Half hitch

Twist   Overhand knot

Some basic elements of bends

beneaped, used of a vessel which has gone aground at the top of the *spring tides and has to wait for up to a fortnight (during which the *neap tides occur) for the next tide high enough to float her off. Vessels beneaped at around the times of the *equinoxes when the highest spring tides occur may have to wait up to six months to get off.

Bermuda or **Bermudian rig,** a sail plan in which the main and/or mizen sail, or the foresail of a *schooner, is of triangular shape, very long in the *luff and set from a tall mast by slides running on a track or by the luff rope fitting in a mast groove. The rig was commonly used by sailing craft in and around the West Indies from about 1800 and was introduced for small racing craft in Britain about 1911–12, spreading to larger racing yachts and cruising yachts in the twenty years between the two world wars. The rig is now almost universal in all modern yachts. The Bermuda rig is claimed to be more efficient to windward and also requires a smaller crew to handle it than the *gaff rig. See also RIG.

berth, (1) a place in which to sleep on board ship, now normally a *bunk. A snug berth, a situation of not too arduous labour on board a ship. **(2)** The place in harbour in which a ship rides to her anchor or is secured alongside. **(3)** A term used to indicate a clearance of danger, e.g., to give a wide berth to a rock, shoal, or a point of land, to steer a ship well clear of it.

Berthon boat, a folding or collapsible boat, of painted canvas stretched on a wooden frame, invented by Edward Berthon.

best bower, the starboard of the two *anchors carried at the bow of a ship in the days of sail. That on the port side was known as the small bower, even though the two were identical in weight.

bibbs, pieces of timber bolted to the *hounds of a mast of a square-rigged ship to support the *trestle-trees.

bight, (1) the name by which the loop of a rope is known when it is folded, or any part of a rope between its two ends when it lies or hangs in a curve or loop. **(2)** The area of sea lying between two promontories, being in general wider than a gulf and larger than a bay, is also known as a bight.

bilge, that part of the *floors of a ship on either side of the *keel which approaches nearer to a horizontal than a vertical direction. It is where the floors and the second *futtocks unite, and upon which the ship would rest when she takes the ground. Hence, when a ship is holed in this part, she is said to be bilged. Being the lowest part of the ship inside the hull, it is naturally where any internal water would collect, and where the suction of the *bilge pump is placed. These spaces on either side of the keel are collectively known as the bilges.

bilge keel, also known as a docking keel, longitudinal projections fixed one on each side of a ship, parallel to the central *keel, at or just below the turn of the *bilge and protruding downwards. Their main purpose is to support the weight of the hull of the ship on the wooden *ways when *launching or on the lines of keel blocks when in dry-dock for cleaning or repairs. They are also of service to a ship in a seaway by providing additional resistance in the water when the vessel is rolling heavily, and in a sailing vessel provide a better grip on the water and thus allow her to hold a better wind. For illus. see KEEL.

bilge pump, a small pump designed to pump the *bilges clear of water which lies beyond the suction of the main pumps.

bilge water, the water, either from rain or from seas breaking aboard, which runs down and collects in the *bilges of a ship and usually becomes foul and noxious.

billy-boy or **billy-boat,** an east coast of England, bluff-bowed trading vessel of river-barge build, originally single-masted with a *trysail, and usually with the sails *tanned. Later it took on a *ketch rig, with *gaff mainsail and mizen and square topsails on the mainmast.

binnacle, formerly **bittacle,** the wooden housing of the mariner's *compass and its correctors and illuminating arrangements.

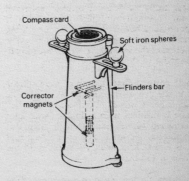

Binnacle

bite, to. An *anchor is said to bite when the *flukes bed themselves into the ground and hold firm without *dragging.

bitt stopper, a length of rope, in the days when ships had hemp cables for their anchors, used to bind the cable more securely to the *bitts to prevent it slipping. When a ship anchored and enough cable was run out, it was brought to the bitts and secured by several turns round them. The bitt stopper was then passed round the turns to bind the cable in taut so that it could not render round the bitts.

bitter, the name given to any turn of the anchor *cable of a ship about the *bitts. Hence, a ship is 'brought up to a bitter' when the cable is allowed to run out to that turn around the bitts or to its modern equivalent. See also BITTER END.

bitter end, that part of the anchor *cable of a vessel which is abaft the *bitts and thus remains within board when a ship is riding to her *anchor. To *pay a rope or chain out to the bitter end means that all has been paid out and no more remains to be let go. 'Bend to the bitter end' means to reverse a cable, to *bend the inboard end of it to the anchor so that the strain on the cable when a ship is anchored now comes on a part of it that has been less used and is therefore more trustworthy.

bitts, in older ships, a frame composed of two strong pillars of straight oak timber, fixed upright in the fore part of the ship and bolted to the deck *beams, to which were secured the *cables when the ship rode to an anchor. Small bitts were fitted in square-rigged sailing vessels for securing other parts of the running *rigging, such as *topsail-sheet bitts, paul-bitts, *carrick-bitts, *windlass-bitts, *gallows-bitts, *jeer-bitts, etc. They all served the same purpose, providing a convenient means of taking a securing turn with the *fall of whatever piece of rigging was involved.

black squall, a sudden squall of wind, accompanied by lightning, encountered in the West Indies. It is usually caused by the heated state of the atmosphere near land where the warm expanded air is repelled by a colder medium to *leeward and driven back with great force, frequently engendering electrical storms of great intensity.

block, a wooden or metal case in which one or more sheaves are fitted. They are used for various purposes in a ship, either when as part of a *purchase to increase the mechanical power applied to ropes or to lead them to convenient positions for handling. Blocks are of various sizes and powers; a single block contains one sheave, a double block has two, a threefold block has three, and so on. A fiddle block has two sheaves fitted one below the other.

Blocks consist of four parts: the shell, or outside wooden part, the sheave, on which the rope runs, the pin, on which the sheave turns, and the strop, which is of rope or wire spliced round the shell and by which the block can be attached wherever it is required to work. See also PURCHASE.

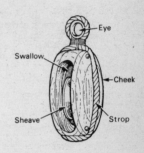

Single stropped block

Blue Peter, the signal that a ship is about to sail and that all persons concerned should report on board. The flag, which is hoisted at the fore topmasthead, or main-topmasthead in ships with only one mast, is a rectangular flag with a blue ground and a white rectangle in the centre. It is P flag in the *International Code of Signals.

board, a word much used at sea with a variety of meanings, but chiefly indicating the distances which a sailing vessel runs between *tacks when working to windward. Thus a ship tacking across the wind to reach a point to windward of her present position can make short or long boards according to the frequency of her tacks; the more frequently she tacks, the shorter the boards. To make a good board, to sail in a straight line when *close-hauled without making any *leeway; to make a stern board, to come up head to wind so that the vessel stops and makes way astern until she falls off on the opposite tack, often a very seamanlike operation when navigating in narrow channels; to board it up, a term often used by older seamen meaning to *beat up to windward.

Other meanings of the word are, to go on board, to go into a ship; to slip by the board, to desert a ship by escaping down the ship's side; by the board, close to the deck as when a mast is broken off close to the deck level, or goes by the board.

boat, the generic name for small open craft without any decking and usually propelled by oars or outboard engine, and sometimes by a small *lugsail on a short mast. Some exceptions to this general definition are fishing boats, sometimes decked or half-decked and propelled by sail and/or inboard diesel engine. Some yachts are also known as boats.

Boat is a word frequently used by people ashore when they really mean ship, and such terms as packet boat, mail boat, etc., are in fairly general use. Railway companies also run boat trains to take passengers to a ship in which they are sailing for some destination. But a seaman will never call any sort of ship, packet, mail, or any other, a boat as the two terms are not synonymous and are to him quite distinct.

boatswain's (pron. bo'sun's) **chair,** a short board, secured in a *bridle, used to sway a man aloft for scraping or painting masts, and treating yards, rigging, etc.

bobstay, a chain or heavy wire rigging running from the end of the *bowsprit to the ship's *stem or *cutwater. Particularly heavy rigging was required in this position since the foretopmast in sailing vessels was *stayed to the bowsprit, exerting a strong upward pull when the sails were full of wind. The bowsprit was also secured by *shrouds from either bow of the ship. Very few sailing vessels are fitted with bowsprits today and in consequence the bobstay is rarely seen as a piece of rigging, the only ships still to use it being the square-rigged school ships which are operated by various nations for training purposes, and some yachts.

boeier or **boier,** a craft used on the inland waterways of the Netherlands, with apple-shaped bows and stern, rounded bottom, and broad fan-shaped *leeboards for sailing in very shallow waters.

bollard, a vertical piece of timber or iron, fixed to the ground, to which a ship's mooring lines are made fast when alongside. They were also sometimes known as nigger-heads.

bolster, a piece of wood fitted in various places in a ship to act as a preventive to chafe or nip. In the older wooden sailing ships the pieces of soft wood, usually covered with canvas, which rested on the *trestle-trees to prevent them getting nipped by the rigging were also called bolsters.

bolt, the standard measurement of length of canvas as supplied by the makers for use at sea. It is a piece, or roll, 39 yards (35.6 m) in length. There is no standard measurement of width, but normally it is supplied in widths varying from 22–30 inches (56–76 cm).

bolt-rope, the name given to the rope which is sewn around the edges of a sail to keep the canvas from fraying. While the whole rope is known as the bolt-rope, it is subdivided in name according to the side of the sail on which it is sewn, as luff-rope, foot-rope, etc. Bolt-ropes are always placed slightly to the left of centre of the edge on which they are sewn to enable the seaman to orient the sail by feel in the dark.

bonaventure, an additional *mizen sail, *lateen in shape, which used to be carried on a fourth mast, known as a bonaventure mizen, in the older sailing ships. It went out of use during the 17th century, when the standard three masts was adopted as the most efficient rig for ships.

bone, the white feather of water under the bow of a ship when she is under way. A ship moving fast through the water and throwing up an appreciable feather is said to have a bone in her mouth, or in her teeth.

bonnet, an additional strip of canvas laced originally to the foot of fore-and-aft sails and *courses in small ships to increase the area exposed to the wind.

booby-hatch, (1) a small opening in the deck of a vessel used as an additional *companion to facilitate movement. **(2)** A name sometimes given to the sliding hatch on the raised cabin top of small cruising yachts.

boom, (1) a *spar used to extend the foot of a sail: thus (a) in square rig, *studding-sails are set on studdingsail booms extended from the ends of the yardarms; such booms (including booms temporarily rigged at deck level to extend the *clews of the lower sails) would normally be rigged only when it was required to make the most of a light wind which would not otherwise fill the

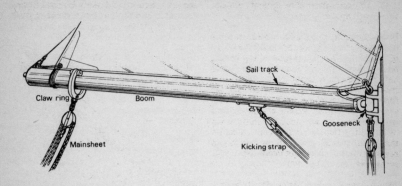

Typical yacht boom

sails. Thus a ship was said to come booming forward when carrying all the sail that she could make. (b) In fore-and-aft rig, however, (i) the boom is usually a permanent and important spar, at the foot of the mainsail, and also of the foresail of a *schooner and the mizen of a schooner, *ketch, or *yawl; it is pivoted at the fore end to the mast by a *gooseneck, and controlled by a *sheet at or near the after end, by which the sail is trimmed. A *spritsail has neither boom nor *gaff, and a gaff sail may be boomless (loose-footed), but for efficient sailing a boom is used in most types of fore-and-aft rig. The sail may be secured to it only at the *tack and clew, but is more often laced to it, or has a foot-rope which slides in a groove on top of the boom.

Traditionally a boom is a solid round wooden spar, tapering slightly towards the ends, or of uniform cross-section; in modern practice it may be of hollow glued wooden construction, or a metal tube, both serving to combine strength with lightness; as greater stiffness is required in the vertical than in the horizontal plane it may be oblong or oval in section. In 19th/20th century racing yachts, before the introduction of *Bermudian rig, main booms were often extremely long, overhanging the *taffrail at the stern, just as the same rig often included a long *bowsprit and a *jackyard topsail, to obtain a very large total sail area. Modern sail plans tend to favour height, generally in the form of a

Bermudian mainsail, and a large fore-triangle without a bowsprit, obtained by stepping the mast well aft from the bows: the boom is kept short and its end may be well inboard, in which case the sheet is led straight down from the boom-end to the *horse or sheet block. In some large *J-class and similar Bermudian cutters, the boom was flat-topped and unusually wide at its widest part (and hence called a *Park Avenue boom, after the street in New York); the object was to obtain the best aerodynamic shape for the foot of the sail; but this peculiarity did not last. The purpose of any boom, however, is to enable the sail to set well, as near flat as necessary, without undue 'belly' or sagging of the upper part of the sail to *leeward when close hauled. To increase flatness, in racing dinghies and small yachts, the boom is sometimes prevented from rising when it swings outwards by a *'kicking strap' (as it is called by dinghy sailors) or *martingale, between a point on the boom and the foot of the mast. (ii) Also in fore-and-aft rig, the *spinnaker is normally set on a boom, which is a light spar used only when the spinnaker is set, in order to extend the foot of the sail. (iii) A fore-staysail may also be set on a boom, which is pivoted to, or just abaft, the forestay. This is not usual, and has the drawback that the staysail cannot then overlap the mast.

(2) A boom is also a spar rigged outboard from a ship's side horizontally to which boats are secured in harbour or when at

anchor in calm weather; the boats thus lie clear of the ship's side and ready for use.

(3) To boom off, to shove a boat or vessel away with spars.

boom crutch, originally **crotch,** a temporary receptacle mounted on the *counter of small *fore-and-aft rigged sailing vessels on which the main *boom is stowed and held secure when anchored or lying on a mooring. It normally takes one of two forms, a metal shaft with semi-circular arms on top into which the boom fits, or a small folding wooden structure in the form of an X, the two feet held firm in slots on the counter with the end of the boom resting in the space between the upper arms. See also GALLOWS.

boom-irons, metal rings fitted on the yard-arms of square-rigged sailing ships through which the *studdingsail booms are traversed in cases where extra advantage is to be taken from a following wind by setting the studdingsails.

booms, the space in the larger sailing vessels, usually between the foremast and mainmast, where the spare spars were stowed on board. The larger ship's boats were carried on the booms when the ship was at sea, either in crutches or between the spare yards themselves.

bora, a violent easterly squall experienced in the upper part of the Adriatic Sea. It is caused by the weight of the cold air from the mountains accelerating its flow to the sea.

bore, or **eagre,** a sudden and rapid flow of tide in certain rivers and estuaries which rolls up in the form of a wave. Bores are caused either by the meeting of two tides, where the excess of water results in a rapid rise, or by a tide rushing up a narrowing estuary where the closeness of the banks or a shelving bottom encloses the tide so that it is forced to rise rapidly to accommodate the volume of water coming.

Although the two terms are virtually synonymous, each locality uses one of the two exclusively, thus in England the River Severn has a bore, the River Trent an eagre.

botter, originally a Dutch fishing boat based normally between Volendam and Haderwijk in the South Zuider Zee. Many botters were converted into yachts, the

large amount of space below decks providing comfortable and reasonably spacious accommodation, and many Dutch cruising yachts are still built on general botter lines.

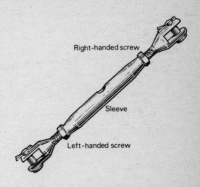

Right-handed screw

Sleeve

Left-handed screw

Bottlescrew

bottlescrew or **turnbuckle,** a rigging screw used to adjust any rigging equipment for length or tension, the correct maritime term being to 'set up' the rigging. A bottlescrew consists of an internally threaded sleeve into which a right-handed screw takes at one end and a left-handed screw at the other. As the sleeve is revolved, the two contra-threaded screws are drawn together, thus increasing the tension of those parts of the rigging to which they are attached. Bottlescrews are largely used for setting up the *shrouds of sailing vessels and the *guardrails and davit guys fitted in ships.

bow, the foremost end of a ship, the opposite of *stern. From bow to stern, the whole length of a ship. The word is frequently used in the plural, as 'the bows of a ship'. It is also used to give an approximate *bearing of an object in relation to the fore-and-aft line of the ship, as, e.g., 'the buoy bears 15° on the port bow' or 'two *points on the starboard bow', as the case may be. On the bow, within an arc of four points (45°) extending either side of the bow.

bower anchor, one of the two largest *anchors in a ship carried permanently attached to their *cables, one on either *bow with the cables running through the *hawseholes so that the anchors are always ready for letting go in an emergency. They were originally known as *best bower and small bower, not from any difference in their size since they were the same weight, but from the bow on which they are placed, the best bower being the one on the starboard side and the small bower on the port. Today they are known purely as the starboard and port bower.

bowline, (pron. bōlin), **(1)** a knot tied in such a way as to produce an *eye, or loop, in the end of a rope. It is a knot with many uses at sea, whether to join two large hawsers together, with one bowline tied

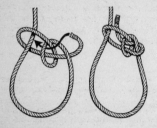

Running bowline

with its eye inside the eye of the other, or tied in the end of a hawser to provide a loop for dropping over a *bollard. It is a knot which will never slip and cannot jam.

Variants of this knot are a running bowline, where the knot is tied around a bight of the rope to form a noose, and a bowline on the bight, where the knot is made with the bight of the rope to produce two eyes. This variant is often used to form a temporary *boatswain's chair when a man is needed to work aloft. **(2)** The name of the rope attached with a bowline to, and leading forward from, a bridle between *cringles on the *leeches of sails in a square-rigged ship. Its purpose, when hauled hard in, is to keep the weather edge of the sail taut and steady when the ship is *close-hauled to the wind. Thus a square-rigged ship is said to 'sail on a bowline', or 'stand on a taut bowline', when she is being sailed as close to the wind as possible. For illus. see RIGGING.

bowse, to, haul with a *tackle in order to produce an additional measure of tautness; thus the *tack of a *lugsail is bowsed down with a tackle after the sail has been hoisted so that the *luff is drawn tauter than can be achieved merely by hauling on the *halyards in hoisting. 'Bowse away', the order for all men on the hauling part of a tackle to haul away together.

bowsprit, (pron. bō), orig. **boltsprit,** a large spar projecting over the *stem

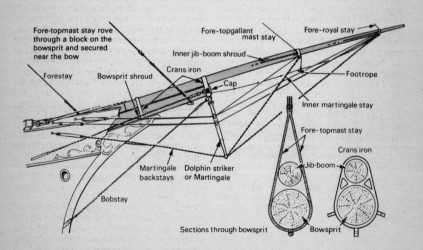

Fore-topmast stay rove through a block on the bowsprit and secured near the bow

Fore-topgallant mast stay

Fore-royal stay

Inner jib-boom shroud

Forestay

Bowsprit shroud

Crans iron

Cap

Footrope

Inner martingale stay

Fore-topmast stay

Crans iron

Jib-boom

Martingale backstays

Dolphin striker or Martingale

Bobstay

Sections through bowsprit

Bowsprit

Bowsprit

of large sailing vessels to provide the means of staying a fore-topmast and from which the *jibs are set. When a fore-topgallant mast is set, the bowsprit is extended by a *jib-boom, to the end of which is led the fore-topgallant mast stay on which the flying jibs are set. The bowsprit itself is held rigidly in place by *shrouds led to each bow of the vessel and by a *bobstay led from its outer end to the stem of the vessel just above the waterline. In some smaller *cutter-rigged sailing vessels the bowsprit was often fitted so that it could be run in, or furled, by sliding inboard and was known as a running bowsprit as opposed to a standing one.

With the wide adoption of the *Bermuda rig for most modern sailing craft and yachts, the bowsprit has virtually disappeared except in the few big sailing vessels still retained as school or training ships, and in the growing number of these ships which are being preserved for historical and museum purposes. In some yachts a small *bumpkin is fitted to the stemhead in the nature of a bowsprit.

box-haul, to, *wear a square-rigged ship in rough weather when the force of the waves makes it impractical for her to *tack by means of the following procedure: the helm is put *a-lee (1), as in tacking, to bring the bows up into the wind, when the strength of the waves as they strike the weather bow will force the bows down to *leeward (2). With the helm reversed, this movement is accelerated, and at the same time the aftermost sails are brailed up to spill the wind out of them in order to give the foremost sails an added turning moment. As the stern of the ship crosses the wind the aftermost sails are braced to catch the wind (3) and increase the rate of turn until the wind is forward of the beam and the yards can again be braced (4). Box-hauling, as well as being a rough weather tactic, was also used when ships were too near the shore to *wear in the usual way.

box off, to, haul the head-sheets to windward and lay the head-yards flat *aback in a square-rigged ship to *pay the ship's head out of the wind when *tacking, when the action of the helm by itself is insufficient to produce that result. It is a means of ensuring that the ship does not miss stays, that is, remain head to wind and unable to pay off on either *tack. In *fore-and-aft rigged ships the same result can be achieved when the vessel hangs head to wind by hauling out the *clew of the *jib to windward.

box the compass, to, know and be able to recite the *points and quarter points of the magnetic compass from north through south to north again, both clockwise and anti-clockwise. It is now nearly a lost art.

brace, one of the ropes or wire ropes rove to the ends of all *yards in a square-rigged ship by which the yards are *braced, or swung, at different angles to the fore-and-aft line of the ship to make the most of the wind. For illus. see YARD.

brace, to, swing round, by means of *braces, the *yards of a square-rigged ship to present a more efficient sail surface to the direction of the wind. By bracing the yards at different angles to the fore-and-aft line of the ship, the best advantage can be taken of any wind which may be blowing. Thus, the yards are braced *aback to bring the winds on the forward side of the sails to take the way off her, are braced *about to bring the ship on the opposite tack when going about, are braced *abox to bring the headyards flat aback to stop the ship, are braced *by to bring the yards in contrary directions on different masts to *lie the ship to or *heave-to, are braced **in** to lay the yards squarer to the fore-and-aft line for a *free wind, and are braced **sharp** to bring the yards round to make the smallest possible angle with the fore-and-aft line when sailing *close-hauled.

'brace of shakes, a', originally a maritime term which has found its way into everyday language. It denoted a moment of time which could be measured by the shaking of a sail as a ship comes into the wind: 'I will be with you before the sail can shake twice.'

Wind

1   2   3   4

Box-hauling

brails, ropes leading from the *leech on both sides of a fore-and-aft loose-footed sail and through leading *blocks secured on the mast *hoops of the sail to deck level. Their use is to gather in the sail close to the mast so that it is temporarily *furled when coming up to a mooring or as required.

breach, to, break in of the sea, either in a ship or through a coastal defence such as a sea wall. A sea which breaks completely across a ship is called a clean breach.

breakers, waves breaking over rocks or shoals, often a useful warning to ships off their course that they are standing into danger.

break ground, to, of a ship's anchor at the moment when the *cable lifts it off the bottom and the anchor breaks out of the ground into which its *flukes have bitten.

break sheer, to. When a ship lying to her anchor is forced, perhaps by wind or current, to swing across her anchor so as to risk fouling with her own cable, she is said to break sheer. When she swings clear the other way, she is said to keep her sheer.

breakwater, an artificially placed construction in or around a harbour designed to break the force of the sea and to provide shelter for vessels lying within.

breast backstay, one of a pair of *stays led from the head of a topmast or a topgallant mast in a square-rigged ship to *chain-plates forward of the standing *backstays to provide support for the upper masts from to windward. They formed part of the standing rigging of the ship. See also RIGGING.

breeches buoy, a ring lifebuoy fitted with canvas breeches and used for life-saving when a ship has run aground and is in danger of breaking-up or sinking. Contact with the wrecked ship is made from the shore by means of a line fired from a rocket ~un, a *jackstay is then rigged between ~ and shore, and the breeches buoy, ~rted in a sling attached to a traveller,

is hauled back and forth between ship and shore by an endless *whip along the jackstay, the seaman being rescued having his legs through the breeches to give him support as he is hauled ashore. The breeches buoy is then hauled back empty to the ship for the next man to be rescued.

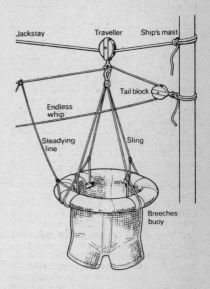

Breeches buoy

breeze, sea or land, a coastal wind which blows regularly in warmer climates from the sea in daytime and from the land at night. It is caused by the action of the sun in raising the temperature of the land during the day faster than that of the sea so that the warm air rises, thus drawing in a breeze from the sea. The process is reversed at night as the land cools more quickly than the sea, which retains its temperature, so that the cooler air from the land flows seaward to replace the warmer sea air, which rises. See also METEOROLOGY.

bridle, (1) a length of rope, wire, or chain secured at both ends to a spar or other object, to the *bight of which a *purchase can be hooked on. The purpose is to provide a better balance in an unhandy object for lifting purposes. **(2)** The upper end of fixed *moorings laid in harbours and anchorages. When a ship lies to moorings, it is the bridle, or the *buoy at the end of it, to which she is secured.

bridle-port, a square port cut in the bows on either side of the stem of wooden ships on main deck level through which mooring *bridles were led.

brig, originally an abbreviation of *brigantine, but later a type of ship in her own right after some modifications in the original rig. The true brig is a two-masted vessel square-rigged on both fore and main masts. A *hermaphrodite brig, sometimes called a brig-schooner, has the usual brig's square-rigged foremast and a *schooner's mainmast, with *fore-and-aft mainsail and square topsails. Brigs were widely used in the days of sail for short and coastal trading voyages, and there are still a few to be found today employed in local trades. They were also used widely in several navies as training ships for boys destined to become naval seamen, and in many navies were retained for this purpose long after sail had disappeared in them for good. For illus. see RIG.

brigantine, a two-masted vessel, as a *brig, but square-rigged on the foremast and *fore-and-aft rigged on the mainmast. The name comes from the fact that these ships were favourite vessels of the sea brigands, particularly in the Mediterranean, although in their case the vessel they used was of the galley type used with oars. But as sea brigandage spread to the more tempestuous waters of the Atlantic and North Sea, the ship used by these new brigands took the Mediterranean name even though the type of ship changed. For illus. see RIG.

bring up, to, bring a ship to an anchor or a *mooring. The normal practice, particularly in small ships or vessels under sail, is to bring up head to tide; at the periods of slack water when there is little or no tide, a vessel would bring up head to wind.

bring-to, to, bring a sailing vessel to a stop with her sails still set. In the case of square-rigged ships this was achieved by *bracing the yards on her foremast *aback to counter the effect of those that were still drawing; in the case of a *fore-and-aft rigged vessel it is achieved by bringing her head to wind so that no sail will draw. When anchoring, the correct term is to bring a ship to an anchor, because in the days of sail it was

usual to bring-to for anchoring by laying the foresails aback to take off the ship's way.

Bristol fashion, everything neat and seamanlike. The expression had its origin when Bristol was the major west coast port of Britain before the growth of Liverpool brought competition, and during the palmy days when all its shipping was maintained in proper good order. The full expression is shipshape and Bristol fashion.

Broaching-to

broach-to, to. A sailing vessel's tendency to fly up into the wind when *running free or with the wind blowing strongly from the *quarter is called broaching to. In square-rigged ships the chief danger of broaching-to arose from the habit of many skippers of driving their ships too hard, keeping aloft too large a press of canvas to make the most of strong winds, particularly on main and *mizen-masts. In extreme cases of broaching-to, the sails could be caught flat *aback, in which situation the masts were likely to go *by the board, and the ship might even *founder stern first. *Fore-and-aft rigged ships are less likely to suffer from broaching-to, though it does remain a major danger, particularly when sailing with a *spinnaker set. See also POOP.

bubble horizon, an attachment which can be screwed to the frame of a *sextant immediately in front of the horizon glass to provide an artificial true horizon in weather conditions, or at night, when the real horizon is indistinct or invisible. When taking an *altitude of a celestial body, the navigator's line of sight through the telescope passes through the clear part of the horizon glass and enters the attachment where, by means of mirrors and a lens, the rays of light from a bubble inside the attachment are projected in a true horizontal direction. This provides an artificial true horizon, and when the reflected image of the body, seen in the silvered part of the horizon glass, is brought down to the artificial horizon, its altitude can be read off on the sextant scale.

Builders Old Measurement, a formula adopted in Britain by Act of Parliament passed in 1773 to calculate the *tonnage of a ship as a figure on which port and harbour dues, etc., could be based. The formula was

$$\frac{(L - \frac{3}{5}B) \times B \times \frac{1}{2}B}{94}$$

where L equals the length of the ship measured along the *rabbet of her keel and B equals her maximum beam, the result giving her measurement in *tons. This formula remained in force until the mid-19th century when the introduction of iron as the most efficient material for shipbuilding and steam as the means of propulsion resulted in the design of ships with longer, fine-lined hulls, to which the older measurement rule no longer applied. See also THAMES MEASUREMENT.

bulb keel, a deep fin with a large bulb of lead on the bottom, widely used in racing yachts during the late 19th and early 20th centuries. Its purpose was to achieve the maximum resistance to the excessive heel of racing yachts, produced by the vast areas of sail they carried, by placing the centre of gravity as low as possible. Its use led eventually to the development of extreme and unseaworthy yachts, and was discouraged by the adoption of *rating rules which severely penalized yachts built in this fashion. See also KEEL.

bulge, often used in the same sense as *bilge. A ship which is bulged (or bilged) is one whose bottom has been holed.

bulkhead, a vertical partition, either fore and aft or *athwartships, dividing the hull into separate compartments.

bull rope, (1) a rope used for hoisting a topmast or topgallant mast in a square-rigged ship. It is rove from the *cap of the lower mast, through a sheave in the *heel of the topmast, and then back through a *block on the lower masthead, with the hauling part led to the deck. When a topmast is hoisted, a pull on the hauling part of the bull rope sends the topmast up to the height where the *fid, which holds it securely in place, can be inserted. The reverse operation lowers the topmast. (But see also TRIPPING LINE.) **(2)** A line rove temporarily through a *bullseye on the end of a yacht's *bowsprit and secured to a mooring-buoy, designed to hold the buoy well clear of the yacht's bows and prevent it striking or rubbing against the hull.

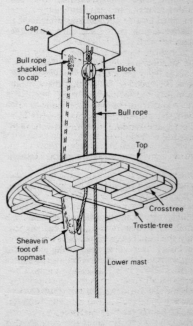

Bull rope

bullseye, (1) a circular piece of *lignum vitae, hollowed in the centre to take a rope and grooved round the outside to accommodate a *strop which enables it to be fixed in position where required. Its main purpose is to change the lead, or direction, of a rope in cases where a *block for this purpose is not required. (2) It is also the name given to a piece of thick glass set flush in the deck of a ship to admit light to the deck below. (3) The small expanse of blue sky seen in the centre of a tropical storm is also known by many seamen as the bullseye.

bulwark, the planking or woodwork along the sides of a ship above her upper deck to prevent seas washing over the *gunwales and also persons on board inadvertently falling or being washed overboard in rough weather.

bumpkin or **bumkin,** originally a short *boom projecting forward on either side of the bows of a sailing ship which was used to extend the *clew of the foresail to windward. It had a *block fixed to the outer end through which the *tack was rove and hauled aboard. Similarly, it was the name of a short boom which extended from each quarter of the sailing vessel to carry the main *brace blocks. In its modern meaning it is a short *spar extending directly over the stern of a sailing vessel to *sheet the *mizen sail in those cases where the mizen-mast is stepped so far aft that there is not enough room inboard to bring down the sheet and trim the sail. The name is also used, in some modern yachts, to describe a short spar extending from the *stemhead in place of a *bowsprit.

bunk, a built-in wooden bed on board ship.

bunt, the middle section of a square sail where it is cut full to form a belly. It applied more especially to topsails, cut to form a bag to gather more wind, than to lower sails which were generally cut square with only small allowance for bunt. In a full-rigged ship the bunt of the topsails was frequently so heavy and voluminous that a **bunt-jigger** was fitted to the sails to assist the men on the yards in *furling them. This was a small *tackle of two single blocks by means of which the bunt of the sail was hauled up to the yard so that the *gaskets could be secured. **Buntlines,** ropes attached to the footropes of the square sails, were also fitted in the larger sailing vessels and led up through blocks attached to the yards. When hauled up they spilled the wind out of the sails for reefing or hoisted them right up to the yards for furling. **Bunters,** the topmen working the centre

of the yards who gather in the bunt when furling sails. **Bunt-fair,** said of a square-rigged ship when sailing before the wind. For illus. see SAIL.

bunting, a thin cloth of woven wool supplied in various colours from which are made signal and other coloured flags.

buntline band, a strip of canvas *tabled on to the forward side of a square sail to prevent the buntlines (see BUNT) from chafing the sail.

buoy, a floating mark used mainly for navigational purposes to mark a channel, bank, *spoil ground, or similar area of which the navigator needs to know. The system in force in any particular area is given in detail in the *Sailing Directions appropriate to those waters.

Buoys have other uses besides navigational, such as *watch buoys to enable a *lightship to check that she is not drifting off her station, buoys to mark the position of telegraph cables or submarine mining grounds, sewer outfalls, etc. All these can have distinctive shapes and colours, of which details are marked on navigational *charts. Admiralty Chart 5011, issued by the British Admiralty, which lists all the symbols and abbreviations used on charts, has a section which deals with buoys and beacons.

Some buoys, particularly those marking main navigational channels, are lighted for identification at night, cylinders of compressed gas being used for the purpose; others may be fitted with a whistle operated by compressed air or with a bell activated by the movement of the waves or by other means to assist in their location in thick weather. Since the wide introduction of *radar in ships, many buoys are now fitted with reflectors to facilitate their detection by this means and to overcome the problem of sea-clutter.

buoyage, systems of, codes of practice, adopted multinationally or nationally, under which *buoys of various shapes and colours are used for the same navigational purpose. The system of buoyage in use in any particular country is given in full detail in the *Sailing Directions appropriate to those waters.

buoy rope, the rope which attaches a small buoy to an *anchor when it is on the bottom to mark its position. In length it needs to be slightly more than the depth of water at high tide where the anchor lies, and in normal practice it is of sufficient strength to lift the anchor in the event of the cable parting. Anchor buoys are generally used when anchoring on a rocky bottom, and the buoy rope is bent on to the *crown of the anchor with a running *eye over one *fluke and with a hitch taken over the other arm. If the anchor is jammed in the rocks and cannot be weighed normally by the cable, the buoy rope can then be used to break out the flukes by hoisting the anchor bottom upwards.

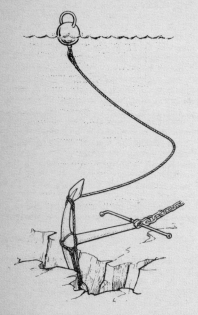

Buoy rope

burgee, a broad, tapering pendant, normally with a swallow tail but occasionally without. Burgees of yacht clubs are normally triangular, of a length twice that of the depth at the hoist, and carry on them the insignia of the club concerned. Commodores of yacht clubs usually fly swallow-tailed burgees again carrying the insignia of the club. Burgees without a swallow tail are used as the substitute flags in the *International Code of Signals.

buss, a 17th- and 18th-century fishing vessel, mainly used in herring fishery,

broad in the beam with two, and sometimes three, masts with a single square sail on each and usually of from 50 to 70 tons.

buttock, the breadth of a ship where the *hull rounds down to the stern. A ship is said to have a broad or a narrow buttock according to the convexity of her hull below the *counter.

buttock lines, longitudinal sections of a ship's hull parallel to the *keel.

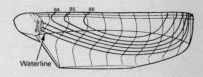

Buttock lines

Buys Ballot Law, a rough and ready method of discovering the direction of the centre of a circular storm. If an observer faces the direction of the true wind, the centre of low pressure will be between eight and twelve *points (90°–135°) on his right hand in the northern hemisphere, and on his left hand in the southern. It takes its name from C.H.D. Buys Ballot, Dutch meteorologist, who published it in his *Comtes Rendus* (1857).

by, in relation to the wind, to sail a vessel **by the wind** is to sail her on or close to the wind with the *sheets hardened in. **Full and by,** to sail on the wind keeping the sails full of wind without their *luffs lifting or shivering. **By and large,** to sail a vessel near the wind but not full on it, i.e., about five *points off the wind with the *fore-and-aft rig and about seven points with the square rig. **By the lee,** the situation when a ship is *running free and the wind, either through a shift of direction or through careless steering, comes across the stern and blows on the *lee side of the sails, thus laying them *aback on the other tack and usually causing an involuntary *gybe. In small sailing ships it is a frequent cause of *capsizing or dismasting. See also BROACH-TO.

by the board, close to the deck or over the ship's side. When a mast carrries away it is said to have gone by the *board.

by the head. A ship is said to be by the head when she draws more than her normal depth of water forward, with her bows lying deeper than her stern. Similarly, a ship is said to be **by the stern** when she is drawing more than her normal depth of water aft.

by the stern, see BY THE HEAD.

C

cabin, a room or space in a ship partitioned off by *bulkheads to provide a private apartment for officers, passengers, and crew members for sleeping and/or eating.

cabin sole, a yachting term for the floorboards of the cabin accommodation, or cabin deck space. The planks rest on sole bearers which are carried athwartships beneath the *floor.

cable, (1) basically any very large hemp or wire rope, but normally associated with the *anchor of a ship, and thus the means by which the ship is attached to the anchor as it lies on the bottom or is stowed in the *hawsepipe or inboard. The size of chain cable is measured by the diameter of the links. The length of a rope cable is 100 to 115 *fathoms, a *hawser-laid cable 130 fathoms. Chain cable is measured for length in *shackles of 12½ fathoms, eight shackles being considered as a cable length. **(2)** A measure of distance at sea, 100 fathoms or 200 yards (183 m).

cable-laid rope, a very thick and strong rope used only for the heaviest work and for the towing cables of tugs. It is made by laying-up (twisting) together three ordinary ropes, which have themselves been

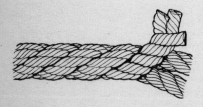

Cable laid rope

made by laying up three strands. Whereas in ordinary rope, known as *hawser-laid rope, the three strands are laid up from left to right, in cable-laid rope the three hawsers must be laid up from right to left, otherwise the strands in the hawser become untwisted and lose much of their strength and durability. If three hawser-laid ropes of 120 *fathoms in length each are laid up

in this way, they will make a cable-laid rope of 100 fathoms.

Cable-laid rope is sometimes known as cablet, and also as water-laid rope, because it absorbs less water than hawser-laid rope.

caique, from the Turkish *kaik*, a boat or skiff. **(1)** In its strict meaning it refers to the light boats propelled by one or two oars and used in Turkish waters, particularly the Bosphorus, but it was also used as a term for the Sultan's ceremonial barge when he went by water to a mosque or to his harem. The word has since been loosely applied to most small rowing boats and skiffs in the Levant. **(2)** A small Levantine sailing vessel, usually with a *lateen rig, but here again the name has been loosely expanded to include a variety of modern sailing and motorized vessels, used mainly for island trade, as far west as Greece and Corfu.

calashee (or coolashi) watch, a watch on deck in a full-rigged ship in which all hands, including the *watch below, must stand by for a call. They were most frequently required when a sailing ship was *tacking in narrow waters or in a particularly heavy sea. The word came apparently from the Hindustani *khalasi*, sailor, as the system on board native ships was to work their watches in this fashion.

call sign, a particular group of letters or numbers in the *Morse code used for identification. Radio beacons, used by vessels fitted with *radio direction finders for obtaining navigational *bearings, have individual call signs, or characteristics, by which they can be immediately identified.

camber, (1) the athwartships curve of a ship's deck, usually giving a fall towards the sides of a quarter of an inch to each foot. **(2)** A small enclosed dock in a dockyard in which timber for masts and yards was kept to weather and pickle in salt water; used also to provide a shelter for small boats.

can buoy, a *buoy in the form of a truncated cone, normally painted in red or red and white chequers and numbered with an even number, used to indicate the port hand side of a channel when entering with the flood tide. The starboard hand side of the channel is marked with *conical buoys.

canoe. The word was originally used for the small open boats of primitive peoples but was extended to embrace all similar craft, in which paddles were the motive force, all over the world as it was opened by the great geographical discoveries of the 17th and 18th centuries. Some canoes, particularly among the Pacific islands, were remarkably large vessels in which two banks of paddlers, up to twenty or thirty a side, were used. Today the term covers any very light craft propelled by a paddle. In recent years the number of canoes in use has increased immensely since canoeing has been developed as an inland water sport, the modern canoe being either of very light wooden construction or of canvas stretched across a light wooden frame. See also KAYAK, UMIAK.

cant, to, turn a ship's head one way or the other, according to the requirement at the time, when weighing *anchor or slipping from a *mooring. It may, for example, be necessary to cant the ship's head to *port (or *starboard) in order to avoid other shipping or navigational hazards in the immediate vicinity.

canvas, a cloth properly woven from hemp (the word 'canvas' derives from *kannabis*, the Greek for hemp). It is used at sea mainly for sails, *awnings, etc. It is numbered according to the thickness and weave, the lowest number being the coarsest and strongest, the highest number being the lightest. It is also a synonym for sails, a ship under sail being said to be under canvas. See also BOLT.

cap, the wooden block on the top of a mast through which the mast above is drawn when being *stepped or lowered when being struck. It has two holes, one of them square which is fixed firmly to the top of the lower mast, the other circular through which the topmast is hoisted, until its *heel is nearly level with the base of the cap, in which position it is then secured with a *fid and sometimes also with a *parrel lashing, being held upright by *shrouds and *stays. In ships where *topgallant masts were stepped, there were similar caps on the tops of the topmasts. A *bowsprit cap serves a similar service for the *jib-boom. See also BULL ROPE.

Cape Horners, originally the American full-rigged ships which used to run regularly from the east to the west coast of America around Cape Horn during the 19th century. More recently the term has been adopted by societies of men who have rounded Cape Horn under sail and who meet to dine together and talk about their experiences.

capping, a strip of wood, usually of Canadian elm, fitted to the top of the *gunwale or *washstrake of wooden boats to strengthen it. In boats fitted to take oars, it is pierced at intervals to take *crutches or *thole pins, or cut away to form *rowlocks.

capsize, to, upset or overturn a vessel at sea or in harbour. In general capsizing results from natural causes, such as high winds or heavy seas, but it can also result from human error, such as faulty stowage of cargo which may cause a ship to become unstable and overturn.

capstan, a cylindrical barrel fitted in larger ships for heavy lifting work, particularly when working anchors and cables. It is normally placed on the centre line of the ship and is driven mechanically either by steam or electricity. In smaller ships the function of the capstan is taken over by a *windlass. The difference between a capstan and a windlass lies mainly in the fact that the spindle on which the barrel of a capstan is mounted is vertical, while that on which the drums and gypsies of a windlass are mounted is horizontal.

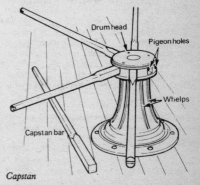

Capstan

caravel, the relatively small trading vessel of the Mediterranean in the 14th–17th centuries, taken up in the 16th century by the Spanish and Portuguese authorities for voyages of exploration as well as for trade.

Originally they were *lateen rigged on two masts (*caravela latina*), but the inconvenience of this rig for longer ocean voyages resulted in their development into three-masted ships with square *rig on the two forward masts and a lateen-rigged mizen (*caravela rotunda*). The average overall length of a three masted caravel was 75–80 feet, although a few were built with an overall length of up to 100 feet.

cardinal point, one of the four *points of north, south, east, and west on a magnetic compass card. The points halfway between these—north-east, south-east, south-west, and north-west—are known as half-cardinal points.

careen, to, in older days to heave a ship down on one side in order to expose the other for the purposes of cleaning the bottom of weeds and barnacles or of repair.

careenage, a suitable beach with a steep, sandy shore-line, where ships could be *careened for cleaning their bottoms of weed and barnacles or for repair.

carlings or **carlines,** pieces of squared timber fitted fore and aft between the deck *beams of a wooden ship. Their purpose is to provide support for the deck planking. In yacht and small wooden vessel construction, carlings carry the half-beams in the way of *hatches and other deck openings, supporting the *coamings of the hatches or the *coachroof above them.

carrack, the larger type of trading vessel of northern and southern Europe of the 14th–17th centuries, developed as a compromise between the typical square *rig of the northern European nations and the *lateen rig of the Mediterranean. Carracks were very similar in rig to the later three-masted development of the *caravel (*caravela rotunda*).

carrick bend, a round knot used to join two rope *hawsers when they are required

Single carrick bend

to go round the barrel of a *capstan, the need for such a special knot being that any

other, such as a *reef knot which is flat, could get jammed between the whelps of the capstan barrel.

carry away, to, break or part, used especially of objects on board ship, particularly *masts and *yards. It is an expression used also in the case of ropes and *hawsers when they break as a result of sudden violence, such as a particularly heavy gust of wind or a ship with too much way on her when attempting to secure alongside.

cartography, the science and practice of projecting an area of the earth's surface on to a flat plane, like a sheet of paper. There are a number of methods of projection, all of them with some advantages and some drawbacks. See, for example, GLOBULAR PROJECTION, MERCATOR PROJECTION.

carvel, a small *lateen-rigged vessel of the Mediterranean, normally with two masts, used for the carriage of small cargoes. Its period was the late middle ages, though it is thought by some to be a synonym for *caravel.

carvel construction or **carvel-built,** a method of building a wooden vessel or boat in which the side planks are all flush, the edges laid close and *caulked to make a smooth finish, as compared with *clinker-built, in which the side planks overlap.

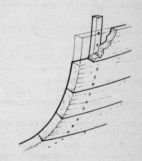

Carvel construction

casco, the local name given to a flat-bottomed, square-ended boat of the Philippine Islands, used as a lighter for ferrying cargo from ship to shore and vice versa.

cast, to, bring the bows of a sailing ship on to the required *tack, just as the anchor is leaving the ground on being *weighed, by hauling on the sheet of a headsail so that the wind will force the bows off in the required direction. When there is insufficient wind to cast with a headsail but a *tide is running, it is often possible to cast on to the required tack by putting the helm over and letting the force of the tide act on the rudder to turn the bows.

cast of the lead, the act of heaving the *lead and line to ascertain the depth of water. At each cast, the leadsman calls out the depth in fathoms of the water alongside the ship according to the *marks or *deeps of the line.

cast off, to, let go a *cable or rope securing a ship to a *buoy, another ship, or to a permanent structure.

cat, (1) the purchase by which a ship's *anchor, before the days of the stockless anchor, was hoisted to the *cathead in preparation for stowing or for letting go. (2) A small open sailing boat in the USA, more accurately known as a *cat-boat.

cat, to, hoist an anchor by its ring so that it hangs at the *cathead either in readiness for letting go or, after it has been weighed, in preparation for securing it on the anchor bed. Anchors were catted by means of a two-fold or three-fold *purchase according to the size and weight of the anchor, either the fixed block of the purchase being secured to the end of the cathead or, more usually, the sheaves being incorporated permanently into the cathead itself. The whole process of catting an anchor was necessary only with anchors fitted with *stocks; the invention and almost universal adoption of the stockless anchor made the process of catting the anchor in preparation for letting go obsolete in all modern vessels.

catamaran, from the Tamil *katta*, to tie, *maram*, wood, has several nautical meanings, the most common being a twin-hulled sailing *yacht, normally used for racing but also recently developed for cruising purposes. The twin hulls are connected by an above-water deck which carries mast and rigging, cockpit, and cabin. Normally rigged with *Bermuda mainsail and jib, catamarans can by reason of their low immersion area attain speeds considerably in excess of conventionally hulled sailing boats. See also MULTI-HULL, TRIMARAN.

cat-boat, a type of sailing boat which originated in the middle of the 19th century in the Cape Cod region of America, primarily for fishing in shallow waters but later adopted as a favourite type of *sandbagger for racing, as well as for coastal cruising.

catenary, the curve of an anchor *cable as it lies between the *anchor on the sea bottom and the vessel which lies to it. The deeper the curve, the more the catenary. A good catenary is essential for two reasons, the first being that the eventual pull on the anchor is horizontal, which tends to bury the anchor *flukes deeper into the ground; the second being that with the elasticity provided by a deep curve in the cable a vessel is prevented from *snubbing to her anchor as she rides to a sea. It is for this reason that most anchor cables, except in the very smallest craft, are made of chain, where the weight of the chain tends to form a natural catenary.

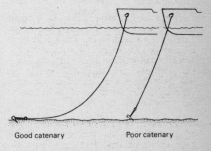

Good catenary   Poor catenary

cathead, a heavy piece of curved timber projecting from each bow of a ship for the purpose of holding *anchors which were fitted with a *stock in position for letting go or for securing them on their beds after weighing. It holds the upper sheaves of the *cat purchase which is used to draw the anchor up to the cathead, a process known as catting the anchor. Since the invention of the stockless anchor, which is now almost universal in its use except in the few square-rigged ships still in commission, ships no longer have these large catheads, or need to cat their anchors before letting them go. But when a large ship secures to a mooring buoy with her cable, she first secures her anchor to a clump cathead where it remains hanging while the cable is in use to hold the ship to the buoy.

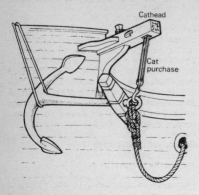

Cathead

cat rig, see UNA RIG.

catspaw, (1) a twisting hitch made in the bight of a rope to form two eyes, through which the hook of a tackle is passed for hoisting purposes. **(2)** The name given to a ruffle on the water indicating a breath of wind during a calm. Old sailors, on seeing a catspaw on the surface of the water, would frequently rub the ship's backstay (as though fondling a cat) and whistle to induce the wind to come to the ship.

Catspaw

caulk, to, drive, with a caulking iron, *oakum or rope *junk into the *seams of a ship's wooden deck or sides in order to render them impervious to water. After the oakum is driven in hard, the gap between the planks is filled with hot pitch or some other composition to prevent the oakum from rotting through contact with water.

cavitation, the loss of effective propeller thrust caused by the blades of a propeller cutting across the column of water sucked along by the propeller instead of working in it. It can be caused by a propeller being too small, or too near the surface for the head of water pressure to supply a solid stream for the propeller to work in, by poor streamlining of the blades or of the after *run of the hull form, or by too thick a leading blade on the propeller itself.

cay, see KEY.

celestial navigation, see NAVIGATION.

celestial sphere, the imaginary sphere on to which the heavenly bodies appear to be projected. For illus. see ECLIPTIC.

centreboard, a device to increase temporarily the *draught of some sailing vessels. In most shallow-draught vessels, such as sailing *dinghies, etc., it is basically a plate pivoted at one end which can be lowered to increase the lateral underwater area and provide resistance to *leeway. It is normally housed inboard in a case with its

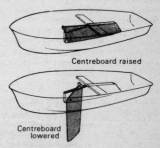

Centreboard raised

Centreboard lowered

bottom open to the sea. Although it is accepted that certain Chinese river *junks were the first to employ a wooden drop, or sliding, keel which was raised and lowered on *tackles through a watertight case whose top came above the deck, the invention of the centreboard for small craft is generally attributed to America during colonial times. The need to be able to sail to windward, *close-hauled, with an entirely flat-bottomed work boat arose from the great stretches of very shallow waters found in Chesapeake Bay and along the Atlantic seaboard from Long Island Sound to Florida, and so the centreboard was born. It was introduced into England in 1774 by Lord Percy when he had a small vessel built at Boston, Massachusetts, on the lines of the local boats and fitted with one centreboard which was almost as long as the boat's keel, and had the boat shipped to England for trials.

By altering the shape of the centreboard and hanging it on a pivot at the fore end, Captain Shuldham of the Royal Navy introduced a distinct improvement in 1809 which became the most common form of centreboard today. In the USA a number of local types of work boat such as *scows, *skipjacks, bugeyes, *cat-boats, oyster *sloops and trading *schooners up to 150 feet in length, as well as many yachts, were built with pivoted centreboards. In the larger vessels the centreboard is generally built up from wooden planks, weighted to make it sink; schooners over 80 feet in length sometimes had two such centreboards. While centreboards and dagger plates are normally used in sailing and racing dinghies and yachts of shallow draught, metal centreplates, usually of bronze, have been fitted within the lead *ballast keels of some racing yachts in recent years. With their use the yacht can gain a little over a similar fixed keel competitor by increasing the lateral resistance to leeway when sailing on a wind (*close-hauled), and when the course brings the wind free the plate is raised and the amount of *wetted surface friction is accordingly reduced, allowing the yacht a little extra speed down wind. See also DROP KEEL.

centre of buoyancy, a point through which the resultant of all buoyant forces on an immersed hull is assumed to act. It is about this point that a vessel afloat could be said to be poised. It is also sometimes known as the centre of displacement, of cavity, or of flotation.

centre of effort, a point of the sail plan of a sailing vessel through which the resultant of all wind forces is assumed to act. In a sail plan each sail is assumed to have its centre of effort at its geometric centre, and on a drawing of a vessel's sail plan the resultant of these forces is assumed to be the centre of effort of the whole sail plan. In practice,

however, the sails are never completely flat as shown on the plan, and the actual centre of effort moves at every fresh trimming of the sheets.

centre of lateral resistance, a point assumed to lie at the geometric centre of a sailing vessel's underwater profile. On a vessel's design plans this is indicated with the hull floating upright on its designed waterline. In practice, however, with sailing vessels heeled under a press of canvas and lifting and pitching over seas, the actual centre of lateral resistance is constantly shifting.

chafe, see BAGGYWRINKLE.

chain, see CABLE.

chain, or **cable, locker,** a compartment below decks in which a ship's *cable is stowed when the *anchor has been weighed and secured and the cable is all inboard.

chain-plate, one of the strips of iron or bronze with their lower ends bolted to the ship's side under the channels of sailing vessels. They carry the *deadeyes or rigging screws to which the standing rigging is secured. In the older sailing ships these deadeyes were attached to short lengths of chain secured to the ship's side, and the name remained when chains were superseded by a plate. For illus. see SHROUDS.

chapelled. A ship is said to be chapelled, or to build a chapel, when, after losing her *way through the water in a light or baffling wind, she turns completely round or, when *close-hauled, goes *about without bracing her head-yards and then comes back on to the same tack as before. It can be caused either by the inattention of the helmsman or by a quick change in direction of the wind.

chapels, the grooves in a built-up, or 'made', wooden *mast in which several pieces of timber are used to fashion it. In large sailing ships the lower masts were all 'made' *spars, the *topmasts and *topgallant masts were whole spars. The chapels occurred where the various pieces of which the mast was made were joined together.

characteristics, the distinguishing qualities of a navigational light, whether from a *lighthouse, *lightship, or lighted *buoy, by which the navigator of a ship can easily identify it. In addition to their colours, white, red, or green, individual lights can be recognized by whether they are alternating, fixed, flashing, fixed and flashing, or occulting, and by the number or group of exposures in each cycle.

An alternating light is one in which two colours are used, exposed alternately in each cycle of the light and always in the same order. The colours are sometimes separated by periods of darkness, and sometimes alternate continuously. A fixed light shows a steady beam with no period of darkness, and thus has no cycle; a fixed and flashing light is one which shows a steady beam varied at regular intervals with a flash of brighter intensity. A flashing light is one in which the period in which the light is visible is less than the period of darkness between flashes in each cycle; an occulting light one in which the period of darkness is less than the period of light in each cycle.

These five main types are further varied for recognition purposes by what is known as grouping, in which a series of flashes or a series of eclipses (occulting) is separated by intervals of darkness or light. Thus in a group flashing light two or more flashes are visible at regular intervals in each cycle; in a group occulting light there are two or more short intervals of darkness in each cycle. As an example, a light indicated on a chart as a group flashing light with four flashes every 15 seconds (Gp.Fl.(4)15 sec.) would show to the navigator four bright flashes with an interval of a second or so between them followed by a period of darkness occupying the rest of the 15 seconds. The 15 seconds is the period, or cycle, of the light, and is measured from the first flash in one group to the first flash in the next succeeding group.

Another differentiation of characteristics, introduced since the the the Second World War, is the quick flashing light, which is a modification of the flashing and group flashing systems. This comprises a light which displays rapid flashes at a greater rate than once every second. These quick flashing lights can be divided into three characteristics, quick flashing (Qk.Fl.) in which the flashes are continuous, interrupted quick flashing (Int.Qk.Fl.), in which a number of quick flashes are separated by an interval of darkness, and group interrupted quick flashing (Gp.Int.Qk.Fl.), in which a group of quick flashes, each separated by a short interval of darkness, is itself separated from the succeeding group by a longer interval of darkness.

The characteristics of every light, though not every lighted buoy, are clearly marked on all charts and are also listed, with the exception of lighted buoys and wreck-marking vessels, in the *Admiralty List of Lights*. Details of lighted buoys are listed in the *Sailing Directions* appropriate to the waters in which they are situated and are also marked on the largest scale chart of each area.

chart, a representation on a plane surface (paper) of an area of a spherical surface (the earth) for use for navigational purposes. In general terms, two types of charts are produced for use navigationally, a straightforward navigational chart, on the *Mercator or equivalent projection, in which the *rhumb line courses appear as straight lines, and *gnomonic charts, on which great circle bearings appear as straight lines. In general navigation terms, ships steaming from one place to another across the gnomonic projection are used when wireless and direction-finding bearings, which travel in great circles, need to be plotted. A modern development, following the wide introduction of radio aids to navigation such as Decca, Loran, etc. is the combination of these two charts into one by the superimposition of hyperbolic graticules in colour on the navigational detail of the ordinary chart.

A chart is essentially a map of a sea area, showing on it any coastlines, rocks, etc., within the area covered, the positions of buoys, lighthouses, and other prominent features, the *characteristics of all lights, and depths of water below the *chart datum. A compass rose on every chart shows the direction and annual rate of increase of *variation.

chart datum, the level below which depths indicated on a chart are measured and above which heights of the *tide are expressed in *tide tables. The level is essentially one below which the sea surface seldom falls. It is normally the mean level of low water at ordinary *spring tide (M.L.W.O.S.). The datum used is usually expressed on the chart, always if a different datum from M.L.W.O.S. is used.

charter, the contract for the employment of a ship or yacht. Charters are of two main types, a time charter, in which the owners of the vessel provide the crew and all other requirements for operating the ship; and bare hull, or bare pole, charter, in which the charterer provides the crew and all other requirements. Yachts are frequently chartered for short periods for holiday purposes, with or without a crew.

chasse-marée, the French name for a coasting vessel, one which works the tides.

check, to, (1) ease away slowly, particularly used in connection with a *purchase such as the falls of a lifeboat or the *sheets of sails. **(2)** Bring a vessel to a stop, by letting go an *anchor, by a mooring wire made fast to a wharf, or by going astern on the engines.

cheeks, pieces of timber bolted to the mast of a sailing ship below the masthead to support the *trestle-trees.

cheese down, to, coil down the tail of a rope on deck to present a neat appearance. The end of the tail is in the centre and the remainder coiled flat round it in a tight spiral, each *fake touching those on either side of it so that the finished coil looks like a spiral rope mat lying on the deck. When a fall has been cheesed down, the final result is itself called a cheese. The end of a rope should never be cheesed down if it is required to *render quickly through a *block, as the tight coiling which forms a cheese is apt to make the rope kink when uncoiled quickly and thus to jam in the block. A rope so coiled is also known as a *Flemish coil.

chesstrees, two pieces of oak secured to the *topsides of a square-rigged sailing ship at the point where the curve of the bow began to straighten for the run aft, one on each side of the ship. Normally they had a hole through them in the centre, but occasionally they were fitted with a sheave. The *bowlines with which the main *tacks were hauled down were led through the hole or the sheave in the chesstrees to give the crew a clear haul.

chine, (1) the angle where the bottom *strakes of a boat meet the sides. In a hard-

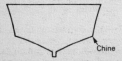
Chine

chined boat this angle is pronounced; in a soft-chined boat it is rounded off gradually.

(2) That part of the waterway along the edges of the upper deck of a wooden vessel which projects above the deck-plank so that the lower seams of spirketting can more conveniently be *caulked.

Chinese gybe, a type of wild and unpremeditated *gybe which occurs in a sailing vessel when the main *boom lifts over to the *lee side of the vessel while the *gaff does not follow. It is so called because it is common with the Chinese *junk rig with its light bamboo *battens and no boom to hold the *foot of the mainsail steady.

chock, to, secure articles in a ship to prevent their taking charge in rough weather when the vessel is rolling excessively.

chock-a-block, the position when two *blocks of a *tackle come together so that no further movement is possible. It is also known as 'two blocks'.

chocolate gale, the sailor's name for the brisk north-west wind which is the prevalent wind in the West Indies and off the Spanish Main.

Choking the luff

choke the luff, to, temporarily stop all movement of a rope through a *block by placing the hauling part across the *sheave of the block, where it jams the sheave and holds it tight. A pull on the hauling part releases the sheave.

chops, the area where tides meet to cause an irregular sea, or where a channel meets the sea. 'Chops of the Channel', the western entrance of the English Channel when approaching from the Atlantic.

chronometer, in the words of the *Admiralty Manual of Navigation*, '...simply an enlarged watch...and its mechanism is by no means complicated although its construction demands the most accurate workmanship, and its adjustment requires a high degree of skill'. The *longitude of a ship at sea may readily be found by comparing the local time and the corresponding *Greenwich Mean Time.

The essential feature of the traditional type of chronometer is the contrivance known as the compensated balance. This is a bimetallic device which compensates for temperature changes. Without a compensated balance an increase in temperature causes the rate of a timekeeper to be retarded; conversely, a decrease causes an accelerated rate.The object of the compensated balance is to correct this defect. But since the advent of radio time signals, the need for expensive chronometers no longer exists. It is an irony of navigational history that now that the need for a chronometer is almost non-existent a new type of marine chronometer which is reputed to have an accuracy of one part in a million has been produced. This degree of accuracy means that its *rate of change is within a little more than a second per month.

chubasco, the name by which the violent easterly squall which blows on the western coast of Nicaragua and in the mouth of the Orinoco River is known to mariners.

cirrus, a type of cloud formation. See METEOROLOGY.

clamps, (1) pieces of timber fixed longitudinally to the *masts or *yards of square-rigged ships to strengthen them if they showed signs of weakness or bursting under strain. See also FISH. **(2)** Planks laid fore and aft under the *beams of the orlop and lower decks in wooden ships and *fayed to the timbers to add strength to the ship's structure. **(3)** *Strakes fastened to the inside of wooden ships' sides to form a support on which the ends of the deck beams can rest, the *knees being bolted or fastened with *treenails or bolts to the clamps.

clap on, to, add something temporarily to an existing part. Thus, a *purchase is clapped on to a *guy or *fall when additional hauling power is required. Some masters of sailing vessels used to order additional sails to be clapped on to take advantage of a fair wind. A *whipping is clapped on to the end of a rope, particularly in the case of a *West Country Whipping where the two ends are brought up and changed from hand to hand, with an overhand knot at top and bottom.

class or **classification,** the degree of seaworthiness of a ship as determined by a survey based upon her construction and the size, or *scantlings, of the materials used in her building. A vessel is classed in this way for a definite period of years, and on its expiry she must be resurveyed if she wishes to retain her original classification. In addition, after any disaster such as fire or shipwreck, a ship has to be resurveyed to re-establish her classification.

In Britain the body which issues such classifications is Lloyd's Register of Shipping, which has committees representing it in all maritime nations in the world. The modern Lloyd's classification is 100 A, with the figure 1 following the A if the survey includes her anchors and cables. The famous old classification, A 1 at Lloyd's, is used now only for ships that operate in local waters, such as rivers, estuaries, etc. Many of the principal maritime nations now have their own method of classification.

claw off, to, beat to windward in a sailing vessel to avoid being driven on to a *lee shore. The expression implies danger of shipwreck because of a combination of a rough sea and a strong onshore wind.

claw ring, a fitting on the main *boom of a yacht to take the main sheet where roller reefing (see REEF) is fitted.

clean, used of the lines of a vessel's hull when they give a fine and unobstructed *run from bow to stern so that she moves through the water smoothly without undue turbulence. A clean entrance, a clear run of the hull from a ship's bows so that she goes through the water without the swell of her bow creating undue resistance and turbulence in the water. A clean run aft, the same conditions at the ship's stern, a smooth tapering of the hull lines into the stern so that no *cavitation or drag is produced at the stern as the vessel moves through the water.

clean slate, originally a log-slate, on which the *courses steered by a ship and the distances run as indicated on a *log were entered during the course of a *watch. At the end of the watch, the information on the slate was entered in the deck-log and the slate wiped clean so that the officer keeping the next watch could enter on it the courses and distances made good during his watch. The term has entered the English language as an expression meaning that past actions and occurrences are forgotten (wiped off the slate) and a new start can be made.

cleat, (1) a piece of wood or metal with two arms placed at convenient stations on board ship to which ropes or *falls can be made fast by taking two or three turns under and over the arms. (2) Cleats were also small wedges of elm or oak fastened to the *yards of square-rigged sailing ships to prevent ropes or the *earings of the sails from slipping off the yard.

clench, to, make a permanent join. Thus a clenched *shackle, with which the end of a chain *cable, for example, is secured to the bottom of the *chain locker, has its bolt hammered over so that it cannot be removed, thus closing the shackle permanently. See also CLINCH.

clew or **clue,** in a fore-and-aft sail, the lower aftermost corner; in a square sail, the two lower corners. In cases where fore-and-aft sails are not normally *laced to a *boom, such as *jibs, *staysails, etc. It is the corner of the sail to which the *sheet, by which the sail is trimmed, is secured; in fore-and-aft sails which normally are laced to a boom, the clew is usually fitted with an *outhaul so that the *foot of the sail can be stretched tautly along the boom. For illus. see SAIL.

clew, or **clue, cringle,** a spectacle iron (i.e., with two or more eyes) stitched into the *clews of a square sail so that two or more ropes or *tackles may be hooked into the eyes and led in different directions. They are used to give a greater movement to the *yards of a square-rigged ship when they are being *braced to the wind.

clew, or **clue, garnet,** the clew line or *tackle of a lower square sail in a square-rigged ship, by means of which the clews

are hauled up to the *yard and trussed when the sail needs to be furled or *goose-winged. In such a situation the sail is said to be clewed (or clued) up. Clew garnets are used only on the *courses of square-rigged ships, clew lines being used for all the smaller sails.

clinch, to, (1) fasten or knot large ropes to heavy objects by a half hitch with the end stopped back on its own part by a seizing. (2) Fasten the hull planking of small craft to the *frames or *timbers by turning over, or clinching, the ends of the copper nails in place of riveting them.

clinker-, or **clinch-, built,** a method of boat building in which the lower edge of each side plank overlaps the upper edge of the one below it. It is a method normally used only in small boat building as in larger vessels the added wetted surface produced by the overlapping planks would cause additional skin friction as the vessel progresses through the water. In the USA this method of building is known as lap-strake. For a comparison, see CARVEL CONSTRUCTION.

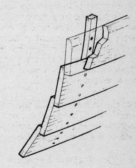

Clinker construction

cliphooks, two hooks of similar shape facing in opposite directions and attached to the same *thimble. They have a flat inner side so that they can lie together to form an *eye and are much used in small tackles where an ordinary hook might jump out.

clipper, the generic name used very loosely to describe types of very fast sailing ships. It was applied first to the speedy *schooners built in Virginia and Maryland, known as the Baltimore clippers (though in fact they were not really clippers) which became famous during the War of 1812 as blockade runners and privateers, and subsequently notorious as slave ships carrying human cargoes from Africa to the USA. Their hull design, long and low, with a draught deeper aft than forward, a very sharp-raked *stem (the true mark of a clipper), and an inclined, overhanging *counter stern, thus reducing the area of hull in contact with the water, was later combined with the three-masted square rig in the beautiful clipper ships of the mid-19th century, the finest productions of the age of sail.

The term itself is said to have been coined because these very fast ships could clip the time taken on passage by the regular packet ships, themselves very fast in their day.

close-hauled, with the sails trimmed so as to sail as close to the wind as possible with all sails full and not shivering. In a square-rigged sailing ship this condition is achieved when her *yards are *braced as near to the fore-and-aft line as possible so that the wind, coming over the bow, fills the sails and drives the ship forward. When close-hauled, the square-rigged ship could get as near as about six *points off the wind. In ships with a fore-and-aft rig, to sail close-hauled is to harden in the *sheets as much as possible to bring the sails in flatter so that the wind strikes them at an acute angle. With this rig a vessel can keep her sails full without shivering when about four points off the wind, although with the modern high and narrow *Bermuda rig it is sometimes possible to sail even a little closer to the wind. See POINT OF SAILING.

close-reefed, the description of a square-rigged ship when all the *reefs of the topsails have been taken in.

cloths, the strips of *canvas or other cloth which are *seamed together to form a *sail. They are normally the width of the *bolt from which they are cut in order that they may be seamed along the selvedges, which are considerably stronger than a cut edge.

clove hitch, a *bend formed by two half hitches, the second reversed so that the standing part is between the hitches, used at sea for making a line fast to a spar or a smaller line fast to a larger rope. It is also used when securing the *painter of a dinghy to a *bollard. It will not slip because the second half hitch rides over the standing part of the rope.

club haul, to, tack a square-rigged ship in a narrow space by letting go the *lee anchor from the bow, though with the hawser led aft and stopped on the quarter, as soon as the wind is out of the foresails. As the ship gathered sternway the pull of the anchor brought her head round on the other tack and the anchor hawser was cut. This method was only used in an emergency in heavy weather and when the ship was embayed.

clump block, a large single block with a wide *swallow, used for a variety of daily purposes on board ship. They are made with a thicker case than the usual run of blocks carried in a ship so as to provide added strength to the *purchases in which they are used.

coach-roof, the name by which the cabin top in older yachts is known.

coachwhipping, a form of decorative square *sinnet work made with an even number of strands to form a herring-bone pattern. It was used occasionally in the decorative *pointing of a rope but more usually for covering *stanchions with a patterned sinnet to make a ship look smart and *tiddley.

coak, originally a wooden dowel, but the meaning has been extended to describe the small brass bearing in the centre of the sheave of a *block to keep it from splitting and to prevent wear by the pin on which it turns.

coaming, the name given to the raised lip, usually about six to nine inches high, with which openings in the upper deck, such as *hatchways leading to the deck below, are framed to prevent any water on deck from

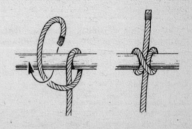

Clove hitch

running down the openings. In yachts, coamings are the vertical sides of the coach-roof or hatches above the deck.

coastal navigation, see NAVIGATION.

coble, a flat-bottomed, *clinker-built fishing boat used in coastal waters, particularly on the north-east coast of England, with a mast and *lug-sail, and occasionally a *jib on a temporary *bowsprit, and fitted for rowing with three pairs of oars. It was in a coble that Grace Darling and her father rowed out to the rescue of the crew of the *Forfarshire* when she went aground off the Outer Farne Island light in 1838 during a storm.

cock, the maritime term for what is called a tap on shore. Many of the essential pipes used in a ship or boat have their outlet to the sea, and it is necessary to fit a cock at the outboard end to prevent seawater coming and flooding through the pipe.

cockbill or **a-cockbill, (1)** the situation of the *anchor, in the days when ships carried anchors with *stocks, when it has been lifted clear of its anchor bed, its cable bent on, and hangs 'up and down' at the *cathead ready for letting go. Similarly, when brought to the cathead after weighing in preparation for being secured on the anchor bed, it hangs a-cockbill. **(2)** The yards of a square-rigged sailing ship are a-cockbill when they are trimmed by topping them up with one *lift so that they lie at an angle to the deck. Yards a-cockbill used to be a sign of mourning for the death of a member of the crew.

cocked hat, the small triangular space usually found at the intersection of position lines on a chart when a ship's position is determined by plotting three bearings. With perfect observation and plotting, the three position lines should intersect at a common point; if they do not, a cocked hat is formed. This provides sure proof of error in the process of fixing the ship, often caused by a small error in the *compass, and, in general, the larger the cocked hat, the greater the error. Navigators normally take the centre of the cocked hat, when it is not large, as the position of the ship.

cockpit, the well of a yacht or small sailing vessel where the steering wheel or *tiller is located. It normally gives access to the saloon, but in some modern yachts a separate central cockpit is incorporated where the steering wheel and navigational instruments are situated.

cockscomb, the name of a serrated *cleat often fitted to the ends of the *yards in square-rigged ships to which the *reef earings are hauled out and lashed when a sail is being reefed.

codline, small line laid up with eighteen threads. It was originally the line used in fishing for cod, but has also a variety of uses on board ship for purposes where small rope would be too large and clumsy.

cog, a type of small sailing craft used for local commerce on the rivers Humber and Ouse in north-east England.

coil, the normal method for the stowage of rope on board ship, laid up in circular turns known as *fakes. The direction in which the coils are laid up depends on the *lay of the rope; if it is laid-up right-handed the rope is coiled clockwise from left to right, if laid-up left-handed, it is coiled anticlockwise from right to left. The reason for this is that the correct direction of coiling keeps the lay of the rope tight. Hemp rope is always coiled clockwise since it is always laid up right-handed. A range of fakes in the same plane is known as a tier, and a complete coil of rope consists of several tiers each consisting of several fakes. Wire rope is almost invariably coiled on a drum, though still consisting of fakes and tiers, as if not coiled on a drum it will not hold its shape as will rope made from fibres.

A Flemish coil, or cheese, is rope coiled flat on the deck in concentric turns forming only one tier, with the end of the rope in the centre. Its purpose is to give a neat, or *tiddley, finish to the *falls of *running rigging, etc., when a vessel is anchored or secured to moorings and at rest.

coir, rope made from the husks of the coconut, light enough to float but with only about one-quarter the strength of *manila rope. It has many uses, particularly when bringing assistance to a ship in distress at sea when coir rope can be floated down across her bows enabling her to haul in a heavier cable for towing purposes. In a small sailing vessel running before a following wind and sea, a coir rope towed astern steadies the vessel down and allows the seas to pass under her. See also GRASS-LINE.

cold front, the line in a typical depression where the cold air coming in to fill the low pressure area meets with warm air and pushes it up in a wave-shaped bulge. This line is known as a cold front, and always follows a *warm front, which is the line in front of the bulge where the warm air has not yet been overtaken by the cold. As a cold front always travels faster than a warm front, it eventually catches it up and pushes underneath the warm air to fill up the *depression, a process known as occlusion. See DEPRESSION for illus., and MET-EOROLOGY.

collar, (1) a name given originally to the lower end of the principal *stays of a mast in a square-rigged ship, but later to the rope, with a *deadeye in its end, to which the stay was secured at its lower end. Thus, the collar of the forestay was the short length of rope attached to the stem of the ship to which the stay was set up and secured. **(2)** The *eye in the upper end of a stay or in the *bight of the *shrouds which is threaded over the masthead before being set up taut to hold the mast secure. **(3)** The neck of a ring bolt.

collision mat, a large square of very stout canvas roped and fitted with hogging lines at each corner to allow it to be drawn under the hull of a ship. The canvas is *thrummed with small stuff or *oakum to act as a sealing agent. When drawn over a damaged part of the hull, the pressure of the seawater forces it tight against the ship's side and limits the inflow to little more than a trickle.

colours, the name by which the national flag flown by a ship at sea is known.

come, to, a verb with many maritime meanings. When a helmsman in a sailing vessel receives an order to come no nearer, he is to hold the vessel as close as she already is to the wind and not attempt to sail any closer. A ship comes to an *anchor when she lets it go. 'Come up to the *capstan', an order to walk the *cable back to take off the strain or to *veer some of the cable; 'come up the *tackle', an order to let go the *fall.

come home, to, an *anchor is said to come home, or be coming home, when its *flukes are not holding in the ground and it *drags.

common log, see LOG.

common whipping, a whipping widely used to prevent the strands at the end of a rope from unlaying or fraying. The end of the whipping twine is laid along the rope towards its end and a number of turns of the twine passed round the rope against its *lay, each turn being hauled taut. At about

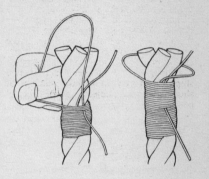

Common whipping

half the length of the required whipping, the other end of the twine is laid along the rope in the opposite direction and the whipping continued with the bight of the twine, taking the bight over the end of the rope with each turn. When the bight becomes too small to pass over the end of the rope, the second end of the twine is hauled through the turns until the whole whipping is taut. The two ends are then cut off. See also SAILMAKER'S WHIPPING, WEST COUNTRY WHIPPING.

companion, nowadays refers to the covering over an upper deck hatchway which leads to the companion-way, or staircase, to the deck below. The word is also loosely used today in place of companion-way and is generally understood to mean the stairs themselves.

compass, the instrument by which a ship may be steered on a pre-selected course and by which *bearings of visible objects may be taken to fix a ship's position on a chart. There are two types of compass in use at sea, the magnetic compass, of which the north mark points to the magnetic north pole, and the gyroscopic, or gyro, compass, of which the north mark points to the true north pole. The magnetic compass depends for its action on the horizontal component of the earth's magnetic field while the gyroscopic compass is electrically driven and owes its directional properties to a spinning wheel.

A third type of compass, the Azimuth compass, was designed to observe the amount of magnetic *variation. It is no longer in use, as an azimuth ring, which fits over the top of the standard compass and can rotate around it, enables an azimuth bearing to be taken simply and easily. A magnifying prism is the only sight required. Today there is no need to observe the amount of variation anywhere in the world, since it is recorded on every chart, and azimuth rings are used mainly when *swinging ship to discover the individual ship's *deviation, or to take bearings of shore and other objects in the normal course of navigation.

compass error, the combination of *variation and *deviation, is the horizontal angle between the direction indicated by the north point of a magnetic compass card and the true north. It is named east or west according to whether the compass points to the right or to the left of the true direction. It must be applied to all true *courses taken from a chart in order to ascertain the corresponding compass courses. Likewise it must be applied to compass *bearings in order to find the corresponding true bearings for laying down on a navigational chart.

composite built, planked with wood on an iron or steel frame. A great many of the *clipper ships of the mid-19th century were composite built, as also were many yachts up to about the beginning of the 20th century.

composite great circle sailing, a method of sailing between two positions along the shortest route possible without crossing to the poleward side of a parallel of specified *latitude. A feature of *great circle sailing is that a great circle route, unless it be along a *meridian, lies on the poleward side of the corresponding *rhumb line route.

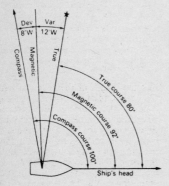

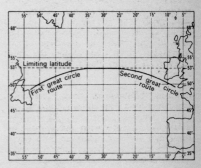

Composite great circle

concluding line, a small line rove through the centre of the wooden steps of a Jacob's ladder or a stern ladder. It is used for hauling up the ladder for stowage, when each step collapses on top of the step below it.

conical buoy, a *buoy in the shape of a cone used to mark the *starboard hand side of a channel when entering with the flood

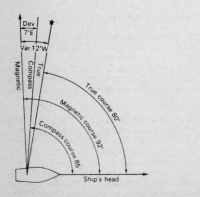

Compass error with westerly (above) and easterly (below) deviation

tide. They are generally painted black or some other solid colour and are usually marked with odd numbers. The *port hand side of a channel is indicated with *can buoys, marked with even numbers. In the USA a conical buoy is known as a nun buoy.

consol, see NAVIGATION.

continental shelf, the area of sea around a land mass where the depth increases gradually before it plunges into the deeps of the ocean.

contline, the modern name of the spiral grooves between the *strands of a rope after it has been *laid up. It is, perhaps, a less suggestive and more refined name for these grooves than the original term cunting.

co-ordinates, the definition of the exact position of a point on the surface of the globe in relation to two lines, *latitude and *longitude, which intersect at right angles.

coppered, used of the hull of a wooden ship when sheathed below the waterline with thin sheets of copper to prevent the teredo worm eating into the planks and also to limit weed and barnacles building up on the ship's bottom.

coracle, from the Welsh *corwgl*, carcass, or Irish *curach*, boat, a small boat, occasionally circular but more often rectangular with rounded corners, constructed of wickerwork and made watertight originally with animal hides but more recently with pitch or some other watertight material. It was originally used for river and coastal transport by the ancient Britons, and is still used by fishermen, mainly for salmon, on the rivers and lakes of Wales and Ireland. It is light enough to be carried easily on a man's back.

Corbie's aunt, a term sometimes used by fishermen in the north-east of Scotland to describe *St. Elmo's Fire or *corposant.

cord, small laid-up rope of an inch or less in circumference, more often referred to in ships as 'line'. It is about half-way between twine and rope, and is used on board for a variety of purposes where rope would be too large and clumsy. It is also widely described as *codline.

Corinthian, a 19th- and early 20th-century term for an amateur yachtsman

who sails his own yacht, i.e., without the aid of a professional skipper. The term originated in the USA in the mid-19th century to describe a rich amateur sportsman, and spread to Britain mainly in its yachting connotation.

corposant, from the Italian *corpo santo*, the fiery balls or brushes which appear at the masthead or at the yardarms of ships when the air is surcharged with electricity. See ST. ELMO'S FIRE.

counter, the arch forming the overhanging *stern of a vessel above the waterline, its top, or crown, being formed by the aftermost *deck beams and its lower ends terminating the wing *transoms and *buttocks. The term is also loosely used to indicate the small area of deck abaft the sternpost or rudder-head. Most yachts are built with counter sterns, particularly racing yachts where the counter is often pronounced, with a long overhang. **Counter stern,** the overhang of the stern abaft the rudder used in the sense of describing a type of stern. **Sawn-off counters,** as above, but with the aftermost part terminating abruptly in a vertical end instead of being carried on in the normal line of the hull form.

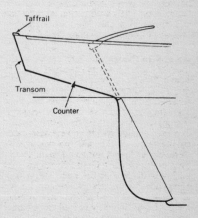

Taffrail

Transom

Counter

Typical yacht counter

counter brace, to, *brace the head-*yards one way and the after-yards the other when going *about, or lying to the wind, in a square-rigged ship. The counter brace is the *lee brace of the fore topsail yard at the time of going about. When the fore topsail begins to shake as the ship is brought up into the wind, the lee brace is hauled in hard to flatten the sail against the weather side of the topmast to force the ship's head across the wind.

counter current, that part of the water which is diverted from the main stream of a current by an obstruction or by the formation of the land and which as a result flows in the opposite direction. It is also the term given to the reverse movement of water caused by many of the big ocean currents, such as the Humboldt, Gulf Stream, etc., which have their own counter currents just outside the limits of their main stream where the water flows in the opposite direction as a compensatory movement.

course, the horizontal angle contained between the direction of north or south and that of the fore-and-aft line of a vessel extended ahead. The angles between true, magnetic, and *compass norths and souths and the path of a vessel are known respectively as true course, magnetic course, and compass course. The angular difference between the true and magnetic course is known as *variation, and that between magnetic and compass course as *deviation. The combination of variation and deviation is the *compass error. See also GREAT CIRCLE, RHUMB LINE.

course, in theory, the sails set upon the lower *yards of a square-rigged ship to which *bonnets could be attached. The original spelling for these sails was corps or corse. But the original definition of course was extended to sails set on the lower yards irrespective of whether they were adapted to carry bonnets, and they were designated by the name of the mast on which they were set, as fore course and main course (and mizen course). Gradually staysails set on lower masts and the main staysails of *brigs and *schooners also became known as courses. A ship which set only foresail, mainsail, and mizen was said to be under her courses. For illus. see SAIL.

cove, (1) a small coastal inlet frequently protected from the worst of the prevailing winds by high cliffs or promontories. **(2)** A thin, hollowed line cut along a yacht's sheer strake below deck level, and traditionally gilded. It is also known as a caveta.

covering board, the name given, particularly in yacht construction, to the outermost plank of the main deck, which is usually wider than the other deck planks.

cow-hitch, any *bend or *hitch which slips as a result of being improperly tied; or a 'home-made' knot which is not a recognized maritime knot as used at sea. The great majority of knots used on board a ship have recognized purposes and each has stood the test of time as the best and most efficient knot for its purpose, and if a different knot is made up or 'invented' for such a purpose, it would qualify to be called a cow-hitch.

cowl, a ventilator with a bell-shaped top, which can be swivelled on deck to catch the wind and force it below.

CQR, a type of *anchor introduced for small vessels and yachts shortly before the Second World War. The *fluke is roughly in the form of two plough shares set back to back and is held to the *shank by a pin about which it can pivot to some extent. The CQR anchor has no *stock, but when it reaches the bottom, any pull on it automatically turns it over so that the point of the fluke digs into the ground. It has considerably greater holding power than a fisherman's anchor of comparable weight and, having no stock, cannot be fouled by the anchor cable. The CQR is not suitable as an anchor for large vessels because of the difficulty of stowing it on board, but it has proved admirably efficient for small craft, such as yachts, and is deservedly popular.

It was designed by Sir Geoffrey Taylor who originally proposed to name it the 'secure' anchor, but decided that the letters cqr, which give approximately the same sound, would be better remembered. In the USA it is usually known as a plow anchor. See also DANFORTH ANCHOR, and for illus. ANCHOR.

crab, a *capstan but without a drumhead, in which the bars are inserted right through the top of the barrel instead of into pigeon-holes in the upper perimeter (drumhead) as in a capstan proper, the holes for the bars in a crab being in different planes.

cradle, in general, any device which supports another when at rest.

crance, crans, or **cranze,** an iron band on the outer end of a *bowsprit fitted with eyes to take the bowsprit *shrouds and the *bobstay.

crane lines, (1) small ropes which were set up to keep the *lee *backstays from chafing against the *yards of a square-rigged ship when running with a quarter-ing wind. **(2)** The lines which were rove from the *spritsail topmast to the centre of the *forestay to steady the former, acting somewhat in the manner of a backstay. With the spritsail topmast set up on the *bowsprit, there was no way of staying it except by such temporary means.

crank, a sailing ship which, either by her construction or the stowage of her *ballast or cargo, heels too far to the wind, or one which through lack of ballast or cargo cannot carry sail without the danger of overturning, is said to be crank.

cringle, a short piece of rope worked *grommet fashion into the *bolt-rope of a sail and containing a metal thimble.

Cringle

cross-jack (pron. crojeck) **yard,** the lower *yard on the mizen-mast of a square-rigged ship, to the arms of which the *clews of the mizen topsail are ex-tended. In some sailing ships a sail, called a cross-jack, used to be set on this yard.

The term also applied to any fore-and-aft rigged ship which sets a square sail below the lower *crosstrees.

cross lashing, a method of lashing with a rope in which the consecutive turns, instead of lying close up against each other in the same direction, are crossed diagon-ally. This type of lashing, by binding in upon itself with each turn, is less liable to give or *render.

cross sea, a sea running in a contrary direction to the wind. During a gale in which the direction of the wind changes rapidly, such as during a cyclonic storm, the direction of the sea, whipped up by the wind, lasts for some hours after the wind has changed, throwing up a confused and irregular wave pattern which can be dan-gerous for ships caught in such a gale.

crosstrees, light timber or metal spread-ers fixed *athwartships across the *trestle-trees at the upper ends of lower masts and topmasts to give support to the tops and to spread the topmast and topgallant mast *shrouds. For illus. see also RIGGING.

crowd, to, carry excessive sail, particu-larly in square-rigged ships, or approach too closely another ship which has the right of way (SEE RULE OF THE ROAD).

crown, (1) a knot formed by tucking the strands of a rope's end over and under each other to lock them and prevent them unravelling. A crown knot made on top of a *wall knot is the basis on which a manrope knot is formed. **(2)** The lower part of an anchor where the arms are fixed to the *shank.

crow's foot, the name given to the method of attaching *reef-points to a sail. The points are cut to the required length and each end *whipped. A crow's foot is then

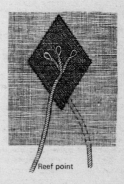

Crow's foot

formed in the middle by twisting against the lay so that the individual strands are separated, pulling each one out and letting it twist up on itself. The crow's foot is then sewn to the starboard side of the sail (if possible on a seam) after the reef point has been drawn through the sail.

crow's nest, a small shelter on the foremast for the masthead lookout, originally made from a cask.

crutch, (1) a *stanchion with two short, curved arms at the end shaped to take the main *boom of a yacht, or other fore-and-aft rigged vessel, when the sails are stowed. It is fitted on the vessel's *counter and is used to secure the boom and prevent it swinging from side to side when the vessel rolls. See also GALLOWS. **(2)** A metal pin with jaws at the top of a size to take the shaft of an *oar. They fit into sockets in the *gunwale of the boat placed just abaft the *thwarts in a position convenient for pulling an oar. To avoid being lost overboard, they are secured with a *lanyard to a *stringer in the boat. See also THOLE PIN, ROWLOCK.

cuddy, originally a *cabin in the after part of a sailing ship under the poop deck for the captain and his passengers. The term is also sometimes used to denote a small cabin on board a boat, or very occasionally a small cookhouse on board, though caboose was a more usual word for this.

Cunningham hole, a semi-circular space cut near the bottom of the *luff of a mainsail in a racing yacht to enable the luff to be set up more tautly while racing. In many racing classes there are restrictions against hoisting the mainsail higher than a particular mark on the mast or lowering the inboard end of the boom below a similar mark. A Cunningham hole allows a *tackle to be attached so that the luff of the sail above can be tensioned as necessary.

currach or **curragh,** a boat peculiar to Ireland, especially its western coast, used for local traffic. It is of great antiquity, contemporary with, and very similar to, the *coracle, being originally constructed of animal skins attached to a wicker frame, often nearly circular in shape and operated by paddles. Currachs are today constructed of two skins of calico or canvas, tarred to make them watertight, most frequently stretched over an interlaced framework of elm laths, although other woods are used when elm is not easily available. They are now of conventional boat shape and have been constructed for use with as many as eight oars, though they are normally of

rather smaller size. A small mast and square sail is usually carried for use when the wind is favourable. The currach is particularly associated with the Aran Islands, off the west coast of Ireland, where it is used for the transport not only of people and goods but also of cattle.

current, the flowing of the sea in one direction. Currents may be periodic in relation to the tides, seasonal in relation to a prevailing wind which blows only at certain times of the year, or permanent in relation to the main rotational winds (i.e., winds affected by the earth's rotation, such as the *trade winds) which blow over the wide ocean surfaces. Differences in water temperatures also affect the formation of currents, in very much the same way as differences in air temperatures affect the force and direction of winds.

Atmospheric circulation over the oceans, where the wide uninterrupted surfaces give stability and permanence to air flows such as the recognized trade winds, is the most effective producer of the drift movements of the surface waters which we know as currents. Thus, in the Atlantic Ocean, the two patterns of trade winds on either side of the equator, the north-east and south-east trades, give rise to two westward-moving drifts, known as the equatorial currents, which themselves generate between them a compensatory counter-current flowing in the opposite direction along the equatorial belt. When the southern equatorial current reaches the coast of South America at about Cape St. Roque it divides into two parts. One branch, the Brazil current, flows south following the coast as far as the River Plate, where it comes under the influence of the strong westerly winds known as the *'Roaring Forties'. It then flows eastward across the South Atlantic as far as the Cape of Good Hope, part continuing into the Indian Ocean, part being deflected northward by the African land mass to become the Benguella current, eventually reaching and joining the South Atlantic drift. The other part of the southern equatorial current flows north and joins the northern equatorial current. These two drifts, blocked by the shape of the land, escape into the Caribbean Sea and Gulf of Mexico where, unable to continue their drift westward because of the total land block formed by the Isthmus of Panama, they raise the level of the sea. This congestion of water must escape, and the only direction available is north-east up the coast of North

America. This is the *Gulf Stream. It is deflected off the coast of Newfoundland by the south-flowing Labrador current (see below) and flows eastward across the North Atlantic until it is blocked by the coast of Europe, where it divides. The southern part becomes the Canaries current and eventually rejoins the northern equatorial drift; the northern part divides into three branches, one flowing west of Britain to Norway and into the Arctic basin, the second known as the Irminger stream, passing up the western side of Iceland, the third flowing up the Davis Strait to Baffin Bay. These three branches are separated by south-flowing compensatory currents from the Arctic basin, known as the Greenland current and the Labrador current, and it is the latter which deflects the Gulf Stream eastward off Newfoundland.

In the Indian Ocean, north of the equator, the dominant factor in the creation of currents is the *monsoon winds. The currents in the open sea change with them, forming north-east and south-west drifts. During the summer the south-west monsoon sets up a strong north-easterly drift in the Arabian Sea, and the water which this draws from the African coast is replaced by cold water rising from below. South of the equator the dominant factor is the powerful Equatorial current which flows westwards between the approximate latitudes of $7°$ and $20°$ S. This sets up an eastward-flowing counter-current, known as the Indian counter-current, which follows approximately the line of the equator. When the Equatorial current meets the coast of Africa it divides into two parts, the smaller, north-flowing, following the coastline until it meets and is absorbed by the Indian counter-current. The larger part flows south to form the Mozambique current, which becomes the Agulhas current south of Cape Corrientes and is one of the most powerful currents in the world, at times flowing at a rate of 4–5 knots. As soon as it reaches open water south of the Cape of Good Hope it meets the west wind drift caused by the 'Roaring Forties' and joins it to form a strong east-flowing stream. On reaching Australia, a part of this is diverted northward by the continental land mass to form the West Australia current until it reaches and merges with the Equatorial current.

The Pacific currents are, in general, less pronounced than those of the Atlantic and Indian Oceans. The North Equatorial current, a westerly stream caused by the action of the north-east trade winds, splits into two parts when it meets the Philippine Islands, one part flowing north and repeating very much the characterstic pattern of the Gulf Stream in the Atlantic. It is known as the Kuro Siwo, or Black, Stream and it feeds a drift circulation influenced by the North Pacific winds, becoming the Californian current when it meets the North American coast. This follows the coastline until it divides, one part continuing down the coast to form the Mexican current, the other rejoining the North Equatorial current.

Further south, the South Equatorial current is the dominant feature. It is produced by the south-east trades. It divides when it reaches the western Pacific, part flowing southwards to the east of New Zealand and Australia and known as the East Australian current, and part northwards. Most of this joins the Equatorial counter-current, which flows eastward between the North and South Equatorial currents, but during the north-east monsoon some of this northern drift makes its way through the China Sea to the Indian Ocean. During the south-west monsoon period it is reversed and joins the Kuro Siwo. Between the Kuro Siwo and the Asiatic coast, a band of cold water known as the Oya Siwo flows southward following the coastline.

Still further south, the surface movement of the waters again comes under the influence of the 'Roaring Forties' to form an east-flowing stream. When it reaches South America, the southern portion continues past Cape Horn but the part that meets the coast is diverted northwards to form the Humboldt, or Peruvian, current, which eventually joins the South Equatorial current.

The setting, or direction, of a current is that point of the compass towards which it flows, the drift of a current is the rate in *knots at which it runs. Information on currents is given in the *Current Atlas of the World* and is also included in the appropriate *Sailing Directions*.

cut splice, two ropes spliced together to form an *eye. The splice is not made with the two ropes end to end, as in a short splice, but overlapping to the extent required to form the eye, the end of each rope being spliced into the body of the other rope and the splices then *whipped.

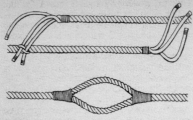

Cut splice

cutch, a preservative dressing used to prolong the life of canvas sails. It consists of broken up gum catechu boiled in fresh water in the proportion of 5 lb of gum to eight gallons of water. See also TAN.

cutter, a term which embraces a variety of vessels, but which nowadays normally means a sailing yacht with, in much of the world, a mainsail and two foresails; but in the USA such vessels are called *sloops, and the term cutter refers only to the old-fashioned rig where such vessels had a very long bowsprit. Modern cutters are almost invariably *Bermuda-rigged though there are still some older boats *gaff-rigged with a jib-headed topsail.

'cutting his painter', an expression meaning, in terms of a ship in harbour, to make a clandestine departure, but also, in seaman's language and in terms of an individual, to depart this life.

cutwater, the forward curve of the *stem of a ship. It was also sometimes known as the *knee of the head or beakhead.

cyclone, see TROPICAL STORM.

D

Dacron, see POLYESTER.

dagger-board, a drop *keel, or sliding *centreboard of wood or metal which can be raised or lowered inside a case through a slot in a shallow-draught boat's keel, to increase the effective draught and thereby reduce *leeway when sailing *close-hauled. It was one of the earliest types of sliding keel, originally used by the Chinese in some of their river *junks. It is so called because it is generally narrow in proportion to its length and, not being pivoted like a true centreboard, slides down from its case like a dagger from a sheath.

dahabeeyah or **dahabiah**, from the Arabic *dahabiyah*, golden, a large river sailing vessel with high *lateen sails associated with the River Nile. Originally the term applied to the gilded state barges of Egyptian rulers, hence its derivation.

damelopre, a Dutch sailing barge or coaster in which the mast is stepped in a *tabernacle so that it can be lowered for passing under a bridge.

dan buoy, a small temporary *buoy used for marking a position at sea. It consists of a float, made of cork or similar substance, with a staff passing through it, to the top of which a small flag is attached for ease in recognition, and it is anchored on the bottom by a weight and lines. Dan buoys are used extensively for marking the position of fishermen's nets, for marking wrecks until permanent wreck buoys can be moored in position, and in all such similar cases at sea. Dan buoys are also required equipment for yachts racing under I.Y.R.U. rules, to mark the position if any member of the crew should fall overboard.

dandy-rig, another name for the *ketch and *yawl rigs, but sometimes used to describe the rig when the mizen-sail is about one-third the size of the mainsail, the true ketch rig having a mizen-sail about half the size of the mainsail and the true yawl rig having its mizen-sail a quarter or less. In some English west country (Devon and Cornwall) craft the mizen-mast was stepped just forward of the *transom stern either to one side of the *tiller or with an iron tiller crooked around the mast. The sail, of triangular or 'leg o'mutton' shape, sheeted to an *outrigger or *bumpkin, was called the dandy, and a boat so rigged, such as the Falmouth Quay punt, was called dandy-rigged. The term is very rarely used today.

Danforth anchor, an American-designed anchor in which the two pivoting *flukes are placed close together with the *shank between them. The *stock is across the crown of the anchor instead of in the more usual place at the top of the shank, and this makes it impossible for the anchor to be fouled by the cable. It has great holding power for its weight, though slightly less than that of the *CQR anchor, but has the advantage that it stows flatter on deck. It is deservedly popular for small craft such as yachts. For illus. see ANCHOR.

davit, a small cast-iron crane, from which a ship's lifeboat is slung. Davits are fitted with hoisting and lowering gear in the form of blocks and falls and are placed along both sides of large passenger-carrying vessels. Some yachts and power boats carry their tenders from davits positioned over the *stern.

Davy Jones, in nautical slang the spirit of the sea, usually cast in the form of a sea devil. 'This same Davy Jones, according to the mythology of sailors, is the fiend that presides over all the evil spirits of the deep,' Tobias Smollett, *Peregrine Pickle* (1751), Ch. XIII. Thus also, Davy Jones's Locker, the bottom of the sea, the final resting place of sunken ships, of articles lost or thrown overboard, of men buried at sea. Thus it has become also a seaman's phrase for death, as in the saying 'He's gone to Davy Jones's Locker' when referring to anyone who has been buried at sea. The term is often shortened to Davy.

deadeye, orig. **dead-man's-eye**, a circular block usually of *lignum vitae*, though sometimes of elm, grooved around the circumference and pierced with three holes. In older sailing vessels deadeyes were used in pairs to secure the end of a *shroud to the *chain plate. A lanyard was threaded through the holes in the deadeyes and by this means a *purchase was created whereby the shroud could be set up taut. The triangular block of wood with a single large hole in the centre and known as a *heart, which was used to set up a *stay, was also at one time called a deadeye.

Officially the term 'dead' was used because although deadeyes perform the function of triple *blocks, they have no revolving sheaves, though no doubt the original name of dead-man's-eye arose from the remarkable resemblance of these blocks with their three holes to a human skull.

Lanyard

Deadeye

deadlight, a metal plate, today usually of brass but originally of wood or iron, which is hinged inboard above a *scuttle or *port and can be let down and secured by a butterfly nut to protect the glass of the scuttle in heavy weather.

dead men, *reef and *gasket ends left flapping instead of being tucked in out of sight when a sail has been furled. See also IRISH PENNANTS.

dead reckoning position, usually abbreviated to D.R., a position which is obtained by applying *courses and distances made through the water from the last known observed position.

Dead reckoning, as a system of navigation, implies charting the position of a ship without the use of any astronomical observation whatever, merely arriving at the ship's position by laying off on the chart courses steered and distances run, with due allowance for currents, tidal streams, and *leeway, from the last fixed position. Before the days of modern navigational aids, there were always likely to be periods of storm and overcast during a voyage during which the navigator was unable to see sun, moon, or stars, and his only means of reckoning his ship's position was by dead reckoning. When at last he did see the sun or stars again and was able to take an observation, he had to use his D.R. position as the basis for working out his sight, having no position more accurate on which to work.

Dead reckoning is still a useful adjunct of navigation, though with the number of modern navigational aids available it is becoming less important. But it remains a useful guide to a vessel's position between fixes and also serves as a permanent check on the reliability of bearings obtained by direction finders, which can be erratic, particularly around dawn and dusk.

dead water, the eddy formed under the *counter of a ship by the angle of her *run aft as she passes through the water. It is so called because it passes away more slowly than the water along her sides. See also CAVITATION, to which it is closely allied in its effect on the vessel's way.

deadweight, a measurement of a ship's *tonnage which indicates its actual carrying capacity. The figure is arrived at by calculating the amount of water displaced by a ship when she is unloaded, but with her fuel tanks full and stores on board, and the amount of water similarly displaced when she is fully loaded with her cargo holds full. The difference expressed in tons (35 cubic ft of seawater = one ton) gives the ship's deadweight tonnage. It is usually expressed in shortened form as d.w.t.

deadwood, the solid timbering in *bow and *stern of a sailing vessel just above the *keel where the lines narrow down to such an extent that the separate side timbers cannot each be accommodated. Generally the fore deadwood extends from the *stem to the foremost *frame, the after deadwood from the sternpost to the after balance frame. Both deadwoods are firmly fixed to the keel to add strength to the ship's structure.

Decca navigation system, see NAVIGATION.

deck, the horizontal platform in a ship which corresponds to the floor in a house. Properly speaking, a deck extends the full length of the ship, but in cases where they do not extend the full length the word is still used, if improperly, to describe the built-up portions forward and aft of a ship, the fore portion being known as the forecastle deck and the after portion the poop deck. That portion of the upper deck which lies between forecastle and poop is often known in merchant ships as the well deck, and in many other types of ship as the *waist.

deck beam, one of the transverse beams which run across the width of a ship supported at each end by the *frames or ribs. They form an integral part of the basic structure which gives a ship her constructional strength and at the same time provide a continuous support for the upper deck.

deck house, a square or oblong *cabin erected on the deck of a ship.

declination, a term used in celestial *navigation to indicate the angular distance of a celestial body north or south of the equator measured from the centre of the earth. It corresponds, therefore, to the geographical latitude of the body. Tables of declination for those bodies used by navigators in working out positions by celestial navigation are included in *nautical almanacs.

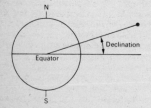

deep, a position in the oceans, often also known as a trench, where the water is of exceptional depth in comparison with adjacent areas. Depths of over 3,000 fathoms in the oceans are given the generic name of deeps.

deep, a point on a *lead line which corresponds to a *sounding in *fathoms but has no distinguishing mark on the line. The hand lead line, with which soundings are taken from a ship in relatively shallow water, has different distinguishing *marks, recognizable both by sight and touch, at 2, 3, 5, 7, 10, 13, 15, 17, and 20 fathoms, and when one of these marks is on the sea level after the lead is hove as the line is vertical, the leadsman knows exactly the depth of water he is getting. If, however, after heaving the lead, there is no distinguishing mark on the sea level he must estimate the depth of water by the nearest distinguishing mark that he can see above the level of the water. This is known as a deep, and he will call the depth of water with the words 'Deep—', by which the navigator will know that he has not got an exact depth by means of a mark on the line.

degree, a unit of measurement applied to the surface of the earth, the length subtended at the equator by one degree of *longitude.

de Horsey rig, a sail rig for use in the larger pulling boats carried by British warships, introduced by Admiral de Horsey in the early 20th century. It consisted of a single mast stepped in a *tabernacle and carrying a *gaff mainsail with a loose foot, i.e., without a *boom, and a single fore staysail.

demast, see DISMAST.

departure, (1) the last position on a *chart, when a ship is leaving the land, fixed from observations of shore stations. Thus a ship, when starting on a voyage, takes her departure not from the port from which she sails but from the position where the last *bearings of points ashore intersect on the chart. It is the correlative of *landfall at the end of the voyage. **(2)** The number of *nautical miles that one place is eastwards or westwards of another. Where the two places are on the same parallel of *latitude the departure between them is equivalent to the difference of *longitude in minutes of arc multiplied by the cosine of the latitude. See also DEAD RECKONING, NAVIGATION.

depression, an area of low barometric pressure around which the wind circulates in an anti-clockwise direction in the northern hemisphere and clockwise in the southern hemisphere. Depressions are basically bad-weather

systems in which the strength of the wind
increases considerably towards the centre
of low pressure, frequently giving gales and
storms, often with heavy rain. They are
relatively fast moving, the average rate
being about 25 miles an hour. See also
METEOROLOGY.

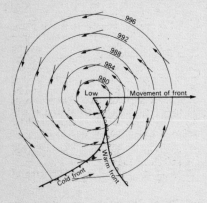

Depression with associated fronts

derelict, any vessel abandoned at sea.
When a ship is abandoned, whether by
consent, compulsion, or stress of weather,
she is a derelict, although legally if any live
domestic animal, such as a cat or dog, is on
board when found, the owner may recover
the ship within a year and a day by paying
*salvage if he so wishes. See also WRECK.

deviation, an error of a magnetic *compass caused by a ship's own residual
magnetism. If a ship had no residual
magnetism, the needle of her magnetic
compass would point direct towards the
north magnetic pole, but as every modern
ship has metal fittings which affect the
compass, there is always some error. Deviation varies according to the heading of the
ship because, as a ship changes course, the
metal in her changes its position in relation
to the compass as the ship swings round.
Deviation is therefore read off for every
quarter *point (about 4°) as the ship is
swung through 360° and is tabulated on a
deviation card so that it can be applied,
together with *variation, to every compass
course or bearing to convert them to *true
courses or bearings. It can rarely be
completely eliminated in a ship's magnetic
compass though it can be very considerably
reduced by the use of soft iron balls

mounted on each side of the compass and
by bar magnets, known as Flinders bars,
hung in the *binnacle below the compass
bowl.

devil, the caulker's name for the *seam in
the upper-deck planking next to a ship's
waterways. No doubt it was given that
name as there was very little space to get at
this seam with a caulking iron, making it a
particularly difficult and awkward job.
This is the origin of the saying 'between the
devil and the deep blue sea', since there is
only the thickness of the ship's hull
planking between this seam and the sea. See
also CAULK, 'DEVIL TO PAY'.

'devil to pay', an old seafaring term
meaning very difficult or awkward. It
originates from the name given by caulkers
to the *garboard *seam in a ship's hull,
which was universally known as the *devil,
as it was difficult to *pay in the *oakum and
hammer it home. 'Devil to pay and no pitch
hot', a situation so difficult that no means
of solving it is immediately apparent. See
CAULK.

dhow, in its strict meaning a trading vessel
of 150 to 200 tons, *lateen-rigged on a
single mast, and indigenous to the Red Sea,
Persian Gulf, and Indian Ocean, but the
name has been extended to embrace any
trading vessel of similar size in those
waters, irrespective of the number of masts
rigged. Some modern dhows are fitted with
diesel engines. They were formerly used
extensively in the slave trade from East
Africa to the Arabian countries.

diagonal built, a method of planking the
sides of a wooden vessel in which the
*strakes are laid diagonally instead of
horizontally. A diagonal built vessel is
normally double-skinned, with the inner
skin fastened diagonally in one direction on
the *timbers and the outer skin laid
diagonally in the opposite direction. The
main purpose of diagonal planking is to
give the hull of a vessel additional strength.
It is a system of construction used for small
naval vessels, some yachts, and also in
sailing *dinghies in the glued plywood
method of construction, such as the Fairey
Firefly class.

diamond knot, a stopper knot made in a
length of rope, the *strands being unlaid,
the knot formed by tucking the strands
through the bights of each other, and
laying up the rope again. A double diamond

knot is made by tucking the strands twice. The purpose of a stopper knot is to prevent a rope from running through an eye, for example the foot-rope of a *jib- boom, and it is also used for certain ornamental work.

Single diamond knot

diamond shrouds, masthead stays in the rigging of some yachts, made of steel wire or rod and carried in pairs over short struts to a lower position on the mast, thereby forming a diamond outline to support the upper part of a yacht's mast. They are used only with the *Bermuda rig, and not necessarily in all yachts so rigged.

diaphone, a type of sound signal emitted from *lighthouses and light vessels in fog, characterized by a powerful low note ending with a sharply descending tone known as the grunt.

dinghy, from the Hindi *dengi* or *dingi*, a small boat used on rivers, originally a small open rowing boat, pulled by one pair of oars, usually *clinker-built, and used as a general work-boat or as a tender to a yacht. By about the end of the 19th century some dinghies were being built partly decked and were used for racing under sail in many parts of the world, but it was not until after the First World War (1914–18) that dinghy racing began to take a major part in the sport, particularly after the introduction of the International 14-ft and National 12-ft classes. With the enormous growth of all kinds of pleasure boating that took place after the Second World War racing dinghies and dinghy classes proliferated, and in Britain alone there are over 300 different

racing classes of dinghies. Both national and international racing events for dinghy championships are held in all yachting countries.

dip of the horizon, the allowance which must be made when observing the *altitude of any heavenly body with a *sextant for (a) the refraction of light passing through the atmosphere from the horizon to the observer, and (b) the height of the observer's eye above the level of the sea. The effect of these two is to increase the observed altitude and the correction is made by subtracting from the observed angle the angular distance of dip, which is calculated and given in dip tables included in all compilations of nautical tables. The result is known as the apparent altitude. For illus. see HORIZON.

dipping lug, a rig in which the forward end of the *yard carrying a *lugsail projects forward of the mast, entailing lowering the sail two or three feet and dipping the yard round the mast whenever the vessel goes

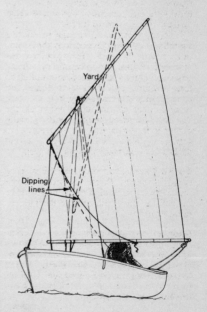

Dipping lug

*about and rehoisting the sail for the other tack. For this purpose dipping lines are secured to the end of the yard, one on either

side of the sail, by which the yard is pulled down and dipped round the mast as the sail is lowered.

dismast, to, carry away a mast. A vessel is dismasted when her mast goes by the *board.

displacement, the weight of water which a ship displaces when she is floating with her fuel tanks full and with all stores on board. The size of yachts is usually expressed by their waterline length but where tonnage is mentioned, it is calculated by the *Thames Measurement Rule.

distress signal, a means of calling for help or assistance at sea.

In 1857 an *International Code of Signals was established and a special flag was allocated for distress; other signals which came into use during the 19th century were a square flag with a ball above it, a cone point upwards with a ball above or below it, continuous sounding on *foghorns, and, for night use, flames or shells or rockets throwing stars of any colour. It was not until 1954 that agreement was reached that distress rockets had to be red.

The most profound change in distress signalling was brought about by the invention of the wireless. In 1933 wireless installations became compulsory on all passenger ships and on cargo ships of 1,600 tons upwards, and since 1954 it has been internationally compulsory for all such ships to keep a continuous watch on the distress frequency, either with a radio officer or an auto-alarm. The distress call to actuate the auto-alarm is twelve 4-second dashes with one second between each.

docking keels, also known as *bilge keels, small subsidiary *keels projecting downwards from the *hull of a ship at about the turn of the *bilge, and run parallel with the main keel.

dodger, canvas screens rigged at chest height that used to protect the open bridges of ships, which are now invariably enclosed. The term is now only normally used to describe canvas screens rigged in yachts to protect those in the cockpit from breaking seas and spray.

dog, to, back the tail of a block with several turns around a *stay or *shroud, with the tail going with the lay of the rope. This is one way of *clapping on a *purchase where additional hauling power is required.

dogger, a development of the original *ketch, square-rigged on the main and carrying a *lugsail on the *mizen, with two *jibs on a long *bowsprit. Short, wide-beamed, and small, she was a fishing vessel engaged in trawling or lining on the Dogger Bank in the North Sea, hence her name. The Dogger Bank got its name from the Dutch fishing vessel called a *dogger*.

doghouse, a yachting term introduced from the USA to denote the short *deck house or main hatchway which is raised above the level of the cabin top or coachroof.

dogs, the metal hand clips fitted around watertight doors, small hatch covers, etc., which when turned, force the rubber gasket lining the doors and hatches hard up against the sealing to ensure a watertight seal.

dog watch, one of the two half *watches of two hours each into which the period from 4 p.m. to 8 p.m. is divided. The purpose of dividing this watch into two is to produce an uneven number of watches in the 24 hours, seven instead of six, thereby ensuring that watchkeepers in ships, whether organized in two or three watches, do not keep the same watches every day. These two watches are known as the First Dog and Last Dog, and *never*, except by landlubbers, as First Dog and Second Dog. How they came by these names is not known; they were certainly in use by the 17th century. One suggestion that they were called dog watches because they were curtailed, though ingenious, does not appear to have any foundation in fact.

doldrums, the belt of calm which lies inside the *trade winds of the northern and southern hemisphere. This area, which lies close to the equator except in the western Pacific where it is south of the equator, had great significance during those years when the trade of the world was carried by sailing ships; today it is of no significance except, perhaps, for occasional yachts. The areas immediately north and south of the trade winds also used to be known as doldrums but are now known as variables.

dolly, a timber similar to a single *bollard which is set horizontally in the *bulwarks of a ship and used as a convenient means for securing temporarily the *fall of a *purchase by taking a jamming turn round it when there is no *cleat conveniently placed.

dolphin, a large wooden pile, or collection of piles, serving as a *mooring post for ships or occasionally as a beacon.

dolphin striker or **martingale,** a short perpendicular spar under the *cap of the *bowsprit of a sailing vessel used for holding down or guying the *jib-boom by means of *martingale stays. It was a necessary spar to support the rigging needed to counteract the upward pull on the jib-boom of the fore top-gallant stay. The name, of course, comes from the position of the spar—pointing vertically downwards towards the sea just beyond the *bows of the vessel, i.e., it would strike a dolphin were one to leap out of the water just beneath it. For illus. see BOWSPRIT.

dory, a small flat-bottomed boat associated with the coast of New England and also used widely for line fishing on the Grand Banks off the coast of Newfoundland. More recently it has come to mean a type of hard-*chined dinghy with flared sides, suitable for an outboard motor and widely used by yachtsmen and amateur fishermen, being properly considered as a useful weight-carrying work-boat.

double-clewed jib, a sail introduced in 1934 for the *America's Cup races in that year. The sail consisted virtually of an extra large *jib with the clew cut off to form a four-sided foresail *sheeted with two sheets. The new fourth side, corresponding to the *leech of a normal four-sided fore-and-aft sail, was either loose or laced to a small boom sheeted at either end. In the USA it was given the slang name 'Greta Garbo', but though it proved to be powerful it never caught on as a racing sail.

doubling, the name given to that portion of the mast of a large sailing vessel where an upper mast overlaps the lower, as a topmast with a lower mast, a *topgallant mast with a topmast. It is a word more often used in the plural than in the singular, as in normal square-rig each mast will have two doublings.

down-easter, a colloquial term for the American three-masted ships and *barques which followed the *clipper ships in about 1859. The down-easter originated on the coast and rivers of Maine and more often than not was commanded by a Maine

captain, but the term spread to embrace most of the wooden three-masted ships of the USA which extended the life of trading sail by a quarter of a century or more. If it was the rewards of Californian gold which brought the clipper ship to her final stages of excellence, it was the wealth of Californian wheat which inspired the birth of the down-easter.

downhaul, a single rope fitted in large sailing ships for hauling down a *jib or *staysail when shortening sail. It was led up along a stay and through the *cringles of the sail and then made fast to the upper corner of the sail. Downhauls were also rigged for similar use with *studdingsails, being led through blocks on the outer *clews of the sails to the outer yardarms of the studdingsail. But in general any rope fitted for the purpose of hauling down a sail would be called a downhaul. In racing yachts, the rope attached to a *spinnaker pole to hold it down is known as a downhaul, and frequently the boom *vang is also called a downhaul.

drag, the amount by which a ship floats lower *aft than *forward. See also COME HOME.

drag, to, fail to hold, used when the *flukes of a ship's *anchor are not holding in the ground. It is the anchor itself which drags when the flukes do not hold; the ship drags her anchor, although colloquially the last two words are frequently omitted, e.g., 'the ship is dragging', meaning in fact that the anchor is dragging, or the ship is dragging her anchor.

draught, sometimes written as draft, the depth of water which a ship draws, which of course varies with the state of her loading.

draw, to, (1) a sail when it is full of wind is said to be drawing. To let draw, to trim the *jib of a small sailing vessel with the *lee *sheet after it has been held to *windward by the *weather sheet in order to assist in forcing the *bows across the wind when *tacking. In very light winds, where the vessel may not have sufficient way to make tacking easy, the jib is held out to windward when the vessel is head to wind to assist the bows across. As soon as this is achieved, the order to let draw ensures the jib being sheeted normally on the new tack. After a ship is hove-to (see HEAVE-TO) at sea, in which condition the jib is permanently sheeted to windward, the order to let draw gets her sailing again. **(2)** Said of a ship to indicate her *draught, e.g., 'the ship draws, or is drawing, so many feet *forward and so many *aft'.

drift, (1) the distance a vessel makes to *leeward, by the action of either the tide or the wind. **(2)** The term used to indicate the rate in knots of ocean currents, as for example the 'west wind drift' which circles the globe in southern latitudes under the influence of the *Roaring Forties.

drive, to. A ship drives when her *anchor fails to hold the ground and she is at the mercy of wind and tide. In the case of a sailing vessel, a ship drives to *leeward when the force of the wind is so great that she cannot be controlled by sails or rudder. In a full gale, too violent for the sails to be hoisted, she drives under bare poles before the wind (see also SCUD).

driver, an additional sail hoisted in the form of a *studdingsail to take advantage of a following wind.

drogue, usually an improvised contraption by which a sailing vessel is slowed down in a following sea to prevent her from being *pooped by waves coming up astern. It can vary from a long *warp towed astern in small sailing craft to a spar with a weighted sail in larger sailing ships. A drogue is very widely confused with a *sea anchor, but in fact the two serve different purposes.

An extremely efficient drogue is made by sailmakers for use in yachts, etc. It consists of a hollow cone of canvas with a line attached to a *bridle at the base of the cone and another line attached to the top. With the cone towed from the bridle and top line loose, it forms an efficient drogue to slow the yacht down; when this is no longer required, a pull on the line connected to the top of the cone collapses it so that it no longer acts as a drogue.

When an open boat approaches the shore through lines of breakers, a *grass line over the stern acts as an efficient drogue, both slowing the boat down and holding it steady so that the waves do not turn it broadside to the beach and upset it or wash it ashore.

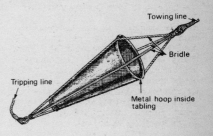

A drogue

drop keel, a term often used, though erroneously, to describe a *centreboard or dagger plate.

E

eagre, see BORE.

earing, a small rope used to fasten the
upper corners of a square sail to its *yard.
The outer turns of the earings, after being
passed through the head *cringles on the
sail, are then passed beyond the *lifts and
rigging on the yardarm and are designed to
stretch the head of the sail tight along the
yard, while the remaining turns, known as
inner turns, draw the sail close up to the
yard and are passed within the lifts. Below
the earings are the *reef earings, by which
the reef cringles are similarly made fast to
the yard when the sail is reefed.

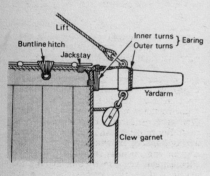

Earing

ease, to, or **easy,** a good maritime term
meaning, in general, to take the pressure
off. A sailing ship, on the order 'ease her', is
*luffed, or brought closer into the wind in
order to reduce the wind pressure on her
sails in a heavy blow. Similarly, in sailing
yachts, the sheets are eased, sometimes to
take the pressure off the sail to reduce the
angle of heel, at others to produce a squarer
aspect of the sail to the wind.

ebb, the flow of the tidal stream as it
recedes, from the ending of the period of
*slack water at high tide to the start of the
period of slack water at low tide. Its period
is about 6 hours, which is approximately
divided into three parts, the first 2 hours

being known as the first of the ebb, the
middle 2 hours as the strength of the ebb,
and the last 2 hours as the last of the ebb.
See also FLOOD.

echo sounder, an instrument based on the
principle of sonar by which the depth of
water can be measured. By using a vertical
sonar pulse and measuring the time taken
between emission of the signal and the
receipt of the echo off the bottom, the
depth of water can be accurately calculated.

ecliptic, from the Greek *ekleipsis*, disap-
pearance, the *great circle on the *celestial
sphere traced out by the sun in the course
of a year. It is so called because for an
eclipse of the sun or moon to occur, the
moon must lie on or near the ecliptic. The
ecliptic intersects the celestial equator, or
*equinoctial, twice during the year at dates
known as the equinoxes; on 21 March at
the 'first point of Aries', which is 0° Right
Ascension, and on 23 September at the
'first point of Libra', at 180° Right Ascension, and is furthest from the equator (23°
23' N. or S.) at the points marking the
summer solstice (June) and winter solstice
(December).

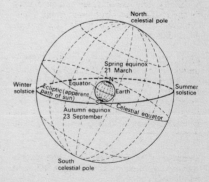

Ecliptic

eddy, a small local current in the sea usually caused by tidal streams as they ebb and flow round or against objects fixed or moored to the sea bed. A pier or jetty will produce eddies according to the direction of the tidal stream, as also will a buoy moored in tidal waters. Points of land or other similar obstructions produce their eddies. They can also be formed by particular winds, especially on mountainous coastlines where the wind can be deflected or accelerated by the contours of the coast and act on the surface water of the sea to give it a temporary eddy. An eddy flows in a different, often opposing, direction from the main current.

embark, to, a verb with three meanings: **(1)** to put on board a vessel, **(2)** to go on board a vessel, **(3)** of a ship, to receive on board. **Embarkation**, the process or action of embarking.

ensign, the national flag as worn by the ships of a nation. Many countries which have navies as well as merchant ships use two ensigns, one for naval ships and one for merchant vessels. For British ships three ensigns are used, the White Ensign flown by a ship or naval shore establishment indicates a unit of the Royal Navy, the Blue Ensign is flown by naval auxiliary vessels, and the Red Ensign by vessels of the merchant navy. The White Ensign may also be flown by yachts above a certain tonnage belonging to the Royal Yacht Squadron. Many yacht clubs also have approval for their yachts to fly the Blue Ensign defaced with the badge of the club in the *fly. Any British vessel not naval may fly the Red Ensign, but again many yacht clubs have permission to fly this ensign defaced as above.

entry, the form of the fore-body of a ship under the load line as it thrusts through the sea. A ship with a slim bow is said to have a fine entry. It is in many ways the complement of *run, which is the shape of the after-body of a ship in relation to the resistance it causes as it moves through the water.

equator, the *great circle on the earth's surface equidistant from both north and south poles.

equinoctial, from the Latin *aequus*, equal, and *nox*, night, the *great circle on the *celestial sphere in the plane of the earth's equator, sometimes called the celestial equator. The sun is on the equinoctial on two occasions each year, these occurring on 21 March and 23 September, days known as the equinoxes. On these days the sun rises at 6 a.m. and sets at 6 p.m. (local time) at every place on earth. The two points of intersection of the equinoctial with the *ecliptic are called the spring and autumnal equinoctial points respectively, or more usually the First Points of Aries and Libra for the spring and autumnal equinoxes.

The word is also used as an adjective to describe phenomena happening at or about the time of the equinox, e.g., equinoctial gales, equinoctial rains, etc.

equinox, the two dates each year (21 March, 23 September) when the sun crosses the plane of the earth's *equator. On those dates the sun rises at 6.0 a.m. and sets at 6.0 p.m. local time at every place on earth.

even keel. A vessel is said to be on an even keel when she floats exactly upright in the water without any *list to either side.

eye, properly speaking, the circular loop in a *shroud or *stay where it passes over a mast at the *hounds. It is formed by *splicing the ends of two ropes or wires into each other to form a loop to fit over the mast. But by extension it has come to mean any loop spliced or *whipped at the end of a rope or wire, usually round a *thimble. A Flemish eye was a method of making the eye in a shroud or stay by dividing the *strands, knotting each part separately and then *parcelling and *serving. This method, though very neat, was frowned upon by all good seamen as it lacked strength where, for the safety of the ship, it was most needed.

The word has other nautical meanings. The eye of the wind, or wind's eye, is a term used to describe the exact direction from which it blows, or dead to windward. The eyes of the ship, or 'eyes of her', is used to describe the extreme forward end of a ship, the term being derived from the old eastern and Mediterranean custom of painting an eye on each bow so that the vessel could see where she was going. By some it is considered that the *hawseholes are equivalent to the eyes in a modern ship, but this is a somewhat doubtful attempt to fit the physical fact of more modern ship construction to an older derivation. The

eye of a tropical storm, the area in the
centre where all is still.

eyebolt, a metal bolt with an *eye in the
end secured in various convenient places on
board ship to which the *blocks of *purchases can be hooked or other lines secured.

eye splice, a loop or **eye** made in the end
of a rope or wire by turning the end back
and splicing it through the standing part,
usually around a *thimble, with the length
of the *splice *served to prevent fraying
and to make a neater job.

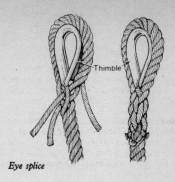

Thimble

Eye splice

F

fag-end, the end of any rope, but particularly applied to the end of a rope where the *strands have become unlayed and have frayed out.

fag out, to, fray, especially used of the tendency of the *strands of a rope to fray out at the ends. It is stopped by holding them securely in place with a small whipping, by a *back splice, or by pointing the rope. See WHIP.

fair, a term applied to the direction of the wind when it is favourable to the *course being steered in a sailing vessel. It is more comprehensive than *large, which indicates a wind which blows from the beam or abaft it, while a fair wind can blow from about four points on the bow to right astern. Any wind which will enable a sailing vessel to *fetch a desired point without *tacking or *pinching is a fair wind.

fairlead, a means of leading a rope in the most convenient direction for working, perhaps with a leading *block to alter its direction or with *eyes or *cringles to keep it clear of obstructions.

fairway, the navigable channel of a harbour for ships entering or leaving. It is, in all harbours of any size, marked by *port and *starboard hand *buoys, and usually in the smaller harbours by withies or similar marks. Obstructions in a fairway, such as a *middle ground, are also marked by buoys.

fake, a complete turn of a rope when it has been coiled either on deck or on a drum. When a rope has been properly faked down, it is clear for running, each fake running out without fouling those below it. The word is used as both a noun and a verb.

fall, the hauling end of a *tackle, the end of the rope, rove through *blocks, on which the pull is exerted in order to achieve power.

fall off, to, sag away to *leeward, said of a ship when she falls further off the wind. It is the opposite to *griping, and similarly requires the movement of ballast inside the vessel to correct the tendency. The shifting of ballast forward to trim the vessel by the head gives a greater grip of the water in the bows and thus less tendency to sag away from the wind.

fancy line, (1) a line rove through a block at the jaws of a *gaff and used as a *downhaul when lowering the sail. It was only necessary in larger vessels setting a gaff-rigged sail. **(2)** A line used for crosshauling the lee *topping-lift to hold it clear of the sail to leeward so that it will not beat or rub against the canvas or reduce the sail's aerodynamic properties by creating a ridge in the sail when it stands *taut.

fantail, the overhanging part of a ship's *stern, a term used particularly in the case of large yachts and passenger liners. Although the correct word for the stern overhang of all ships, it is not often used in this connection except in the USA. It has not quite the same meaning as *counter, but comes very close to it.

fast, in terms of a ship, secured, attached, fixed. Thus, to make something fast is to secure it firmly, e.g., a ship alongside a *mole or jetty, a boat to a *boom, etc. It is also a word used to designate the lines or hawsers which secure a ship to a wharf or pier, generally indicated by the position in which they are used in relation to the ship, as bow-fast, breast-fast, stern-fast, etc. These particular terms are, however, very rarely used today.

fathom, the unit of measurement in most maritime countries for the depths of the sea or the lengths of rope and *cables. The word comes from the Old English *fœthm,* to embrace, and is a measurement across the outstretched arms of a man, approximately 6 feet in a man of average size; the length of a nautical fathom is therefore 6 feet. The term is becoming obsolete with the growing tendency in most countries to adopt the metric system of measurement.

In most British *charts the *soundings are still shown in fathoms though gradually they are being replaced by soundings in metres. It is a process which will obviously take many years to complete because of the great number of charts which must be altered. A fathom is equal to 1.8256 metres.

When used as a measurement of ropes and cables, the length of a *hawser-laid cable is 130 fathoms. As a measurement of distance a cable is 100 fathoms, and a chain anchor cable, made up of eight *shackles, is the same length, although of course in large ships many more than eight shackles of cable are attached to the *bower anchors.

fay, to, fit together two pieces of timber in ship- and boat-building so that they lie close to each other with no perceptible space between them.

feather, to, (1) alter the angle of the blades of a *propeller so that they lie with the leading edge more or less in the line of advance of the vessel, normally a sailing vessel, to which they are fitted. The object of feathering a propeller is to reduce the drag when the vessel is under sail alone. (2) The turning of the blade of an *oar from the vertical to the horizontal while it is being taken back for the next rowing stroke, performed by dropping the wrists at the end of the stroke. The object of feathering an oar is twofold: it lessens the effort by reducing the windage of the blade on the backstroke and it does not take the way off the boat if it hits the water during the backstroke, which may easily occur when rowing in a choppy sea. Feathering an oar is, however, much more practised in inland waters than at sea, and few seamen, when *pulling an oar, bother to feather it.

felucca, a small sailing or rowing vessel of the Mediterranean, used for coastal transport or trading. The larger feluccas were narrow, decked, galley-built vessels, with *lateen sails carried on one or two masts, occasionally also with a small *mizen. Smaller feluccas were propelled with six or eight oars, though some of the smaller sailing feluccas used oars and sail simultaneously. The sea-going type has almost completely died out, but they are still in use on many Eastern Mediterranean rivers, particularly the Nile.

fender, something let down between the side of a ship and a wharf or other ship to prevent chafing when ships are lying alongside or to take the shock of a bump when going alongside. They come in many shapes and sizes, such as large bundles of withies lashed together, large bags of granulated cork, the ends of large coir cables, even old rubber motor tyres. Boats' fenders used for the same purpose were traditionally made of canvas stuffed with granulated cork but are now more often formed of rubber or synthetic moulding. But see also RUBBING STRAKE.

fend off, to, bear a vessel off, by a spar, boathook, or *fender, in order to prevent violent contact when coming alongside.

ferrocement, or cement-mesh or ferro-concrete, a material used in the construction of small craft. The method employs several layers of wire mesh, generally of the welded type, which are wired to the intersections of steel rods and tubes forming a close-knitted framework of the vessel's hull. The whole fabric when complete is rendered waterproof by an application, simultaneously from both inside the hull and outside, of a semi-liquid mortar mix. The mortar is composed of cement and very fine sand, which may include pozzolano or volcanic ash as used in ancient Roman mortar for its adhesive properties; when cured and set over a period of a week or more, the resulting surface of the hull is smooth, hard, and resilient. A ferrocement hull might be likened to a steel mesh reinforced plastic, and is far removed from the popular notion of concrete, as in harbour piling, buildings, or even the early concrete ships introduced during the First World War (1914–18).

Thousands of yachts, harbour launches, and other small craft up to 80 feet or so in length have been constructed in ferro-cement, and the production of the traditional wooden *sampans in China has been virtually stopped in favour of mass production of similar boats in ferrocement.

fetch, to, reach, or arrive at, some place or point, particularly in conditions of an adverse wind or tide. The word is used only in relation to sailing vessels when *close-hauled or *on the wind, and implies being able to arrive at the desired point without having to *tack to windward. As a noun the word signifies the distance of open water traversed by waves before they reach a given point, such as a ship's position or a stretch of coast. The longer the fetch, the higher generally are the waves, and the more strongly the *swell will run after the wind has dropped. It is also used to indicate the distance a vessel must sail to reach open water, thus a yacht can anchor in an inlet on a coast, and have a fetch of so many miles to reach the open sea.

fibre glass, or glass reinforced plastic (GRP), as used for the moulding of boat hulls, decks, superstructures, and other parts, consists of very fine fibres of glass made up into strands or in chopped mat formation, to which is applied a polyester resin in liquid form when the necessary thickness of glass fibres or mat is laid over the pre-formed mould. A catalyst, such as methyl ethyl ketone peroxide, together with a hardener is applied as a liquid which will cause the glass fibre to set hard at normal workshop temperature (about 15°C) and form a plastic shell. On the hull of a GRP vessel the outside is normally given a finishing coat, known as a gel coat, producing a smooth, shiny, and exceedingly hard surface.

Once a suitable mould or pattern has been constructed, hulls can be reproduced from it in large numbers. At first, immediately after the Second World War only *dinghies and small boats were produced in GRP, but as demand grew and techniques improved, yacht hulls were moulded in ever-increasing sizes. Manufacturers with premises far inland could produce the shells of hulls in quantity for the boatyards to complete and fit-out to customers' requirements, and much time in building new yachts was thereby saved. Advantages claimed for fibre glass, such as its freedom from rust and corrosion, wet or dry rot, and shipworm, its lightness in relation to its proved strength, its resilience to knocks and minor collisions, and the additional space given inside by the thin shell, encouraged many boat-building yards to give up wooden construction altogether in favour of plastics. As a result, in America, Holland, France, and Great Britain, some 90 per cent of dinghies, yachts, and small craft up to about 75 feet (22.8 m) in length are produced in GRP, the remainder being of wood, steel, aluminium, or *ferrocement.

fid, (1) a square bar of wood or iron, with a wider shoulder at one end, which takes the weight of a topmast when *stepped on a lower mast. The topmast is hoisted up through a guide hole in the *cap of the lower mast until a square hole in its *heel is in line with a similar hole in the head of the lower mast, when the fid is driven through both and the hoisting *tackles slacked away until the fid is bearing the weight. The two masts are then generally secured firmly together with a *parrel lashing. Similarly a fid would support the weight of a topgallant mast at the head of a topmast. **(2)** A round pin of hard wood, usually *lignum vitae*, tapered to a point and used for

opening the strands of large cordage for splicing. It has a groove down one side used for feeding in the strand being tucked.

fiddle, a rack fixed to mess tables on board ships in rough weather to prevent crockery, glasses, knives and forks, etc., from sliding to the deck as the ship rolls and pitches. The simplest fiddles were merely battens fixed to the edges of the tables and projecting about an inch above the table level so that if the plates, etc., slid, they were brought up by the battens, but more elaborate fiddles, used in liners and other such ships, usually fitted the tables exactly and had compartments in them to hold each item firmly in position so that they were unable to move whatever the ship's motion.

fiddle block, a double *block in which the two *sheaves lie in one plane one below the other instead of being mounted on the same central pin as in more normal double blocks. The upper sheave is larger than the lower so that it vaguely resembles a violin in shape. They were used chiefly for the lower-yard *tackles of square-rigged ships as they lay flatter to the *yards.

fiddlehead bow, the stemhead of a vessel finished off with a scroll turning aft or inwards, as at the top of a violin.

fife rail, the circular or semi-circular rail around the base of a mast of a small sailing vessel which holds the *belaying pins to which the *halyards of the sails are secured. The masts of modern yachts do not normally have fife rails as the halyards are brought down inside the hollow mast and secured below deck to avoid creating windage.

figure of eight knot, a knot made in the end of a rope by passing the end of the rope over and round the standing part, over its own part and through the bight. Its purpose is to prevent a rope from unreeving when passed through a block.

fill, to, *trim the sails of a fore-and-aft rigged ship, or *brace the yards of a square-rigged ship, so that the wind can fill the sails. In square-rigged ships it was possible to move ahead, to stop, or to move astern all on the same wind by bracing the yards so that the sails could fill, shiver, or *back with the wind, i.e., with the wind blowing on the front of the sail.

fin-keel, see KEEL.

fish, a long piece of wood, concave on one side and convex on the other, used to strengthen a mast or a *yard of a sailing vessel that has been sprung or otherwise damaged. Two such fish are placed one on each side of the weak point and secured either with metal bands or with a strong lashing known as a *woolding.

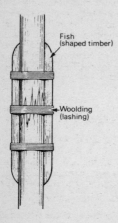

Fish (shaped timber)

Woolding (lashing)

A fished spar

fish, to, (1) strengthen a yard or a mast in a sailing vessel by binding on *fish with a lashing known as a *woolding in those places where it has been sprung or otherwise damaged. Broken spars can also be temporarily repaired with fish in cases where no spare yard is carried. **(2)** To fish an *anchor, the operation of drawing up the *flukes of a *stocked anchor to the *cat davit preparatory to its being stowed on an anchor bed. The modern stockless anchors have no need to be fished as their permanent stowage when weighed is in the *hawseholes and not on anchor beds.

fisherman's bend, a knot very similar to a *round turn and two half hitches, differing from it only in that the first of the two half hitches is made through the round turn and round the standing part of the

Fisherman's bend

rope instead of round the standing part only. It is the recognized knot with which a hawser is bent to the ring of an anchor, and when used for this purpose the end of the rope, after the knot has been formed, is usually *seized to the standing part with two or three turns of *marline as a safety measure.

fitting-out, the general preparation of a ship to make her in all respects ready for sea.

To the yachtsman who takes care of his boat himself, fitting-out entails a period of hard work shortly before the sailing season opens. All last season's varnish is scraped off, rubbed down, and a new coat applied, the topsides are repainted, and the vessel's bottom scrubbed and an anti-fouling composition painted on. All the wire and mild steel standing *rigging is inspected and overhauled, and the rope running rigging, *warps, *hawsers, *blocks, *tackles, etc., are checked and tested, being replaced where necessary. The anchor and chain cable are cleaned and placed on board, the *wardrobe of sails inspected, and the engine, batteries, fuel tank, and all other auxiliary equipment checked to make sure it is in good working order. After the mast is hoisted in and stepped, the standing rigging set up, and the running rigging rove, the yacht is ready for launching.

In the case of a wooden-hulled yacht, it is usual to leave her on her mooring for a short period before sailing so that the planking may 'take-up', or swell, in order to close up all seams.

fix, to, ascertain the position of a ship from observations of *land- or *sea-marks or by astronomical, radio, or electronic methods of navigation. The word 'fix' is often used as a noun to denote a position obtained from observations and is synonymous with the term 'observed position'.

fixed and flashing light, a navigational light in which a steady beam constantly visible is varied at fixed intervals by a flash of brighter intensity. See CHARACTERISTICS.

fixed light, a navigational light displayed by a *lighthouse, *lightship, or lighted *buoy in which the light exposed is a steady *beam with no intervals of darkness. See CHARACTERISTICS.

flags, see INTERNATIONAL CODE OF SIGNALS.

flake, to, lay out the chain anchor *cable of a ship on the *forecastle for examination.

flare, (1) the outward curve of the bows of a ship, which is designed to throw the water outwards when meeting a head sea, instead of letting it come straight up over the bows. **(2)** A signal, often to indicate distress, used in ships at night. A proposal to use rockets or flares of different colours to indicate various other requirements or conditions of a ship, such as her position or the need for a pilot, has been put forward for international agreement but no firm decision has yet been reached. See also ROCKET.

flashing light, a navigational light displayed by a *lighthouse, *lightship, or lighted *buoy in which the period of light is shorter than the period of darkness separating the flashes. See CHARACTERISTICS.

fleet, to, a verb with a number of different meanings, but generally used to describe a means of obtaining a better haul on a rope, purchase, or cable. To fleet a rope is to move up on it to get a more convenient haul. When a *tackle is approaching *two blocks so that no more movement is possible, the moving block is fleeted along to give a more advantageous haul. When *shrouds become stretched in sailing vessels so that the *deadeyes come too close together, the upper set of deadeyes is fleeted further up the shroud so that there is room to haul it tauter. When an *anchor was weighed by hand, the *swifter was fleeted round the ends of the *capstan bars to provide space for additional men to be used on the capstan.

Fleet is also used as a verb colloquially by fishermen of a vessel's first movement when she drags her keel along the ground as the rising *flood tide is just beginning to float her off.

Flemish coil, a flat coil made on deck with the tail of a rope or *fall to present a neat appearance. The end of the tail is in the centre of the coil, the remainder coiled flat around it in a tight spiral. See also CHEESE DOWN.

Flemish horse, the short foot rope at the end of a *yard used by the man at the outer corner of a square sail when *reefing or *furling. The outer end of the Flemish horse is normally spliced round the *gooseneck of the *studdingsail boom iron and the inner end secured to the *jackstay.

flood, the flow of the tidal stream as it rises from the ending of the period of *slack water at low tide to the start of the period of slack water at high tide. Its period is about six hours which is divided into three parts of about two hours each, the first two hours being known as the young flood, the middle two hours as the main flood, and the last two as the last of the flood. An approximate rule both for the amount of the rise and the speed of the flow of a flood tide for each of the six hours of the period of tide is one-twelfth for the first hour, two-twelfths for the second hour, three-twelfths for the third and fourth, two-twelfths for the fifth, and one-twelfth for the sixth.

floor, the lower part of a transverse *frame of a ship running each side of the *keelson to the *bilges.

flotsam, any part of the wreckage of a ship or her cargo which is found floating on the surface of the sea. It was originally in Britain a part of the perquisites of the Lord High Admiral, but is today considered as *derelict property and goes to the finder or salvor. To be flotsam, however, it must be floating and not on the bottom of the sea, when other questions of ownership arise. See also JETSAM.

flowing, (1) used of the *sheets of a sail in fore-and-aft rigged ships when they are eased off as the wind comes from broad on or abaft the beam, and the *yards of a square-rigged ship when they are braced more squarely to the mast. A ship is said to have a flowing sheet when the wind crosses her beam and the sails are trimmed to take the greatest advantage of it. **(2)** A term used in connection with the *tide, a synonym of flooding. See FLOOD.

fluke, the triangular shape at the end of each arm of an *anchor immediately below the bill or point which, by digging into the ground when any strain or pull comes on it, gives an anchor its holding power. Flukes are also sometimes called *palms. Many seamen do not sound the 'k', pronouncing it as 'flue'. For illus. see ANCHOR.

fluky, used of a wind at sea when it is light and variable in direction and has not settled down to blow steadily from any one quarter. It is a term used more often in connection with sailing vessels than with other types of craft.

flush deck, a continuous deck of a ship laid from fore to aft without any break. Strictly speaking, the only true decks of a ship are those which continue from forward to aft without a break, the remainder being only part decks, but the generally accepted meaning of the word has been expanded to include every deck, whether whole or part.

fly, the part of a flag or pendant farthest from the staff or *halyard on which it is hoisted, i.e., the part which flutters in the wind.

flying jib, see JIB.

foghorn, a sounding appliance fitted in ships, or a portable horn carried on board small craft, used for giving warning of a vessel's presence in fog. Smaller ships may be fitted with a steam whistle in place of a foghorn, but use the same signals. *Fog signals are also made by *lighthouses and by *lightships when they are in their correct position.

fog signals, a series of sound signals in fog laid down in the *International Regulations for Preventing Collisions at Sea. A steamship under way sounds one prolonged blast on her steam whistle or foghorn every two minutes, a vessel under way but stopped sounds two prolonged blasts, and a vessel towing, a cable ship at work, a fishing vessel engaged in fishing, or a vessel not under command sounds one prolonged and two short blasts. Ships at anchor ring a bell rapidly for five seconds every minute. A sailing ship gives blasts on her foghorn every minute, one blast meaning that she is under way on the starboard tack, two blasts on the port tack, and three blasts running with the wind abaft the beam. Short blasts are used to indicate changes of course, one blast meaning altering course to starboard, two to port, and three going astern.

foot, the bottom side of a sail, whether triangular or four-sided. Thus, also, footrope, that part of a *bolt-rope, to which the sides of a sail are sewn, which bounds the foot of the sail. For illus. see SAIL.

'foot it in', an order given to the men *furling the *bunt of a square sail when it was required to stow the sail especially snugly. It entailed the *topmen stamping this part of the sail in as hard as they could, supporting themselves by hanging on to a topsail *tye. It was a process also known as 'dancing it in'.

footrope, one of the ropes in square-rigged ships, supported at intervals by ropes from the *yard known as *stirrups, which hang below a yard and on which the *topmen stand when aloft *furling or *reefing sail. They were sometimes also known as horses of the yard, possibly because of the connection with stirrups. For illus. see YARD.

fore-and-aft rig, the arrangement of sails in a sailing vessel so that the *luffs of the sails abut the masts or are attached to *stays, the sails, except in the case of *jibs and *staysails, being usually extended by a *boom. See RIG.

forecastle (pron. fo'c'sle), the space beneath the short raised deck forward, known in sailing ships as the *topgallant forecastle, to be seen usually in smaller ships. The origin of the name lies in the castle built up over the *bows of the oldest fighting ships in which archers were stationed to attack the crew of enemy vessels or to repulse boarders. It used also to be the generic term to indicate the living space of the crew in the forward end of the ship below the forecastle deck, but this meaning has gradually died out as better living conditions for crews have made their way into all modern ships. In this connection, it was also the name given to the deckhouse on the upper deck of large sailing ships in which the seamen had their living quarters.

forefoot, the point in a ship where the *stem is joined to the forward end of the *keel.

foregirth or **fargood,** a short wooden spar lashed to the mast and used to boom out the leading edge, or *luff, of a *lugsail. It was sometimes known as a 'wooden bowline', as it served the same purpose of keeping the leading edge of the sail as far forward as possible when sailing *on the wind. It was chiefly used in small French and English fishing craft from about the middle of the 19th century, being probably an importation from a similar spar sometimes used in North American waters.

foreguy, a rope leading forward from the end of a mainsail *boom to the *bitts to prevent the boom from swinging inboard when broad-reaching or running before a following wind which is patchy in force or direction. It applies mainly to *gaff-rigged vessels.

fore-reach, the distance a sailing vessel will shoot up to windward when brought head to wind in the act of tacking. If a vessel has a good fore-reach, which is a function of her underbody design and her sailing speed at the time, it can sometimes be useful to make this distance to windward while remaining on the same *tack, e.g., in those cases where it might mean rounding a mark or fetching a point without having to go *about on the opposite tack. The term can also be used as a verb to indicate that a vessel can make progress to windward when coming about or hove-to. See also FETCH, PINCH.

forestay, the stay supporting the foremast, or the only mast in a single-masted vessel, in the fore-and-aft direction. It is part of the standing *rigging and runs from the *stemhead to the top or *hounds of the mast.

fore-triangle, in yachts, the area formed between the masthead, the base of the mast at deck level, and the lower end of the fore masthead *stay, whether it reaches the stemhead or the fore end of a *bowsprit. In the rating rules for offshore racing the size and area of the fore-triangle plays an important part in making it possible to increase a yacht's sail area forward of the mast without incurring a handicap penalty; this has resulted in the modern sail plan in which yachts are rigged with small mainsails and correspondingly large headsails.

foreturn, the twist given to the *strands of which *rope is made, before they are laid up into rope. See also AFTERTURN.

forge over, to. A ship forges over a shoal or sandbank when she is forced over by the wind acting on a great press of sail. If the wind was fair it was often possible to free a ship which had been caught on a shoal by setting additional sails and using the wind to push or forge her over.

forward (pron. forrard), towards the bows of a ship, or in the fore part of a ship. It has no particular boundary line in the ship, being used more in a relative or directional sense than as a definition of any area.

fothering, see COLLISION MAT.

foul, an adjective with various nautical meanings, generally indicative of something wrong or difficult. Thus a foul *hawse is the expression used when a ship lying to two *anchors gets her *cables crossed; a foul bottom is the condition of a ship's underwater hull when weeds and barnacles restrict her way through the water; a foul wind is one which, being too much ahead, prevents a sailing ship from laying her desired course. When used as a verb it indicates much the same thing. One vessel can foul another when she drifts down on her, or can foul a ship's hawse by letting go an anchor and cable across that of the other. In a yacht race, one can foul another by bumping into her.

foul, or **fouled, anchor,** an *anchor which has become hooked in some impediment on the ground or, on weighing, has its *cable wound round the *stock or *flukes. The fouled anchor is also the official seal of the Lord High Admiral of Britain and another version of it is the decorative device on his flag which, until the office of Admiralty was merged into the Ministry of Defence in 1964, was flown day and night from the Admiralty building in London. It is now the personal flag of the Queen, who assumed the title of Lord High Admiral in 1964.

The use of the foul, or fouled, anchor, an abomination to seamen when it occurs in practice, as the seal of the highest office of maritime administration is purely on the grounds of its decorative effect, the rope cable around the shank of the anchor giving a pleasing finish to the stark design of an anchor on its own.

Foul anchor

founder, to, sink at sea, generally understood to be by the flooding of a ship's hull either through springing a leak or through striking a rock. Other causes of a ship sinking, such as explosion, etc., are not usually associated with the word.

frame, a *timber or *rib of a ship, running from the *keel to the side rail. A ship's frames form the shape of the hull and provide the skeleton on which the hull planking or plating is secured. In a wooden ship the frames are built up of sections called *futtocks, in steel ships they are normally of angle iron bent to the desired shape. A ship with her frames set up and ready for planking or plating is said to be 'in frame'.

frap, to, bind together to increase tension or to prevent from blowing loose. Thus *shrouds, if they have worked loose, are frapped together to increase their tension; a sail is frapped with turns of rope round it to prevent it from flapping in the wind.

free. A ship is said to be **sailing free** when her sheets are eased, and **running free** when the wind is blowing from astern. 'To free the sheets', to ease them off to present a squarer aspect of the sails to the wind. For illus. see POINT OF SAILING.

freeboard, the distance, measured in the *waist, or centre, of a ship, from the waterline to the upper deck level.

Frenchman, the name given to a left-handed loop when coiling down wire rope right-handed. Wire rope, especially in long lengths, does not absorb turns as easily as fibre rope, and if the wire being coiled is not free to revolve during coiling it will become twisted. An occasional left-handed loop introduced into the coil will counter-act the twists.

Frenchman

full and by, the condition of a sailing vessel when she is held as close to the wind as possible with the sails full and not shivering. See also BY.

furl, to, take in the sails of a vessel and secure them with *gaskets, in the case of square-rigged ships by hauling in on the *clew-lines and buntlines (see BUNT) and rolling them up to the *yards; in the case of fore-and-aft rig, by lowering *gaff-rigged sails and similarly securing them to the *booms or rolling up triangular sails and securing them to the *stays on which they are set. To take off the sails of a ship and stow them in sail lockers below decks is not, strictly, furling although the final result in respect of the ship is the same. **To furl in a body,** a method of furling sail in square-rigged ships occasionally practised when the ship is expected to remain for some time in harbour; it entailed gathering the sail into the *top at the heel of the topmast by releasing the *earings at the *yardarms so that the sail could be drawn in towards the centre of the yard.

furniture, the whole movable equipment of a ship—rigging, sails, spars, anchors, boats, and everything with which she is fitted out to operate her, but not including her consumable stores, such as fuel and victuals.

futtock, one of the separate pieces of timber which form a *frame or *rib in a wooden ship. There are normally four, or occasionally five, futtocks to a rib in a ship of moderate size, the one nearest the *keel being known as a ground or naval futtock, the remainder being called upper futtocks.

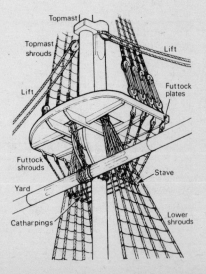

Futtock shrouds

The word would appear to be seaman's pronunciation of foothook.

futtock shrouds, originally short *shrouds of chain or large hemp, but later metal rods, which give support to the *top on a lower mast. They run from the futtock plates, secured to the sides of the top, downwards and inwards towards the lower mast being secured either to a stave in the lower shrouds close under the top, from which the catharpings (see HARPINGS) are led to the mast, or to a futtock band round the mast itself. The futtock plates, to which the upper ends of the futtock shrouds are secured, carry the futtock chain plates to which the topmast shrouds are set up.

G

gaff, a spar to which the *head of a four-sided *fore-and-aft sail is laced and hoisted on the after side of a mast. The forward end, against the mast, is built up laterally to form jaws, or pivoted to a wrought iron saddle, to fit round the mast. To hold the gaff against the mast in all conditions, the gaff jaws are usually joined by a stout jaw rope on which are threaded wooden balls known as *trucks or *parrels to allow the gaff to slide easily up and down the mast. Two *halyards are used to hoist a gaff sail, a *throat halyard at the mast end and a *peak halyard at the outer end, but on many traditional types of Dutch craft the gaff is a very short spar, usually cut into an arched curve, and only a single halyard, attached to a span on the gaff, is used to hoist it.

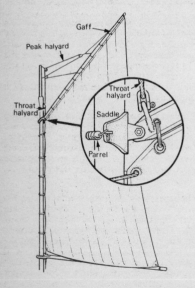

A typical gaff

For some centuries, up to the introduction of mechanical power, the gaff rig was the sailing rig of the great majority of small craft, with the exception perhaps of those plying in eastern waters and the Mediterranean where the *lateen rig predominated. It remained as such until the gradual introduction, in the first two decades of the 20th century, of the *Bermuda rig for small yachts, extended after the First World War (1914-18) to the larger ocean-going and racing yachts (see also J-CLASS). A considerable number of older yachts in commission still have their gaff rig, and there are some signs of its revival in cruising yachts. Although the rig requires more running rigging than the Bermuda rig, the comparatively shorter mast required poses fewer problems in structural strength and support than the tall mast demanded by a Bermudian mainsail. For illus. see RIG.

gage, sometimes **gauge,** a term used at sea in relation to the direction of the wind. A ship which is to *windward of another has the weather gage of her; one to *leeward has the lee gage.

gale, a wind blowing at a speed of between 34 and 47 knots, force 8 and 9 on the *Beaufort scale. Winds of this strength are usually divided into two general descriptions, a gale when the wind speed is between 34 and 40 knots and a strong gale when it blows between 40 and 47 knots.

Gales are associated with *depressions, and when the *synoptic evidence indicates an approaching depression deep enough to produce gale force winds, gale warnings are broadcast to shipping giving the probable area and strength. Although winds of above 47 knots are officially designated as *storms, they are usually still broadcast as gale warnings of force 10 and above.

An indication of gale strength winds is also provided by the state of the sea. When the waves are high and the crests begin to break into spindrift, a gale is blowing. Crests beginning to topple and roll over, with dense streaks of foam along the direction of the wind, are signs of a strong gale. See METEOROLOGY.

galley, the ship's kitchen.

gallows, (1) a raised wooden frame consisting of two uprights and a cross-piece on which the spare *booms and spars in a square-rigged ship rested. These booms ran from near the *forecastle along the *waist of the ship and were used for the stowage of the ship's boats, giving rise to the name 'booms' as the proper place for the stowage of boats on board. (2) A temporary wooden structure erected on the *counter of a small *fore-and-aft rigged sailing craft on which the main boom is stowed and secured when the vessel is at anchor or lying on a mooring. See also BOOM CRUTCH.

gammon iron, a circular iron band used to hold a *bowsprit to the stem of a sailing vessel. When a bowsprit is fitted in a yacht, the gammon iron has two metal sheaves fixed on either side which act as fairleads for the anchor cable.

gammon lashing or **gammoning,** seven or eight turns of a rope lashing passed alternately over the *bowsprit and through a hole in the *stem of a sailing vessel to secure the bowsprit at the knightheads. Good gammoning was a skilled operation, and when properly performed made a *cross lashing. Nowadays a *gammon iron replaces the old gammon lashing.

gantline, the modern corruption of girt-line, a single *whip originally used to hoist to the masthead or *hounds the standing *rigging which was to be secured there while the ship was *fitting-out, and also to hoist the *riggers, in *boatswain's chairs, to do the work. The gantline was also used for hoisting sails in square-rigged ships from the deck when required to be bent on to their *yards, as they were far too heavy to be carried up the rigging by the *topmen.

garboard or **garboard strake,** the first plank on the outer hull of a wooden vessel next to the *keel, into which it is *rabetted. It runs from the *stem to the *sternpost, and is similarly rabetted into those timbers. The term was also used in wooden ships to describe the first *seam nearest the keel, the most difficult of all to *caulk.

garland, a collar of rope round a mast to support the standing *rigging and prevent it from chafing the mast. In the early sailing days when ships only had single pole masts, the *tops were circular or semi-circular platforms built round the masts, and that part of the pole mast above the top was known as the topmast. The only mark on the mast above the top was the garland which supported the *stays, and that part of the pole mast above the garland was known as the 'top-garland' mast, which may have become *topgallant.

gasket, a rope, plaited cord, or strip of canvas used to secure a sail, when *furled, to a *yard or *boom of a vessel. In large square-rigged ships gaskets were passed with three or four turns round both sail and yard, with the turns spaced well out. The *bunt gasket, which had to hold the bunt or heaviest part of a square sail when furled, was sometimes made of strong netting. In the old seamanship manuals of the 17th and early 18th centuries the word is sometimes written as casket. The modern term, used in yachts, is 'tier'.

genoa jib, a large *jib or foresail used in racing and cruising yachts, almost invariably in conjunction with a *Bermuda mainsail. Its features are (a) its size, considerably larger than a standard jib and often larger than the mainsail, and (b) its shape, with the *clew extended much farther aft than in an ordinary jib, overlapping the mainsail by an appreciable amount, its *foot often parallel with the deck sheer. In effect, it combines jib and fore staysail in a single large sail. As well as transferring the main driving power of a yacht's sails to the *fore-triangle, it also, by the sheeting of its clew well abaft the mast, increases the speed of the airflow over the *luff of the mainsail and thus increases the partial vacuum there which helps to pull the yacht forward. See AERODYNAMICS for an analysis of this forward pull.

ghost, to, make headway in a sailing ship without any apparent wind to fill her sails. By taking advantage of such breaths of wind as may occur, a well-trimmed sailing vessel can often make quite an appreciable way through the water, appearing to move, or ghost, even in a flat calm.

ghoster, a light-weather sail set in yachts *hanked to the topmast *stay for use in very light winds. It is very similar in shape to either a *genoa or a *yankee, according to choice, but with its *luff extending the whole length of the stay instead of short of the masthead as is often the case with a genoa or yankee. It is made of much lighter cloth (usually 6-oz *Terylene) than a genoa and is suitable for use in winds of up to force 2 on the *Beaufort scale.

gimbals, two concentric metal rings which form the mounting and suspension for *compasses and *chronometers on board ship. Gimbals are also used to mount table lamps, cooking stoves, etc., in small vessels.

gird, to, haul in or bind something together with the object of securing more space. It is an expression used particularly in regard to *rigging and more especially to the rigging of a square-rigged ship, where extra space was needed to *brace the lower *yards round when sailing *close-hauled. The standing rigging of a mast when it reached the *hounds often formed a limit to the degree a lower yard could be braced round; if this rigging could be girded in to the mast, extra space for the yard was made and it could be braced sharper.

girt. A ship is girt when she is moored with two anchors out with both cables hauled in so taut that they prevent her swinging to wind or tide. The cables as they *grow out tautly to the anchors catch her *forefoot as she attempts to swing and prevent any such movement. It is a situation easily corrected by *veering one of the cables slightly.

girtline, the old, and more correct, word for *gantline.

glass, the seaman's name for a telescope and the ship's barometer.

glass reinforced plastic, see FIBRE GLASS.

globular projection, a form of map-making in which the central meridian and the periphery are arbitrarily marked off in equal parts for lines of *latitude to be drawn, and the equator equally divided up to accommodate the meridians of *longitude. The resultant map shows less distortion of land areas than other methods of projection, but is useless for plotting distances or directions. See GNOMONIC CHART.

glut, a strengthening piece of canvas sewn into large square sails at the *bunt, with an eyelet hole in the middle, for the bunt *jigger to go through when the sail was being *furled. These big sails were too heavy for the men working on the yard to lift by hand, and so a small purchase (jigger) was used to haul up the foot of the sail, hence the need to strengthen the canvas where the jigger was hooked on.

gnomonic chart, a chart of great utility in *great circle sailing based on the gnomonic projection. This is a perspective projection in which part of a spherical surface is projected from the centre of the sphere on to a plane surface tangential to the sphere's

surface. The principal property of this projection is that great circle arcs are projected as straight lines.

In order to draw a great circle on a *Mercator chart—the projection being a relatively complex curve always concave to the equator—the route is first drawn on a gnomonic chart by connecting the plotted positions of the places of departure and destination with a straight line. Positions of a series of points on this line are taken from the gnomonic chart and marked on the Mercator chart. A fair curve is then drawn through these points, this being the required projection of the great circle route on the Mercator chart.

The gnomonic chart became popular with the publication by Hugh Godfray in 1858 of two polar gnomonic charts covering the greater part of the world, one for the northern, and the other for the southern hemisphere. Although it was generally believed that Godfray was the original inventor of this method of great circle sailing, it is interesting to note that a complete explanation of the construction of a polar gnomonic chart, with a detailed example of a great circle route from the Lizard to the Bermudas, appeared in Samuel Sturmey's *Mariners' Mirror* of 1669.

Gnomonic charts are also used navigationally for the plotting of wireless directional bearings which follow a great circle route.

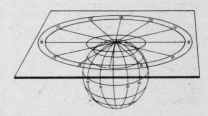

Projection of a gnomonic chart

go about, to, see TACK.

gooseneck, a metal fitting on the inboard end of a *boom of a sailing vessel by which it is connected to a metal ring round the base of the mast on which the sail, spread by the boom, is set. It has reference only to the fore-and-aft sailing *rig or to the *spanker of a square-rigged ship. The fitting allows for the swing of the boom sideways and is also hinged to allow the boom upward movement.

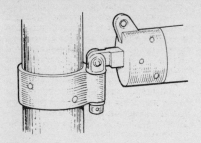

Gooseneck

goose-wings, originally the *clews of a *course or topsail of a square-rigged ship used to *scud under when the wind was too strong for the whole sail, fully reefed, to be used. With the *bunt of the sail hauled up to the *yard, only the clews would remain spread. More recently, as **goose-winged**, a term applied in *fore-and-aft rigged sailing craft to indicate the *jib or *staysail being *boomed out on the opposite side to the mainsail in a following wind to present the largest possible area of sail to the wind. The assumption in such a case is that the vessel concerned does not carry, or does not wish to set, a *spinnaker, which is the most efficient means of getting the most out of a following wind in fore-and-aft rig.

gore, (1) a *cloth of canvas cut on an angle to increase the breadth or depth of a square sail or to shape the *leech of a fore-and-aft sail. In a four-sided fore-and-aft sail, the leech is always longer than the *luff, and some cloths must be cut on an angle whether they are *seamed vertically or horizontally. **(2)** An angular piece of plank in a wooden vessel inserted to fill up the planking at any part requiring it.

grapnel, sometimes **grapple,** a small four-pronged anchor often used in dinghies and similar small boats. A grapnel can also be used for dragging the bottom for articles lost overboard.

grass-line, a rope made of sisal, not particularly strong but with the property of floating on the surface of the water. It has several uses at sea, particularly in cases of rescue and salvage, when a grass-line floated down across the bows of a disabled ship in rough weather can be easily picked up and used to haul across a towing cable. It is used by naval ships when streaming a fog-buoy. It is also of value in small sailing or rowing vessels in a following sea; when a length of grass-line is towed astern it acts as a *drogue and steadies the vessel down so that the seas pass under her and do not carry her along dangerously on the crests of the waves. Similarly, when a small boat approaches a shore on which waves are breaking, a grass-line towed astern provides an extra grip on the water and helps to prevent the boat being turned broadside on to the breakers, rolled over, and capsized.

graticule, (1) the network of projected parallels of *latitude and *meridians on a map or chart. **(2)** The scale, traditionally made from filament spun by spiders, inserted into rangefinders and marine binoculars.

great circle, the largest circle which can be inscribed on the surface of a sphere. In terms of the earth, the *equator, and all the *meridians of longitude, since they pass through both poles, are great circles, i.e., the centres of all these circles lie at the centre of the earth. It follows therefore that any circle inscribed around the earth which has its centre at the centre of the earth is a great circle.

These circles are of great importance in the art of *navigation. The shortest distance between any two points on the earth's surface lies along the great circle which passes through them both. Wireless signals, and hence wireless direction-finding bearings, follow the path of great circles. See also GNOMONIC CHART, MERCATOR PROJECTION.

great circle sailing, a method of navigating a ship along the shortest distance between the point of departure and the point of arrival, subject of course to no land or other navigational hazard lying between the two points. On any sphere, the shortest distance between any two points is the circumference of the circle which joins them and whose centre is at the centre of the sphere. In terms of the earth, this is a *great circle, and if it were possible for a ship to sail along the great circle connecting her point of departure with her point of arrival, she would sail the shortest distance between the two. But unless both these points lie on the equator, which is of course a great circle, and along which she can steer a steady *course east or west, she cannot do this unless she sails a continuing curve, permanently altering course to keep herself on the great circle.

The theory of great circle sailing has been known and understood almost from the days when it was realized that the earth was a sphere, and it is described in many of the early books written about the art of navigation. But it was of little use to a ship which depended on the wind and her sails to get from one place to another. It was quite impossible for any such ship to adhere to a predetermined course, and she had to make the best of her way according to the vagaries of the wind. But when, during the 19th century, steam began to take the place of sails as the means of ship propulsion and enabled a ship to steer a course irrespective of the wind, the economies of great circle sailing in terms of fuel consumption and time on voyage were quickly appreciated.

One of the properties of a *gnomonic chart is that a great circle appears on it as a straight line, and a ship's navigator, if he wants to plot a great circle track on a *Mercator chart, which he uses for navigation, needs to join his point of departure and his point of arrival by a straight line drawn on a gnomonic chart and then to transfer a series of positions on this straight line, read off in *latitude and *longitude, on to his Mercator chart. These positions will then lie on a curve, which he can sketch in. Although he will not be able to steer his ship along this exact curve, he can approximate to it with a number of short, straight courses, known as *rhumb lines, which are chords of the great circle and which appear as straight lines on a Mercator chart. If he keeps his ship on these straight courses, always altering course to the next one when necessary, he will be keeping his ship as close as conveniently possible to the great circle joining the two points. By this means he is sailing the shortest reasonable course between them, thus saving fuel and time. See NAVIGATION, and for illus. see MERCATOR PROJECTION.

Greenwich Mean Time (GMT), the present basis of all navigational measurement of time by which the results of observations of heavenly bodies are worked out and the position of a ship fixed at sea. It was not until 1880 that international agreement was reached to accept the *longitude of Greenwich, the home of the Royal Observatory, as the *prime meridian from which all time at sea should be measured; until that year many maritime nations had their own prime meridians, resulting in a variety of navigational times according to the nationality of the particular ship whose position was being fixed. That of France, for example, was the meridian of Paris, that of Spain the Azores. Greenwich Mean Time, therefore, now means the exact time which is being recorded at Greenwich at any moment of local time around the earth. This exact Greenwich time is discoverable on board ship by means of *chronometers, in conjunction with their known *rate of change, and/or by the many periodical time signals broadcast by wireless from a multitude of stations all round the earth.

gregale, a Mediterranean wind blowing from the north-east, usually in sudden squalls and particularly associated with Malta and Sicily.

'Greta Garbo', the slang name which was given to a quadrilateral or *double-clewed jib used in a few large racing yachts around the years 1934 and 1935.

gripe, to. The tendency of a sailing vessel to come up into the wind when sailing *close-hauled, and thus to carry too much weather *helm to correct this tendency, is known as griping. It is sometimes an effect of the overall *trim of the vessel and if so can be reduced by lightening the vessel forward or trimming down aft to make her stern draw deeper into the water. This is of course normally done by the movement of *ballast from forward to aft. But more usually it is the effect of an ill-balanced *hull, too bluff a bow causing an excessive bow-wave, a short *run aft causing *drag or turbulence. An unbalanced rig can also cause a vessel to gripe, which can be corrected by reducing the fore canvas. In cases where griping is more or less built into the design, there is little that can be done to remove it.

gripes, broad plaited bands of small rope used to secure boats on deck when at sea.

grommet (pron. grummet), a ring formed by laying up a single *strand of rope three times, and used originally to fasten the upper edge or *luff of a sail to its stay. Its place for this purpose has been taken by the modern spring-loaded hank or clip-hook. Grommets have various other uses on board ship and, when the two sides of one are brought together by a *serving, it forms a couple of connected *eyes, always a useful article to have available on deck. In boatwork grommets are used to hold the oars to *thole pins when rowing.

gross register tonnage, see TONNAGE.

ground tackle, a general term embracing all the gear (*anchors, *cables, etc.) carried by a ship to enable her to anchor or to *moor. By some it is also held to include permanent moorings for ships and smaller vessels including trots, but more usually the term refers only to a vessel's own means of anchoring.

group, a navigational term which indicates the number of exposures of a fixed navigational light, whether from *lighthouse, *lightship, or lighted *buoy, in each cycle of operation. See CHARACTERISTICS.

grow, to, used of an *anchor *cable, to lie in a particular direction in relation to the ship when it is at anchor. ('How does the cable grow?').

growler, a piece of low-lying ice floating in the sea in high northern or southern *latitudes which is difficult to see from a ship approaching it because of its dark colour. Growlers are formed of blocks of ice which have broken away from the ice pack or from icebergs, and have been blown or have drifted clear.

GRP, see FIBRE GLASS.

guardrail, the upper deck rail along both sides of a vessel to prevent anyone falling overboard. In smaller ships guardrails are usually of wire, supported at intervals by *stanchions and secured at each end to the foremost and aftermost stanchion by small Senhouse slips. Ships with *bulwarks do not need a guardrail as the bulwark takes its place.

gudgeon, orig. **googing,** the metal plate carrying an eye bolted on to the *sternpost or the *transom. Normally two gudgeons and two *pintles are fitted to hold a rudder steady. In almost all ships today, even the smallest, a balanced rudder is fitted and so pintles and gudgeons are not required, since the rudder is fixed to a rudder post which rises through the vessel's *counter.

Gudgeons and pintles are today used only in boats and very small yachts. The main value of this fitting, apart from its simplicity, is that the rudder can be easily unshipped when not in use.

guest-rope, a rope thrown to a boat from a ship, either to tow her or to enable her to make fast alongside; it is also sometimes known as a guess-rope or gift-rope.

Gulf Stream, sometimes also known as the North Equatorial Current. It starts in the Caribbean Sea where the water, expanded by the heat, escapes into the Gulf of Mexico. Here it is warmed still further and expands to a vast bulk, escaping through the Florida Straits and to the eastward of the Grand Banks off Newfoundland, continuing in great depth across the North Atlantic to northern Europe. Its warmth ensures a temperate climate in all countries which lie in its path. Its velocity is calculated at about 80 miles a day. A counter-current flows to the south of it westward across the Atlantic to the Caribbean Sea. See also CURRENT.

gull, to, wear away, used especially of the action of the pin of a *block when it wears away the *sheave, round which the rope of a tackle revolves. When the sheave begins to wobble in the block because of wear by the pin, it is called gulling. Similarly, when the *yards of a square-rigged ship rubbed up against the mast, they were said to gull the mast.

gun tackle, a *tackle comprising a rope rove through two single *blocks with the standing part of the rope made fast to the *strop of one of the blocks. It multiplies the power exerted on the fall of the tackle by three when rove to *advantage. Its original use was to run out a gun after it had been loaded so that the muzzle projected through the gunport ready for firing, but being a useful tackle for many purposes it is still widely used in ships and yachts. See also PURCHASE.

gunter rig, a development of the *lugsail rig in which the sail is cut with a very short *luff and very long *leech. The *head of the sail is laced to a *yard, which when fully hoisted, and with the *tack of the sail *bowsed hard down, lies virtually as an extension of the mast, making the sail in effect very similar to a *Bermuda sail. It is a rig which is included in the generic term of *standing lug.

Typical gunter rig

gunwale (pron. gunnel), **(1)** a piece of timber going round the upper *sheer strake of a boat to bind in the top work. **(2)** The plank which covers the heads of the *timbers in a wooden ship. **(3)** In modern terms, the projection above the upper deck level of the two sides of a small vessel as a means of preventing the influx of seawater when the vessel heels over.

guy, (1) a rope or *tackle used to control the lateral movement of a derrick. **(2)** A rope or wire led forward from a *boom as part of the running *rigging of a fore-and-aft rigged vessel. In sailing yachts a guy, called a boom guy, may be rigged between the end of the boom and a point well forward when running before the wind, particularly in light winds or when the yacht is *rolling in a swell, to prevent the *sheet from going slack and the boom swinging excessively; a *spinnaker boom nearly always needs a boom guy (or spinnaker guy) because this sail is less under control by the sheet than a mainsail.

gyassi or **gaiassa,** the traditional sail trading vessel of the upper Nile.

gybe, or **jibe, to,** swing across, used when *wearing a fore-and-aft rigged sailing vessel when the *boom of the mainsail swings across as the wind crosses the stern. The word can also be used as a noun, e.g., a ship can make a gybe.

The stronger the wind, and the greater the area of the mainsail and weight of the main boom, the more strain a gybe will put on gear and crew, but if properly sailed a *fore-and-aft rigged vessel should be able to gybe in any strength of wind in which she can carry normal canvas. The force of the gybe is broken by hauling in the main sheet before the boom is allowed to swing across, thus considerably reducing the strain as the gybe takes place. If the wind is so strong that a gybe would be dangerous, this may be a reason for setting a *trysail, smaller in area and with no boom, in place of the mainsail. An involuntary gybe, caused by running *by the lee through bad steering, or by a sudden squall from an unexpected quarter, is always dangerous.

If the vessel is not fitted with a permanent *backstay, the operation of gybing requires the setting up of the weather (when the vessel is on her new *tack) *runner before the boom swings across the stern and the *overhauling of the lee runner to allow the boom to swing forward as the wind takes it. To gybe without attending the runners, or to do so involuntarily, is known as to 'gybe all-standing', and is dangerous. See also CHINESE GYBE.

gypsy, an attachment to a ship's *windlass shaped to take the links of a chain cable for anchor work in a small ship where no *capstan or cable holders are fitted. Normally two gypsies are fitted, one each end of the horizontal shaft of the windlass inside the warping drums, in order to work the two *bower anchors which a ship normally carries in her *hawseholes. They can be disconnected from the windlass shaft by means of clutches when they are required to run freely, as when letting go an anchor. They take the place of the cable-holders of larger ships.

H

half hitch, a single turn of a rope around a spar or other object with the end of the rope being led back through the *bight. It is the basis on which many knots used at sea are constructed.

'half seas over', the condition of a ship stranded on a *reef or rock when the seas break over her deck. In this condition she is usually unable to take any action to ease her situation. The expression has passed into the English language to describe the situation of a person incapacitated by drink and incapable of steering a steady *course.

half-sprit, see GAFF.

halyards, halliards, or **haulyards,** the ropes, wires, or *tackles used to hoist or lower sails, either to their *yards in square-rigged ships with the exception of the fore, main, and mizen *course or on their *gaffs or by their peaks in fore-and-aft rigged ships. The courses, which are very heavy sails, are hoisted by the *jeers.

hambro, or **hamber, line,** also widely known as cod line, a three-stranded small size rope tightly laid up and used for lacing sails and for lashings where strength is essential. It is normally supplied in hanks whereas smaller stuff (twine, *marline etc.) is usually supplied in balls.

hand, (1) as a verb, to furl the square sails of a ship to the *yards. In a strong wind the two *leeches of the sail were first brought to the yard since if the leeches were left to belly or fill with wind, it would be impossible for the men on the yard to get the sail in. The order given in a square-rigged ship was **'hand in the leech'. (2)** As a noun, a member of the ship's crew. **'All hands',** the order for all seamen to come on deck either in an emergency or to assist in some operation which is beyond the capacity of the watch on deck. **(3) Hand-over-hand,** to haul rapidly on a rope or *tackle by men passing their hands alternately one before the other and thus keeping the hauling part in motion. A seaman was said to go hand-over-hand when he went up the mast by means of a *stay or *shroud without using the *ratlines. The expression also means rapidly,

as, e.g., 'we are coming up with the ship ahead hand-over-hand'.

handsomely, gradually and carefully, used for example when easing off a line or *tackle. 'Lower away handsomely', the order when lowering a seaboat or a lifeboat from the *davits of a ship so that she may go evenly down the ship's side and be kept level during the process.

handy billy, the name of a small *jigger purchase or watch *tackle, used on board ship for a variety of purposes. It is rove with one double and one single block and multiplies the power by four when rove to *advantage.

hank, (1) a small ring or hoop of metal by which the *luff of a *jib or *staysail is bent to the *stays of a sailing vessel. Modern hanks are usually spring-loaded so that they can easily be slipped on or off the stays as desired. **(2)** A skein of small line or twine, used on board for small work such as *whipping the ends of ropes, passing a *seizing, etc.

harbour dues, the amount of money the owner of a ship has to pay to a harbour authority for the use of the harbour and its facilities. It is usually quoted as a charge per ton based on the ship's gross registered *tonnage, or in the case of a yacht, per foot of her overall length. In many ports, the bare harbour dues are increased by an additional charge for the use of navigational beacons and lights.

harbourmaster, an official of a port who is responsible for seeing that the port regulations are enforced, particularly in respect of *moorings and the proper berthing of ships. Queen's, or King's, Harbourmaster, an official post in the British Navy, usually filled by a captain, responsible for all the navigational requirements of a naval base or port, again including moorings or berthing.

harden-in, to, haul in the *sheets of a sailing vessel to present the sails at a more acute angle to the wind.

harmattan, an easterly wind which occasionally blows during the dry season (December, January, February) on the west coast of Africa, coming off the land instead of the more normal wind which blows off the sea. It is a very dry wind, usually accompanied by dust storms which the wind has picked up from the desert. It is sometimes also known as the 'doctor', as it is cooler than the normal temperatures of the coast.

harness. 'One hand for the ship, the other for yourself' has been the seaman's adage through the ages, but aboard a small yacht battling through the seas in an offshore race, both hands may have to be used in an emergency and it is then all too easy for a member of the crew to fall overboard and be lost astern. With the intention of preventing such accidents the Royal Ocean Racing Club, together with other associations connected with offshore yacht racing, introduced a rule that safety harness must be worn at night and in very heavy weather by the watch on deck when racing. The Royal Society for the Prevention of Accidents has encouraged this precaution among all who go to sea in small boats. It is an unwise skipper who permits any of his crew to work on deck at night without some form of harness, attached to part of the yacht. The harness is usually of strong webbing which passes round the chest and over both shoulders, with a length of line having a metal clip on its end for easy attachment to a handy *stanchion, one of the *shrouds, or any really strong object, leaving the wearer free to use both hands.

harpings or **harpens, (1)** the forward parts of the *wales at the *bows of a wooden ship where they are fixed into the *stem. They are normally thicker than the after part of the wales in order to provide additional strength at the bows, where most of the strain on a ship falls. **(2)** Lengths or ribbands of timber used to bind the *frames at bow and stern of a wooden ship until the ship is planked. **(3)** Catharpings are the cross pieces at the end of the *futtock staves used for *girding, or hauling in, the standing *rigging to allow the lower *yards of a square-rigged ship to be *braced sharp up. By holding the standing rigging as close in to the mast as possible, there is more room for the lower yards to be braced at a sharper angle to the fore-and-aft line of the vessel and thus enable her to carry a better wind when sailing *close-hauled.

hatch, an opening in the ship's deck for ingress and egress of either person or cargo. The cover that closes it is known as a hatch cover, though many seamen call this also a hatch. The term hatchway is generally taken to mean the vertical space through a series of hatches, one below the other, through the decks of a vessel.

hawse, strictly, that part of a ship's *bow where the *hawseholes and the hawsepipes are situated through which the anchor *cables pass. But it is by extension and in its most generally accepted meaning also the distance between the ship's head and her anchor as it lies on the bottom. Thus another vessel which crosses this space is said to cross the hawse. When a ship lies to two anchors, she has a clear hawse when the two cables *grow from the ship without crossing; when they do cross, the ship has a *foul hawse. The normal practice in ships when they lie to two anchors is to insert a *mooring swivel between the two cables so that the ship swings in a restricted circle without the cables becoming crossed.

hawsehole, the hole in the forecastle deck, or upper deck in the case of vessels without a forecastle, right forward in the bows of a ship, through which the *anchor cable passes. The hawseholes form the entries to the *hawsepipes which lead the cables from the deck to the outside of the ship's hull.

hawsepipe, the inclined pipe or tube which leads from the *hawsehole of a ship, on the deck close to the *bows, to the outside of the vessel. The anchor *cable is led through the hawsepipe and the *anchor, bent to its end with a shackle, lies with its *shank in the hawsepipe when it is hove up close and secured for sea.

hawser, a heavy rope or small *cable with a circumference of 5 inches or more. On board ship hawsers are used for a variety of purposes which require a strong and heavy rope, as, e.g., a *warp for a *kedge anchor, and for breast-ropes and *springs when a ship is secured alongside a wharf. In smaller vessels, such as yachts which have no chain cable, the rope used as an anchor warp is sometimes called a hawser, even though less than the size normally accepted as the minimum to qualify for the name.

hawser-laid rope, rope in which three *strands are laid up against the twist to form the rope. It is the normal form of rope used for most purposes at sea. In Britain, most hawser-laid rope is laid up right-handed, or anti-clockwise, but left-handed ropes are sometimes found. Three strands each of 150 *fathoms in length will make a hawser-laid rope of 120 fathoms. See also CABLE-LAID ROPE, and for illus. see S-TWIST.

head, a much used maritime word meaning the top or forward part. The top edge of a four-sided sail is called the head, the top of the mast is the masthead, the head of a ship is the bows (but the ship's head means the compass direction in which she is pointing). Headsails are the *jibs and *staysails hoisted at the forward end of a sailing vessel; a headboard is the small wooden insertion at the top of a *Bermuda mainsail. The word is also used as a verb in very much the same sense: a sailing vessel is headed by the wind when it swings round towards the vessel's bows so that the original course can no longer be laid.

By the head, a ship which is drawing more water forward than aft.

headboard, of a *Bermuda mainsail, see HEAD.

head rope, that part of the *bolt-rope of a sail which lies along the head of a four-sided sail. Triangular sails, of course, have no head and therefore no head rope.

heads, the name given to that part of the older sailing ships forward of the *forecastle and around the beak which was used by the crew as their lavatory. It was always used in the plural to indicate the weather and lee sides, seamen being expected to use the lee side so that all effluent should fall clear into the sea. They were floored with gratings so that the sea could assist in washing them clean, though there was always a small working party told off from each *watch to clean the heads, never a very popular task and one usually reserved as a punishment for small misdemeanours.

The name has been largely retained among seamen, even in these days of lavatory bowls and modern flushing arrangements.

headsails, the collective name used to describe the sails set before the *mast of a sailing vessel or the foremast in a ship with more than one mast. It embraces the jibs and staysails, etc., which may be set before the forward mast.

heart, a form of *deadeye which was used for setting up the *stays of a square-rigged ship in the same way as deadeyes were used for setting up the *shrouds. It was in the form of a triangular block of wood, sometimes cut heart-shaped, with a single large hole in the middle grooved for the rope or lanyard (according to the size of ship) to provide a degree of purchase when setting the stay up taut.

heave-to, to, lay a sailing ship on the wind with her helm *a-lee and her sails shortened and so trimmed that as she comes up to the wind she will fall off again on the same tack and thus make no headway. Vessels normally heave-to when the weather is too rough and the wind too strong to make normal sailing practicable. A steamship can similarly heave-to in stormy weather by heading up to the sea and using her engines just enough to hold her up in position. The whole idea in heaving-to is to bring the wind on to the weather bow and hold the ship in that position, where she rides most safely and easily.

heaving line, a light line with a small weighted bag at the end used for heaving from the ship to shore when coming alongside; a heavier wire rope or hawser is attached which can then be hauled over by the heaving line.

heel, (1) the after end of a ship's *keel and the lower end of the *sternpost to which it is connected. **(2)** The lower end of a mast, *boom, or *bowsprit in a sailing vessel. The heel of a mast is normally squared off and is lowered through a hole in the deck until it fits into a square step cut in the *keelson of the ship, or alternatively is held in a *tabernacle on deck in the case of masts which can be lowered, or raised, at will.

heel, to, in relation to a ship, to lean over to one side. It is not a permanent leaning over, as with a *list, or spasmodic, as when a vessel *rolls in a sea, but somewhere between the two. Thus a sailing vessel will heel over when the winds catches her sails, unless she has the wind directly astern, and she will retain that heel until she alters course by coming nearer the wind or bearing away or the wind changes in strength or direction. When used as a noun, the word refers to the amount, or angle, to which a vessel is heeled.

heeling error, an error in a yacht's magnetic *compass which can be caused when she *heels. Whereas most ships' compasses are stabilized and corrected with small magnets to prevent errors when the vessel is rolling or takes a slight list, the compass of a sailing yacht is more liable to become affected when the yacht heels more sharply under the pressure of the wind on her sails. This is usually caused by the shifting positions of adjacent ferrous metal objects in relation to the compass card, which remains level to the horizon by means of its *gimbals. While any error in the compass may have been corrected by magnets when the yacht was upright, this correcting influence can be upset as soon as the yacht heels to port or to starboard, and the iron, steel, or electrical objects causing the error move above or below the compass card. A separate correction card for compass error at different angles of heel may have to be made out, or, if the error is excessive at certain angles of heel, it may become necessary to relocate the compass.

helm, another name for the *tiller, by which the *rudder of small vessels, such as yachts, dinghies, etc., is swung, and also the general term associated with orders connected with the steering of a ship. Steering by tiller was the general form of steering for all ships, after the replacement of the original steering oar by the rudder, and although the tiller gave way long ago to the steering wheels in ships of any size, the original helm orders (applicable to the tiller) remained in operation. The steering wheel is connected to the rudder so that the direction of turn is the same as the movement of the rudder, i.e., when the wheel is put over to *starboard, the rudder moves to starboard and the ship's head swings the same way. The reverse is the case with the tiller which moves in the opposite way to the rudder; when the tiller is put to starboard the rudder moves to *port and the ship's head swings also to port.

For some three centuries all helm orders given in ships remained applicable to the tiller, and an order from the navigator of a ship to a helmsman of, for example, 'port 20' meant that the helmsman put the wheel over 20° to starboard, the equivalent direction of moving the tiller 20° to port, and the rudder and the ship's head moved to starboard.

This practice was universal until after the First World War (1914–18), when some nations began to adopt the practice of relating helm orders to the rudder and no longer to the tiller, so that an order of, for instance, 'starboard 20°' meant turning the wheel, the rudder, and the ship's head all to starboard. By the mid-1930s all maritime nations had adopted this practice, which removed the anomaly of a navigator giving the order 'port' when he wanted to turn the ship to starboard, and vice versa.

hemp, the plant *Cannabis sativa*, from the fibres of which the best natural rope is made. Hemp rope is usually tarred as a preservative against perishing, but when not so treated is known as white rope. Although for centuries regarded as the best kind of rope for use in ships, it is today being rapidly replaced by rope made from synthetic or man-made fibres, which are impervious to weather, do not shrink when wet, and size for size are of greater strength, if sometimes less kind to a seaman's hand and apt to slip when knotted.

hengst, a typical Dutch fishing vessel of south Holland with a flat bottom, two *chines a side, a rounded low stern, narrow *leeboards, and straight *stem at about 45° rake. Hengsts are small craft with an average overall length of 30–35 feet with the traditional Dutch rig of a foresail set on the stemhead *forestay and a tall, narrow, loose-footed mainsail with a short *boom and curved *gaff. Later fishing hengsts, and those converted into private yachts, were fitted with auxiliary petrol or diesel engines.

hermaphrodite brig, sometimes known as a brig-schooner, a two-masted sailing ship rigged on the foremast as a *brig with square sails set on *yards, and as a *schooner on the mainmast, with a square topsail set above a *gaff mainsail. She differed from a *brigantine by the square topsail set on the mainmast, brigantines being fully fore-and-aft rigged on the main.

Highfield lever, a form of hand-operated lever used aboard sailing yachts as a rapid method of setting up or tautening running backstays or forestays. It was invented about 1930 by J. S. Highfield, then rear-commodore of the Royal Thames Y. C., for trial aboard his 15-metre racing yacht *Dorina*. Casting off the *lee runners (or *backstays) and setting up the weather ones every time the yacht changed tacks showed up the degree of smartness or otherwise of a racing yacht's crew. With the advent of the *Bermuda rig with its lofty mast and taut rigging in the 1920s, the *blocks and *purchase of the old-fashioned backstays were no longer swift or taut enough, and the Highfield lever solved the difficulty. The end of the backstay wire is led to a block which slides along a lever pivoted above deck so that the lever works in a fore-and-aft direction. When the lever is turned aft and its end pressed down on to the deck, the block holding the backstay wire comes below the line of the pivot bolt, thus holding the stay taut. To slacken the stay, the end of the lever merely has to be tripped up, and the stay is immediately released. Forestays can be set up and released in the same manner. Variations and improved designs of the Highfield lever are to the found aboard yachts in all parts of the world.

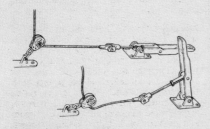

Highfield lever

high seas, in international law all the area of sea not under the sovereignty of states with a seaboard. For many years various claims had been made by different states on the extent of their *territorial waters, some choosing an arbitrary figure such as 100 miles, others the range of visibility, and so on. As the interests of navigation and trade grew, it was universally accepted that the dictum *terrae dominium finitur ubi finitus armorum vis* applied to the definition of territorial waters, and so the utmost range of a cannon-shot, accepted as 3 miles, was taken as the limit of sea which could be claimed nationally. All sea outside this limit was high seas and open to all without hindrance.

In recent years this limit of territorial waters has been challenged by many seafaring nations, mainly to preserve to themselves their inshore fishing grounds, and the limit has been gradually extended, with most nations now accepting 12 miles as marking territorial waters. But this, too, presents great difficulties with some nations claiming an extended limit ostensibly to preserve their fish breeding grounds, and in view of the growing exploitation of the seabed in drilling for oil and natural gas.

hitch, one of a series of knots by which one rope is joined to another or made fast to some object, such as a spar. There are many types of hitches used for various purposes, such as a *half hitch, a *rolling hitch, a *clove hitch, a running hitch, etc. They come within the overall genus of *bends, which include all the more common knots in use at sea.

hoist, (1) the name given to the *luff of a *fore-and-aft sail; the distance which it must be hoisted to get a taut luff. In a square sail it is the depth of the sail measured from its mid point. **(2)** That part of a flag or ensign which lies along the flagstaff and to which the *halyards are bent.

hoist, to, haul something up, particularly a sail or a flag, though the word is used in connection with most things which have to be lifted. An exception is a *yard of a square-rigged ship which is *swayed up, never hoisted.

holiday, a gap unintentionally left uncovered when painting or varnishing on board ship and applying equally to a ship herself or to her *masts and spars. It is also a gap left, equally unintentionally, in *paying a deck seam with *oakum and pitch.

holystone, a piece of sandstone used for scrubbing wooden decks on board ship.

hood, the canvas cover set up over a *companion-hatch or a skylight to give protection from sun and rain and, in older sailing ships, the tarred canvas covering the *eyes of the standing rigging to keep water out and thus preventing the rope from rotting. It was also the name given to the top of the galley chimney, which was made to turn round so that the galley smoke might go down to *leeward.

hooker, a development of the original *ketch, a short, tubby little vessel with main and mizen-masts, originally square-rigged on the main and with a small topsail above a fore-and-aft sail hoisted on a *gaff on the mizen. She usually set two jibs on a high-*steeved *bowsprit. She was a fishing vessel, and probably, as her name suggests, was used mainly for line fishing.

The name is also used, slightly contemptuously, for any vessel when she grows old and has lost her early bloom, or perhaps has come down a bit in the maritime world.

hoop, (1) in older *gaff-rigged sailing craft the *luff of the mainsail was secured to the mast by wooden hoops which slid up or down the mast as the sail was hoisted or lowered. **(2)** Although square in form, the metal bands which held the *stock of the old-fashioned anchors to the *shank were called hoops.

horizon, from Greek *horos*, 'a boundary', *horizo*, 'form a boundary', 'limit'. **(1)** The line which limits an observer's view of the surface of the earth and of the visible heavens. In astronomical navigation three meanings must be distinguished: (a) the visible horizon, that which is actually seen. This however is affected by the *dip of the horizon which depends on the refraction of light by the atmosphere and the observer's height above the sea; (b) the sensible horizon, the true horizon at sea level at the observer's position on the earth's surface, corrected for dip; it is the projection on the celestial sphere of a plane tangential to the earth's surface at that point; (c) the rational horizon, the projection on the celestial sphere of a plane parallel to the sensible horizon but passing through the centre of the earth instead of tangential to

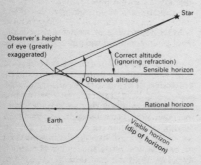

Horizon

its surface. In measuring the *altitude of a heavenly body considered as infinitely distant, the radius of the earth is insignificant, and normally the sensible and rational

horizons coincide. For some purposes, however, they must be distinguished. **(2)** The broad ring, most frequently of wood, in which a globe of the earth is fixed. The upper surface of the ring, level with the centre of the globe, represents the plane of the rational horizon. See also BUBBLE HORIZON.

horizontal sextant angle, the angle in the horizontal plane between two *land- or *sea-marks. By measuring such an angle the navigator is able to plot a position circle on his chart somewhere on which his ship may be fixed. A second position circle obtained in the same way, or a straight position line, which intersects the first position circle indicates the ship's position at the point of intersection. See also NAVIGATION.

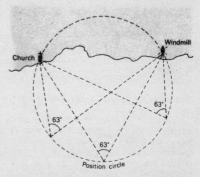

Horizontal sextant angle

horns, (1) the points of the jaws of a *boom or *gaff in a sailing vessel where they embrace the mast. Normally a boom is attached to the mast with a *gooseneck, but in some cases jaws were used instead, as jaws allow a spar to slide up and down the mast, while a gooseneck is fixed in position. A gaff always has jaws. **(2)** The name by which the outer ends of the *crosstrees of a mast are known. **(3)** Two projecting bars sometimes bolted to the after part of a *rudder from which chains can be led as an alternative method of working the rudder should the rudderhead be damaged or broken off.

horse, (1) the footrope of a *yard in a square-rigged sailing ship on which seamen stand when they are working aloft on the sails. It is supported at intervals from the yard by *stirrups. **(2)** An elevated rod, fixed at both ends and parallel with the deck of a sailing vessel to which the *sheets of sails can be led, lateral movement of the sheet being made possible by means of a *traveller which can slide from side to side of the horse according to the trim of the sail. Before the evolution of the modern high, narrow sail plan with the foresail overlapping the main, a horse was fitted mainly for use with headsails. In smaller sailing craft, the mainsail sheet is almost invariably led to a small horse fitted on the *counter or *taffrail of the vessel. See also FLEMISH HORSE.

horse latitudes, the areas of the ocean which lie between the generally westerly winds of the higher latitudes and the *trade winds, usually areas of prolonged calms.

hounds, wooden shoulders bolted below the masthead to either side of a wooden mast of a sailing vessel which originally supported the *trestle-trees. In smaller vessels without trestle-trees, hounds are used to support the *shrouds by which the mast is stayed laterally. In the days of large sailing ships the hounds of the lower masts were more properly known as *cheeks.

house, to, in general terms a word meaning to secure or make secure. Thus a topmast or *topgallant mast is housed by being lowered until its top is level with the top of the mast next below it and its *heel secured to the lower mast by a *parrel lashing or a *frapping line so that its rigging does not chafe or rest on the *cap. Topmasts and/or topgallant masts were normally housed when it was expected that the wind would increase into a gale of such force that the upper masts would be in danger. In gales of exceptional severity, topmasts and topgallant masts were struck down to the deck. See also STRIKE DOWN.

hoy, a small coasting sailing vessel of up to about 60 tons, in England usually with a single mast and *fore-and- aft sail, sometimes with a *boom and sometimes loose-footed, and used largely for carrying passengers from port to port. Hoys in Holland mainly had two masts, usually *lug-rigged on both. The hoy had no definite characteristics, being any small coasting vessel which might, in other places, be called a *sloop or a *smack.

hulk, (1) originally a large ship used either as a transport or for carrying merchandise, particularly in the Mediterranean where hulks ranged up to about 400 tons. It was contemporary with the *carrack and occasionally described as such. In general, any large and unwieldy ship of simple construction with a rounded bow and stern was described as a hulk. (2) Another name for the *hull of a ship, but this use of the word had fallen into disuse by the end of the 18th century. (3) An old ship converted for some use which did not require it to move.

hull, probably from the German hulla or hulle, a cloak or covering, the main body of a ship apart from her masts, rigging, and all internal fittings, including boilers, engines, etc. It consists virtually of the upper deck, sides, and bottom of a ship. Hull down, a ship so far distant that only her masts and/or sails, funnels, etc., are visible above the *horizon.

hull, to. A ship is said to be hulling when she drives to and fro without rudder or sail or engine movement. To strike hull, in a sailing vessel, to take in all sail in a storm and to lie with the *helm lashed *a-lee. This is also known as lying a-hull.

hurricane, see TROPICAL STORM.

hydrodynamics, a branch of physics concerned with pressures and behaviour of fluids, closely connected with the study of the design of ships and sailing yachts. When it was discovered by William Froude that the behaviour characteristics of scale models of ships towed at scale speeds through water along a testing tank varied exactly in accordance with their full size prototypes, he was able to propound his law of comparison, which later became more widely termed the Law of Mechanical Similitude. Froude showed that the behaviour of water as it flowed past a moving hull could be measured in terms of resistance and drag on the hull, and could be applied with reference to a full-size ship of identical design. It was clearly demonstrated that scale models, therefore, could be used to determine in advance the seagoing and performance characteristics of any new design of ship, in smooth water and in waves and rough weather conditions, and so to discover more accurately the ship's resistance and the engine power needed to give the requisite service speed. Running model tests was less time-consuming and considerably less costly than building the ship first and making modifications afterwards.

Study of the movements of liquids in the

allied subject of hydrokinetics also resulted in the discovery of what came to be termed the streamline form, which presents the lowest resistance to a liquid flowing past the object. For example, if a floating rectangular box is towed through water, or is anchored and the water is allowed to flow past, a wave will build up against the front face of the box, forming an area of pressure. The disturbed water then flows round both sides and underneath the box, producing friction drag along the surface of the box. Behind the flat rear end the water flow endeavours to close in upon itself, and does so with a series of eddies and whirlpools which break up the flow, producing a disturbed wake for some distance downstream. This disturbance forms a distinct suction at the rear of the box that, added to the pressure at the forward end and friction along the sides, creates a considerable amount of drag (Diagram 1).

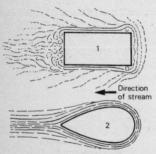

Direction of stream

1 Box in flowing stream
2 Sheet of ice in flowing stream

Streamlined flow

If a block of ice is cut into a rectangular shape similar in plan to the box, and it is held fast in a moving stream of slightly warmer water, the edges of the ice will begin to melt. The water flowing both round and under the ice will steadily erode it until the ice assumes a sleekly curved form which reduces the overall drag to a minimum. This naturally moulded teardrop shape, fuller at the front than at the tail end, offers minimal resistance to the flow of the water, and is said to be streamlined. Whatever shape the ice might be to begin with, its erosion by melting will inevitably reduce it to a curved shape approximating to Diagram 2: approximating, because the exact form and relation

between the length and the breadth will depend upon the rate of the stream, i.e., the speed of the water past the ice. The greater the speed of flow the narrower and sleeker the figure will become in proportion to its length.

It might be thought that such a streamline form would be eminently suitable for the design of a ship's hull, for like a fish it seems ideal for offering the minimum amount of resistance to the ship's forward progress. During the 18th and 19th centuries shipbuilders did in fact copy a modified 'cod's head and mackerel tail' form of hull below the waterline in sailing ships, small coasters, pilot boats, and revenue *cutters. These excessively full bows with a very fine run aft were normal over a period from about 1700 to 1850, and many yachts were built on the same principle, until a more balanced form was introduced, leading to modern designs. Other considerations in commercial ship design make such a fully streamlined hull impracticable: the full bow causes high resistance, if not damage, to the ship herself, when driven into a head sea, while the very fine lines aft create a condition of 'squatting', or settling by the stern, which is aggravated by the suction of the *propeller(s). Consideration of cargo carrying, passenger accommodation, and machinery space also rules out any fully streamlined vessel in favour of the conventional straight-sided ship with suitably designed bow and stern. A more recent development of the streamline principle, designed to minimize the bow waves and to reduce pressures of water along the ship's hull and so reduce drag and wash, is to be seen in the bulbous bow fitted below the waterline to many fast ships and giant tankers.

The fact that liquids are virtually incompressible makes it possible for a suitably shaped object which attains sufficient speed to rise above the water and skate along the surface, like a small flat stone skimmed by a child. When only steam machinery was available its weight in relation to the power it developed (i.e., the power/weight ratio) rendered it impracticable to drive a boat fast enough for it to begin to skim over the surface, and it was only when development in internal combustion engine design and lightweight boat construction produced a more advantageous power/weight ratio that boats could be made to plane, or skim along the water.

For this purpose the old conception of the fast launch with a fine entrance forward, narrow beam, and a fine run to the stern, so as to make as few waves as possible, went by the board. A new type of hull was designed on the principle of a water sledge which would rise on to the surface at high speed and plane, with only its after part, rudder, and propeller in the water. The design was found to need a broad flat stern to prevent squatting at speed, and sharply V'd sections at the bow. At velocities of 40 knots and over, water can be treated as though it were almost solid, and to assist boats to start planing in the early days of power boating many boats were built with one, two, or more steps on the underside of the hull, on which the boat was designed to ride like a sledge.

Based on the same principle as this stepped hull is a further development with some commercial uses—the hydrofoil. In this craft a series of curved vanes or hydrofins is fitted to a leg attached to each side of the hull forward, and similar vanes to another pair of legs fitted aft. As soon as the speed reaches a certain point the vessel rides up until its hull is completely clear of the water, and so runs on only the hydrofins. Hydrofoil craft operate as fast (50- to 60-knot) ferries in different parts of the world, particularly in the Mediterranean and on Russian rivers.

To be able to start planing under sail power alone it is essential for a conventional boat to be of exceedingly light construction with V'd bow sections and a flat bottom at the stern like the engine-powered speedboat, together with a highly efficient rig to supply the necessary drive. Although some light displacement yachts, such as Half-Ton Cup competitors and some multihull racers, can sail down wind with short bursts of speed in a state bordering on planing, true planing—riding along the surface at high speed for considerable periods—is normally achieved only by certain classes of high performance racing dinghies. See also PLANE, WAVE LINE THEORY.

hydrography, the science of marine surveying and of determining the position of points and objects on the surface of the globe, depths of the sea, etc.

I

iceberg, a floating island of ice. Icebergs in the northern hemisphere almost all originate in Disko Bay in Greenland. The mountains of northern Greenland are covered by a vast ice-cap which moves slowly down the valleys until it reaches the sea, where great sections break away in a process known as calving. They float out to sea and are then carried southward by the Labrador Current. Their usual life-span is about two years, the second summer finding them at their most southerly point in the region of the Grand Banks off Newfoundland. Small portions which break away from the main icebergs and are still large enough to constitute a danger to navigation are known as growlers. Only one-ninth of the total mass of an iceberg is visible above water level.

Today an ice patrol, directed from Halifax, is maintained in the North Atlantic to observe the position of all icebergs, the rate and direction of their drift, and to report them so that all shipping can be warned of their presence. In many cases the warning comes to a ship in the form of a chart transmitted by wireless, so that the navigator has a copy of the actual chart in front of him when plotting his course.

in soundings. A vessel is said to be in soundings when she is being navigated in water sufficiently shallow for soundings (see SOUND) to be made and used as a means for ascertaining the approximate position of the ship. Traditionally a ship is reckoned to be in soundings when she is within the 100-fathom line, this *isobath being taken as marking the edge of the *continental shelf.

in stays. A sailing vessel is said to be in stays when she is head to wind and temporarily unable to pay off on either *tack, though in its original meaning the term was used to indicate the act of tacking.

intercept, the difference, measured in nautical miles, which the navigator obtains when he works a *sight of an astronomical object. It is the difference between his estimate of the ship's position by *dead reckoning and the position obtained from his *altitude observations. He transfers this to the *chart by measuring the length of his intercept along the *azimuth of the observed object and drawing his position line at that point at right angles to the azimuth. See also MARCQ ST. HILAIRE METHOD.

International Code of Signals, a series of signal flags and *pendants, one flag for each letter of the alphabet and one pendant for each number between 0 and 9, with three additional pendants for substitutes and four for special meanings, which has been agreed and adopted by all maritime countries for communication between ship and ship, and ship and shore. It was founded in 1817 on Captain F. Marryat's code of signals and consisted originally of only fifteen flags and pendants. By 1855 it was being widely challenged by codes developed in France by Captain Reynold de Chauvaucy, in Great Britain by Rohde (1836) and Watson (1842), and in the USA by Rogers, but an international committee was set up in 1856 to try to reach agreement on a single code for universal use. Its final recommendation was based almost entirely on Marryat's original flags and it published a *Commercial Code of Signals* which received universal recognition. In 1887 the existing code ran into difficulties because of the adoption of the four-letter group for ship identification. Additional coloured flags and pendants were incorporated into the code, making a total of forty in all. The revised code, universally agreed in 1900, was brought into use in 1902.

International Convention for the Safety of Life at Sea, the official body, composed of government representatives of all maritime nations, which among other responsibilities draws up the International Regulations for Preventing Collisions at Sea, more widely known as the *Rule of the Road. The Convention is called together from time to time by member governments to review the existing rules and to propose amendments when required.

international dateline, a line running mainly along the *longitude of 180° but with adjustments to avoid the division of certain island groups which lie astride that longitude, the Aleutian Islands in the north and the Fiji, Tonga, and Kermadec groups, with New Zealand, in the south. It is on this international dateline that the *zone times of + 12 hours and − 12 hours meet and the date changes. If a traveller round the world sets out from Greenwich, on 0° longitude, and travels eastward, he puts his clock forward by one hour as he crosses each 15° of longitude, so that by the time he reaches the longitude of 180°, he has put his clock forward by one hour twelve times. If he continues his journey eastward, he will still have to put his clock forward by one hour as he crosses each 15° of longitude, so that by the time he reaches Greenwich again, his clock has been put forward by 24 hours and he is one day ahead in date. To correct this anomaly, he changes the date when he crosses the international dateline, subtracting one day when he crosses it eastward and adding one day when he crosses it westward. Thus in the former case the same calendar date is used for two successive periods of 24 hours; in the latter case one calendar date is omitted altogether. The time apparently gained or lost is compensated for by the separate hours gained or lost by the adjustments to the clock at 15° intervals in the rest of the circumnavigation, or of course by recrossing the international dateline in the other direction.

International Metre Class Yacht, a yacht designed under the International Yacht Racing Union rules to rate as 12, 10, 8, 6 or 5.5 metres, according to the rule restrictions of the classes. The 8-, 10-, and 12-metre classes were introduced to meet the need for thoroughbred racing yachts equipped with acceptable cabin accommodation for making coastal passages from regatta to regatta, and were appreciably less costly to build and maintain than the *J-class and similar big racing yachts.

The metre yachts of the same class are not all identical, as in a *one-design class, but bear the characteristics of the individual designer and his interpretation of the formula. The rating is calculated by a formula which takes into account such measurements as the yacht's length overall, length on waterline, breadths at different points between bow and stern, depths inside the hull, *draught, total displacement, and the measurements of various sails including the overall height of the rig. In each yacht in its class these measurements can differ, but when applied to the rating formula the resultant figure must produce the class rating of 12-metres, 8-metres, and so on.

Because of the greatly increased costs of racing a *J-class yacht, 12-metres were selected for the *America's Cup challenges from 1958 onwards. In Scandinavia, and notably in Sweden, towards the end of the 1920s two new classes were introduced as lighter, faster, and less expensive racing boats than the English 6-metres. Both the 22 sq metre (236 sq ft) and the 30 sq metre (322 sq ft) class have cabin accommodation, although both are of lighter displacement than the normal cabinless 6-metre. These, nevertheless, have remained essentially a continental type, not much favoured in British waters.

International Regulations for Preventing Collisions at Sea, the official title of the internationally agreed rules by which ships at sea keep clear of each other, more generally known as the *Rule of the Road. They are drawn up and approved by the *International Convention for the Safety of Life at Sea. The regulations are binding on all ships using the sea and govern every case in which a danger of collision may arise when ships meet at sea or congregate in narrow waters. But the fact that a strict interpretation of the rules may give the right of way to one of two vessels where there is a risk of collision if they both continue on their present *course, does not absolve the master of the vessel with the right of way from taking the necessary action if a collision appears imminent. For example, although the regulations lay down that in all cases of danger of collision a vessel under steam power gives way to a vessel under sail, it would be unreasonable to expect a giant tanker navigating in narrow waters to give way to a yacht under sail. It is for reasons such as these that the regulations lay down on all masters of vessels, whether they have the official right of way or not, a duty to avoid a collision by taking whatever action is necessary.

The steering and sailing rule currently in force, with the rules governing sound signals in fog, are set out under RULE OF THE ROAD.

International Yacht Racing Union, see YACHTING, Racing rules.

Irish hurricane, a sailor's name for a flat calm, when no wind blows. It was also sometimes referred to by seamen as a Paddy's hurricane.

Irish pennants, the seaman's name for loose ends of twine or ropes left hanging over a ship's side or from the rigging, a sure sign of a slovenly crew. Similarly, the name given to the ends of *gaskets and *reef-points left flapping on the *yard when the sail is furled in a square-rigged ship. See also DEAD MEN.

irons, a sailing ship is in irons when, by carelessness or through a fickle wind, she has been allowed to come up into the wind and lose her way through the water so that she will not pay off again on either *tack. It is in the process of tacking, which entails a vessel coming up head to wind and bringing the wind on the other side, that a ship most frequently becomes in irons.

irradiation, an optical phenomenon whereby bright objects viewed against a darker background appear to be bigger than they are, and dark objects viewed against a lighter background appear to be smaller. The sun viewed against the darker background of the sky, and the sky viewed against the normally darker background of the sea, result in irradiation effects for which an allowance should be made when correcting the observed *altitude of the sun in astronomical navigation. The same conditions apply to moon altitude observations. An interesting effect of irradiation of the moon is often to be seen when the moon is crescent-shaped and the remainder of the moon's surface is faintly illuminated by reflected earth-shine. When the moon is young—not more than three or four days after new moon—this phenomenon is referred to as 'the old moon in the new moon's arms'.

isobar, a line on a weather chart linking points of equal barometric pressure usually measured in millibars, 3.4 millibars equalling one-tenth of an inch on a mercury barometer. See also METEOROLOGY.

isobath, from the Greek *iso*, equal, and *bathos*, depth, a line on a *chart linking points of equal depth, sometimes called a depth contour.

isobathytherm, a line connecting points in vertical sections of the sea which have the same temperature.

isogonic lines, lines drawn on a *chart which connect points of equal *variation of the compass. The first world chart to incorporate isogonic lines was published by Edmund Halley in 1701, a notable landmark in the history and development of cartography and *navigation.

isohalsine lines, lines on a chart joining parts of the sea which have an equal salinity.

J

jack, the national flag which is flown from a *jackstaff on the *stem of a naval ship when at anchor.

jackass-barque, a four-masted sailing ship square-rigged on the two foremost masts and fore-and-aft rigged on the two after masts. A number of these jackass-barques were used in the late 19th- and early 20th-century nitrate trade around Cape Horn to the Chilean ports, many owners and skippers considering them to be more efficient in the particularly stormy weather so frequently experienced around the Horn.

jack in the basket, a mark in coastal waters, consisting usually of a wooden box or basket on the top of a pole, to show the edge of a sandbank or other obstruction.

jackstaff, a short pole mast erected perpendicularly on the *stem of a modern ship, or at the end of the *bowsprit in the days of large sailing vessels, on which the national flag is hoisted in naval ships when at anchor. In many ships the jackstaff has a piece of gilded decoration, a crown or some other symbol, at the top.

jackstay, a wire or hemp rope or pendant secured firmly between two points and used as a support. Thus, when using a *breeches buoy for saving life from a ship aground, a jackstay is rigged between ship and shore along which the breeches buoy is hauled to and from the ship. When an awning is spread over a deck in hot weather as protection from the sun, it is supported centrally on a jackstay, though in this particular case the jackstay is often called a ridge-rope.

Jackstays are rigged with a minimum safety factor of four, i.e., the load supported by a jackstay including its own weight should not be more than one-quarter the breaking strain of the wire or rope used. The rope, batten, or iron bar on the top edge of the yards in square-rigged ships to which the head of the square sail is bent is also known as a jackstay.

jackyard topsail, a triangular topsail set above the mainsail in a gaff-rigged vessel, setting a larger area of sail than a *jib-headed topsail as both the *luff and the *foot of the topsail are laced to jackyards which extend beyond the top of the mast and the *peak of the *gaff.

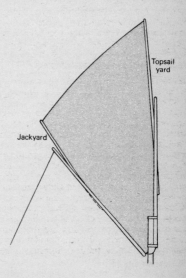

Jackyard topsail

jaegt, the typical sailing boat of the Norwegian coast, now virtually obsolete.

jaw, the distance between adjacent *strands on a rope. It gives a measure of the hardness or tightness of the *lay—the shorter the distance, the harder the lay. When a rope has been much used and the lay has become slack, the rope is said to be long-jawed or slack-jawed.

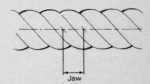

J-class yacht, a racing yacht of the largest class, built to the American *Universal Rule during the 1930s, with a waterline length varying from 75 to 87 feet (23–6 m).

Only ten were ever built, six in the USA and four in Britain, though several of the 'Big Class' yachts which raced in the British regattas were converted during the early 1930s to conform to some of the J-class rules.

The J-class yachts are often regarded as the peak of yacht-racing history and the peak of extravagance in pleasure sailing. As a class they were remarkably short-lived in comparison with other, healthier, classes of racing yacht, no doubt because they were the playthings of only the very rich. With a professional skipper and crew of up to twenty-four men, with new sails and new equipment always being tried to improve their sailing qualities, as for example the *Park Avenue boom, the costs of keeping such a yacht in racing commission were prodigious.

During the summer yachting season they raced at the major yacht club regattas round the coasts, from, in Britain Harwich to the Clyde, taking in French regattas at Le Havre and the Irish regattas, and in the USA, along the length of the East coast. But, apart from the *America's Cup races for which they were primarily built, the J-class yachts of Britain and the USA rarely raced together. They were essentially light weather craft and could not stand up to winds above about force 5. It used to be said of this class of yacht, rather cruelly, that the owners would put a lighted candle on their booms at night, and if it was still burning in the morning would decide there was not enough wind for racing, and if it was out, that there was too much.

Rising costs of construction, maintenance, and professional crews brought the J-class, as a racing class, to an end in 1937, though some of the existing British yachts in the class had their rig cut down and were used as cruisers. A recent revival of interest in these historic racing yachts has led to several of them being rebuilt, though only *Velsheda* retains her original rig.

jeers, a heavy *tackle with double or treble *blocks used for hoisting the lower *yards in square-rigged sailing ships, an operation known as *swaying up the yards. A jeer *capstan was one fitted between the fore and main masts used for heaving on the jeers. In the square-rigged ships of today, mainly used as school ships, auxiliary power is normally used in place of the jeer capstan.

jetsam, the legal term for goods or equipment thrown overboard from a ship at sea, differing from *flotsam in that the goods are deliberately thrown overboard from a ship, for instance to lighten her if she is in danger, while flotsam covers goods accidentally lost overboard or which may float up from the hull of a wrecked ship. In the strict and original legal sense, jetsam is the place where such goods are thrown overboard, and not necessarily the goods themselves, and also implies total abandonment of such goods to a later finder.

jettison, to, throw goods or equipment overboard to lighten a ship in stress of weather or other danger. See also JETSAM.

jetty, normally considered to be a solid structure built out, usually into the sea but in some cases along the shore as part of a port or dockyard, alongside which ships can lie for loading or discharging cargo, repair, etc.

jewel blocks, the blocks attached to *eyebolts on those *yards (lower and topsail yards) on which *studdingsails were set in square-rigged ships and through which the studdingsail *halyards were rove.

jew's harp, a name sometimes given to the *shackle with which a chain *cable is attached to an *anchor. It is always secured with the bow of the shackle outboard so that, when the anchor is let go, the lugs of the shackle do not catch up on the rim of the *hawsehole.

jib, a triangular sail set by sailing vessels on the stays of the foremast. The largest square-rigged sailing vessels of the late 19th century and early 20th century carried as many as six jibs, named from aft forward, storm, inner, outer, flying, spindle, and jib-of-jibs. Smaller sailing vessels, particularly those *fore-and-aft rigged, normally set only one jib, other triangular sails set before the foremast being known as *staysails. In the older design of the fore-and-aft rig, where a *bowsprit carried a fore topmast stay beyond the *stem of the vessel to give additional support to the mast, it was on this stay that the jib was carried, with a staysail set on the forestay. In the modern rig design, where no bowsprit, or only a very short bowsprit, is fitted, the single forestay is set up on, or even inboard of, the *stemhead and this usually carries only one large jib, no staysail being set. These large jibs, of which the *clew extends well abaft the mast, are known as *genoa or *yankee jibs; for a period between 1934 and 1937, some of the larger racing yachts set a four-sided jib, known as a *double-clewed jib, or 'Greta Garbo', which was virtually a genoa jib with its after corner cut off.

In most modern sailing vessels of any size, the jib is sheeted to winches to trim the sail instead of using manpower, which was the normal means of trimming up to comparatively recently. Jibs vary in size according to the strength of the wind, ranging from the genoa, made of light cloth for use in winds of up to about force 4 on the *Beaufort scale, to the storm jib, made of heavy duty canvas, for heavy blows.

The jib and *jib-boom were introduced in 1705 for smaller ships as a replacement for the older *spritsail and spritsail topsail, and by 1719 had also been adopted by the largest ships then built. From its inception it proved a great step forward in the efficiency of a sailing vessel on a wind. For illus. see SAIL.

jib-boom, a continuation of the *bowsprit in large ships by means of a spar run out forward to extend the *foot of the outer *jib and the *stay of the fore *topgallant mast. Flying jib-boom, a further extension with yet another spar to the end of which the *tack of the flying jib is hauled out and the fore *royal stay secured.

jibe, to, see GYBE.

jib-headed topsail, a triangular topsail set above the mainsail in a gaff-rigged vessel. The *peak of the topsail is hoisted to the masthead and the foot is stretched along the top of the *gaff, so that the sail just fills the triangle formed by the mast-head, the peak of the gaff, and the *jaws of the gaff. See also JACKYARD TOPSAIL.

jib-of-jibs, a sixth *jib set as a jib topsail on the fore *royal stay in a square-rigged ship. It is a light weather sail set only in a gentle breeze when sailing *on the wind.

jigger, (1) a light *tackle consisting of a double and single *block, multiplying the power by four when rove to *advantage and used for many small purposes on board ship. Originally it was designed to hold on to the *cable as it was being hove on board

in the form of a temporary stopper when *anchors were weighed by hand, but in fore-and-aft rigged ships (see RIG) a jigger was also often used on the standing part of the *throat and *peak *halyards to give them the final *sweating up. A boom jigger was one used to rig the *studdingsail booms in and out from the lower and topsail yards of square-rigged ships. It is in effect a *luff tackle used with a rope of smaller size. (See also PURCHASE.) **(2)** The name given to the small sail set on a *jigger-mast.

jigger-mast, a small mast set right aft in some smaller sailing craft, and a name frequently given to the after mast of a small *yawl, though this is more properly called a *mizen, and to the small mast set right aft in some *spritsail barges. It is also the name given to the fourth mast in a five- or six-masted *schooner.

jockey pole, a metal *spar used to prevent the *spinnaker guy rope fouling the *stanchions on a modern yacht of beamy design. The jockey pole runs athwartship from the mast to the guy and is rigged only when the spinnaker boom is trimmed well forward, close to the forestay.

joggle shackle, a long, slightly curved *shackle used in anchor work to haul the *cable of one *anchor round the bows of a ship when *mooring to two anchors. The occasion of its use is when a mooring swivel is inserted into the two cables to prevent a foul *hawse with two anchors on the ground.

jolly-boat, possibly from the Dutch and German jolle, Swedish jol, a small *bark or boat, though this may be the derivation of the English *yawl; or possibly a perversion of gellywatte, a small ship's boat, generally of the 18th and 19th centuries, used for a variety of purposes, such as going round a ship to see that the *yards were square, taking the steward ashore to purchase fresh provisions, etc. It was *clinker-built, propelled by oars, and was normally hoisted on *davits at the stern of the ship.

jugle or **joggle,** a notch cut in the edge of a plank to admit the narrow butt of another when planking up a wooden vessel. Its purpose is to make a more watertight joint and also to make it less likely for the butt of the plank to start or *spring.

'jumbo', the name often used for the fore *staysail in a *fore-and-aft rigged ship. It is the largest of the foresails, which perhaps explains the name, and in general terms corresponds to the *genoa jib of the modern yacht rig.

jumper, a chain or wire *stay which leads down from the outer end of the *jib-boom to the *dolphin striker in a square-rigged ship. It provides support for the jib-boom in staying the fore *topgallant mast, countering the upward pull of the fore topgallant stay. Jumper stay, a truss stay which leads from the root of the lower crosstrees in a sailing vessel to the fore side of the masthead, given additional spread at the top by means of a *jumper strut.

jumper strut, a short metal or wooden strut on a yacht's mast canted forward at an angle of about 45° which spreads the effective angle of a short masthead or jumper *stay. Its purpose is to add stiffness and support to the long mast used in the *Bermuda rig.

Junior Offshore Group, an organization formed in 1950 to provide ocean races for owners of smaller and less costly yachts than those which normally race in the main Royal Ocean Racing Club's events. The yachts racing in this group are limited to between 16 and 24 ft (5–7 m) in waterline length and normally compete in races up to 250 miles. In the USA the Midget Ocean Racing Club caters for a similar demand.

junk, (1) a native sailing vessel common to Far Eastern seas, especially used by the Chinese and Javanese. It is a flat-bottomed, high-sterned vessel with square bows, with two or three masts carrying *lugsails often made of matting stiffened with horizontal battens. The name comes from the Portuguese *junco*, adapted from the Javanese *djong*, ship. (2) Old and condemned rope cut into short lengths and used for making swabs, mats, *fenders, *oakum, etc.

jury, temporary, makeshift, used of any such means to bring a disabled vessel back to harbour. A jury mast is one erected to take the place of a mast which has been *carried away; a jury rig is the contrivance of masts and sails to get a ship under way after she has been disabled; a jury *rudder is a makeshift arrangement to give a ship the ability to steer when she has lost her rudder.

K

kapal, a square-rigged trading vessel, usually two-masted but very occasionally with three, used in Far Eastern waters, particularly in Malaysia, for inter-island trade. It is rapidly becoming obsolete under competition from the diesel engine.

kayak, an Eskimo word for a light, covered-in, *canoe-type boat used for fishing, common in northern waters from Greenland to Alaska. It is made by covering a wooden framework with sealskin, with a hole in the centre of the top of the boat into which the kayaker, also dressed in sealskin, laces himself to prevent the entry of water. It is propelled by a double-bladed paddle. The word kayak, in its strict meaning, applies only to one of these boats when it is occupied by a man; if a woman uses one, it is called a umiak. It is thought by some people that the word is derived from the Arabic *caique, the name having been given to these native boats when they were first seen by the early explorers and subsequently taken into the Eskimo language, but this seems unlikely as the name is the same in all Eskimo and Greenland dialects. In recent years kayaks have been widely used for recreational purposes on inland waters in many other parts of the world.

keckle, to, cover a hemp cable spirally with old rope to protect it from chafing in the *hawsehole, a necessary precaution in the days before chain *anchor cables. In the days of large sailing vessels, anchors and cables were normally worked on the main deck, the hawsehole being cut in the ship's side close to the *stem. As there was no hawsehole in the modern sense of a sloping pipe, the wear through the hawsehole on an unprotected hemp cable as a ship swung to her anchor was prodigious, hence the need for keckling it. Chain cable was not generally adopted for anchor cables until the third or fourth decade of the 19th century.

kedge, a small ship's anchor formerly carried on board to *warp a ship from one harbour berth to another or to haul her off into deeper water after grounding; also the name by which the spare anchor normally carried in yachts is known.

The original name was *cagger*, an early derivation from *catch* (i.e., to catch the ground), which dates back certainly to the 14th century, but it had developed into kedge at least by the end of the 16th century. In addition to its main uses as a means of hauling off a ship after grounding or shifting berth in calm waters, it was also frequently used in harbour by sailing vessels as the main anchor to which the ship lay in order to save labour when the time came to *weigh it for departure. In the days of sail a kedge was also sometimes used to back up the *bower anchor when a ship was anchored in bad holding ground or when heavy weather was expected. In modern ships, with their more efficient ground tackle and powerful engines, the kedge anchor has lost much of its former usefulness and is rarely carried on board larger ships.

A kedge anchor is part of the standard ground tackle of yachts, and the name embraces whatever type of spare *anchor is carried; e.g., fisherman's, stockless, mushroom, cqr, etc. It is frequently used to hold a yacht against an adverse tide when there is insufficient wind to make headway against it, and also for anchoring a yacht in water too deep for the cable of the main anchor.

keel, the lowest and principal *timber of a wooden ship, or the lowest continuous line of plates of a steel or iron ship, which extends the whole length of the vessel and to which the *stem, *sternpost, and *ribs or *timbers are attached. It could be called the backbone of the ship and is its strongest single member. In the sailing barges of the Thames the keel is a continuous run of oak 16 inches square, an indication of the great strength required in the keel of any ship.

In large steel ships, two additional keels, known as *bilge keels, are fitted to the hull one on either side of and parallel to the central keel, running along the turn of the *bilge approximately along the length of the hull where the sides are parallel. Their main purpose is to support the weight of the hull on the launching *ways in a building slip or on blocks on the floor of a dry-dock when the ship is docked for cleaning or repairs, but they serve a subsidiary purpose in a seaway by providing additional resistance to the ship's rolling. Some modern small yachts are built with twin bilge keels, which are appendages fitted under the turn of the bilge to *port and *starboard and approximately at right angles to the hull at this point, and which act in the same way as a normal centreline ballast keel. The first recorded yacht to have two keels abreast in this fashion was the *Iris*, a 60-ft (18.3 m) long by 12 ft 6 in (3.8 m) beam *ketch built in Dublin Bay in 1894, whose draught upright was only 3 ft 6 in (1 m). In 1924 the Hon. R.A. Balfour designed a 23-ft *sloop *Bluebird* with twin keels fitted to the bilges, and cruised extensively in her. The advantages of twin bilge keels are that they enable a yacht with shallow draught to sail to windward as well as any similar *centreboard boat, to sit upright when on level ground, and to be self-supporting without the need for shoring-up on *slipways or

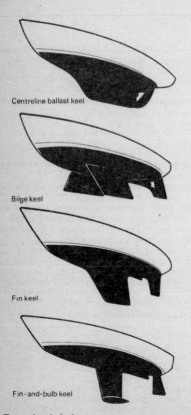

Centreline ballast keel

Bilge keel

Fin keel

Fin-and-bulb keel

Types of yacht keel

road trailers. These advantages were recognized after the Second World War when deep water anchorages became congested and yachts had to accept more and more mooring sites where they must take the ground at low water. Cruising yachts with twin bilge keels in addition to a centreline ballast keel were built in large numbers from 1950 onwards to designs by Robert Tucker and Maurice Griffiths, pioneer designers of this type of yacht, and numerous *fibre glass production yachts of twin bilge keel type have since been manufactured in the UK.

An additional type of keel used in yachts, particularly for racing, is the fin keel. It is a comparatively deep and narrow keel short in the fore-and-aft line, and fitted about amidships. Like a lowered centreboard it presents a long leading edge to give sufficient 'bite' to the water for working to windward, while its short fore-and-aft length makes the boat quick on the helm and very handy to steer. A fin keel can be built up in wood with a cast iron or lead base for ballast, or it can be a steel plate with bulb-shaped cast ballast at its base. This latter type is known as a fin-and-bulb keel.

A recent development in racing yachts is the winged keel, a short lateral addition at the bottom of a fin keel. It is still (1986) in an experimental phase, but was used successfully for the 1983 *America*'s Cup challenge on *Australia II* which defeated the American defender, *Liberty*, by 4 races to 3, and has subsequently been used by other yachts competing in the International 12-metre championship.

keelson or **kelson,** an internal *keel in the form of a *stringer bolted on to the keel, to provide additional strength and to support the *floors.

ketch, a sailing vessel with two masts, the recognized description being that the *mizen is stepped before the rudder-head, while in a *yawl it is stepped abaft it. This, however, is not an exact definition, the true difference between the two rigs depending more on the size of the mizen-sail; if the difference depended on the position of the mizen-mast, most of the yawl-rigged beach boats, including the well-known Norfolk yawls, would be ketches. The original name in England was 'catch', but although this suggests that they were used primarily for fishing, their main use was in fact as small coastal trading vessels. Suggestions have also been made that the name indicated vessels used to chase or pursue others in time of war, but this appears to be negated by a description by Glanville in 1625 that 'catches, being short and round built, be very apt to turn up and down, and useful to go to and fro, and to carry messages between ship and shore almost with any wind'. They were small vessels, originally of 50 tons or less, but they roughly doubled in size during the reign of Charles II (1660–85), who used the ketch design for his royal yachts. They were square-rigged on both masts to the full ship rig, and were often described as 'a ship without a foremast', the reference being to sail rig and not to the vessel as a type.

Large numbers of small ketches were built by the English, French, and Dutch navies during the wars of the late 17th and early 18th centuries to act as *tenders to the fleets, and the design was also adopted by the English to serve as bomb vessels, the large open space forward of the mainmast being ideal for the accommodation of a large mortar, by which the bombs were fired. For this particular use the size of the average ketch was increased through adding to her length, and as a result they became fast and weatherly, and a new use for them was developed as packet vessels. From the ketch rig was also developed the *hooker and the *dogger.

With the wide naval use of bomb vessels dying out in the mid-19th century, the naval value of the ketch diminished and it largely resumed its original use as a coastal trading vessel until, with the growing popularity of *yachting during the 19th century, the advantages of the rig again became apparent. The substitution of *fore-and-aft rig for the older square rig during the 19th century enhanced their weatherliness and greatly increased their popularity among yachtsmen. See also DANDY-RIG.

kevel, sometimes known as **kennet,** a large *cleat formed of two upright pieces of wood usually fitted on the *gunwale of a sailing vessel and used for *belaying ropes. Kevel-heads are the ends of a vessel's top *timbers projected beyond the level of the gunwale and similary used for belaying ropes.

kevlar, a man-made chemical from which unstayed masts, combining great strength with lightness, are made. It can also be made into a woven fabric used for some sails.

key or **cay,** from the Spanish *cayo*, rock, a small islet in the West Indies covered with scrub or sparse vegetation. The word was introduced into the English language by the buccaneers who infested that area of the sea in the late 17th and early 18th centuries. They are sometimes coral formations, sometimes outcrops of sand and rock.

khamsin or **kamsin,** a hot wind, usually from the south-west, which blows over Egypt and the eastern Mediterranean Sea, normally only in the months of March and April. It is a source of much discomfort, very similar to the *sirocco of the central Mediterranean. When blowing strongly it causes sandstorms, sometimes far out at sea.

kicking-strap, the name usually given by helmsmen of racing *dinghies and yachts to the *martingale which prevents the *boom of the mainsail from rising when it swings outwards, and thus presents a flatter sail to the wind and increases its driving power.

king spoke, that spoke of the hand steering-wheel in a ship which is uppermost when the helm is amidships. It is often marked with a ring carved on it or by a *turk's head knot fixed round the spoke.

kites, a general name for the additional light sails spread in a square-rigged ship to make the most of light following winds. Originally they included all sails set above the topsails but as the square rig was extended in the 18th and 19th centuries, and the *topgallant sail became standard, the term referred only to sails set above that sail, but included *studdingsails and jib-topsails.

knee, a timber or metal bar fashioned into a right angle to provide strengthening and support at the points of intersection of *timbers in a wooden ship. They are of various kinds, such as a hanging knee, which fits vertically under a deck *beam and supports its ends; a lodging knee, which is fixed horizontally between the forward side of a beam and the ship's side; a bosom knee, which performs the same purpose on the after side of a beam; and a *carling knee, which strengthens the right-angle between a carling and a beam. Knees in ships' boats, which support the *thwarts, or in small sailing craft, which support the deck beams, are preferably fashioned from naturally grown timber in which the grain of the wood follows the right angle round.

knock down, to, roll a small vessel over with her mast(s) and sails in the water, caused by a sea breaking over her or by a violent squall.

knot, (1) the nautical measure of speed, one knot being a speed of one *nautical mile (6,080 feet) per hour. The term comes from the knots on the line of a chip *log which were spaced at a distance of 47 feet 3 inches. The number of these knots which ran out while a 28-second sandglass emptied itself gave the speed of the ship in nautical miles per hour. As a measure of speed the term is always knots, and never knots an hour. **(2)** It is also a generally used term to describe a *bend or *hitch in ropes, but in its strict maritime sense only refers to a tucking knot in which the strands of a rope are tucked over and under each other to form a *stopper knot, or a knob or enlargement of the rope, such as a manrope knot, a *Matthew Walker, a *turk's head, etc., or a *splice, such as a long, short, back, or eye splice. In more general terms, a knot is meant to be permanent, a bend or hitch temporary. The word is very rarely used in this strict sense today and is widely employed to embrace every form of knot, bend, or hitch.

L

labour, to, roll or pitch excessively in a rough sea. The expression, though applied to all ships, is most apt in its application to sailing ships, since pronounced rolling produces a great strain on masts and rigging and may lead, in sailing vessels with wood hulls subjected to such a strain, to an opening of the *seams.

lace, to, attach, in a sailing vessel, a sail to a *gaff or *boom by passing a rope or cord alternately through eyelet holes and round the spar. In the case of a boom the eyelet holes are in the foot of the sail, in the case of a gaff they are in the head. The rope or cord itself is known as a lacing.

ladder, the general nautical term for what on shore would be called a staircase. Ladders leading from deck to deck are known as accommodation ladders; gangway ladders, rigged over the side when a ship is anchored or at a mooring, extend from a small platform level with the upper deck down to the level of the water for use when embarking or disembarking from small boats.

lagan, a term in maritime law for goods which are cast overboard from a ship with a *buoy and buoyrope attached so that they may be later recovered. It is a term also sometimes used to refer to articles still within a sunken ship as she lies on the bottom. The word comes from the Old French *lagand*, lying. By extension, the term has now come to mean any goods lying on the bottom of the sea, whether buoyed, inside the hull of a ship, or loose on the bottom. See also FLOTSAM, JETSAM.

lagoon, a stretch of water enclosed, or mainly enclosed, by coral islands, atolls, and reefs.

laid, a term associated with rope-making, from *lay, meaning the twist of the rope. Single-laid rope is one *strand of rope, the strand consisting of fibres twisted up. *Hawser-laid rope consists of three strands twisted together into a rope against the lay of the strands; *cable-laid rope is three hawser-laid ropes twisted together to form a cable. Cable-laid rope was also frequently known as water-laid rope.

laminar flow, the pattern of motion of particles in a thin zone of water which a vessel of normal ship or yacht form draws along the surface of its hull. In this zone, which in the case of a smooth racing yacht's hull may be of the order of 3 mm in thickness, layers of water slide over each other in a direction parallel with the surface of the hull. Around rough hulls, pitted with rust or coated with weed or barnacles, this zone will be much thicker and will in consequence greatly increase the drag or resistance to the vessel's forward motion.

In the water immediately beyond and at a distance which depends on the size, shape, speed, and smoothness of the vessel's hull the laminar flow becomes disturbed and gives place to a much thicker zone of turbulently flowing water also drawn along with the hull. It is the drag induced by these layers which causes the resistance to rise so sharply as the speed of a vessel increases. See also WAVE LINE THEORY.

laminated construction, a method of construction of many parts of small wooden vessels when suitable planks and crooks, in which the grain of the wood follows the required curve, are not readily available. With this method such members of the hull as the *stem, the *sternpost, the *keel, fore-and-aft *stringers, *frames, *knees, *deck beams, etc., are formed of several thin layers of timber which are bound together with water-resistant glue into the various curves required. By means of prefabricated jigs or rigid patterns, various parts of the hull can thus be laminated in large numbers, enabling production of identical wooden hulls to be carried out with a reduction in time and labour costs. A familiar form of laminated construction is plywood which is formed of three or more thin layers or veneers of wood bonded together with glue.

Lanby buoy, a special *buoy developed to take the place of a *lightship. It is a very large buoy with a diameter of 12 metres (40 ft) and a depth of 2.5 metres (8 ft), surmounted by a lattice mast which carries a *characteristic light at a height of 12 metres (40 ft) above sea level with a visibility of 16 miles in clear weather. In addition to the light, Lanby buoys are fitted with a sound fog signal and a radar beacon. They can be moored in position in any depth of water up to 90 metres (300 ft) and are designed to operate for up to six months without attention. At all times their performance and position are monitored by a shore station. As they are unmanned, they can operate much more economically than a lightship, which normally has a crew of three or four, and it has been estimated that the ratio of cost of Lanby buoy to lightship is one-tenth. The name comes from the initials of large automatic navigational buoy.

land breeze, an evening wind which blows from the land to seaward when the temperature of the land falls below that of the sea. As the sun sets, areas of land cool more quickly than the sea adjoining them, and the air over the land thus becomes heavier and flows out to sea to establish an equilibrium with the lighter air over the sea.

landfall, the first sight of land at the end of a ship's voyage.

landmark, any fixed object on the land whose position is marked on a *chart. Some, such as *lighthouses, beacons, leading-marks, are set up specifically as guides to navigation or warnings to seamen; others, such as prominent buildings or church towers, can be used as navigational guides if the chart in use shows their positions. Cross-*bearings of any landmarks will fix a ship's position in coastal waters with complete accuracy.

lanyard, a short length of rope or small stuff used for a variety of purposes on board. In sailing vessels, before the introduction of *bottlescrews and similar modern fittings, the *shrouds of all masts were set up taut by means of lanyards rove through the *deadeyes. A sailor carries his knife on a lanyard.

lap-strake, see CLINKER-, or CLINCH-, BUILT.

larboard, the old term for the left-hand side of a ship when facing *forward, now known as *port. During the early years of the 19th century the term larboard began to give way to port as a helm order in order to avoid confusion with the similar sounding *starboard, and the change was made official in 1844. Opinions differ as to how larboard originated as describing the left-

hand side of the ship. The most favoured theory is that larboard derives from ladeboard, as many of the old merchant ships had a loading, or lading, port on their left-hand side.

large, a point of sailing where the *sheets which control the sails in a sailing vessel can be eased well away to make the most of a quartering wind. In square-rigged ships it was the point where *studdingsails would draw if set. The term does not refer to a wind from dead astern but to one from abaft the beam. To sail large, to ease away the sheets and sail further *off the wind.

lash, to, secure anything with a rope or cord.

lateen, (from *latin*, meaning Mediterranean), a narrow triangular sail set on a very long *yard of which the forward end is *bowsed well down so that it sets obliquely on the mast and produces a high *peak.

The lateen rig is one of great antiquity, believed to be pre-Christian and probably of Arab origin. The yard was formed of two or more pieces bound together so that the outer ends would whip more easily than the middle. Because no forestay could be fitted, the *mast usually had a pronounced *rake forward, and the yard was held to the mast by a form of easily released slip knot. Two bow *tackles were used to haul down the forward end of the yard, while the after end was checked by braces, thus producing a curve in the yard. The Arab version of the sail is not a true lateen but a seltee-lateen, having a short luff to the forward edge of the sail, thus making a four-sided sail. The yard on which the sail is set is often longer than the ship herself, on occasions by as much as one-third. The rig is today virtually restricted to the Mediterranean, the upper Nile, and the northern waters of the Indian Ocean, being hazardous in any but calm waters. It is the typical sail of the Mediterranean *felucca and the Arabian *dhow. For illus. see RIG.

latitude, from the Latin *latitudo*, breadth. It is one of the spherical *co-ordinates used to describe a terrestrial position, the other being *longitude. Treating the earth as a perfect sphere, the latitude of a point on its surface is the angular measure between the point and the plane of the *equator along the *meridian on which the point is located. This is equivalent to the corresponding angle at the earth's centre. The earth's shape, however, is not that of an exact sphere so that these two angles do not coincide exactly except for points on the equator (latitude 0°) or the poles of the earth (latitude 90°).

Geographical latitude, also called true latitude, is equivalent to the true *altitude of the elevated celestial pole at the place. This is always greater (except at latitude 0° or 90°) than the corresponding angle at the earth's centre, which is called the geocentric latitude of the place.

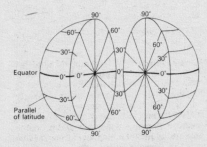

Parallels of latitude showing angular measurement

The latitude of a ship at sea may be found by observing the meridianal altitude of the sun by day and, very approximately, of the pole star at night.

launch, the generic name for the small steam or power boat carried as a *tender in the larger cruising yachts. Although most of these were at first steam propelled, in present times the use of petrol engines, either inboard or outboard, or small diesels is virtually universal.

launch, to, send the completed *hull of a newly built vessel from its place of construction into the water.

lay, the twist given to the strands of a rope.

lazaretto, a compartment set aside in smaller ships for the stowage of provisions and stores.

lazy guy, a small *tackle or rope used to prevent the *boom of a sail swinging unduly when a sailing vessel is rolling heavily.

lazy painter, a small rope for securing a boat lying alongside a ship in fine weather

when her own painter is unnecessarily large for the job.

lead line, a means of finding the depth of water near coasts and probably the earliest of the devices used by coastal navigators to facilitate safe navigation, especially in thick or hazy weather. It consists of a hemp line to which is attached, by means of a leather *becket or a rope *strop, a lead weight or plummet of about seven pounds. The lower end of the plummet is cup-shaped to accommodate the arming of the lead, this being a lump of tallow pressed into the hollow at the base of the lead to indicate the nature of the bottom deposits. Sand, mud, shingle, etc., adheres to the tallow and tells the leadsman the type of bottom he is finding; when the tallow comes up clean, he is finding rock.

The hand lead line of about 25 *fathoms is used in shallow water and an experienced and skilful leadsman is able to measure depths of as much as 20 fathoms with a ship making moderate headway of about 10 knots by heaving the lead ahead of the ship so that when it reaches the bottom it will be vertically beneath him. The line is marked in a traditional way with pieces of leather at 2 (two strips), 3 (three strips), and 10 (a square piece with a hole in it) fathoms; white duck at 5 and 15 fathoms; red bunting at 7 and 17; and blue serge at 13 fathoms. The mark at 20 fathoms is a piece of cord with two knots in it. The unmarked fathoms between the marks of the lead line are called *deeps. When sounding with the lead line in darkness, the leadsman can tell the depth by feeling the number of leather strips or the type of cloth.

For measuring depths greater than is possible with a hand lead line, the deep sea lead line is used. By its use depths of up to about 100 fathoms may be measured. The lead, in this case, is about 14 lb in weight and the line is marked at each multiple of 10 fathoms with cord having a number of knots equal to the number of tens of fathoms. Each intermediate fifth fathom is marked with a piece of cord having a single knot.

The lead is always cast from the weather side of the ship.

leading block, a single block, frequently a *snatch block, used as a *fairlead to bring the hauling part of a rope or the *fall of a *tackle into a more convenient direction, or to lead it on to the barrel of a winch. In the case of a tackle, the fall is known, after it has been led through a leading block, as the leading part.

leading light, see LEADING MARK.

leading mark, a mark sometimes set up on shore or fixed on the bottom in shallow water which, when brought into line with another mark or prominent object ashore, will lead a ship clear of a local danger, such as a rock or shoal, when approaching the shore. They are sometimes lighted at night, displaying the light to seaward, for the same purpose.

leading wind, a wind which is blowing *free in relation to the desired *course of a sailing vessel; i.e., any wind which enables the *sheets of a sail to be eased off to present a square aspect of the sail to the wind.

league, a measurement of distance, long out of use. A league at sea measured 3.18 *nautical miles, though for practical purposes the odd fraction was omitted.

lee, probably from the Dutch *lij*, shelter, or the Old English *hleo* with the same meaning, though some authorities quote the Scandinavian *loe* or *laa*, sea, as the derivation; the side of a ship, promontory, or other object away from the wind. Thus the lee side of a ship is that side which does not have the wind blowing on it, lee *helm, the helm of a vessel put down towards her lee side to bring the bows up into the wind. The lee of a rock or promontory, that side sheltered from the wind. Yet a lee shore is a coastline on to which the wind blows directly, i.e., it is down wind from any ship in the offing, and thus can be dangerous as the wind tends to force a sailing vessel down on it. The word can be used both as a noun and an adjective.

leeboard, (1) an early type of drop *keel, usually made of wood and pivoted at its forward end on each side of a flat-bottomed or shallow draught sailing vessel. They were first introduced in Europe, notably in the Low Countries, during the first half of the 15th century. When the board on the *lee side is lowered it increases the effective *draught, thereby reducing the *leeway made when sailing *close-hauled. When the vessel has to turn through the wind to change from one *tack to the other, the board on the lee side is lowered as the sails fill on the new tack while the board on the *weather side is hauled up. According to the Dutch *Dictionnaire de la Marine* (1702),

leeboards were made of 'three boards laid one over another and cut to a shape of a sole of a shoe', but in fact they normally vary slightly in shape according to the waters in which the vessel sails. In those which use inland waters and canals the leeboards are generally very broad in relation to their length, in shape not unlike an opened fan, so as to present the greatest practicable area to resist leeway within the limits of depth of water. In those which work in coastal waters, where rough seas can blow up with great rapidity, the leeboards are usually long and narrow, more like *daggerboards, and a 40-ft fishing vessel, for example, would carry leeboards made up of five or six planks of oak, bound and clad with galvanized sheet iron, about nine feet long with a width of little more than two feet at the lower, and wider, end. These boards are normally cut so as to be concave on the inboard side and slightly hollowed on the outboard side, giving them a flattened aerofoil shape for greater efficiency. Mounted with a slight 'toe-in', or squint, by means of angled *wales attached to the vessel's sides, they are highly effective in reducing leeway when sailing on the wind. **(2)** A board or other preventive fitted to the side of a *bunk on board ship to keep the occupant from rolling out when the vessel is lively in a rough sea.

leech, the after side, or lee edge, of a fore-and-aft sail and the outer edges of a square sail; in the case of square sails they are known as *port and *starboard leeches according to which side of the ship they are nearest. The leechrope is that part of the *bolt-rope which borders the leech of a sail. For illus. see SAIL.

lee-oh, the order usually given in a yacht or small sailing craft when it is required to *tack.

leeward (pron. loo'ard), a term denoting a direction at sea in relation to the wind, i.e., down wind as opposed to windward, up wind.

leeway, the distance a ship is set down to *leeward of her *course by the action of wind or tide. A vessel can make a lot of leeway if a strong cross *tide is running or if her *keel is not long enough or deep enough to give her a good grip of the water and hold her up to the wind. The word has also a colloquial meaning as having fallen behind in something: 'He has a lot of leeway to catch up' to reach the required position or standard.

leg, the seaman's term for the run or distance made on a single *tack by a sailing vessel. Thus, when making for a point directly to windward, a sailing vessel will sail legs of equal length on each tack alternately; if the required *course is not directly to windward but still higher than she can *fetch on a single tack, she will sail by means of long and short legs alternately.

leg, a wooden support lashed each side of a deep-keeled vessel, such as a yacht, to hold her upright when she takes the ground either for cleaning or repair. Legs extend to the depth of the keel.

lemsteraak, a Dutch cargo carrier originating in the Friesland town of Lemmer. They are built with a round bottom, and are generally similar in shape to the *boeier but run up to 55 feet in length. Some lemsteraaks have been built as yachts, others converted into yachts. The traditional rig was a *loose-footed mainsail having a curved *gaff and a large foresail set on the forestay to the *stemhead, with the mast *stepped in the usual *tabernacle to facilitate lowering when required.

let fly, to, let go the *sheets of a sailing vessel so that the sails flap directly down wind and lose all their forward driving force. It is a means, though possibly an unseamanlike one, of losing the way quickly off a boat under sail when bringing her alongside a pier or wharf or picking up a *mooring buoy.

'let go and haul' or **'afore haul',** one of the orders given during the process of *tacking a square-rigged ship, given when the bow of the ship has just passed across the wind and is about to *pay off. 'Let go' refers to the fore *bowline and what are now, after crossing the wind, the weather *braces, and 'haul' refers to the lee braces.

levanter, a strong, raw wind from the east or north-east which blows in the Mediterranean.

lie a-try, to, (used of a sailing vessel in a very high sea) to lie head to the wind, or as near to it as possible, keeping a slight forward motion in order to remain within a trough of the waves. It involves taking in all sails except, perhaps, a *mizen topsail or

*trysail, though it is also a possibility under *bare poles.

lie-to, to. A sailing ship lies-to when, in a gale, she keeps her head as steady as possible about six points off the wind, making a little way ahead as she falls off away from the wind to avoid drifting down to *leeward. For this purpose just enough sail is set to give her forward motion as she falls away from the wind, bringing her back up to it. The main objective in lying-to is to keep the vessel in such a position with the wind on the bow that heavy seas do not break aboard. See also DRIFT, HEAVE-TO.

lifeboat and **life-saving.** A reasonable definition of a lifeboat would be a boat specifically designed for saving life at sea, although ordinary ships' boats are called lifeboats when engaged in saving life (they are normally known as seaboats when employed for other purposes). Britain enjoys the reputation of being the first nation in the world to adopt a comprehensive organization for saving life at sea. Admiral Graves is credited with building a lifeboat in about 1760, but a better claim for being the real initiator is usually that of Lionel Lukin, a coachbuilder, who in 1785 converted a Norwegian *yawl by giving her a projecting cork *gunwale, air chambers at bow and stern, and a false *keel of iron, to provide buoyancy and stability. This he called his 'insubmergible boat', but although he took out a patent for it, the invention had no success. He did, however, design an 'unimmergible' *coble for use at Bamborough, Yorkshire, which saved many lives.

It took the disaster of the *Adventure* in 1798 to dispel public apathy about saving life at sea. This ship was wrecked in rough seas off Newcastle, only 300 yards from the shore, while a large crowd watched helplessly as her crew, one by one, dropped to their deaths in the fierce seas. A public meeting was held and money raised for the design of a lifeboat. A design by Henry Greathead, boatbuilder of South Shields, was selected as the best, and the lifeboats he built did sterling service.

The year 1823 is the next milestone in the history of lifeboats and life-saving, when Sir William Hillary, of the Isle of Man, who had himself taken part in the saving of over 300 lives from ships wrecked on the coast, succeeded in getting the question discussed in Parliament. He founded in 1824 the Royal National Institution for the Preservation of Life from

Shipwreck, which became the Royal National Lifeboat Institution. This institution, which has authority over all life-saving stations in Britain, did noble work up and down the coasts of Britain, but at first was always hampered by lack of money. When the Duke of Northumberland became president in 1851, he successfully aroused public enthusiasm, money flowed in, and the committee of management advertised a prize of 100 guineas to the designer of a self-emptying, self-righting lifeboat. The prize was won by Mr James Beeching of Great Yarmouth, and many examples of his boat were built.

Since then the design of lifeboats has been under constant review and experiment, and immense advances have been made in stability, buoyancy, speed, and robustness of construction. Modern shore-based lifeboats are fitted with two-way wireless communication, searchlights, and medical supplies for treating and maintaining life in cases of injury. Powerful motors give them good mobility in even the roughest conditions. In Britain, the Royal National Lifeboat Institution is run on an entirely voluntary basis.

At most life-saving stations around the coast, *breeches-buoy equipment is kept ready for use in cases where it can be usefully employed. The equipment consists of a line-throwing gun, by which means a light rope can be fired from a position ashore to a ship which has gone ashore. This line is then used to haul across a wire *jackstay which is secured between ship and shore and along which a breeches-buoy travels on a *sheave. Men from the wrecked ship are then hauled ashore one by one in the breeches-buoy.

In the USA the first government life-saving stations were set up in New Jersey in 1848, although one or two local organizations had been operating along the coast since the inauguration of the pioneer Massachusetts Humane Society in 1789. In 1871 Mr S. Kimball was appointed head of the Revenue Cutter Service, which was the governing body of the various life-saving stations in existence, and he undertook a thorough and most efficient reorganization of the entire life-saving service which lifted it into one of the finest such services in the world.

The life-saving service in Belgium was established in 1838, that of Denmark in 1848, Sweden in 1856, France in 1865, Germany in 1885, Turkey in 1868, Russia in 1872, Italy in 1879, Spain in 1880.

Since about 1960 the emphasis on life-saving at sea has been increasingly attached to the helicopter, which has a distinct advantage over the lifeboat in speed, manoeuvrability, and stability. In most advanced nations today, the coastline is divided into sectors, with a helicopter service, normally provided by the armed services, on call in emergency. Although lifeboats still provide the backbone of the normal life-saving service, it seems probable that over the next few years the use of helicopters will continue to expand.

lifebuoy or **lifebelt,** a buoy designed to support a human body in the water. The majority of lifebuoys are circular rings of cork covered with canvas, but some are cruciform, made of copper, and fitted with a calcium flare which burns for 20 minutes when it comes in contact with seawater. These lifebuoys can support the weight of two men in water. In most small craft, including many yachts, one lifebuoy is attached to the vessel by a line to make it easier to haul back on board when supporting a man overboard. In many racing yachts, international rules require, in addition, a *dan buoy to be carried to mark the position when a member of the crew falls overboard.

life-jacket, a short jacket worn across the chest and back for saving life at sea by holding a body upright in the water. They are often inflated automatically by a carbon dioxide cylinder.

lifeline, a rope or wire stretched fore and *aft along the *deck of a ship in rough weather, so that men can hang on to it in heavy seas as a safety measure against being washed overboard. In yachts lines are rigged fore and aft on to which *harnesses are clipped.

life-raft, originally any raft made on board ship from any available timber and used for saving life in shipwreck or other calamity. More recently, many ships carry inflatable rubber rafts for the same purpose.

lifts, the hemp ropes, later replaced by wire ropes or chains, which in square-rigged ships are led from the various mastheads to the two ends of the corresponding *yards to support them.

lighthouse, a building or other construction erected to display a *characteristic light as a warning of danger at sea and an aid to navigation.

Individual lights are recognized by their characteristics, which can vary from a fixed light visible all round or in a certain advertised sector to *flashing, *occulting, or *fixed and flashing lights. The pure mechanics of such lights can be simply achieved by revolving the assembly of lenses, prisms, and mirrors around the light. A flashing light is one in which the period of light displayed is less than the period of darkness between flashes; an occulting light is one in which the period of light is more than the period of darkness. Further variations in characteristics can be reached by arranging the flashes in a flashing light in groups of two or more; the same can be done, of course, with an occulting light. A fixed light can have flashes incorporated in it to make it a fixed and flashing light.

Lighthouses come under the control of the national authorities on whom has been placed the responsibility for all coastal lights and navigational marks.

Light Lists, a periodical publication, in two volumes, of the British Hydrographic Department of the Navy, giving the position and *characteristics of every navigational light, whether from *lighthouse, *lightship, or lighted buoy, in the world. It supplements the information shown on charts, which remain of course the primary navigational documents.

lightship, normally a dumb vessel (i.e., non-navigable), though in some countries lightships are fitted with diesel engines for self-propulsion, moored over a shoal or bank where, because of the distance from the shore or constructional difficulties, a *lighthouse is impracticable. Its purpose is exactly the same as that of a lighthouse, a warning to seamen of danger and an aid to navigation. Like lighthouses they display at night a *characteristic light, carried on a tripod mast, and by day a special mark, both easily identifiable and marked on every chart which covers the waters in which they are moored. They are also equipped with fog and submarine signalling equipment and *radar beacons. Again like lighthouses they come under the control of the national authorities on whom has been placed the responsibility for all coastal lights or navigational marks—in English waters, Trinity House, in Scottish waters the Commissioners of Northern Lights. In British and many other waters,

lightships are always painted red.

Lightships, which normally carry crews of three or four men, are gradually being replaced, on grounds of economy, by *Lanby buoys, which are unmanned but provide the same service for navigators.

'light to', an order, when *belaying a hawser round a *bollard and the first turn has been made, to *fleet the hawser back along the deck to provide enough slack for additional turns round the bollard to be made. When there is tension on the hawser, the first turn round a bollard will hold it momentarily, but additional turns are then required to make it secure, and enough rope to make these additional turns is provided by the order 'Light to'.

lignum vitae, the hard smooth wood of the guaiacum tree, grown in the West Indies. It had many maritime uses, particularly for the *deadeyes and *chesstrees of sailing vessels and the sheaves of wooden *blocks, its hardness standing up well to wear caused by ropes and its smoothness allowing a rope to render through it easily.

limber, a hole cut in the floor *timbers of wooden ships on either side of the *keelson to allow a free passage for the *bilge water to run down to the pump well.

lines, the designer's drawings of a ship. Normally they consist of three plans: the sheer plan which shows the longitudinal vertical section of the ship; the body plan which shows the vertical cross-sections; and the half-breadths plan which shows the longitudinal transverse section at the deck line and waterline and other stations in the same plane.

line squall, a squally wind heralded by a dark cloud stretched across the horizon, sometimes arched in form. It is caused by a narrow area of low pressure passing across the sea with an area of high pressure following close behind it. Where the differences of pressure are considerable, a heavy squall blows up accompanied by a distinct drop in temperature.

lining, an additional piece of canvas sewn to a sail to prevent chafe.

list, the inclining of a ship to one side or other, usually caused by a leak or some other mishap. It is a more permanent situation than a *heel, which is generally due to the pressure of the wind and lasts

LIST

only as long as a ship's course relative to the wind is held without alteration.

lizard, a short length of rope with a *thimble spliced into the end, used for various purposes on board ship.

Lloyd's Register of Shipping, a society formed in the 18th century to draw up rules regarding the construction of merchant ships. It originated in 1760 when a number of merchants engaged in marine insurance and underwriting at Lloyd's formed an association to protect their interests. From this small beginning grew the leading and widely known classification society of to-day called Lloyd's Register of Shipping. The society lays down rules regarding the *scantlings used in a ship's structure, and a list of the ships built according to these rules is published annually in *Lloyd's Register of Shipping.*

log, (1) any device for measuring the speed of a vessel through the water or the distance she has sailed in a given time. In general use in small vessels such as yachts is the patent log, a rotator which is streamed astern from the taffrail where a register records speed and distance travelled. Also used increasingly in small vessels is the electronic log. This is a small impeller fixed externally to the keel which is connected electrically with the main instrument inboard, giving an accurate reading of speed and distance run. **(2)** The short name by which the *log book or deck log is generally known.

log book, usually referred to as a log, a book in which are kept records of a ship's voyage, such as meteorological conditions, courses, and speeds, etc.

log-line, a specially woven line of contra-laid cotton used for towing a patent *log from the *taffrail of a ship. The reason for the special weaving is to prevent twist, so that it will faithfuly repeat the number of revolutions made by the patent log as it is towed through the water.

loll, to, float at an angle of *heel on one side or the other used of a ship which is unstable when upright.

longboat, the largest boat carried on board a full-rigged ship.

longitude, from the Latin *longitudo,* length. It is one of the spherical *co-ordinates used to describe a terrestrial

position, the other being *latitude. It is the arc of the equator or the angle at either pole between the planes of the *prime meridian and the *meridian of the places measured eastwards or westwards from the prime meridian. The longitude of a ship at sea may be found from the methods of nautical astronomy or by calculating the local time of noon on the longitude of Greenwich, the difference in time giving the longitude east or west of Greenwich. Because the earth rotates uniformly on its polar axis, the longitude of a place is proportional to the time the earth takes to rotate through the angle contained between the planes of the prime meridian and the meridian of the place, and thus the measurement of this time is bound to give the longitude. Originally this was done by a ship's *chronometer, but it is today more easily achieved by means of the many time checks broadcast throughout the day and night by radio stations.

long-jawed, the term used to describe rope which, through much use, had had the twist, or *lay, in its strands straightened or pulled out and has no longer the resilience to resume its normal tightness of lay after use.

long splice, a method of splicing two ropes by unlaying the ends to a distance of eight times the circumference of the rope and then laying up the strands in the space

Long splice

left where the opposite strand has been unlayed. By this means the two ropes are joined without increasing the thickness over the area of the splice. A long splice is used where the rope is required to *reeve through a *block after it has been spliced.

long stay, see STAY.

loom, (1) the inboard end of an *oar, that part of it which lies inside the boat from the *crutch or *rowlock when the oar is shipped for rowing, including the grip. **(2)** An effect of refraction in a light fog at sea which makes objects look larger than they are. 'That ship looms large', the dim outline of a vessel seen through fog and appearing larger than she in fact is. The same effect is often observed when the land is seen through a fog from seaward, cliffs frequently appearing much higher than they really are. **(3)** Also an effect of reflection on low cloud in the case of the light from a *lighthouse or *lightship, when the light itself cannot be seen directly although its reflection is visible.

loose, to, cast loose the *gaskets, or stops, of a *furled sail of a square-rigged ship so that the sail may be set.
The word is used only of sails set on *yards, and only when they are furled on the yards, implying the actual casting loose of the gaskets. Thus, if additional canvas such as a *royal is sent up in fair weather, it is set, not loosed, as it was not already in position furled on the yard with gaskets.

loose-footed, a fore-and-aft sail which is set without a *boom, as in the mainsail of a barge, or in the *de Horsey rig. A sail which is set on a boom but with only the *tack and *clew secured, the *foot of the sail not being *laced to the boom, is also said to be loose-footed. Although at one time it was not uncommon to see sails set in this way on a boom in small craft, it is a practice which has almost completely died out.

Loran, see NAVIGATION.

lorcha, a sailing vessel with a European-shaped *hull and a Chinese *junk rig. They are believed to have originated at Macao when it was first settled by the Portuguese. The typical *lateen rig of the Mediterranean, with its somewhat eastern look, led to many ships so rigged being wrongly called lorchas.

low and aloft, a nautical expression describing a sailing ship with sail spread from deck to *truck; every stitch that she can carry. Many people are inclined to

think that the phrase is an abbreviation of alow and aloft, but it is in fact the other way round, alow and aloft being an expansion of the correct term.

lubber's hole, an opening in the floor of the *tops on the fore, main, and *mizen-mast of square-rigged ships, just abaft the heads of the lower masts, to give access to the tops from below. It was so termed because timid climbers up the rigging preferred to go through this hole to reach the top rather than over the *futtock shrouds, the way the experienced sailor went.

lubber's line or **point,** the black vertical line or mark on the inside of a *compass bowl which represents the *bow of the ship and thus enables a *course to be steered by bringing the lubber's line to the point on the compass card which shows the desired course.

luff, the leading edge of a *fore-and-aft sail (for illus. see SAIL). 'Hold your luff', an order to the helmsman of a sailing vessel to keep her sailing as close to the wind as possible and not allow her to sag down to *leeward.
When used as a verb, 'luff', or 'luff her', is an order to the helmsman to bring the ship's head up closer to the wind by putting the helm down, or to leeward. In yacht racing to luff an opponent is to come up closer to the wind, or even head to wind if necessary, to prevent her overtaking to *windward, a legitimate procedure under the rules of yacht racing.

luff rope, see BOLT-ROPE.

luff tackle, a *purchase which has a single and a double *block, the standing part of the rope being secured to the *strop of the single block, and the hauling part coming from the double block. It increases the power by four times when rove to *advantage. It was originally used for hauling down the *tack of a fore-and-aft sail to tauten the *luff, but the term is now used to describe any tackle rove through a single and a double block in which the size of the rope is 3 inches in circumference or greater.
Luff upon luff, one luff tackle hooked on

to the fall of another in order to double the increase in power. See PURCHASE.

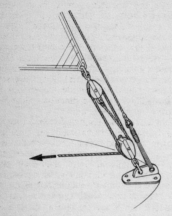

Luff tackle rove to disadvantage

lug, (1) the name, rarely used, of the *yard on which a *lugsail is set, but more often employed to describe the sail of a small boat (see LUGSAIL). **(2)** A projection on a mast or *bowsprit fitting with an *eye to take a *shackle of a *stay or *shroud.

lugger, a sailing vessel with a *lugsail rig, normally two-masted except when they were used for smuggling or as privateers, when a mizen was stepped right aft. The lug rig came in during the late 17th or early 18th century, particularly for fishing and for the coastal trade where its increased weatherliness over the square *rig gave considerable advantages when working the *tides. See also CHASSE-MARÉE.

lugsail, a four-sided sail set on a *lug or *yard, used mainly in small craft. The sail is very similar to a *gaff sail but with a wider *throat, and depends on its *luff for its stability. The yard, or lug, by which the sail is hoisted is normally two-thirds the length of the *foot of the sail and carries a *strop one-fourth of the way from throat to *peak. This strop is hooked to a *traveller on the mast and is hoisted in the normal way until the luff is as taut as possible.

The earliest known drawing, by a Dutch artist, of what may have been a lugsail is dated 1584, but the name itself does not appear for another hundred years. Suggestions that it is of much more ancient origin and first appeared in the Mediterranean in Egyptian and Phoenician craft around the first century BC, are not borne out by any evidence and probably arose through confusing the *lateen rig with the true lug rig. The original lugsails were set on *dipping lugs which, when the vessel went *about, entailed lowering the sail sufficiently to enable the forward end of the lug, together with the *tack of the sail, to be passed round abaft the mast to the (new) *lee side as the vessel came head to wind.

The *standing lugsail, in which the forward end of the lug is *bowsed down so that it becomes virtually an extension of the mast, came in very much later and never became viable except for a short period for small racing yachts. It is more usually known as the *gunter rig, or gunter lug. The balanced lugsail is laced to a *boom which extends a short way forward of the mast, and set flat by a tack *tackle.

It is said to have been a Western adaptation of the short-boomed Chinese lugsail, and became popular in the West around the end of the 19th century.

lutchet, a mast fitting in the form of a *tabernacle used in *spritsail barges and *wherries to enable the mast to be lowered to deck level when passing under bridges, etc.

M

maelstrom, commonly thought to mean a whirlpool, but in fact specifically a strong current which rips past the southern end of the island of Moskenaes in the Lofoten group off the west coast of Norway. It is also known as the Maskenstrom.

Mae West, a large parachute *spinnaker used in yacht racing during the 1930s, so called after the well-known actress because of the large swelling curve it took up when filled with wind.

Magellanic clouds, a popular name for the two *nebiculae,* or cloudy-looking areas in the southern sky, which consist of a great number of small stars much resembling the Milky Way. They were named after the navigator, Ferdinand Magellan.

magnetic compass, see COMPASS.

magnetic pole, the point on the earth's surface to which the needle of a magnetic *compass points. It is not at the North pole but some distance away in the Canadian Arctic, nor is it in a fixed position, but wanders according to the vagaries of terrestrial magnetism. Although its approximate location had been known for many years, it was not until 1831 that Sir James Clark Ross, an explorer of the Arctic regions, discovered that it was on the west side of the Boothia Peninsula. The angular difference between the magnetic pole and the North pole at the point of a magnetic compass is known as *variation, and must be applied to a magnetic *course or *bearing to obtain the true course or bearing.

magnitude, as it applies to nautical astronomy, the apparent brightness or luminosity of any of the navigational stars or planets. First to classify stars according to their apparent brightness was Hipparchus, the prince of ancient astronomers. His system comprised six magnitude classes, the small group of some fourteen of the brighter stars forming those described as being of the first magnitude, and the relatively large number of faint stars just visible to the unaided eye forming the group of sixth magnitude stars. This rough and ready classification was improved

during the 19th century with the introduction of a decimal scale of magnitudes and the extension of the magnitude scale to include telescopic stars, whose magnitude numbers are more than six, and fractional and negative magnitudes. Sir John Herschel, son of the astronomer Sir William Herschel, is credited with having suggested that a star of magnitude 1.0 should be regarded as being 100 times as bright as a star of magnitude 6.0.

Nautical almanacs include tables providing for the navigational use of selected stars of the first and second magnitude, but those of lower magnitudes are never used for observation, although they may form part of the constellations which enable the navigational stars to be identified. With the use of these tables, a navigator can obtain a position line of his ship on a *chart after taking an *observation of a navigational star.

mainsail, the principal sail of a sailing vessel. On a square-rigged vessel this is the lowermost (and largest) sail carried on the mainmast, and is usually termed the main *course. The earliest known mainsails in European waters, as depicted on Roman pottery and mosaics of the 3rd century AD, were set with a *sprit. This rig held good in the Netherlands and North Sea ports until about the 15th century, when the sprit was superseded by the *gaff and *boom, while in the eastern Mediterranean it became the *lateen. Thames sailing barges, however, are still rigged with sprit mainsails for ease of handling with a crew of two.

On *smacks in the past the gaff and boom mainsail was loose-footed, i.e., the *foot was not laced to the boom, but attached only at the *tack and the *clew. On certain types of fishing craft, such as the Thames hatch boat, the cockle bawley, and the Plymouth hooker, the mainsail had an extra long gaff and no boom, the mainsheet being led from two or more points on the leech of the sail to blocks on the stern *horse. In Bermuda from the late 18th century a simple form of triangular or jib-headed mainsail was used on local *sloop-rigged boats, which was set on a sharply raked mast having a long boom but no gaff. In this early version the boom was almost as long as the *luff of the sail. A more sophisticated application of this type of sail was introduced to racing yachts in Europe in the early part of the 20th century. Developed in time into a very tall and narrow sail with a luff-to-foot proportion (*aspect ratio) of about 4:1, this so-called Bermudian mainsail is now almost universal on both racing and cruising yachts throughout the world.

'mainsail haul', the order given during the *tacking of a square-rigged ship to *brace round the after *yards. The timing of the order is vital during the operation if the ship is not to be caught in *stays. The moment comes after the sails on the foremast have been *backed and the ship is very nearly exactly head to wind.

make her number, to, see SIGNAL LETTERS.

manila, a type of rope much used at sea before the introduction of man-made fibres. It is made from the fibre of the wild banana plant, grown in the Philippine Islands, and takes its name from the capital of those islands, Manila. Rope made from these fibres does not need to be tarred, as does rope made from *hemp fibres which will rot when exposed to seawater unless preserved with tar.

Marcq St. Hilaire method, a means of finding a ship's position by nautical astronomy known to the French as the *méthode du point rapproché*, and to British navigators as the *intercept method. It was introduced in 1875 in a paper published in the *Revue Maritime* by a French naval officer, Captain (later Admiral) Marcq St. Hilaire. The basis of the method rests on the fact that for every heavenly body at a given time there is a spot on the earth's surface (its 'geographical position') where it is at the *zenith. For other places, its observed *altitude, subtracted from 90°, gives its *zenith distance, and this determines a circle on the globe, called a 'circle of equal altitude', with its centre at the geographical position of the body; somewhere on this circle the observer's position must be. The navigator, however, is concerned only with the small segment of this circle which runs near his estimated position, and, because the circle is very large compared to the length of the segment in question, this may be plotted on a *chart as a straight line; it is known as a *position line. To obtain such a line, the navigator decides his estimated position by *dead reckoning or other

means, and from the *nautical almanac he obtains by calculation the altitude of a convenient navigational star or other heavenly body (usually the sun), as it would be observed from the estimated position at the time of observation. The bearing or *azimuth of the selected heavenly body is also obtained. Its altitude is observed and this probably differs by a small amount from the calculated altitude, the true position of the ship not being identical with her estimated position. The difference in minutes of arc is known as the intercept, and is set out on the chart either towards, or away from, the bearing of the heavenly body, according to whether the observed altitude is greater or less than calculated. From the end of the intercept a position line is drawn at right angles, and the ship's position at the time of the observation is somewhere on this line. By carrying this line forward according to *course and distance run, and obtaining another position line, the ship's position is found by the intersection of the two lines.

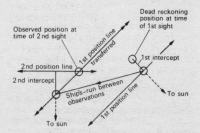

A Marcq St. Hilaire fix

It will be seen that this method does not depend on a noon altitude of the sun, but it does involve the use of a reliable *chronometer or means of knowing the exact time of observation, and the existence of good nautical almanacs; it was therefore not available till a fairly late stage in the history of navigation, but modern navigators find it generally useful except in so far as astronomical navigation has been replaced in larger ships by hyperbolic navigational systems such as Decca or Loran. See also NAVIGATION.

marina, a term which originated in the USA for a modern sophisticated harbour designed specially for the safe berthing of yachts. Variously called yacht station, harbour, haven, or basin, the marina is essentially a complex of floating piers and jetties at which yachts can lie, together with the facilities demanded by the modern yacht owner and his family. These include fresh water, fuel and electric power laid on, shipwright and engineering services, a yacht chandler's store, laundry services, a clubhouse with bar and showers, grocery stores, a car park, and good access roads. Elaborate yacht harbours or marinas are being constructed in almost all countries throughout the world where yachting is an accepted way of life, and range generally from the small harbour holding 100 berths or so to giant marinas in Florida and California where 2,000 and more yachts are regularly based.

mark, one of the fathoms of a *lead line which has a distinguishing mark, those unmarked being called *deeps. The marks on a hand lead line, which is normally 25 fathoms in length, are:

Depth in fathoms	Mark
2	two strips of leather
3	three strips of leather
5	piece of white duck
7	piece of red bunting
10	piece of leather with a hole in it
13	piece of blue serge
15	piece of white duck
17	piece of red bunting
20	two knots

When using a line longer than 25 fathoms, the line is marked with one knot at each five fathoms and with three, four, and five knots at 30, 40, and 50 fathoms.

When a seaman takes a *sounding with a hand lead line he calls out the depth of water according to the mark on the line which is on or near the surface of the sea when the lead reaches the bottom beneath him. If he sees, for example, that the first piece of red bunting is on the surface after his cast, he calls out, 'by the mark, seven'. If he sees that it is approximately six feet above the surface after his cast, he calls out, 'Deep, six'.

marl, or **marle, to,** put on a *serving by which the *worming and *parcelling of a rope is secured. Ropes are frequently wormed and parcelled in places where heavy use may fray or gall them or where it is desired to make them impervious to water. An old rhyme instructs us to

'worm and parcel with the lay,
turn and serve the other way.'

The serving is secured on each turn by a *marling hitch, hence its name.

marline, a small light line used for a variety of purposes on board ship. It is two-stranded, loosely twisted, and was originally used for bending light sails to their *yards or *stays. It is usually supplied both tarred and untarred.

marline spike, a steel spike pointed at one end and used for lifting the strands of a rope to make room for another to be tucked in when splicing.

marling hitch, a series of round turns in which the end is passed over the standing part and under the bight and pulled taut on each turn. Unless there is an *eye in the end of the rope a marling hitch is usually started with a *timber hitch and is used for lashing up sails, etc.

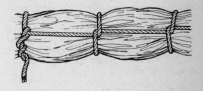

Marling hitch

maroon, an explosive rocket used to attract attention as much by its sound as its colour in cases of emergency at sea. It was originally the name given to a signal rocket which burst with a red flare.

maroon, to, deliberately put someone ashore and leave him there when the ship sails away. The word usually implies being left, or marooned, in some relatively inaccessible place.

marry, to, bring two ropes together, such as the *falls of a boat to be hoisted at the *davits of a ship, so that the haul on them can be combined and the boat is hoisted level. The term is also used in other maritime contexts where two ropes, or other objects, are brought together and laid side by side.

martingale, (1) the *stay which holds the *jib-boom down against the pull exerted by the fore *topgallant-mast stays in a square-rigged ship. It runs from the outer end of the jib-boom to the *dolphin striker. Martingale *guys hold the dolphin striker firm, being run from its end and secured on either bow of the ship. (2) A rope or strap which runs from a point on the *boom of a *dinghy's mainsail to the foot of the mast, designed to prevent the boom from rising when it swings outwards and thus to present a flatter sail surface to the wind. It is normally fitted only in racing dinghies, and is usually known as a *kicking-strap.

mast, in a sailing ship the vertical spar whose prime use is, of course, to carry sails. Masts are normally taken through holes in the deck and their *heels, which are squared off, fitted into *steps in the *keelson of the ship. In larger sailing vessels they are held firm in the deck holes with wedges, and are secured in place by *shrouds, running from the masthead or the *hounds to *chain-plates on the ship's side, and by *stays, which run from the masthead to deck level forward and aft. In square-rigged ships the yards are crossed on the masts, from which they are held in position by *lifts, with the sails set on the yards; in fore-and-aft rigged vessels the sails are set on the masts themselves, by means of slides working on a track fixed to the after side of the mast, or by hoops which slide up and down the mast as the sail is hoisted or lowered, or in modern yachts by means of a mast groove within which the luff rope itself slides.

Originally, before the growth in size of ships which occurred during the 17th century, ships' masts were single spars, cut from the trunk of a fir tree, but as the size of sailing ships developed in the 17th and 18th centuries with the consequent addition of an increased number of sails and of upper masts, the original pole masts fashioned from a single trunk of a fir tree were not strong enough or tall enough to carry the larger *yards and sails, and so had to be made of several pieces of timber in order to get the required strength, circumference, and height and were thus called made masts. In most ships of the 17th century and later, the lower masts were all made masts, topmast and *topgallant masts being pole masts.

Today, only a few small *gaff-rigged craft and small dinghies have solid wooden masts, and only a minority of yachts still have hollow wooden masts, usually built up from spruce, *scarfed and glued. A majority of modern yachts and racing dinghies have masts and booms made from extruded aluminium tubes, the masts shaped aerodynamically in cross-section to reduce windage. For illus. see RIGGING.

Matthew Walker knot, a *stopper knot near the end of a manrope or the end of a *lanyard to prevent it running through an *eye. It is made from forming a half hitch with each strand of the rope in the direction of the *lay and then tucking the strands over and under until the knot is formed. A finished Matthew Walker knot looks similar to other stopper knots. (See illus. of DIAMOND KNOT.)

'Mayday', an international distress signal made by voice radio on a wavelength of 2,182 kHz, a wave which is permanently watched ashore. It is said that the origin of the signal is the French *m'aidez,* help me.

measurement, see BUILDERS OLD MEASUREMENT, THAMES MEASUREMENT, TONNAGE.

Mercator projection, the method adopted by Gerardus Mercator, a Flemish geographer, of producing a sea *chart in which parallels of *latitude and *meridians of *longitude cut each other at right angles, and on which a *rhumb line, which is a line of constant *compass *bearing, will appear as a straight line. As ships normally steer rhumb line *courses, such a chart would obviously be of great navigational value.

Mercator introduced his new projection in 1569, but it was nearly seventy years before its use became widespread at sea. His system depended on the principle that the convergence of meridians as they approached the North and South poles is in proportion to the cosine of the latitude, and that if a proportional misplacement is introduced in the spacing between the parallels of latitude on the chart as they move away north and south from the equator, then a rhumb line, which cuts all meridians at the same angle, must become a straight line.

In geometrical terms, Mercator's projection can be envisaged as a cylinder touching the globe at the equator, on to which the meridians and parallels are projected from the earth's centre, which is then developed (i.e., unwrapped) to form a flat chart. As the axis of the cylinder is the same as the polar axis of the globe, the projection of each pole will be at infinity and the polar regions therefore cannot be shown on Mercator's projection. The dis-

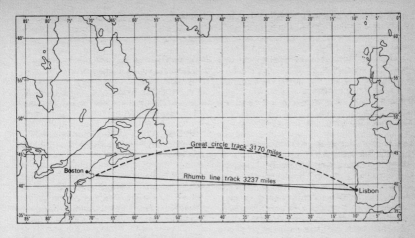

Mercator projection: rhumb lines appear straight

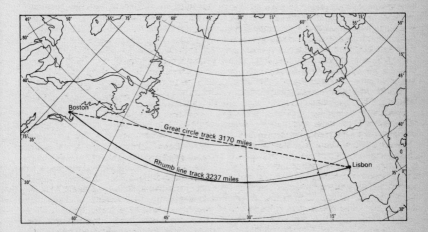

Gnomonic projection: great circles appear straight

tortion is least in the region of the equator and increases progressively towards high latitudes. By 'distortion' is meant that the linear scale for north-south distances becomes more and more divergent from that for east-west distances, increasing with the latitude, though not in the same proportion. This means that in a chart covering an area with a considerable north-south dimension, such as North or South America,

the regions in high latitudes, e.g., Baffin Land or Tierra del Fuego, appear exaggerated in size compared with tropical areas such as the Isthmus of Panama; they also appear distorted in shape, e.g., Greenland on Mercator's projection appears to stretch out almost indefinitely to the north because, as the Arctic is approached, the projection becomes less and less convenient. Nevertheless, for nautical purposes the projection has the unique advantage that rhumb lines always appear as straight lines.

In measuring distances on a Mercator chart, therefore, it is essential to measure the span of degrees of latitude on the sides of the chart which lie on the same latitude as the distance being measured. These degrees will each represent sixty nautical miles for the measurement required. Degrees measured in other parts of the chart (i.e., not on the same latitude as the distance to be measured) will not, and of course the scale of degrees of longitude in the top and bottom margin is useless for measuring distances. For this reason no linear scale of miles can be included in any Mercator chart, except in the largest-scale plans showing a small area only. No linear scale could be drawn that would be accurate for different latitudes on a chart of any considerable area.

Mercator's projection can also be used with the axis of the cylinder not coinciding with the axis of the earth through the poles, and the resulting projections are known as Transverse Mercator (if the axis is at right-angles to the polar axis) or Oblique Mercator. The former results in the projection being least distorted along a given meridian, instead of along the equator, and is useful for mapping regions extending in a north–south direction, e.g., the British Isles on the Ordnance Survey. Oblique Mercator gives a line of least distortion which can be arranged to suit the area being mapped, running at an angle to both meridians and parallels of latitude. Both these varieties, however, are useless for navigation.

meridian, from Latin *medius* meaning middle, and *dies* meaning day, a semi-*great circle joining the earth's poles. Meridians, better known perhaps as lines of *longitude, cross the equator and all parallels of *latitude at right angles. Owing to the uniform rotation of the earth, all celestial bodies appear to revolve around the earth towards the west, making one revolution in a day. When the sun crosses an observer's meridian, the time is reckoned to be midday, that is to say the local time is 12 noon at the instant the sun is at meridian passage.

messenger, a small rope attached to the *eye of a *hawser and used to haul it out to the ring of a mooring *buoy.

metacentre, the point of intersection of a vertical line, in relation to the ship's structure, drawn through the centre of gravity of a ship when she is lying upright and a vertical line drawn through the centre of buoyancy when the ship is heeled. To make certain that a ship is stable so that a righting moment comes into play when she is heeled, the metacentre must be above the centre of gravity.

metacentric height, the vertical distance between the centre of gravity of a ship and her transverse *metacentre. It is an important element of the righting moment exerted to bring a ship back to the vertical when she *rolls under the influence of the sea or wind; the greater the metacentric height, the more the righting moment. At angles of roll of more than about 10°, the position of a ship's metacentre, and therefore her metacentric height, varies, and a designer must arrange the shape and dimensions of a ship's hull to provide not only reasonable initial stability at normal conditions of loading but also reasonable stability at the probable angles of heel to which a ship may roll in heavy weather.

meteorology, the study of weather patterns with the object of predicting change in the weather. It is a complex and still inexact science, based on current weather reports over a large area, but it is of great importance to navigators, particularly of small vessels and yachts, in enabling them to avoid areas in which stormy weather is predicted.

Pressure. The basic cause of all weather change lies in the property of a gas to rise when heated. Air is a gas, and when it is warmed by the sun or by a large hot area such as a desert, it rises, produces an area of low pressure, and colder air from the surrounding area of higher pressure flows in to take its place. This action causes variations in the atmospheric pressure at sea level. To the navigator, therefore, the atmospheric pressure in the vicinity of his position at sea is the most important guide he has to the likely behaviour of the weather in the immediate future.

Atmospheric pressure is measured by the height of a column of mercury in a tube sealed at the top and open at the bottom to the pressure of the atmosphere, as in the ordinary mercury barometer. The average pressure at sea level in winter is 29.9 inches and in summer 30.0 inches, and variations above or below this level indicate areas of high or low pressure. Most maritime barometers are now marked in millibars rather than in inches, 3.4 millibars equalling one-tenth of an inch. Another method of measuring atmospheric pressure is with an aneroid barometer, in which a hermetically sealed chamber of thin metal is partly exhausted of air and thus susceptible to any change in external pressure, which can be read off by means of a pointer on a graduated scale. Aneroid barometers are almost all marked to read pressure in millibars rather than in inches, and pressure on all modern weather charts is today given in millibars. Thus, the average atmospheric pressure at sea level in millibars is 1,013 in winter and 1,016 in summer. A refinement of the aneroid barometer, favoured by many navigators, is a barograph, in which a continuous curve reflecting the changes in atmospheric pressure is traced on a small chart mounted on a revolving clockwork drum which makes one complete revolution in a week. This trace gives an accurate and continuous picture of pressure changes, providing visible evidence from which forecasts can more easily be made. Most large ships, in addition to aneroid barometers and barographs, carry at least one mercury barometer because of their greater accuracy and sensitivity. Smaller ships and yachts, in which the movement in rough weather makes it difficult to accommodate a mercury barometer, normally only carry an aneroid barometer or barograph.

Weather systems. There are two main weather systems in the general weather patterns, *anticyclones and *depressions. In the northern hemisphere an anticyclone is a system of wind which circulates spirally in a clockwise direction around an area of high pressure, which can at times cover an area of immense size. In the southern hemisphere the anticyclonic wind circulates in an anti-clockwise direction, though still around a high pressure area. The stronger winds are found at the outer limits of the anti-cyclone, those nearer the centre being very light or at times non-existent. This is always a fair-weather system, with the air dry and the wind strength never more than moderate. Anti-cyclones are normally slow moving and sometimes stationary for quite long periods. The approach of an anticyclone can usually be predicted by a steadily rising barometer and a clearing sky.

In a depression, basically a bad-weather system, the wind blows in an anti-clockwise direction about a centre of low pressure in the northern hemisphere, and in a clockwise direction in the southern hemisphere. The winds are usually high, sometimes violent, often accompanied by heavy rain, and strongest near the centre of the low pressure area where the barometer gradient is steepest. Depressions usually move swiftly, at an average rate of about 25 miles an hour. A navigator needs to know where the centre of a depression is in relation to the position of his vessel, in order to avoid the area of highest wind, and can do so by applying the *Buys Ballot law. If he faces the wind in the northern hemisphere, the centre lies on his starboard hand just abaft the beam; if he does so in the southern hemisphere, it lies just abaft his port beam. The approach of a depression can be foretold by a falling barometer, a backing wind, and the appearance in the sky of high cirrus cloud, the 'mare's tail' sky of sailors. Further evidence of an approaching depression is a halo, or white luminous ring, around the sun or moon, and a banking up of low, heavy cloud. For illus. see DEPRESSION.

It does not necessarily follow that every rise in barometric pressure foretells an anticyclone and that every fall foretells a depression. Variations of three or four millibars up or down from the average, except in the tropics, are fairly normal and may produce little change in the current weather pattern; it is only when variations of five or more millibars from the normal occur that some predictions are possible. A barometer reading of five millibars below normal, with the barometer steady or still falling, is an indication of a period of unsettled weather; five millibars above and a steady or still rising barometer indicates settled weather with light or moderate winds. In the tropics, where variations of atmospheric pressure are generally limited to a small diurnal oscillation, a fall of three millibars below the average needs to be treated with suspicion, especially if it persists for two or three days, when it is a fairly sure indication of a *tropical storm somewhere within a radius of about 250 miles. In other areas, atmospheric pressure of less than 1,000 millibars, and the barometer falling rapidly at one millibar or more in an hour, is a sure indication of strong winds and rain; a barometer rising rapidly indicates a fine period of a day or two but likely to be followed by a fall in pressure and more unsettled weather. Other weather conditions that can be foretold by the behaviour of the barometer are best illustrated by two simple rhymes that every seaman should know:

'Long foretold, long last,
Short notice, soon past.'

This means that a steady fall in pressure over a long period indicates a long period of bad weather, but that a rapid fall indicates that though the weather will be severe it will be of short duration.

'First rise after low
Foretells a stronger blow.'

The full force of a *gale at sea is frequently felt after the centre of a depression has passed, the first rise of the barometer of course indicating that the centre has passed. Gales with a rising barometer are invariably squally.

Cloud formation is also frequently a useful guide in weather prediction. There are four main types of cloud formation, cirrus, cumulus, stratus, and nimbus, but combinations of these main formations can also be indications of the type of weather ahead. *Cirrus*, the highest of the cloud formations, is cloud in the form of light wisps stretched across the sky. If these wisps are few in number and tend to disappear quickly, the probability is that fine weather will continue. If they are numerous and appear to group themselves in long streaks radiating from a common centre, a depression accompanied by strong winds is likely to be on the way. Sometimes cirrus takes the form of a thin film of cloud across the sky which, at night, produces a halo around the moon. This is almost certain evidence of violent weather.

Cumulus is the cloud which looks like masses of cotton wool billowing up in the sky. When cumulus comes on a summer day and disappears in the heat of the sun, the weather will remain fine and settled. If it appears to increase at the end of the day, a weather change is probable. When it builds itself up in pyramids and appears to topple over, it is a sure sign of thunder.

Stratus is the lowest of the cloud formations, and appears as a bank or pall of shapeless low-lying cloud, often forming in the evening and disappearing at dawn. Although it may at times look threatening, it has little message for the forecaster unless, towards dusk, its edges appear torn and twisted to windward. If then in its advance across the sky it meets cumulus cloud, a period of bad weather can be predicted.

Nimbus, the rain cloud, is the darkest of the clouds, often inky in appearance, and indicates rain. When it has a hard lower edge broken by vortex-like wisps and moving fast, it indicates a line squall approaching with the cloud.

As much, however, can generally be foretold from the nature of all these clouds as from their actual form. When any of them are soft-looking and reasonably low, then the weather will be fine with moderate breezes; when they are hard-edged and oily-looking, it is a sign of increasing wind; when they are small and inky-looking, rain is certain.

Clouds form when the temperature of the air falls below its saturation point. When air has been heated by passing over a warm land or sea area, it expands and rises, and as it mounts it expands still further because of the decrease in atmospheric pressure. This expansion causes it to cool, and if this cooling process continues beyond the point of saturation, the excess water condenses into the droplets which form clouds. The formation of mist and fog is fundamentally the same as that of cloud, except that the air is cooled below its saturation point at ground level. When warm moist air is blown over a cold sea surface, by which the lower layers of the air are cooled, fog will form. Sea fogs are most common in spring and the early part of summer, seasons at which the sea is still cold but adjacent land areas have warmed up. Sea fogs are also prevalent in the areas where cold ocean currents flow.

The difference between mist and fog is purely one of degree, and a generally accepted definition is that when the visibility exceeds 1,000 metres it is classed as mist, and when under 1,000 metres, it is classed as fog.

metre class yacht, see INTERNATIONAL METRE CLASS YACHT.

middle ground, an obstruction in the form of a sand or mud bank, or an outcrop of rock, in a *fairway. Its extremities are marked by *buoys so that vessels entering or leaving can pass either side of it in safety. See BUOYAGE.

mile, see NAUTICAL MILE.

millibar, a unit of measurement of atmospheric pressure, 1,000 millibars equalling the atmospheric pressure required to raise a column of mercury in a vacuum tube to a height of 29.53 in. (750 mm). Lines drawn on a *synoptic chart connecting points of equal atmospheric pressure in millibars are known as isobars. See also METEOROLOGY.

mirage, a natural phenomenon induced by certain atmospheric conditions of temperature and light which can reflect objects below the natural curvature of the earth so that they can be seen although in fact still below the horizon.

mistral, a cold wind from the north-west which blows down the Rhône valley into the western Mediterranean Sea. In the Adriatic and eastern Mediterranean, a similar north-west wind is called the maestrale.

mitre, the seam in a sail where cloths which run in two directions are joined. Triangular sails, such as *staysails and *jibs (and occasionally yachts' Bermudian mainsails), are normally made with the lines of the cloths running in two directions; for example, the upper cloths of a jib might run at right angles to the leech, and the lower cloths at right angles to the foot. The mitre seam usually forms a strengthened narrow cloth running diagonally from the clew to some point on the luff. Different sailmakers have their own ideas of the best method of setting the cloths and the mitre seam, but the latter is usually arranged to run more or less in line of the *sheet so as to distribute the strain of the sheet evenly throughout the sail cloths. For illus. see SAIL.

mizen or **mizzen,** the name of the third, aftermost, mast of a square-rigged sailing ship or a three-masted *schooner, or the small after mast of a *ketch or a *yawl (but see also JIGGER MAST). The word probably came into the English language either from the Italian *mezzana* or the French *misaine,* which in fact are the names in those languages for the foremast, but for some reason its position in the ship was changed round when the word was adopted in Britain. The French word for mizen is *artimon,* and artemon was the name given in England to an additional mast in the forward end of a vessel, probably the forerunner of the *bowsprit.

mole, a long pier or breakwater forming part of the sea defences of a port. It can be built either in the form of a detached mole constructed entirely in the sea or one with an end connected to the shore.

monkey block, a small single *block stropped with a swivel, used on board in places where it is awkward to get a straight haul. The name was also used in square-rigged ships for the blocks fastened to the *yards through which the *bunt-lines are rove.

monk's seam, the seam made by a sailmaker after sewing the overlapping edges of *cloths together to make a sail. It is a line of stitches through the centre between the two rows of edging stitches. See also PRICK.

monsoon, a seasonal wind caused by the summer heating and winter cooling of a large land mass. The most important monsoons occur in the Indian and western Pacific oceans where the huge land mass of Asia is the dominant factor. Only in the western part of the Arabian Sea and the northern part of the China Sea does a monsoon wind reach gale force; for the most part the winds are no more than fresh, about force 5 on the *Beaufort scale. There are three recognized monsoons, the South-West monsoon which blows from about May to September over the northern Indian Ocean and western North Pacific, the North-East monsoon which blows over the same areas from about October to April, and the North-West monsoon which blows from about November to March over parts of the Indian Ocean and western Pacific Ocean south of the equator. This last is in effect the North-East monsoon after it crosses the equator where the reversed effect of the earth's rotation changes it into a north-westerly wind.

moonraker, a small light sail set above a *skysail in a square-rigged ship in very fine weather. It is also often called a moonsail or *raffee.

moor, to, in its strict meaning to lie in a harbour or anchorage with two *anchors down and the ship middled between them. When a ship is moored in this fashion it is usual to bring both cables to a mooring swivel just below the *hawseholes so that the ship may swing to the tide without getting a *foul hawse (that is, without getting her cables crossed). The word is also loosely used to describe other ways of anchoring a ship using two anchors: e.g., when a ship has a stern anchor laid out she is said to be moored head and stern. The word is today also widely used of a vessel which is secured head and stern to a quay or alongside another vessel, or which lies with the bow secured to a quay and an anchor laid out astern. See also MOORING.

mooring, a permanent position in harbours and estuaries to which ships can secure without using their own *anchors. For yachts, a very small buoy, light enough to be lifted easily on board with a boathook, is attached by a length of rope to a light chain, itself attached to a concrete block, and the mooring is hauled up until the chain reaches the surface and the yacht is secured with it.

Morse code, a method of signalling much used at sea until the introduction of the radio-telephone. Its system of alphabetical and numerical symbols made up of dots and dashes made it easy to transmit in sound, as by wireless; in light, as by searchlight or *Aldis lamp; or by motion, with hand signal flags. It was a quick and easy code to master, and has proved invaluable for communication at sea.

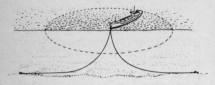

Ship moored

A	Alpha	• —	I have a diver down; keep well clear at slow speed.
B	Bravo	— • • •	I am taking in, or discharging, or carrying, dangerous goods.
C	Charlie	— • — •	Yes (affirmative).
D	Delta	— • •	Keep clear of me—I am manoeuvring with difficulty.
E	Echo	•	I am altering my course to starboard.
F	Foxtrot	• • — •	I am disabled—communicate with me.
G	Golf	— — •	I require a pilot. When made by fishing vessels operating in close proximity on the fishing grounds it means: 'I am hauling nets.'
H	Hotel	• • • •	I have a pilot on board.
I	India	• •	I am altering my course to port.
J	Juliett	• — — —	I am on fire and have dangerous cargo on board: keep well clear of me.
K	Kilo	— • —	I wish to communicate with you.
L	Lima	• — • •	You should stop your vessel instantly.
M	Mike	— —	My vessel is stopped and making no way through the water.
N	November	— •	No (negative).
O	Oscar	— — —	Man overboard.
P	Papa	• — — •	In harbour hoisted at the foremast head, Blue Peter, 'All persons should report on board as the vessel is about to proceed to sea.' At sea, it may be used by fishing vessels to mean, 'My nets have come fast upon an obstruction.'
Q	Quebec	— — • —	My vessel is healthy and I request free pratique.
R	Romeo	• — •	
S	Sierra	• • •	My engines are going astern.
T	Tango	—	Keep clear of me; I am engaged in pair trawling.
U	Uniform	• • —	You are running into danger.
V	Victor	• • • —	I require assistance.
W	Whiskey	• — —	I require medical assistance.
X	Xray	— • • —	Stop carrying out your intentions and watch for my signals.
Y	Yankee	— • — —	I am dragging my anchor.
Z	Zulu	— — • •	I require a tug. When made by fishing vessels operating in close proximity on the fishing grounds it means: 'I am shooting nets.'

1	• — — — —		6	— • • • •
2	• • — — —		7	— — • • •
3	• • • — —		8	— — — • •
4	• • • • —		9	— — — — •
5	• • • • •		0	— — — — —

mouse, a stop made of *spunyarn fixed to the collar of the *stays in a square-rigged ship to hold the running eye of the rigging from slipping down the stay. It is also a mark fixed on the *braces and other rigging of the *yards to indicate when they are square. In general, any small collar made with spunyarn round a wire or rope with the object of holding something in place, such as an *eye threaded on the rope, would be called a mouse.

mouse a hook, to, pass two or three turns of *spunyarn across the jaw of a hook to prevent it jumping out of a ringbolt or *eye into which it has been hooked, or to prevent a rope running across the hook from jumping clear.

Hook half moused; to be finished with more turns and a reef knot

mudhook, the sailor's slang name for an *anchor.

multi-hull, a type of vessel formed of two or more hulls or floats which is propelled by paddles, sails, or mechanical power. Sailing *catamarans (two identical hulls) and *trimarans (a central hull with twin floats) have been built during the 20th century in large numbers and increasing sizes for ocean voyaging and racing. Craft having more than one hull have been known in the Indian and Pacific Oceans for many hundreds of years but their use in the western hemisphere is comparatively recent.

The advantages of a multi-hull design are lightness and stability, and therefore, when used as sailing craft, an increase in speed for a given sail area. In a moderate or fresh wind from the *beam or forward of the beam the catamaran is faster than conventionally rigged yachts, and speeds of more than 20 knots have been recorded in quite small craft. But a disadvantage of a catamaran is that in a strong puff of wind or a squall she is likely to lift her weather hull out of the water, and beyond a certain point she becomes unstable and capsizes. A trimaran cannot capsize, but if she is driven hard she can bury her bows in the sea and turn stern over bows. In both catamarans and trimarans, their stiffness (i.e., inability to *roll because of their basic design) imposes a considerable strain on hull and rigging, and in a seaway the structural stresses are considerable.

Many long voyages, however, including circumnavigations, have been made in multi-hulls.

MY, a prefix used before the name of a yacht to designate a motor yacht.

mylar, see KEVLAR.

N

Nautical Almanac, an annual publication which gives the navigator all the information he needs for working out his position by celestial navigation. For deep-sea sailing, the best nautical almanacs are those produced by the Hydrographic Department of the British Ministry of Defence (published by HM Stationery Office) and the US Department of the Navy. In 1958 agreement was reached that each should be printed with a standard layout, so that both are now identical, and the information provided is in the most convenient form for navigators. *Reed's* and *Brown's* nautical almanacs give the same information in a condensed form but both include much additional information which is not found in the national publications, such as tide tables and tidal constants for British waters, lights, buoys, radio beacons, etc. This additional information makes them invaluable for the small boat sailor who, without them, would need also to carry on board *The Admiralty Tide Tables, The Admiralty List of Lights,* and *The Admiralty List of Radio Signals.*

nautical mile, the unit of distance used at sea, and differing considerably from the standard mile of 1,760 yards used on shore. A nautical mile is the distance on the earth's surface subtended by one minute of *latitude at the earth's centre. If the earth were a perfect sphere, one nautical mile would be equivalent to an arc length of one minute at all places and in all directions, but the earth is not exactly spherical, being an oblate spheroid flatter at the poles, with its axis of rotation having the least diameter.

Because of this shape, the length of the nautical mile varies slightly with the latitude, being shortest at the equator, where the curvature of the *meridians is greatest, and longest at the poles. The arithmetical mean of a nautical mile measured at the equator and one measured at the poles is 6,077 feet, but this figure is rounded off to 6,080 feet (1,852 m), which is the length of the 'standard' nautical mile. The errors of navigation arising from the use of a 'standard' nautical mile instead of its actual length for the latitude in which a ship is being navigated are obviously greatest at the equator, but they are of negligible proportions and are of no significance in practical navigation.

On a navigational *chart, except in large-scale plans where the differences in latitude are very small, it is impossible to incorporate a scale of miles because the projection of the chart (see, e.g., MERCATOR PROJECTION) distorts the latitude; the further north or south of the equator, the greater the degree of distortion on the chart. When measuring a distance on a chart, it is therefore essential that it is measured on the latitude scale, on the east and west borders of the chart, corresponding to the mean latitude in which the distance to be measured lies.

nautophone, an electrically operated sound signal of high pitch used in fog, fitted on *buoys and unmanned *lightships.

naval architect, a person qualified to design ships, within whose brief comes responsibility for the strength and stability of the vessel, her internal and external fittings, and her suitability for the purpose for which she is designed.

naval architecture, the art and science of designing ships, yachts, and other craft for use at sea.

nave line or **navel line,** a rope or small *tackle in square-rigged ships leading from the main and foremast heads and secured to the *parrels or *trusses of the *yards. Its purpose is to hold the parrels up while the yards are *swayed up, and exactly level with the yards so that they can be fully *braced.

navigation, from the Latin *navis,* a ship, and *agere,* to drive, the art of conducting a vessel from one place on the earth's surface to another by sea safely, expeditiously, and efficiently.

Coastal navigation. The difference between coastal navigation and *pilotage is narrow, but a general definition of the former would be the safe conduct of a ship where the navigator has the land on one side of his *course and the open sea on the other, even though he is in fact navigating in what is known as pilotage waters. When a ship is proceeding in sight of a coastline, her navigator need never be in doubt of her exact position, for the largest-scale chart of the area will give him the exact position of all landmarks, lighthouses, lightships, buoys, etc., and by taking compass bearings of suitable objects on the shore and transferring these bearings on to the chart, the point of intersection of the bearings, called a *fix, gives the ship's position. Since all courses and bearings laid down on a chart are *true, the bearings taken with the compass must be corrected before being drawn in on the chart, by the application of *variation and *deviation in the case of a magnetic compass, and of any gyro error in the case of a gyroscopic compass.

of the transferred bearing with the second bearing gives the ship's position.

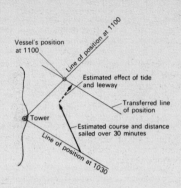

Running fix

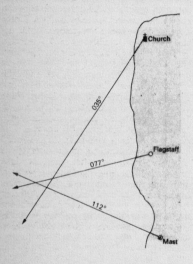

A fix

Where the chart shows only one conspicuous object in a long coastline, a position can be obtained by means of a running fix. A compass bearing of the object is transferred to the chart and, later, when the bearing of the object has altered sufficiently to give an adequate angle of cut, which should preferably be around 90° and never less than 45°, a second bearing is taken and laid off on the chart. If the first bearing is transferred by parallel rulers by the distance the ship has run in the interval between the bearings along the course steered, making due allowance for the distance and direction the ship has been carried by the tide, the point of intersection

Other methods of fixing a ship's position when in sight of land are by sextant angles. If the height above sea level of an object on land, such as a lighthouse or church tower, is known, a *vertical sextant angle, by means of simple mathematics, will give the distance between the observer and the object, and when combined with a compass bearing, provides a position on the chart by bearing and distance. A *horizontal sextant angle (illustrated) between two objects ashore will give a position line which is the arc of a circle on which the ship and the two objects both lie. A second horizontal sextant angle between two other objects gives a similar position line, and again the ship's position is at the point of intersection of the two arcs.

Modern aids to navigation make the task of the coastal navigator even easier. *Radar is a means of providing the navigator with vital information in darkness or in fog, enabling him to 'see' the land and in many cases providing him with an accurate bearing and distance of landmarks which are marked on his chart. Hyperbolic navigation (see below), such as the Decca Navigator system, is another means of accurate fixing, using the principle of phase comparison of continuous wave radio signals.

A wise navigator, unless he has no alternative, does not use buoys as marks with which to fix his ship's position. Buoys can drag their moorings and thus be out of position and, being unmanned, can give no warning of any error. Lightships, however, are manned, and when they drag their moorings and are out of position, they indicate the fact by displaying the marks or lights laid down in the *Rule of the Road to show the navigator that they are not in the position as marked on the chart.

Celestial navigation. The astronomical methods of position-finding at sea used at the present time are the culmination of an evolutionary process which began even before the first Phoenician sea traders navigated their vessels in the waters of the western Mediterranean and along the Atlantic coast of north-west Europe some 3,000 years ago, using the heavenly bodies to guide them.

Perhaps the true origin of nautical astronomy was the realization that the star known today as *Polaris, or the Pole Star, always lay to the north. Certainly the Phoenicians knew this, and it is probable that this fact had not escaped the notice of earlier navigators. The realization that an observation of Polaris, or of the midday sun, also gave the *latitude of the observer followed quickly and naturally, and this is the principle that has been used since the earliest navigations. But the problem of finding *longitude has not been nearly so simple, and it exercised the attention of many brilliant astronomers right down to the middle of the 18th century, when ultimately it was solved by the perfection of the marine *chronometer.

During the 19th century the finding of longitude at sea by the time method was simplified and systematized by the discoveries and ingenuities of Captain Thomas Sumner and Admiral Marcq St. Hilaire, and their methods of obtaining a ship's position by observation of one or more heavenly bodies became the navigator's standard practice. The *sextant, the chronometer, the *Nautical Almanac, and mathematical tables are the indispensable instruments of nautical astronomy, and with them a navigator can find his position on a chart anywhere in the world.

Until the compilation of new astronomical tables to assist the air navigator in obtaining a quick position by celestial observations, the solution of a sun, moon, or star sight, by which a position line on a chart could be obtained, required a knowledge of spherical trigonometry and the solving of what is known as the PZX triangle, where P is the position of the

celestial pole, Z is the observer's *zenith (i.e., the point in the sky directly over head), and X is the celestial body. The triangle is solved by calculations on the lines of the Cosine Theory and involve extensive use of mathematical tables. But the new air navigation tables, now in wide use by many navigators at sea, have made the solution very much simpler, and with these and a Nautical Almanac a navigator can obtain his true position without the long calculations previously necessary.

From his observed altitude of the celestial body a navigator obtains from the tables the true zenith distance of the body and from the Nautical Almanac the zenith distance from his *dead reckoning or assumed position. The difference between these two distances is known as the *intercept, and shows the navigator how far his real position is from his assumed position in one direction. He finds this direction from the exact time at which he took his sight which, from the tables, gives him the Greenwich Hour Angle. His assumed longitude then gives him the Local Hour Angle and, using the body's declination from the Nautical Almanac, the *azimuth, or bearing, is obtained. By drawing this bearing on the chart from his assumed position and measuring off the intercept, a line drawn through that point at right angles to the azimuth provides a position line. A similar sight taken at the same time of a second celestial body on a different bearing will provide a second position line and the observer's true position is at the point of intersection of these two position lines.

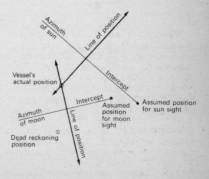

Celestial fix using simultaneous sights of sun and moon

An alternative method for use during daylight hours when the sun is normally the only celestial body in sight is to take a second observation of the sun some 3 or 4 hours later when its azimuth has altered sufficiently to provide a satisfactory angle of cut, which should never be less than 45°. The solution of this second observation produces a position line in exactly the same way as the first. If, now, the first position line is transferred on the chart with a parallel ruler to take account of the distance run and the course steered during the time which has elapsed between the two observations, the point of intersection of the two position lines is the true position of the vessel. This is known as the *Marcq St. Hilaire method (illustrated).

The new tables, though much quicker and simpler to use, do not give quite the accuracy of the older method of calculation. Where the new tables will produce an observed position within about a nautical mile of the true position, navigators using the older method normally worked to a tenth of a nautical mile, or 200 yards, and would expect their sights, providing they were taken from a reasonably steady platform, to produce an observed position within this distance of the true position.

Hyperbolic navigation. In 1946 an international conference to consider radio aids to marine navigation was held in Britain and specifications for radio navigational systems were worked out and agreed. This agreement resulted in the development of four hyperbolic systems which will eventually cover the whole area of the world, known as Consol, Decca Navigator,

Loran, and Omega. Each system varies slightly in its methods of using radio transmissions from master and slave transmitters and in the frequencies they adopt, high radio frequencies giving great ground wave accuracy for distances up to about 50 miles, very low frequencies having to be used where long range coverage is required. There are thus variations in accuracy according to whether the coverage is in coastal areas (high frequency) where continuous fixing of great accuracy is required, or in ocean areas (very low frequency) where such a degree of accuracy is not necessary but the ability to fix at long range is essential.

These systems are all based on the fact that radio waves emanating from transmissions travel in curves known mathematically as hyperbolae and navigationally as *great circles, and since they all travel at the same speed it is possible, by measuring the difference of time between the receipt on board of the signals from two of them, which depends on the difference in distance of the ship from the two stations, to plot the requisite curve on the chart. By repeating this process with another transmitting station in conjunction with one of the first two, usually known as the master, another curve can be plotted on the chart. Since the position of the ship must be somewhere on each curve, the point of intersection is her actual position.

In ships fitted for hyperbolic navigation, these operations are performed simultaneously and continuously by electronic receivers, and over-printed lattice charts or tables are used, so that the point of intersection can be determined quickly and accurately from the readings of the electronic receivers.

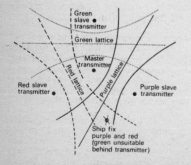

Decca chain; a normal layout with master transmitter and three slave transmitters

navigation lights, the lights which are laid down under the *International Regulations for Preventing Collisions at Sea which vessels must display when under way at sea at night.
(a) A power-driven vessel under way at night, less than 150 feet in length, carries one white steaming light, port and starboard bow lights, and a white overtaking light. If over 150 feet in length, she carries two white steaming lights, port and starboard bow lights, and a white overtaking light.
(b) A power-driven vessel towing another vessel at night carries her bow lights, overtaking light, and steaming light. If the length of tow is less than 600 feet an

Navigation lights—arcs of visibility

additional steaming light is carried; if the length of tow is more than 600 feet a third steaming light is carried.

(c) Vessels engaged in trawling at night show an all-round green light above an all-round white light, both visible for two miles. They may carry in addition one steaming light, lower than and abaft the all-round green and white lights. When making way through the water they show bow lights and overtaking light. Drift net vessels show an all-round red light above an all-round white light. When making way through the water they show bow lights and overtaking light. If outlying gear extends more than 500 feet an additional all-round white light shows the direction of the gear.

(d) A vessel under way at night but not under command and drifting hoists two all-round red lights, one above the other, visible for two miles, and switches off all other navigation lights. If she is making way through the water she shows bow lights and overtaking light in addition.

(e) A power-driven pilot-vessel on duty and under way at night carries bow lights, overtaking light, and at the masthead a white all-round light above a red all-round light, both visible for three miles. She also shows one or more flare-ups at intervals not exceeding 10 minutes or an intermittent white light visible all round.

(f) A sailing vessel under way at night carries bow lights and an overtaking light. In addition she may carry on the top of the foremast a red light above a green light, visible for two miles and showing from ahead to two points abaft the beam.

(g) A vessel of less than 150 feet, when at

anchor at night, carries in the forepart a white all-round light visible for two miles. If of 150 feet or more in length, she carries two white all-round lights, visible for three miles, one near the bow, the other at or near the stern and 15 feet lower.

(h) A light-vessel at night when driven from her proper station shows a red fixed light at the bow and stern, and red and white flares shown simultaneously every 15 minutes.

neap tides, those tides which occur during the first and third quarters of the moon when the pull of the sun is at right angles to that of the moon. The effect of this counteraction is to make the high water lower and the low water higher than when the sun and moon both exert their pull in the same direction, a condition which causes *spring tides. **To be neaped,** the expression used of a vessel which goes aground on the spring tides and has to wait for the next springs before there is enough depth of water to float her off.

net, lines rigged from the mast to the forestay of a racing yacht when running before the wind with a *spinnaker set. Their purpose is to prevent the spinnaker wrapping itself round the forestay if it should collapse as a result of a lack of wind or an unexpected backdraught.

net register tonnage, see TONNAGE.

nimbus, a type of cloud formation. See METEOROLOGY.

nip, (1) the name given by seamen to a short turn or twist in a rope or *hawser (see also FRENCHMAN). **(2)** That part of a rope bound by a *seizing round a thimble or round the tucks of an *eye splice.

nugger or **nuggar,** the traditional sail trading vessel of the lower part of the River Nile. They were two-masted with a very large *lateen sail on the mainmast and a much smaller lateen on the *mizen.

null, see RADIO DIRECTION FINDER.

'number', the somewhat odd designation of a group of four letters assigned to a ship for identification purposes. She makes her 'number' by hoisting the alphabetical flags in the *International Code of Signals which represent the four letters which have been assigned to her. The allocation of these distinguishing letters is done on an international scale, every maritime nation being given groups of letters from which they assign individual distinguishing letters.

nut, the ball on the end of the *stock of an Admiralty pattern *anchor. Its purpose is to prevent the stock from penetrating the ground, thus forcing it to lie flat on the bottom so that the *flukes, at right angles to the stock, are driven into the ground to provide good holding.

nylon, the strongest of the man-made fibres used in rope-making, with the great advantage, as of all man-made fibres, that it does not swell or harden when wet and does not rot from the action of seawater. It has too much elasticity for use as *halyards, or headsail and mainsail *sheets, but can be used for anchor *warps and other purposes where some stretch is an advantage. As a cloth nylon has too much elasticity for working sails but is used occasionally in sailing craft for *spinnakers and sometimes *ghosters, but will pull out of shape if used for long in a strong wind.

O

oakum, tarred hemp or manila (tow) fibres made from old and condemned ropes which have been unpicked, used for *caulking the *seams of the decks and sides of a wooden ship in order to make them watertight.

oar, a wooden instrument which, working as a lever, is used to *pull a boat through the water. It has three parts: the blade, the part of the oar which enters the water; the shaft, the main body of the oar; and the *loom, the inboard end on which the rower pulls. The point of leverage is the *rowlock, *crutch, or *thole pin in the *gunwale of the boat.

observation, a navigational term used to indicate the taking of a *sight of the sun, moon, or a star by which a ship's position line can be worked out and drawn on a chart.

occulting light, a navigational light displayed by a *lighthouse or *lightship in which the period of darkness is shorter than the period of light. See CHARACTERISTICS.

ocean, in its proper meaning, the whole body of water which encircles the globe with the exception of inland seas, lakes, and rivers. For more precise geographical purposes, the ocean is divided into five separate oceans—the Atlantic (North and South), Indian, Pacific, Arctic, and Antarctic. It has been calculated that the oceans cover 71 per cent of the whole area of the globe.

ocean racing, see YACHTING.

Ocean Rating Council, an international body which supervises the rules under which racing yachts are rated. It is a complementary body to the International Yacht Racing Union. (See YACHTING, Racing rules).

offing, the distance that a ship at sea keeps away from the land because of navigational dangers, fog, or other hazards. The term is generally, though not necessarily, understood to mean that the ship remains in waters too deep for anchoring. To keep, or to make, a good offing, to lay a *course which takes a ship well off the land and clear of all danger.

off soundings, or **beyond soundings.** A ship is off soundings when she is in waters which lie to seaward of the 100-fathom line. Before the days of sounding machines and *echo-sounders, the deep sea *lead line could measure depths up to about 100 fathoms, so that this was in those days the limit of soundings, all greater depths being off, or beyond, soundings.

off the wind, said of a sailing ship when she is sailing with the *sheets well eased off with the wind coming *free or from broad on the *bow. When a vessel sails as close to the wind as she can, she is *on the wind.

one-design class, a class of yachts or boats all of which have been built to one accepted design. In an attempt to give all yachts of a class an equal chance in racing, and to eliminate the complications of handicapping, one-designs are built and rigged so as to be as nearly identical one to another as is practicable. All the yachts of the class should, in theory, have precisely the same sailing performance, and the race results should depend therefore on the individual skills of the helmsmen and their crews. In practice, yachts reflect the amount of maintenance they receive and the care the owner gives to his boat's tuning up and details of sails and gear, and the relative performance of one-designs can accordingly vary widely. The principle of one-design, however, limits the advantage the wealthy owner can have over the less opulent, and on the whole racing in any one-design class tends to be very fair. For this reason, the majority of sailing clubs which organize races number at least one one-design class among their racing fleets, as for example the Royal Burnham and Royal Corinthian one-design classes, the Bembridge one-design class, etc., which race exclusively in those clubs. Other one-design classes can be international or national in character, such as the International Star class, the National Flying Fifteen class, etc.

on the wind, said of a sailing vessel when she is sailing with her *sheets hauled as far aft as possible, or as close to the wind as the ship will go. See also OFF THE WIND.

outhaul, a line or purchase by which a sail is hauled outboard along a spar. Aboard a square-rigged ship the *studdingsails and their booms were hauled out along the yards by means of outhauls. On old-fashioned yachts with long *bowsprits, the *tack of the jib was hooked on to a traveller, a large iron ring running along the bowsprit, which was then hauled towards the outer (or *crans iron) end of the bowsprit by the outhaul.

outrigger, (1) an extension to each side of the *crosstrees of a sailing vessel to spread the *backstays, in a *schooner the topmast backstays, and in a full-rigged ship the *topgallant and *royal backstays. **(2)** A counterpoising log of wood rigged out from the side of a native canoe in the Pacific and Indian oceans to provide additional stability when carrying sail in a stiff breeze.

overfall, a condition of the sea when it falls into breaking waves caused by wind or current over an irregular bottom, or by currents meeting. *Tide-rips and *tide-races frequently cause overfalls.

overhaul, to, (1) increase the distance apart of the *blocks of a *tackle by running the rope back through the sheaves. **(2)** (Of a ship) overtake, or catch up with, another ship at sea.

over-raked. A vessel is said to be over-raked when she is riding to her *anchor(s) in bad weather and the seas break continuously over her *bows. It is a condition which can often be ameliorated by increasing the *scope of the *cable through *veering an extra amount so that the vessel may lie more easily.

overtaking light, a white light displayed at the *stern of a vessel under way at night, forming part of the compulsory *navigation lights which a ship must show under the regulations laid down by the *International Convention for Preventing Collisions at Sea. The overtaking light, also widely known as a sternlight, must have a visibility of two miles on a clear night and must show through an arc on either side of the vessel from right astern to two *points *abaft the *beam.

ox-eye, a name given to a small cloud which occasionally appears in the sky off the eastern coast of Africa and spreads quickly to cover the whole of the sky, presaging a severe storm accompanied by a violent wind. It gets its name from its resemblance, when first seen, to the eye of an ox.

P

pacific iron, the cast-iron cappings at the *yardarms of a square-rigged ship which support the *studdingsail *boom irons and to which a *Flemish horse is made fast.

painter, a length of small rope in a boat used for securing it when alongside a pier or jetty or a ship, at the gangway, astern, or at the lower *boom. The inboard end is usually spliced with a *thimble to a ringbolt in the stem of the boat, the outboard end being stopped from unravelling with a *whipping or, more fancifully, by being *pointed.

palm, (1) the triangular face of the *fluke of an Admiralty pattern *anchor. (2) The sailmaker's thimble used in sewing canvas, consisting of a flat thimble in a canvas or leather strip with a thumb hole. The whole is worn across the palm of the hand, which gives it its name.

pampero, a violent squall, accompanied by heavy rain, thunder, and lightning, which blows up with great suddenness on the pampas of the Rio de la Plata plain and frequently drifts out to sea where it blows with the force of a hurricane, the wind usually coming from the south-west. The great five-masted *barque *France* was struck by a pampero in 1901 and later foundered as a result of the damage she sustained.

papagayo, a gale from the north-east which occasionally blows with great force off the coast of Central America, often without any adequate signs to warn a navigator of its imminence.

parallax, in its navigational meaning, an *altitude correction necessary to moon altitude observations, owing to the relative proximity of the moon to the earth. The true altitude of a heavenly body is a measure of an arc of a vertical circle contained between the celestial *horizon of an observer and the true direction of the body from the earth's centre. For all celestial bodies except the moon, their true directions from the earth's centre are regarded as being the same as from the observer located on the earth's surface. This is acceptable because of the great distances between the earth and these bodies compared with the radius of the earth, i.e., the distance between the earth's centre and an observer on its surface. For the moon, however, the angle subtended at the moon between lines which terminate respectively at the observer and at the earth's centre may be as much as nearly a degree of arc. The parallax correction for moon sights depends upon the distance between the earth and moon, the *latitude of the observer, and the altitude of the moon. Tables of parallax for moon observations are normally included in all compilations of nautical tables.

Parallax can also refer to the margin of error in reading a *compass *course where the observer or helmsman stands to one side and there is an appreciable space between the graduated edge of the card and the *lubber's line. This of course can be eradicated by standing directly above the compass when reading off the course.

paraselene, sometimes known as a 'mock moon', a weakly coloured lunar halo, a result of refraction through ice crystals, identical in form and optical origin to the solar *parhelion, which is frequently observed in high *latitudes. It is often taken as a sign of approaching wet weather.

parcel, to, wind strips of tarred canvas round a rope after it has been *wormed and before it is *served or *marled. Parcelling, like worming, is always done with the lay of the rope, and serving against the lay. As the old seamanship rule has it:

> 'Worm and parcel with the lay,
> Turn and serve the other way.'

The object of worming, parcelling, and serving a rope is to make it watertight, and thus prevent it from rotting in those parts which are continually subject to immersion.

parhelion, sometimes known as 'mock sun' or 'sun dog', either or both of two luminous spots having a reddish tinge on the inner edge, that appear on both sides of the sun, usually in high *latitudes. The effect is caused by the refraction of sunlight within hexagonal ice crystals whose axes are vertical. See also PARASELENE.

Park Avenue boom, a main *boom fitted for a period in *J-class yachts during the 1930s when these racing yachts were at their most exotic. It was triangular in section with a wide flat top, which was why it was named after the very wide street in New York. On this top was fitted a series of transverse rails at short intervals along the boom's length into which metal slides sewn along the *foot of the *Bermuda mainsail fitted. Stops, which limited the movement of the slides, were positioned on the rails to allow the *foot of the sail to take up a gentle curve, in order to prevent any turbulence and to get a better aerodynamic flow as the wind passed across the sail. The width across the top of the Park Avenue boom was sufficient to allow a reasonably generous curve, an effect which is today often achieved more economically by the use of metal booms with inbuilt flexibility.

Park Avenue booms proved no more than a passing phase in big yacht racing, the fractional gain in sail efficiency being probably at least counterbalanced by the loss caused through the additional windage of the over-large boom.

parrel, originally a rope threaded with *trucks but later an iron collar by which the lower *yards of a square-rigged ship were held to the mast giving them freedom to be *braced round to the wind. The *topgallant and smaller yards were held to the mast with a parrel lashing, which was a length of rope with an *eye at each end. It was passed round the yard and round the after part of the mast, the ends being then brought back, one over and one under the yard, and the two eyes lashed together. As square-rigged ships, and of course their yards, grew larger with the years, these smaller yards were generally held to the mast with a parrel rather than with a parrel lashing. A parrel lashing was also sometimes used to secure the *heel of a topmast or topgallant mast to the head of a lower mast or topmast as an additional security to the *cap and *fid. For illus. see YARD.

passaree, a rope used in square-rigged ships when running before the wind, with the lower *studdingsail *booms rigged, to haul out the clews of the foresail to the ends of those booms in order to get the maximum spread of the sail.

patent log, see LOG.

pawl, one of a series of metal dogs, hinged at one end, at the bottom of the barrel of a *capstan, which drop into scores in a pawl-ring round the capstan at deck level and prevent it from taking charge and overrunning when being used for *weighing an *anchor or lifting a heavy load.

pay, to, pour hot pitch into a deck or side *seam after it has been *caulked with *oakum, in order to keep out water.

pay off, to. A sailing vessel's head pays off when it falls further off the direction of the wind and drops to *leeward. It is a term used particularly in relation to *tacking when the bows of the ship have crossed the wind and she continues to turn away from the wind until she reaches the position when her sails are full and drawing.

pay out, to, slacken a cable or rope so that it can run out freely to a desired amount. It differs from casting off in that when a rope or cable is paid out it is re-secured in a new position, when it is *cast off it is let go completely.

peak, (1) the upper, after corner of the four-sided fore-and-aft sail extended by a *gaff. The halyards used to hoist the outer end of a gaff sail are known as peak halyards. For illus. see SAIL. (2) The bill or end of the *palm of an *anchor; the 'k' is not pronounced when used in connection with an anchor and the word is often written as pea.

pelorus, a circular ring fitted to the rim of a *compass bowl and carrying two sighting vanes, used for the taking of azimuths (*bearings) of celestial objects. The ring can be easily revolved and the compass bearing read off by sighting the vanes on the required object. Alternatively, the ring can be fitted to a 'dumb' compass which can be set by hand to the *course of the ship before taking a bearing.

pendant, (1) a *strop, or short length of rope or wire with a *thimble spliced into the end, fixed on each side of the main- and foremasts of a square-rigged ship just below the *shrouds, and to which the main and fore *tackles were hooked. They received their name as they hung vertically downwards as low as the catharpings. (2) Any length of rope or wire used in those places where it is required to transmit the power of a purchase to a distant object. Generally they have a thimble or a *block *spliced into one end. They usually also have a qualifying name attached to indicate their use, as a *cat pendant, used in catting an *anchor, a mooring pendant, used to haul the end of a chain cable round the bows of a ship when two anchors are down and it is required to insert a mooring swivel.

pendant, sometimes written and always pronounced pennant, a narrow tapering flag used for signalling or to designate some particular purpose. There are ten numbered pendants and fourteen special pendants used in British naval signalling, and ten numbered pendants and an answering pendant in the *International Code of Signals.

pennant, see PENDANT.

phosphorescence, a glowing condition of the sea when the surface is broken by a wave, the dipping of oars, the bow wave and wake of a ship, etc. The cause of phosphorescence is not completely established but is generally considered to be a secretion emitted by jellyfish and other similar dwellers in the sea when disturbed, which emits light through oxidization when the surface of the sea is broken. It is known that many deep sea fish can become phosphorescent when excited, and in some varieties of mollusc the secretion of a glandular organ not only glows through the transparent body but continues to glow after being ejected into the water.

pier, a structure, usually of timber and supported on wooden piles, built out into the sea and used as a promenade or landing-stage.

pillow, a block of timber fixed to the deck of a sailing vessel just inside the *bow on which the inner end of the *bowsprit was supported. Its use was to take any wear on the deck caused by the working of the bowsprit.

pilot, a qualified coastal navigator taken on board a ship at a particular place for the purpose of conducting her into and from a port or through a channel, river, or approaches to a port.

pilotage, from the Dutch *peillood*, sounding lead, the act of navigating a vessel coastwise, especially when the land is close aboard and the water shallow. The expert *pilot is able to navigate his vessel in and out of harbour using his local knowledge of the disposition of channels and shoals and

their land- and sea-marks; and of *tides and currents and other factors which influence safe navigation. At most harbours licensed pilots are available, and the services of these expert craftsmen are invariably engaged by masters of vessels who are unfamiliar with local conditions.

pinch, to, sail a vessel so close to the wind that the *luffs of the sails are continually lifting. There are obviously some few occasions when it is desirable to pinch a sailing vessel, as for instance when it would be possible by pinching a little to *fetch a mark or other desired point of sailing without having to make a *tack, but in general a sailing vessel loses speed quite considerably when she is being pinched.

pinky, one of the oldest types of New England fishing and trading vessels. These small craft, from 50 to 70 feet in length, were generally *schooner-rigged with or without a forestaysail or *jib.

pintle, a vertical metal pin attached to the leading edge of the *rudder of a small boat. Normally two pintles are fitted to such a rudder, and they drop into *gudgeons, or rings, fixed to the boat's *stern, when the rudder is placed or hung, in position. This method of hanging a rudder allows it to be swung as desired through the use of the *tiller and unshipped when not required.

pipe cot, a hinged cot fitted in many yachts and small vessels where the space available does not permit the inclusion of a fixed *bunk. When not in use they are folded up and secured against the vessel's side.

pirogue or **piragua,** a seagoing *canoe formed out of the trunks of two trees, hollowed out and fastened together, usually of cedar or balsa wood.

pitch, (1) a mixture of tar and coarse resin, fluid when heated and hard when cooled, used to cover the *oakum when caulking the *seams of a vessel's deck or sides. (2) Pitch of a propeller, the distance which a ship is moved forward in calm water by one revolution of her propeller.

pitchpole, to, overturn, of a vessel upended by heavy seas so that it turns *stern over *bows.

plain sailing, an expression which has come into the English language to mean anything that is straightforward and easy. The origin of the term arose from the plane charts of the 16th century which were drawn on the assumption that the earth was flat, even though by then all navigators knew that it was not. It was not until the first *Mercator chart was produced in 1659 that the solution to the chartmaking problem of how to draw *meridians as parallel lines without distorting the navigational process was solved, but for more than a century after Mercator, most navigators continued to use plane charts for their navigation, usually explaining their errors in *longitude calculation on an easily invented ocean current. The use of these charts is known as plane sailing, often written as plain sailing, and since the use of this type of chart did not involve any calculations to convert *departure into difference of longitude, it was obviously easier for the navigator.

plane, to, (of a boat) to attain sufficient speed to cause the forward part of the hull to rise and the boat then to run along the surface of the water. In order to start planing the hull must be of a suitable form and very light in weight in relation to its sail area or power. Power boats with a V-sectioned bow and a broad flat hull are noted for their ability to start to plane above a certain speed, and to skim along the surface with only the after part of the hull and the propeller and rudder in the water. Lightweight, high-performance racing dinghies, given suitable wind and sea conditions, can get up and plane for short or longer periods depending on the continuing strength of the wind and the skill of the helmsman. While planing, a boat's speed can rise to twice or even two and a half times the theoretical maximum sailing speed of a displacement (normal heavy) boat of the same length obtained from the speed formula 1.4 times the square root of the waterline length in feet (1.4 √LWL knots). Thus a dinghy with a waterline length of 16 ft has a theoretical maximum speed under sail of 5.6 knots if it cannot plane, but if it is of the planing type with a sufficiently high power/weight ratio, under the right wind and sea conditions its speed may rise to 8 or 9 knots, when it will surge along the surface with speed rising in bursts to 12 or even 14 knots. While the boat is poised on the surface thus, and the tiller feels almost rigid in the helmsman's hand, great skill must be displayed by the helmsman to prevent a violent sheer to one side or the other and a sudden capsize. The power-driven speedboat, on the other hand, is usually quite stable as the thrust driving the boat is beneath the water surface, and the flat form of the underwater body enables the boat to be steered in sharp turns without such a high chance of a capsize.

Planing requires a suitable shape and bow on a lightweight hull which, once it reaches a certain critical speed, suddenly encounters much less resistance as the fore part of the hull lifts above the surface. In these circumstances the bow no longer has to force the water aside, so that speed immediately rises dramatically. See also HYDRODYNAMICS.

plank sheer, the outermost deck plank covering the *gunwale of a wooden vessel or the plank covering the timber heads of the *frames when they are brought up above the level of the gunwale. Another name for the plank sheer, particularly in the construction of yachts, is *covering board.

plotting sheet, a sheet of plain or squared paper on which a navigator plots position lines obtained from nautical astronomical observations to facilitate finding his ship's position. Since the scale of most navigational ocean charts is too small to allow of accurate results when used for plotting position lines, navigators generally use a plotting sheet on which they can select the most convenient scale, say one inch to one mile, with which to plot the *intercepts and position lines. By using such a scale, either the differences of *longitude and *latitude or the bearing and distance between the ship's *dead reckoning and observed positions can be accurately measured off on the plotting sheet and then transferred direct to the chart.

plug, (1) a tapering piece of wood or a screwed metal stopper, used to stop the drain hole in the bottom of a small boat. (2) The name given to the pattern, or male former, on which the hulls of small craft, such as yachts and harbour boats, are moulded in *fibre glass.

point, a division of the circumference of the magnetic compass card, which is divided into thirty-two points, each of 11° 15'. The compass card shows four cardinal points (N., S., E., W.) and four half cardinal points (NE., SE., SW., NW.), the remaining twenty-four divisions being full points. Each point on the card is subdivided into half and quarter points. When *boxing the compass, the points are always read from the cardinals and half-cardinals, and the points and their nomenclature, from north to east, in the first, or north-east, quadrant of the card, are N., N. by E., NNE., NE. by N., NE., NE. by E., ENE., E. by N., E., and so on for the other quadrants.

A point of the compass was, in the days of the older square-rigged ship, about the smallest division to which an average helmsman could steer by wheel, but with the growing efficiency in the rig of these vessels it was possible for a good helmsman to hold a *course between the points. This led to the introduction of half and quarter points, the half point measuring $5° 37.5'$ and the quarter point $2° 48.75'$.

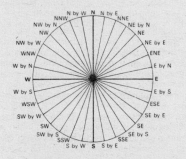

Points of the compass

The requirements of more efficient coastal navigation which came from the growing volume of shipping, and particularly with the realization of the effect of *variation and *deviation on both the course steered by a ship and the accuracy of compass *bearings in fixing her position on a *chart, led to the abandonment of points as a means both of steering a vessel and of taking bearings and their substitution by degrees, each quadrant being divided into $90°$. With the exception of due east and due west, all courses and bearings are read from the two cardinal points of north and south. Thus a ship with a magnetic compass which might formerly have steered a course of, say, NE. by E. would today steer a course of N. $56°$ E. Since both variation and deviation are always expressed in degrees east or west of north, this system of subdivision of the compass card makes it a simple matter to apply the corrections which are entailed in converting compass courses and bearings into true courses and bearings.

The term is still used, however, in expressing approximate bearings in relation to the ship's head. A lookout, on sighting another vessel at sea, may report its position as, for example, two points on the *starboard bow, or a point abaft the *port *beam, as the case may be. But even this use of the term is gradually dying out with the growing tendency to report such positions in relation to red (port side) and green (starboard side), and a report, for example, of a vessel bearing green 45 is rapidly taking the place of its equivalent of four points on the starboard bow.

point, to, taper the end of a rope to prevent it becoming *fagged out and also to make it more handy for reeving through a *block. The rope is unlayed for a short distance from the end and the *strands gradually thinned down until they finish in a point. The length of the pointing is then *whipped with a *West Country whipping to hold the strands together.

point of sailing, the heading of a sailing vessel in relation to the wind. When a vessel is sailing as near to the wind as she can, she is said to be *close-hauled to the wind, i.e., with her sails sheeted (hardened) well in and just full of wind without any shivers in the sails. With a *Bermuda racing rig, a yacht can sail close-hauled about $3\frac{1}{2}$ *points ($39°$) off the wind, a Bermuda cruising yacht about 4 points ($45°$), a gaff-rigged vessel about $4\frac{3}{4}$ points ($50°$–$55°$), and a square-rigged vessel about 6 points ($70°$). When her desired course takes her further off the wind, she is said to be sailing *free, i.e., she can begin to free her sheets to present a squarer aspect of her sails to the wind. When the wind is within the angle of about two points ($22°$) before the beam and four points ($45°$) abaft the wind, a vessel is said to be *reaching across the wind, and in many cases this is her fastest point of sailing, particularly when the wind is blowing from abaft the beam. On this point of sailing, her sheets are eased well away so that the angle of the main *boom is at a little less than a right angle to the direction of the wind.

When the wind is blowing within the angle of 4 points ($45°$) either side of the stern, the vessel is said to be running with the wind, and she has her sheets eased right away to allow the boom to take up the

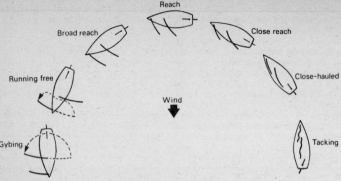

Reach

Broad reach

Close reach

Running free

Close-hauled

Wind

Gybing

Tacking

Points of sailing

broadest possible angle to the wind direction. See also BY THE LEE, a condition of sailing which frequently arises when a vessel is running before the wind.

polacre, a ship or *brig peculiar to the Mediterranean. In the ship version, with three masts, they were usually *lateen-rigged on the fore and *mizen and square-rigged on the main, but occasionally square-rigged on all three. In the brig version they were normally square-rigged on both masts. A feature of their design was that the masts were formed from a single spar so that they had neither tops nor *crosstrees. There were no *footropes to the yards, the crew standing on the topsail *yards to loose or *furl the *topgallant sails and on the lower yards to loose, *reef, or furl the topsails, the yards themselves being lowered sufficiently for that purpose.

Polaris or **Ursae Minoris,** the brightest star in the constellation of Ursa Minor, more commonly known as the Pole Star, and sometimes as Stella Maris, the seaman's star. It is a star of the 2nd magnitude, and by describing a circle of only 2° 25′ daily about the North pole, is of great service to navigators since it points, within a degree or two, to the true north. The *altitude of Polaris is also virtually equal to the *latitude of the observer.

polyester, a family of man-made fibres, which includes Terylene and Dacron, with a slightly lower tensile strength and less elasticity than *nylon but with a good all-round performance. Polyester rope is made either braided or in three-strand form and is widely used in sailing vessels for *halyards, headsail and mainsail *sheets, and

many other purposes on board. As a cloth it is used extensively for sails, where its small stretch under load is not enough to affect its efficiency.

poop, to. A ship is pooped, or pooping, when a heavy sea breaks over her *stern or *quarter when she is *scudding before the wind in a gale. It is a situation of considerable danger, and in smaller craft, such as yachts, it will bring a great weight of water inboard. The danger of being pooped in a heavy following sea can always be reduced by slowing down the ship's speed in relation to the speed of the sea by towing a *drogue.

A vessel pooped

poppet, a small squared piece of wood fitted inside the *gunwale or *washstrake of a boat which has *rowlocks to take the oars when the boat is being rowed. Poppets are shaped to the rowlocks and provide support to the gunwale at these points. See also SHUTTER.

port, (1) the left-hand side of a vessel as viewed from aft. The name probably owes its derivation to the fact that the old-fashioned merchant ships had a loading, or lading, port on their left-hand side, and the later sailing warships also had their entry port on that side. Originally, the left-hand side of the ship was known as the *larboard side, but this was changed officially to port in 1844 to avoid any confusion with the similar sounding *starboard, or right-hand, side. (2) A harbour with facilities for berthing ships, embarkation and disembarkation of passengers, and the loading and unloading of cargo.

port gybe. A *fore-and-aft rigged sailing vessel is sometimes said to be on the *port *gybe, instead of on the port *tack, when the wind comes from abaft the beam on the port side.

port tack, the situation of a sailing vessel with her sails trimmed for a wind which comes over the *port side of the vessel. Although the verb 'to tack' postulates a vessel sailing *close-hauled, a vessel on any point of sailing is on the port tack if the wind comes over her port side. But see also PORT GYBE.

position line, a line drawn on a *chart or *plotting sheet, as a result of a *bearing or *sight, on which the ship from which the bearing or sight is taken must lie. A position line is usually indicated by a single arrow head at each end, this serving to distinguish it from other lines on the chart or plotting sheet. For details of the part it plays in fixing a ship's position, SEE NAVIGATION.

pram, a *dinghy usually used as a small *tender to a yacht, frequently with a truncated or sawn-off bow.

preventer, the name given to any additional rope or wire rigged temporarily to back up any standing *rigging in a ship in heavy wind and weather. It is most usually associated with sailing vessels, and particularly with the mast *stays of such ships.

prick, to, sew an additional central seam between the two seams which are normally employed to join the *cloths of a sail. This was normally only done when the sails were worn and the original stitching weakened by long wear.

prime, to, in general nautical terms, make ready in relation to immediate use. A *lead is primed before taking a *sounding, and in the days of hand pumps the pump was primed by having water poured into the barrel so that the leather washers would take up firmly on the lining of the barrel.

prime meridian, from Latin *primus*, first and *medius dies*, middle-day, the terrestrial *meridian from which *longitudes are measured eastwards or westwards. The longitude of the prime meridian, which is the meridian of Greenwich, is 0°.

proa, (Malay *prau*), in the Malay language the term for all types of ship or vessel but generally looked upon by Westerners as the vessel used by pirates in eastern waters. Proas carried a very large triangular, usually *lateen, sail and an *outrigger to prevent excessive heel.

propeller, the rotating screw of any engine-driven ship by which she is forced through the water. For sailing yachts with auxiliary power, propellers are usually made to fold, to *feather, or to rotate freely when the vessel is under sail, in order to minimize drag as she goes through the water.

protest, an objection by a racing yacht to a rival on the grounds of a breach of the racing rules. To signify a protest a flag or *burgee is flown from the *shrouds of the yacht immediately after the incident which has occasioned the protest. The grounds of the protest are heard after the race by a committee of the yacht club organizing the race, and can be upheld, if it is proved that a breach of the racing rules has occurred, or dismissed if the grounds of the protest are held to be inadequate.

'puff-ball', a slang name used by seamen in sail to describe a *bonnet laced to the foot of a square sail. It was also sometimes known as a 'save-all'.

pull, to, the operation of rowing with an *oar in a boat.

pulpit, a metal tubular frame, U-shaped in plan, at a yacht's stemhead or *bow, carrying the forward ends of the lifelines or guardrails for the safety of hands working on the foredeck. See also PUSHPIT.

purchase, a mechanical device to increase power or force, whether by means of levers, gears, or blocks or pulleys rove with a rope or chain. In its maritime meaning it is only the last of these which is known as a purchase, a rope rove through one or more blocks by which the pull exerted on the hauling part of the rope is increased according to the number of sheaves in the blocks over which it passes.

Where two or more blocks are involved in the purchase, it is generally known as a *tackle (pronounced taykle), though there are exceptions to this general rule when two double or two treble blocks are used, these being known as two-fold and three-fold purchases respectively. The blocks of a tackle are known as the standing block and the moving block; the rope rove through them is known as the fall and is divided into three parts known as the standing, running, and hauling parts. The amount by which the pull on the hauling part is multiplied by the sheaves in the blocks is known as the mechanical *advantage.

The mechanical advantage of a purchase is reckoned by the number of parts of the fall at the moving block, and it follows therefore that any tackle, with one exception, can be rove to advantage or disadvantage according to which block of the tackle is made into the moving block. Where the two blocks concerned each have the same number of sheaves, if the block from which the hauling part comes is made the moving block, the tackle is rove to advantage; where the two blocks concerned have a different number of sheaves, that which has the greater number should be made the moving block if advantage is to be gained.

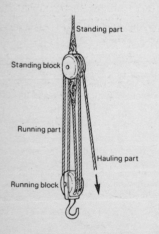

Two-fold purchase rove to disadvantage, mechanical gain 2·26

There are several combinations of blocks in a tackle, each with a name that indicates its general use or size. Where one single block is used for a straight lift, it is known as a single whip and used where speed of hoisting is required. There is no mechanical advantage as the block does not move. When rove so that the block does move, as for example when hauling taut the back-stays of a yacht, it is known as a *runner and the mechanical advantage, ignoring the loss due to friction, is 2, since there are two parts of the fall in the moving block. Double whips are tackles using two single blocks with the standing part of the fall secured to, or near to, the upper block. They are used for hoisting and the mechanical advantage is 2, again ignoring the loss due to friction. This is the one tackle which cannot be rove to advantage as the hauling part must come from the standing block.

The gun tackle also has two single blocks but is not used for hoisting and so cannot be called a double whip. When rove to advantage the mechanical gain is 3; to disadvantage it is 2. A *luff tackle has one double and one single block with the standing part of the fall made fast to the single block. It is used for general lifting or hauling and when rove to advantage gives a mechanical gain, ignoring the friction loss, of 4, and of 3 when rove to disadvantage. A luff tackle using smaller rope is usually known as a *jigger.

Two-fold and three-fold purchases are used only for heavy lifting, such as hoisting boats inboard. When rove to advantage, their theoretical mechanical gains are 5 and 7 respectively, when rove to disadvantage, the gains are 4 and 6, though in each case the loss due to friction of the sheaves is considerable since more sheaves are used. Allowing for average friction these gains are reduced to 4.37 and 3.75 when rove to advantage, and 2.26 and 3.57 when rove to disadvantage.

pushpit, a modern term for the curved tubular frame at the stern of a yacht which carries the after ends of the guardrails. It was perhaps introduced as an antonym for the *pulpit in the bows of a yacht. To many sailing people it is an inelegant word; perhaps a more sensible one, to preserve the ecclesiastical connection with pulpit, might have been reredos.

Q

quadrant, the quarters of the magnetic compass are known as quadrants when they are graduated by degrees instead of by *points. Such a compass card has 90° in each quadrant, measured from the north and south points and running to east and west. A compass card thus graduated is known as a quadrantal card. It is a method of graduation of the magnetic compass which is rapidly becoming obsolete. See COMPASS.

quarantine, a harbour restriction placed on a ship which has an infectious disease on board or has arrived from a port or country which is notoriously unhealthy. While under quarantine she must fly Q flag in the *International Code of Signals, a square yellow flag usually known as the yellow *jack, and her crew may not land until either the infectious period (a maximum of forty days in the case of plague) has elapsed or she is granted pratique as free from disease.

quarter, one of the two after parts of the ship, one on each side of the centreline. Strictly, a ship's *port or *starboard quarter is on a bearing 45° from the *stern, but the term is more often rather loosely applied to any point approximately on that bearing. The term is also applied to the direction from which the wind is blowing if it looks like remaining there for some time, e.g., the wind is in the south-west quarter. For illus. see RELATIVE BEARINGS.

quarter-blocks, two single blocks fitted on the quarters of a *yard of a square-rigged ship, one on each side of the point where the *lifts are secured, through which the topsail and *topgallant *sheets, and topsail and topgallant clewlines, are rove. Quarter-blocks on the main yard take the topsail sheets and clewlines, those on the topsail yard take the topgallant sheets and clewlines. (For illus. see YARD.) On board yachts, blocks on the deck at the quarters, on each side of the *stern, through which the main *sheets are rove are also known as quarter-blocks.

quarterdeck, that part of the upper deck of a ship which is abaft the mainmast. It is the part of a sailing ship from which she was commanded by the captain or master, or by the officer of the watch. It was also traditionally the part of the ship where the captain used to walk, usually on the *starboard side, when he came on deck to take the air or oversee the conduct of the ship, and also from which the navigator took his *sights when *fixing the vessel's position.

quay, a projection, usually constructed of stone, along the boundaries of a harbour to provide accommodation for ships to lie alongside. When a quay is built out from the harbour boundary into the water, it is usually called a *mole.

quick flashing light, a navigational light displayed by a *lighthouse or *lightship in which quick flashes of less than one second duration are shown. See CHARACTERISTICS.

R

rabbet, from the word rebate, an incision in a piece of timber to receive the ends or sides of planks which are to be secured to it. It is used as a verb as well as a noun. Thus the *keel of a wooden ship is rabbeted to receive the sides of the *garboard *strakes and the *stem and *sternpost are similarly rabbeted to take the ends of the side strakes. A strake is rabbeted into a keel or stem and sternpost.

race, (1) the name generally used to describe strong and confused currents produced by the narrowness of channels, an uneven bottom producing *overfalls, or the crossing of two tides. **(2)** The contest of skill and seamanship when yachts take part in a race. See YACHTING.

race, to. The lack of resistance from the water will cause a ship's engine, and thus the propeller, to race, with a consequent strain on the engine, when the ship *pitches to an extent that the propeller is occasionally lifted out of the water.

rack, to, hold two ropes together temporarily with *marline or other small stuff to bind them firmly and prevent rendering or slipping. This is done by taking the marline under and over each rope alternately and crossing it between them two or three times, much in the fashion of a series of figures of eight. It is often used to prevent a *tackle slipping while the hauling part is being secured if the strain on it is so great that the tackle cannot be held with the hands without overrunning. If a more permanent junction of two ropes is required, this is done by passing a racking *seizing round them, as above but with more turns of the marline and the ends of it secured by tucking back under the turns.

radar, an abbreviation of 'RAdio Direction And Range', a method of detecting objects by sending out pulses of radio waves; if these strike anything they are reflected back and the time taken for these 'echoes' to return is measured in a cathode ray tube. As the speed of radio waves is known, this time can be automatically translated into the distance of the object. Direction is given by the direction in which the transmitting aerial points at the time.

The information is presented to navigators in plan form on the face of the cathode ray tube. As the transmitting aerial revolves to 'scan' all round a ship, so a 'trace' revolves in exact synchronism with it on the fluorescent face of the tube, and each echo arriving back from an object brightens the trace at a distance from the centre of the tube corresponding to the distance of the object. Thus a complete picture of all surrounding radio-reflective objects is painted on the screen. The range is conditioned by the height of the aerial, but is seldom less than 25 miles on modern vessels.

Radar reflector, a metal plate or similar object fitted to buoys or other *sea-marks to reflect radar waves and give a positive identification on the cathode ray tube.

raddle, the name given to small stuff (*marline, *codline, etc.) interwoven to make flat *gaskets, or *gripes, for securing boats when hoisted on the *davits of a vessel.

radio beacon, a land-based radio station which transmits medium frequency signals, by means of which the navigator in a ship fitted with a *radio direction finder can obtain a radio bearing to give him a position line on his *chart. The necessary details relating to radio beacons can be found in the *List of Radio Signals*, a periodical publication issued by the British Admiralty, and in some nautical almanacs. Radio beacons provide a radio aid which is particularly valuable to a mariner making a *landfall, when navigating coastwise in thick weather, or when *landmarks or *sea-marks are not available. They are additional to, and in no way part of, hyperbolic systems of *navigation.

radio direction finder, a navigational instrument by which a *bearing of a radio beacon can be obtained and plotted on a chart. A wireless aerial in the form of a loop is directional, and if it is turned on its axis, there are two points, 180° apart, where the strength of the signal loses volume and fades away. These points are known navigationally as nulls, and they occur when the loop is trained at right angles to the transmitting station. The correct bearing is therefore at right angles to the plane of the loop when the null occurs.

Radio beacons transmit signals regularly on fixed frequencies, varying from 250–420 kHz, and each can be recognized by its frequency and type of signal. The signal is transmitted once every three or six minutes, and as beacons are frequently grouped so that a vessel can often be within the operating range of two or more beacons at the same time, a *fix by two or more position lines can be obtained. The strength of beacons varies considerably, but most of them have effective ranges of between 15 and 200 miles.

Bearings taken at or around sunrise and sunset are liable to distortion, and those which cross land, or cross the coast at a narrow angle, can give readings some degrees in error. A wise navigator, when taking a bearing by radio direction finder, avoids if he can the beacons which entail the signal crossing the land, particularly if the ground is high.

raffee, another name for the triangular sail in a square-rigged ship known as a *moonraker, or skyscraper, set only in light weather. It comes within the general classification of all such sails as *kites.

rake, the angle, in relation to the perpendicular, of a ship's masts. It is a word also sometimes used to describe the degree of overhang of her bow and stern.

ram schooner, a *schooner which does not set *topmasts but is rigged with pole *masts only. It is also sometimes known as a bald-headed schooner.

randan, a method of balancing three rowers in a boat so that equal thrust is generated on either side. Stroke and bow row one oar each while the man in the centre rows a pair of oars.

rap full, the point of sailing where a vessel keeps as close to the wind as she can without any shiver or lift in the *luffs of her sails; in other words her sails are full without a wrinkle in them. It is another way of saying *full and by.

rate of change, a correction which is applied to the reading of a *chronometer when a navigator in a ship works out the *Greenwich Mean Time of an observation of a heavenly body which he has taken for the purpose of fixing his ship's position.

rating, a calculation of a yacht's expected performance relative to another yacht round a racing course, based upon measurement of the yacht rather than observed performance. A rating rule is the rule of measurement and calculation by which a yacht's rating is produced. Rating may be used, together with a time allowance formula, to permit yachts of different rating to race against each other with a handicap based on rating, and may also be used to control the size and proportion of yachts that can race against each other at a fixed rating without handicap.

There have been many rating rules over the years and they have varied in the factors that they have measured, how they have measured them, and in the formulae in which the factors have been combined. The common feature of all rating rules is that they have expressed the ratings in linear units of feet or metres. The earliest rating rules were intended to restrict the variations of proportions of yachts within classes that were to race without handicap. Examples of these rules were the rater classes of the late 19th century, a class of which is still sailing on the Thames at Kingston. Later examples of the same principle were the International classes of the International Yacht Racing Union where the actual rules differed in their values and limits in determining the 6-, 8-, 10-, 12-, 15-, and 23-metre classes. Of these rules the best known today is the 12-metre, which is still used for the *America's Cup contests. In the USA, the Universal rule was used in the same way to control the R-, M-, and

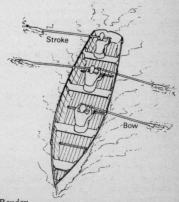

Randan

*J-classes. The J-class rule was used for the 1930, 1934, and 1937 challenges for the *America*'s Cup.

In the years between the two world wars the advent of ocean racing required the use of rating rules under which cruising yachts of different types and sizes could race together. Of these the best known were the rules of the Cruising Club of America (the C.C.A. rule) and the Royal Ocean Racing Club (the R.O.R.C. rule). After the Second World War efforts were made over the years to bring these two rules into line and progress was made in unifying the restrictions on rig and sail dimensions. The two rules were finally brought together in 1970 to become the International Offshore Rating Rule (I.O.R. Mk. II), the forerunner of I.O.R. Mk. III which is in operation worldwide today. This rule is used for handicap racing with time allowance systems in local races and such international events as the *Admiral's Cup. It is also used in the 'Ton Cup' classes for races at fixed ratings without handicap.

The principle underlying any rating rule is that a yacht's ultimate speed is proportional to the square root of its waterline length. However, these speeds are only reached in strong winds, and at lower speeds the amount of sail area that a yacht spreads, and also her displacement, will affect her performance. All rules therefore specify a measurement of length, which is usually some combination of the waterline length and the bow and stern overhangs. There will also be rules for the measurement of sail areas in the different parts of the rig. The displacement of the yacht will be included in some form, either by weighing or by measurement of the immersed depths of the hull at certain points. Corrections are also included for items such as beam, draft, freeboard, engines and propellers, centreboards and keels, all of which have some effect on a yacht's performance. Some measurement of stability or ballast ratio is also necessary to encourage adequate strength in the hull structure. These measurements have finally to be combined to arrive at a rating. As an example, in the I.O.R. Mk. III rule:

$$RATING = \left(0.13 \, \frac{L \times \sqrt{S}}{\sqrt{(B \times D)}} \right.$$
$$+ \, 0.25 \, L + 0.2 \, \sqrt{S} + DC + FC \bigg)$$
$$\times \, EPF \times CGF \times MAF$$

where L is a measure of length, S is a measure of the sail area, B × D is a measure of beam × depth or bulk, DC and FC are draft and freeboard allowances, EPF is the engine and propeller factor, CGF is the stability factor, and MAF is a factor for movable keel surfaces.

ratline, one of a series of rope steps up the *shrouds of a mast, 15 to 16 inches apart, by which men working aloft in square-rigged ships reach the *yards via the *tops and *crosstrees. Ratlines are normally made of 18-thread tarred rope with an *eye in each end *seized to the outermost shrouds, being secured to each intermediate shroud by a *clove hitch.

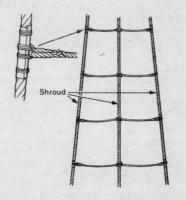

Shroud

Ratline

rattle down, to, secure the *ratlines to the *shrouds with a series of *clove hitches round each shroud except the forewardmost and aftermost, where the ratline is seized to the shroud through an eye.

reach, (1) the *point of sailing of a vessel which can point her *course with the wind reasonably *free and her sails full throughout. A broad reach is the same but with the wind abeam or from slightly abaft the beam. For illus. see POINT OF SAILING. **(2)** A straight, or nearly straight, stretch of a navigable river or estuary.

reach, to, sail with the sails full and the wind free. A sailing vessel which overtakes another is sometimes said to reach ahead of her. It was also a word used to describe a sailing vessel when she was standing off and on, waiting perhaps to pick up a *pilot or for some other purpose. See also FORE-REACH.

'ready about', the order in a sailing vessel to *tack. See also 'LEE-OH'.

reckoning, the record of *courses steered and distances made good through the water since the time at which the ship's position was fixed by shore or astronomical observations. This record used usually to be kept on a log-slate and times of altering course and distances made as indicated by the log on each course were chalked up on the slate. At the end of each watch the record was transferred to the *log book and the relieving officer-of-the-watch started his watch with a clean slate. By applying an allowance for current and *leeway to a *dead reckoning position the navigator arrives at an estimated position, this being his best estimation of his ship's position at any given time until new observations provide a *fix.

red duster, the colloquial name for the Red Ensign flown by all British Merchant ships and also by yachts belonging to yacht clubs which do not have a warrant to fly the White Ensign or a defaced Blue Ensign.

reef (1) the amount of sail taken in by securing one set of *reef-points. It is the means of shortening sail to the amount appropriate to an increase in the strength of wind. In square-rigged ships, sails up to the *topsails normally carried two rows of reef-points, enabling two reefs to be taken in; sails set above them usually had no reef-points as they would normally be *furled or sent down in a wind strong enough to require the sails to be reefed. In *fore-and-aft rigged ships, *gaff or *Bermuda sails usually have three sets of reef-points. Triangular foresails normally have no reef-points, being reefed either with a patent reefing gear which enables them to be rolled up on the *luff or, more usually, by substitution of a smaller sail. In square-rig, the first reef is at the *head of the sail and is reefed up to the *yard; in fore-and-aft rig the first reef is at the *foot of the sail and is reefed down to the *boom. Another method of reefing a mainsail set on a boom, almost entirely restricted to yachts, is to roll the sail down by rotating the boom until the sail has been shortened sufficiently for the weather conditions. This is known as **roller reefing**. (2) A group or continuous line of rocks or coral, often, though not necessarily, near enough to the surface of the sea for waves occasionally to break over it but, generally speaking, at a depth shallow enough to present a danger to navigation.

reef, to, shorten sail by reducing the area exposed to the wind, an operation required when a vessel begins to labour because of the strength of the wind. To double reef, to tie down a second reef in a sail. See also REEF, SPANISH REEF.

reef-band, a strip of extra canvas *tabled on to a sail of a square-rigged sailing vessel along the line of the *reef-points to support the strain on the points when the sail is reefed.

reef-cringles, *thimbles spliced into the *bolt- rope on the leeches of a square-rig sail at the ends of the *reef-bands. When the sail is to be reefed, the cringles are hauled up to the *yard and lashed to it. In fore-and-aft rig sails, the reef-cringles, similarly set in the lines of the *reef-points, become the new *tack and *clew of the sail when a reef is tied down.

reef knot, a square knot formed of two half hitches in which the ends always fall in line with the outer parts. It is used when it is required to join two pieces of rope, particularly if they are of equal thickness, and, of course, when tying *reef-points. It is one of the commonest and most useful knots used at sea.

Reef knot

reef-points, short lengths of small rope set in the *reef-bands of square-rig sails used to tie down a reef. In fore-and-aft rig, the reef-points are usually set direct on to the sail, reef-bands being unusual in these sails. In both cases the reef-points are secured to the sail by a *crow's-foot.

reef-tackle, a *tackle which is hooked into the *reef-cringles of a square-rig sail to hoist it up the yard for reefing.

reeve, to, pass the end of a rope through the *throat and thus on to the *sheave of a *block when forming a *tackle, or through an *eye, *thimble, or *cringle. Generally, when the end of a rope is passed through anything, it is said to be rove through it.

refraction, the bending of light rays as they pass from one transparent medium to another of different optical density, an important consideration when using celestial bodies for fixing a ship's position. Light from an observed celestial body or from the observer's visible horizon suffers atmospheric refraction, that in the former case being called celestial refraction, and that from the horizon terrestrial refraction. The effect of atmospheric refraction is apparently to elevate celestial objects and the horizon, so that it is necessary to make allowance for this effect when converting observed *altitudes to true altitudes. The altitude correction known as mean refraction is defined as the angular measure along an arc of a vertical circle between the true and apparent directions of a celestial body, when atmospheric temperature, pressure, and humidity are normal. Abnormal refraction gives rise to effects such as *looming and *mirage. Mean refraction varies from about 33 minutes of arc for objects on the horizon to nothing for objects at the zenith. See NAVIGATION, Celestial.

register tonnage, see TONNAGE.

relative bearings, the *bearings of objects in relation to a ship's head. They can be expressed in two ways, as bearings on the port or starboard bow, beam, quarter, etc., with the expressions 'fine' or 'broad' to add further definition, or, more accurately, in degrees from ahead on each side of the vessel, with the prefix 'red' if on the port side and 'green' if on the starboard. When relative bearings are given in this way, the word 'degrees' is always omitted.

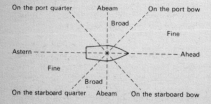

Relative bearings

render, to, (1) ease away gently, for example by taking one or two turns with a rope or *hawser round a *bollard or *winch and easing it slowly to absorb a heavy pull upon it. (2) (Of a rope) to pass over the *sheave of a *block. A seaman talks of a rope rendering through a block, and never passing through it.

reverse sheer, see SHEER.

rhumb line, (from the Old French *rumb*, a compass *point), a line on the earth's surface which intersects all *meridians at the same angle. Meridians and parallels of *latitude are rhumb lines, the angle of intersection being respectively 0° and 90°. Rhumb lines which cut meridians at

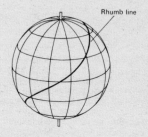

Rhumb line

Rhumb line

oblique angles are called loxodromic curves, from the Greek *loxos*, meaning oblique, and *dromos*, meaning running. The radial lines on a compass card are also called rhumbs, and the term 'sailing on a rhumb' was often used in the 16th to 19th centuries to indicate a particular compass heading. The extension of a radial line of the compass card through the fore-and-aft line of ship ahead clearly will cut all the meridians the ship crosses at a constant angle, this being equivalent to the *course angle. It is easy to see, therefore, that a line of constant course is a rhumb line. On a plane surface, this would be the shortest distance between two points, and over relatively short distances where the curvature of the earth is negligible, it can be considered so, and a rhumb is thus used for plotting a ship's course. Over longer distances at sea, and especially ocean passages, *great circle sailing provides a more direct course, but even so, the inconvenience of having to change course continually when following the path of a great circle between the points of departure and destination of a voyage makes rhumb-line sailing the popular method of navigation. In other words, navigators are content in general to sacrifice distance for convenience.

Because of the importance of rhumb-line sailing, the principal requirement of a navigator in relation to his *chart is that it should be constructed on a projection on which rhumb lines are projected as straight lines. Such a chart is the Mercator chart which is based on the *Mercator projection.

ribband, in *naval architecture the long flexible lengths of fir fixed temporarily to the outsides of the *ribs of a wooden vessel and to the *stem and *sternpost to hold the *timbers together in *frame, until the deck *beams and *stringers are fitted. It is also a term used in connection with wooden boat construction, for which see RIBBAND CARVEL.

ribband carvel, sometimes colloquially termed ribbon *carvel, a form of construction of a lightweight wooden vessel, such as an upriver racing yacht, in which, in place of the more usual athwartship *frames, *timbers, or *ribs, a number of *stringers, splines, or ribbands are laid fore and aft from stem to stern at approximately even spacing, covering the inside seams of the fore-and-aft laid carvel planking.

ribs, another name for the *frames or *timbers of a ship as they rise from the *keel to form the shape of the hull. See also FUTTOCK.

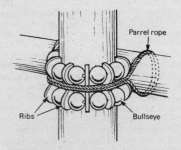

Ribs of parrel

ribs of a parrel. In an old form of *parrel in square-rigged ships, the wooden ribs forming it were separated by *bullseyes. The ribs had two holes in them through which the two parts of the parrel rope were rove with the bullseye between. The bullseyes and the smooth inner edge of the ribs bore up against the mast so that the *yard to which the parrel was applied would slide easily up and down when it was *swayed up or *struck down.

ricker, a short light spar of the kind supplied for the masts of small ships' boats, boat-hook staves, bearing-off spars, etc.

ride, to, a verb with many maritime uses. A ship rides to her *anchor when it is on the bottom and is holding her. When she is at anchor she can ride easily or hard, according to the state of the sea and the *scope of her cable, or *apeak or *athwart, according to the direction in which the anchor and *cable *grows. When at anchor she can ride to the tide or to the wind, or ride out a gale, which she can also do to a *sea anchor in the open sea or, indeed, without a sea anchor by remaining head to the gale. In a square-rigged ship a seaman on the *yards who *foots in the *bunt of a sail is riding it down. A rope round a *capstan or *windlass rides when the turn with the strain overlies and jams the following turn.

rider, a timber secured between the *keelson of a wooden ship and the orlop *beams to give her additional strength if she has been weakened by *stranding or other such cause. Riders are normally only used when the floors or timbers have been broken or damaged in order to give the vessel enough strength to enable her to reach a port for repairs. They are also sometimes known as lower or middle *futtock-riders according to the position in which they are required.

riding light, a navigational light displayed by a ship at night when she is lying to her anchor.

rig, a general term which embraces those characteristics of a sailing vessel in relation to her masts and sails by which her type is determined, such as *cutter, *yawl, *schooner, *barque, *brig, etc.

Square rig. The arrangement of sails in a vessel where the main driving sails are laced to yards which lie square to the mast. It is a rig of the greatest antiquity, originating with the single square sail set on a short mast to take advantage of a following wind. The discovery that it was possible to sail a square-rigged vessel to windward by

Longship

Sixteenth century rig with spritsails

Barque

Barquentine

Brig

*bracing the *yard so that it made a pronounced angle to the fore-and-aft line of the vessel is said to have been made by the Scandinavian longships around the 10th century AD, though possibly it was made by junks as early as the 6th century. This facility, combined with a marked increase in the size of vessel built, quickly led to a much greater versatility in the rig. As ships grew in size, the single mast was replaced by two masts, and later by three, each at first carrying a single square sail. Further growth in hull size was followed by lengthening the mast with the addition of a topmast and increasing the number of sails

set on each mast, first with *topsails and later, by adding a *topgallant mast, with topgallant sails. As in the case of the fore-and-aft rig, local conditions of sea and weather dictated to some extent the type of ship developed.

The general picture of square rig by the 15th and 16th centuries was a two- or three-masted vessel, carrying three square sails (*course, topsail, topgallant sail) on each mast, with a *spritsail carried below the bowsprit and an additional lateen or spritsail on the mizen-mast.

The introduction of staysails into the square rig came about the mid-17th cen-

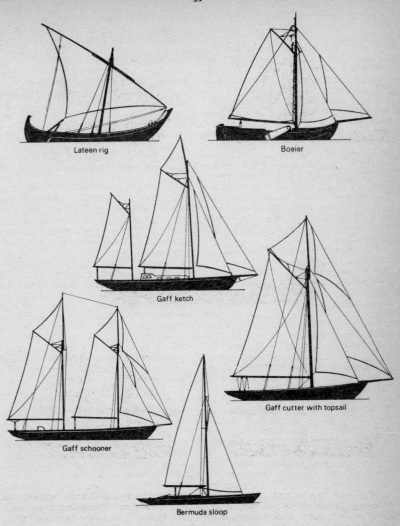

Lateen rig

Boeier

Gaff ketch

Gaff cutter with topsail

Gaff schooner

Bermuda sloop

tury, and the jib replaced the spritsail below the bowsprit about fifty years later. What is known as the ship rig (square sails on all masts) remained more or less standard until the end of the 18th century. But with the great development of world trade during the 19th century and the consequent large increase in hull size to carry it, new sail plans incorporating some features of fore-and-aft rig were developed, the barque and *barquentine for the larger three-masted ships and the *brig or *brigantine for the two-masted. These were found to be as efficent under sail as the ship-rigged vessels and had an advantage, in terms of trade, of requiring a smaller crew through the replacement of square sails by fore-and-aft sails on the mizen-mast.

A further development during the 19th century was the introduction of the *clipper ship, though this was less a development of square rig than one of hull form. In the competition for trade during the early years of the century, the choice was between a hull designed to carry a large amount of cargo at a relatively slow speed or a small cargo at a relatively high speed. The clipper hull was developed in the USA, where speed was accepted as the criterion, the remainder of the trading world largely opting for the deeper, broader hull and larger cargoes. Nevertheless, there were some specialized cargoes, particularly tea and wool, where a premium was placed on speed, and some famous clippers were built in Europe with these cargoes in view.

The final development of the square rig came as late as the early 20th century to take advantage of the last of the great trade routes still open to sailing vessels, the route around Cape Horn for the Chilean nitrate trade. Whereas the steamship had effectively killed the sailing ship on all other routes, she could not compete in the waters south of Cape Horn, partly because of the lack of coaling stations along the route and partly because of the mechanical damage inherent when propellers raced in the troughs of the huge seas, and until the Panama Canal was opened in 1914 this trade remained in the hands of the big sailing ships. Much of it was carried in the big three-masted barques of Britain, France, Germany, Spain, and Finland, but with the world demand for nitrates outstripping cargo capacity, four- and five-masted ship-rigged and barque-rigged vessels were built, with the five-masted full rigged ship in fine weather setting as many as six square sails on each mast together with four jibs, eight staysails, and a *spanker. These big square-rigged ships, the ultimate in power and beauty, were mostly built in Germany for the famous 'Flying P' line.

All square-rigged ships carry a number of fore-and-aft sails, but the criterion as to the correct nomenclature rests on the main driving sails. Where they are set from yards, the rig is considered to be square irrespective of the number of fore-and-aft sails set; where the main driving sails are set by their luffs, the rig is recognized as fore-and-aft. The various hermaphrodite rigs, such as barque, barquentine, and brigantine, are classed as square-rigged ships although in some cases they may carry as many, if not more, fore-and-aft sails as square sails. See also RIGGING, SAIL.

Fore-and-aft rig. The arrangement of sails in a vessel so that the *luffs of the sails abut the masts or are attached to *stays, the sails, except in the case of *jibs and *staysails, being usually extended by a *boom at the foot and, in the case of four-sided sails, by a *gaff at the head. In some cases, such as *barge and *lug rigs, the boom and gaff are replaced by a single *sprit or yard.

The fore-and-aft rig dates back in Europe to the early 15th century, being introduced largely by the Dutch in or about 1420, though there is some evidence of earlier use in the East many centuries before that, some authorities dating its introduction there to the first century AD. This would be the *lateen rig, a hermaphrodite development of a simple square rig into a fore-and-aft rig by elongating the yard and setting it at a pronounced angle to the mast along the fore-and-aft line. It is probable that, so far as Europe is concerned, the earliest form of fore-and-aft rig was a four-sided mainsail set on a sprit, and that the fore *staysail, a triangular sail set on the forestay, was introduced to provide a better sailing balance and prevent excessive *weather helm.

The invention of the gaff and boom came about a century later, the first known example being found in a picture of Dutch ships painted in 1523. Probably it developed naturally as vessels grew in size, for the larger the ship, the longer and heavier the sprit. A massive sprit would well be worth replacing on weight grounds alone by two smaller and handier spars, and even more so when experience showed that such substitution increased in large measure the overall efficiency of the rig, particularly when working to windward. Indeed, for a great many years the gaff was known as a half-sprit.

Local development over the next two or three centuries produced a variety of fore-and-aft types of sailing vessel, the shoal waters of Holland and eastern England lending themselves particularly to types of barge rig, such as the *boiers and *botters of Holland and the *wherries and Thames barges of eastern England, where *leeboards are used in place of a fixed *keel to avoid the danger of grounding when crossing sandbanks, etc. In the Mediterranean, where deep water and steady winds were the governing factors, variations on the lateen rig provided the main types, while in American waters the schooner, carrying more canvas on the foremast than on the main, was widely used as a main type. In very general terms, the overall pattern of fore-and-aft rig, certainly in European waters, was a four- sided mainsail set on a gaff and boom, a triangular staysail, and a jib set on a *bowsprit, and possibly a small four-sided sail set on a mizen-mast, as in *ketches and yawls.

The next major development of the fore-and-aft rig came with the gradual abandonment of sail for commercial purposes and the contemporary growth of yachting as a sport. This period extended from about 1850 until the end of the century, by which time the fore-and-aft rigged commercial ship (with the exception of sailing barges) had been almost completely replaced by steam vessels, and yachting was growing fast in popularity. In the search for extra speed, the gaff mainsail was extended upwards by jib-headed or jackyard topsails, the bowsprit was lengthened to enable additional jibs to be set, and the boom extended beyond the *counter so that a larger mainsail could be spread. The ultimate development of the fore-and-aft rig was the introduction of the *Bermuda rig, first developed in the West Indies at the start of the 19th century and brought to Europe for use in sailing yachts in the years just preceding the First World War (1914–18). It is now the most widely used rig in sailing yachts, and during the last twenty years has been significantly developed on aerodynamic principles to provide greater driving power with a smaller overall sail area.

The main emphasis of this aerodynamic development is the progressive transfer of the driving power of the wind from the main to the fore triangle, by shortening the foot of the mainsail to present a taller and narrower sail area to the wind and by increasing the size of the jib or staysail by extending the luff to the masthead and sheeting the clew abaft the mast. Apart from thus increasing the area of the fore triangle, this has brought an added dividend by funnelling the wind over the luff of the mainsail and increasing the partial vacuum in the lee of the mainsail luff which provides some of the forward pull when sailing close to the wind. See AERODYNAMICS.

A majority of today's racing and cruising yachts use a *sloop or *cutter rig, but *ketches, *yawls, and *schooners are also popular for cruising. These are well established rigs which have been in use for well over a century. A new type is the Freedom rig which has been developed for handling entirely from the cockpit. It employs two unstayed masts, the after one normally but not always shorter than the foremast, on which are set two triangular-shaped sails. These are wrapped around the mast so that they are doubled, and are held out to the wind not by a boom but by a *wishbone spar which protrudes downwards at approximately 45 degrees from about the middle of the mast to the *clew of the sail. The sails are loose-footed and unlike the old wishbone rig (see WISHBONE) both are sheeted in the normal way. The Freedom rig is rated under some handicap rules but is banned by the International Offshore Rating Rule (see RATING).

rig, to, in a sailing vessel to set up the standing rigging, send up the *yards, and *reeve the running rigging; in a powered vessel to set up the standing rigging only, there being no running rigging. The word is also used of many other operations on board ship, such as to rig an awning, to rig a *boom, etc.

rigger, a man employed in boatyards to fit or dismantle the standing and running *rigging of sailing vessels. His duties include all the stretching, *splicing, *serving, and *seizing required before setting up a ship's rigging.

rigging, the term which embraces all ropes, wires, or chains used in ships and smaller vessels to support the masts and *yards and for hoisting, lowering, or trimming sails to the wind. All rigging used in the support of masts and yards, and a *bowsprit when fitted, is known as standing rigging.

In a square-rigged ship this is both extensive and complex, as the number of masts involved varies from two to four in the case of sail training ships still in commission and operational; and in the 19th-century heyday of sail trading there were occasionally as many as six or seven. Each mast consisted of at least three separate parts, and occasionally four when a *royal mast was added, each of which needed its own support. In addition each mast had up to six or seven yards crossed on

Principal elements of a ship's standing rigging

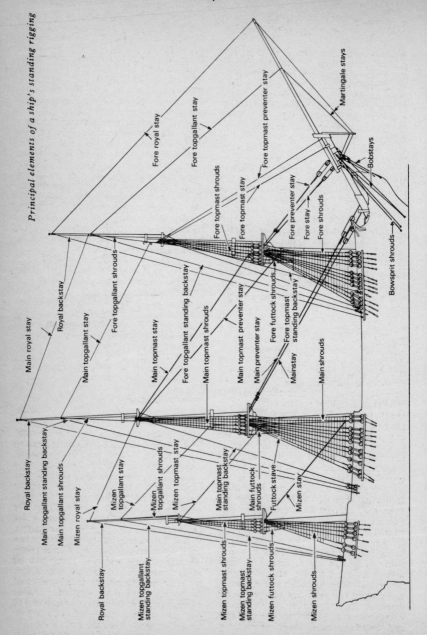

Martingale stays

Bobstays

Fore royal stay

Fore topgallant stay

Fore topmast preventer stay

Fore topmast shrouds

Fore topmast stay

Fore preventer stay

Fore stay

Fore shrouds

Bowsprit shrouds

Main royal stay

Royal backstay

Main topgallant stay

Fore topgallant shrouds

Fore topgallant standing backstay

Main topmast stay

Main topmast shrouds

Main topmast preventer stay

Main preventer stay

Fore futtock shrouds

Fore topmast standing backstay

Mainstay

Main shrouds

Royal backstay

Main topgallant standing backstay

Main topgallant shrouds

Mizen royal stay

Mizen topgallant stay

Mizen topgallant shrouds

Mizen topmast stay

Main topmast standing backstay

Main futtock shrouds

Futtock stave

Mizen stay

Royal backstay

Mizen topgallant standing backstay

Mizen topmast shrouds

Mizen topmast standing backstay

Mizen futtock shrouds

Mizen shrouds

it and each of these, too, had its own
standing rigging to support it.

Athwartship support. A mast is supported athwartships by *shrouds, which
run from the *hounds, or a *stayband
where this is fitted in their place, a short
distance below the top of the mast to the
*chain-plates on the outer side of the hull
opposite the mast. Originally made from
special four-stranded rope, they are today
normally made of steel wire rope or, in
most modern yachts, of mild steel bars.
When made of rope or wire, the lower ends
allow for torsioning, originally by means of
lanyards threaded through *deadeyes but
today by *bottlescrews or similar forms of
rigging screws, so that any temporary
slackness in the shrouds can be taken up. In
large square-rigged ships, multiple
shrouds spaced about 2 feet apart at the
chain-plate are required to take the heavy
strain on the mast exerted by large sails,
and these are secured laterally by *ratlines
which not only assist in maintaining and
equalizing the tension in each shroud but
also form a rope ladder by which men
ascend the mast to work on the yards.

In sailing ships where topmasts and
*topgallant masts are fitted, the supporting
shrouds are led from their hounds or
staybands to the *top of the mast below,
this top being a platform, which rests on
the *crosstrees and *trestle- trees, and
provides an adequate span to spread the
shrouds so that the topmast or topgallant
mast is held rigidly in place laterally. The
trestle-trees are held in place by *cheeks,
bolted to each side of the mast, and the tops
themselves, besides being secured to the
crosstrees and trestle-trees, are further
supported by *futtock shrouds, which are
led from the outer ends of the top downwards to a futtock stave secured to the
shrouds or to a stayband round the mast.
Individual shrouds are designated by the
mast they support as, for example, fore
shrouds, main topmast shrouds, mizen
topgallant shrouds, etc.

Longitudinal support. To hold a mast
firmly in the fore-and-aft direction, *stays
are used. In the case of a foremast,
particularly when extended with a topmast
and a topgallant mast, the support base is
extended by a *bowsprit, with further
extension by a *jib-boom. The bowsprit
and jib-boom must of course be themselves
supported before they can be used to hold
the foremast, and this is done laterally by

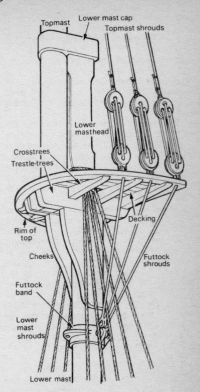

Mast top and fittings

pairs of shrouds led from the end of the
bowsprit and the jib-boom and secured to
plates at the widest part of the bows.
Longitudinal support is provided by a
*bobstay led from the end of the bowsprit
to a fitting on the vessel's stem near the
waterline, and by *martingale stays led
from the end of the jib-boom and similarly
secured to the stem. In order to give a wider
angle of support, a *dolphin striker is fitted
to lead the martingale stays down at a less
acute angle than would otherwise be possible. A foremast is held by a forestay secured
at its bottom end to the *stem, or sometimes to the deck just inside the stem, and
at its top end to the stayband. A fore
topmast is stayed from the bowsprit end to
the fore topmast stayband, and a fore
topgallant mast from the end of the jib-
boom to its stayband. These stays support
their masts against pressures exerted by the

sails which would tend to force the mast over towards the stern of the ship. Main- and mizen-masts are similarly supported in this direction by stays led from the mast ahead of them; a mainmast, for example, by stays from the tops of the three masts which make up the foremast, and so also for the mizen-mast. A stay which extends from masthead to masthead is known as a *triatic stay.

To provide support for the opposite pressure exerted by the sails, i.e., with a following wind which tends to force a mast over towards the bows of the ship, *back- stays are fitted. These are led aft from the tops of the various masts and secured to the ship's sides, one on each side. In a fore- and-aft rigged ship where the mainsail is extended by a *boom, these two backstays are known as *runners, and terminate at the deck in a single *purchase or *Highfield lever so that, when running with the wind *free, the lee runner can be slacked away to allow the boom to swing forward and present a squarer aspect of the sail to the wind. On this point of sailing, the weather runner is set up taut to hold the mast securely against the forward pressure of the sail. In many modern yachts, where the boom is short enough to swing across inside the stern, runners are replaced by a permanent backstay secured to the yacht's *counter.

The yards. In a square-rigged ship, the yards also have their standing rigging. Their weight is supported by *lifts, usually wire rope but occasionally made of chains, one on each side of the mast running from a band round the mast above the yard to each *quarter of the yard. The centre of the yard is secured to the mast itself by a *truss or *parrel, which is loose enough to allow the yard to turn on the mast when it is *braced round to the wind. At intervals along the yard, short perpendicular ropes, known as *stirrups, support the *horse, or footrope, which is held parallel to the yard two or three feet below it to provide a secure foothold for men *reefing or *furling the sails. For illus. see YARD.

Running rigging. All rigging used in hoisting, lowering, or trimming the sails of a vessel, or hoisting or *striking the yards of a square-rigged ship, is known as running rigging. Purchases used for hoisting sails are known as *halyards, those for hoisting the yards as *jeers. In square-rigged ships, only the triangular sails—jibs and stay- sails—have halyards; the square sails are hoisted up to their yards in bundles by *jiggers and then laced to the yards ready for spreading when required. Since they are very heavy sails, they have small lines or purchases, known as *buntlines, leading down from the yard to the foot of the sail to assist in gathering them up when reefing or furling. As with the standing rigging, individual halyards take the name of the mast they serve, as fore halyards, main halyards, etc. In the case of *jibs, they are known as jib halyards.

Fore-and-aft rigged ships have all their sails hoisted by halyards, originally of hemp but today mainly of flexible wire

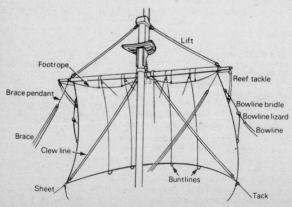

Elements of square running rigging

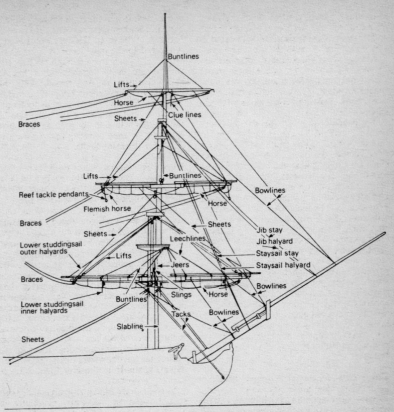

Foremast showing the principle elements of a ship's running rigging

rope, frequently with a Terylene, or occasionally hemp, tail for ease of handling where sails are hoisted by hand. In the case of *gaff rig, the sails have two halyards, one for the *throat and another for the *peak of the sail. *Topping lifts are also fitted to the booms to take their weight and ensure a better set of the sail, while gaff-rig mainsails frequently have *vangs fitted to the peak of the gaff to prevent it sagging away to leeward.

Fore-and-aft sails are trimmed to the wind by *sheets, rove with a purchase except in the case of very small sails where a single rope is adequate. Square sails are not directly trimmed to the wind; the yards are trimmed by *braces attached to each yardarm and led aft, and the sail, laced to the yard along the whole of its length, must therefore take up the same angle. But when a square-rigged ship is *close-hauled to the wind, the individual sails can be trimmed in a little harder by the *bowlines, which are attached to *bridles on the *leeches of the sail, and led forward towards the ship's bows. When the bowlines on the *weather leeches are hauled hard in, they keep the leech taut to the wind so that a better leading edge is obtained. In addition, a tack (led forward) and a sheet (led aft) is attached to the clews of all square sails in order to get a better trim of the sail.

Other running rigging in a ship are, for example, the *guys of *spinnakers and in general any moving rope or wire used in the everyday running of a vessel (with the exception of such specialized articles as anchor *warps, mooring ropes, and wires, etc.) is considered as running rigging. See also RIG.

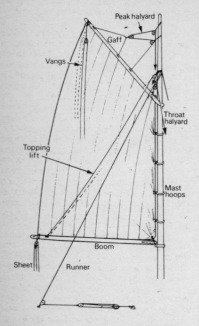

Gaff mainsail—an example of fore-and-aft rig

Labels in diagram: Peak halyard, Gaff, Vangs, Throat halyard, Topping lift, Mast hoops, Boom, Sheet, Runner

rigging screw, a screw clamp for bringing together the two parts of a wire rope and holding them steady while they are *spliced. See also BOTTLESCREW.

righting moment, see METACENTRIC HEIGHT.

ringtail, (1) an extension fitted to the *leech of a *fore-and-aft mainsail to provide a greater area of canvas to spread before a following wind. In earlier days it was rectangular and was attached to the leech of the *spanker and extended by a ringtail *boom attached to the main boom. Later it became triangular, with the peak secured to the end of the *gaff and the foot forming an extension of the mainsail. **(2)** A small triangular sail set on a short mast stepped on the stern of a vessel and extended by a small boom overhanging the stern, used only in light and favourable winds. Ringtails are today used in yachts

making single-handed voyages to form a self-steering device. See also VANE SELF-STEERING GEAR.

rising, a narrow *strake secured to the inside of the *frames of a small rowing boat to support the *thwarts. Risings are often used for this purpose in place of *knees in smaller rowing boats.

roach, the curve in the side or *foot of a sail. Square sails have a hollow roach in their foot to keep them clear of the mast *stays when the *yards on which they are set are *braced up, and this is known as a foot roach. When sails are roached on their sides, as in the *leech of a *gaff mainsail, they are known as leech roaches.

Roaring Forties, the area in the South Indian Ocean between the latitudes of 40° and 50° S. where the prevailing wind blows strongly from the west. Sailing ships in the Australian trade used to make for this area after rounding the Cape of Good Hope, as they could then rely on the westerly gales to lift them along their way. This was known as *running the easting down, and some of the *clippers reported exceptional daily runs in this area. The expression is also frequently used to describe the very rough parts of the oceans in the northern hemisphere between the latitudes of 40° and 50° N., particularly in the North Atlantic.

roband, orig. **rope-band,** a small, sometimes plaited, line rove through the eyelet holes in a sail with a running eye by which the *head of the sail is brought to be *laced to a *yard or *jackstay after the *earings have been secured. Robands are used only on the sails of square-rigged ships.

rocket, a pyrotechnic device used at sea mainly as a signal of distress. Rockets have also been used as recognition signals between vessels of the same shipping line, but this practice has been discouraged as leading to confusion in the meaning of rocket signals at sea, which remain basically signals of distress calling for assistance. Proposals have been made for an international code of rocket signals based on the colour of the rocket fired, such as, for example, red for distress, white to indicate position, blue to call for a pilot, and so on, but as yet no international agreement has been negotiated on this subject. See also MAROON, VERY LIGHT.

rogue knot, the seaman's name for a *reef knot tied 'upside down', the two short ends appearing on opposite sides of the knot after tying instead of on the same side. It is the knot which ashore would be called a 'granny' and is very apt to slip when it takes a strain.

rogue's yarn, a coloured yarn of jute laid up in a strand of rope to identify the materials from which it is made. Commercially made *manila rope is marked with a black rogue's yarn, naval manila rope with red in each of two strands. Commercial *sisal rope has a red rogue's yarn, naval sisal has yellow in each of two strands. Commercial *hemp has no rogue's yarn, naval hemp has red in all three strands. *Coir rope is marked with a yellow rogue's yarn in one strand only. Originally, rogue's yarns were used only in naval rope and indicated from their colour the ropeyard in which they were made. They were introduced to stop thieving by making the rope easily recognizable, as in the days of sailing navies naval rope was considered far superior to all other and there was a great temptation to smuggle it out of the dockyards and sell it to owners or captains of merchant vessels.

Rogue's yarns of different colours are also used in the running *rigging of yachts to identify the individual *halyards, *sheets, etc.

roll, to, the side-to-side motion of a ship in a seaway. See also METACENTRIC HEIGHT.

rolling hitch, a hitch used on board ship for *bending a rope to a *spar. The end of the rope is passed round the spar and then passed a second time round so that it rides over the standing part; it is then carried across and up through the *bight. A rolling hitch properly tied will never slip.

Rolling hitch

rope, the name given in the maritime world to all cordage of over one inch in diameter, whether made from natural or man-made fibres or wire. The natural fibres used in rope-making are *hemp, *manila, *sisal, and *coir, each with its own particular characteristics and uses.

Hemp rope is made from the fibres of *Cannabis sativa*, a hard, smooth rope, pale straw in colour when new but often known as white rope when in this state. It is usually tarred to preserve it against deterioration when it gets wet. It was originally used for *hawsers, running *rigging, etc., but generally today its use is confined to the smaller ropes and lines, except in some yachts, where the white Italian hemp rope is considered the best natural fibre rope for *halyards and *sheets, though it has now been generally replaced on modern yachts by synthetic rope. Manila rope is made from the fibres of the wild banana, which gives it a good strength and spring. When made up into rope it is golden brown in colour and is mainly used for such purposes as a boat's *falls, or in *tackles where considerable weights are liable to be lifted. It is the most dependable of the ropes made from natural fibres, but today is difficult to obtain as the source of supply is limited. Sisal rope is made from the fibres of the *Henniquin* plant which grows widely in Africa. Like hemp, it is a pale straw colour, but is frequently tarred to preserve it. It is a hairy rope, generally used in places where it is not subjected to great strain or the lifting of considerable weights. Coir rope, also known as *grass-line, is made from the fibre of the coconut palm. It is a very rough rope, dark brown in colour, and weaker than the other natural fibre ropes, but has advantages in that it is lighter, more resilient, and floats on water. This last property makes it particularly suitable for use as *warps. Cotton is also occasionally used for rope in yachts, but is hard and difficult to handle when wet and is liable to mildew.

The process of rope-making is the same for all these fibres. Each fibre is generally about five feet in length and, in right-handed rope, known as the *Z-twist, is spun right-handed to form yarns, sufficient overlapping fibres being used to form a continuous yarn. The spinning binds the fibres firmly together, the individual fibres being held in place by friction. The yarns are then gathered together and twisted left-handed into *strands; three strands (or four in the case of four-stranded, or *shroud-laid, rope) being laid up right-handed to form a *hawser-laid rope. The contrary twists of the strands and the rope ensures that it remains compact with no tendency to spread. The twist of the strand is known as the *foreturn, that of the rope, the *afterturn. In left-handed rope, known as the *S-twist, each component of the rope is twisted in the opposite direction.

A rough and ready rule for finding the breaking strain of rope is to divide the square of its circumference in inches by three, the answer being in tons. Thus, the breaking strain in tons of 4-inch rope would be $\frac{16}{3}$ or $5\frac{1}{3}$ tons. A general rule with all rope is to divide the breaking strain by six in order to find the working load, a factor of safety of six to one.

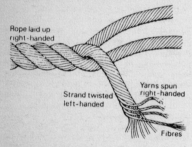

Strand twisted left-handed

Yarns spun right-handed

Fibres

Rope laid up right-handed

Right-handed hawser-laid rope

Synthetic rope, made from man-made fibres, has practically replaced natural rope, particularly in yachts, on account of its greater strength in relation to its size. The main fibres used are nylon, Terylene, and polythene, but when laid up into the normal three-stranded rope it is apt to have an unacceptable elasticity when under strain. This drawback, however, has been largely eliminated by laying up the yarns into braided rope. The strongest of the three is nylon rope. Other synthetic ropes made are Ulstron, which is pale green in colour and has the same degree of strength as Terylene rope, and Courlene, which is orange in colour and highly resistant to chafe. The great advantages of man-made fibre rope over natural fibre rope are that it does not absorb moisture, does not swell or lose part of its strength, as does natural fibre rope, and is not subject to rot.

The breaking strain of synthetic rope can be calculated, as in natural fibre ropes, by using the square of the circumference. In nylon rope the breaking strain in tons is the square of the circumference, in Terylene it is 0.9 of the square of the circumference,

and in Courlene 0.7 of the square of the circumference.

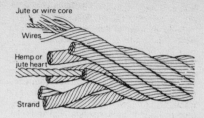

Jute or wire core

Wires

Hemp or jute heart

Strand

Wire rope

Wire rope is made with a number of small wires which extend continuously throughout the length of the rope and give it its great strength. The small wires are twisted left-handed round a jute or wire core to form strands, and six strands are laid up right-handed round a hemp or jute heart to form the rope. The heart has two functions, acting as a cushion in which the strands bed themselves and can take up their natural position as the wire rope is bent and also as a lubricant by absorbing the oil with which wire rope is periodically dressed and forcing it between the individual wires when the rope is bent in the course of its use.

Wire rope is supplied in three grades. Where flexibility is not important, as in the case of standing rigging, SWR (Steel Wire Rope) is the normal type used. Lack of flexibility in SWR is compensated for by its added strength. The individual wires are of larger gauge than in other wire ropes and are wound round a steel wire core, seven wires per strand being used in the least flexible and 19 wires where a certain amount of flexibility is needed. In cases where considerable flexibility is required, as in wire hawsers, a certain loss of strength is unavoidable. FSWR (Flexible Steel Wire Rope) is supplied for these purposes, the individual wires being of medium gauge and wound round a large jute core. The number of wires used in each strand is 30 in very flexible wire, 24 in flexible wire, and 12 in less flexible. The third grade of wire rope is ESFSWR (Extra Special Flexible Steel Wire Rope) and this is supplied in cases where flexibility and strength are both necessities. The wire used is of small gauge wound round a hemp core, 61 wires per strand in extra flexible wire rope and

37, 24, and 19 wires in the less flexible grades. The term 'extra special' refers to the quality of steel used, which is of a higher grade than in FSWR and SWR, thus producing the extra strength.

As in the case of natural and man-made fibre ropes, the breaking strains of wire rope can be simply calculated by multiplying the square of the circumference in inches by factors, that for SWR being 2.75, for FSWR being 2, or 2.5 if the circumference of the wire rope is over $4\frac{1}{2}$ inches (114 mm), and for ESFSWR being 3.6, in each case the breaking strain being in tons.

In Great Britain the size of all rope is denoted by its circumference in inches, in the USA and most other countries the size is denoted by its diameter. See also ROGUE'S YARN.

rose lashing, a *tiddley piece of *seizing by means of which the *eye of a rope is secured to a *spar. The seizing is rove in the form of a cross lashing by being passed over and under the parts of the eye, the end being brought round the whole to finish it off.

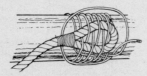

Rose lashing

round, to, a verb with a variety of maritime meanings. To round down a *tackle is to *overhaul it; to round up a tackle is to haul in on it before taking the strain. To round in is to haul in quickly, as on a weather *brace in a square-rigged sailing ship; to round to is to bring a sailing vessel up to the wind.

round of a rope, the length of a single strand when it makes one complete turn round the circumference of the rope.

round seizing, a *seizing used to lash two ropes together with a series of turns of small stuff with the end passing round the turns to finish it off. Two parts of the same rope can be secured by a round seizing to form an *eye.

round turn and two half hitches, a knot widely used when making a boat or small vessel fast to a post or *bollard. It is made by taking a full turn round the post or bollard and finishing the knot off with two half hitches round the standing part of the rope. If there is likely to be much strain on the knot, a better one for the purpose is a *fisherman's bend, as a round turn and two half hitches is liable to jam when there is a heavy pull on it.

Round turn and two half hitches

rouse-in, to, haul in any slack cable, or *slatch, which may lie on the bottom when a vessel lies to a single anchor. The reason for rousing-in such slack cable is that otherwise it might foul the anchor by becoming twisted round the shank or stock as the ship swings to wind or tide.

rowlock, a U-shaped space cut in a boat's gunwale to take the *oars. When the boat is being used under sail, or secured alongside, the rowlocks are closed with *shutters. The term is often used, though wrongly, to describe the metal *crutches used for oars in smaller rowing boats. See also THOLE PIN.

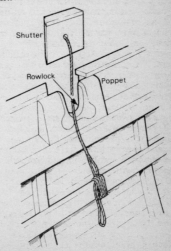

Rowlock

ROYAL

royal, the sail set next above the *topgallant-sail in a square-rigged ship, the fourth sail in ascending order from the deck, except where two topsails, upper and lower, are set, in which case it is the fifth sail in ascending order. The two clews are secured to the ends of the topgallant-yard. It is a light-weather sail, set only when the wind is steady and favourable, and was originally known as the topgallant-royal. For illus. see SAIL.

Royal Yachting Association, the controlling body in Britain for all matters concerning yachting. It was founded in 1875 as the Yacht Racing Association by a representative body of yachtsmen to control yacht racing and the design of racing yachts, with the authority to hold courts of appeal. One of the first rating rules under which yachts could race was initiated by Dixon Kemp, the celebrated designer, who was the Association's first secretary. The rating rules were amended from time to time when it was found that designers were able to produce 'rule cheaters' under the earlier formulae.

In 1881 the Prince of Wales (later Edward VII) became its president, and the influence of the Y.R.A. spread rapidly to other countries. After the Second World War its activities expanded still further as yachting extended in all its branches, until it was involved in matters affecting yachtsmen outside yacht racing. HRH Prince Philip became its new president and in 1952 its name was changed to Royal Yachting Association and it became the national authority representing yachtsmen in the United Kingdom. It is financially supported by the yacht clubs, and general purposes committees have been set up to deal with such diverse problems affecting yachtsmen as the siting of oil refineries, power cables, bridges, and firing and bombing ranges, municipal charges for moorings, river bed and foreshore rights, and pollution of coastal waters. The R.Y.A. has also been instrumental in forming the International Yacht Racing Centre in Portland Harbour and Weymouth Bay, where Olympic events as well as contests for a variety of sailing classes can be held in both sheltered and open water conditions. It is also affiliated to the International Yacht Racing Union (see YACHTING, Racing rules).

rubbing strake, a piece of half-rounded timber or rubber running the length of a small vessel or *dinghy from bow to stern on either side just below the *gunwale to act as a permanent *fender and protect the side of the vessel when coming or lying alongside another vessel or *mole, etc.

rudder, the most efficient means of imparting direction to a ship or vessel under way. The rudder was the logical development of the older steering oar and began to replace it in ships in the mid-13th century. Some of the seals of Hanseatic League ports of this period show local vessels with stern rudders, the earliest known record of this development.

Rudders in *dinghies and many other small vessels are usually hung from the *sternpost or *transom by means of *pintles, which engage in *gudgeons and allow lateral movement from side to side as required. In many yachts they are hung on a rudder stock which is led through the *counter, movement being imparted to the rudder by either a steering wheel or a *tiller. In larger vessels they are also hung on a rudder stock which enters the hull through a rudder port. A quadrant is fixed to the top of the rudder stock, known as the rudder head, and it is by means of the quadrant, with the assistance of a steering engine, that force is applied to turn the rudder as required to steer the ship. A balanced rudder is one that pivots on its central axis in order to distribute the thrust of the water on its surface.

The effect on a ship of turning the rudder depends on the principle of mechanics that to every action there is an equal and opposite reaction. When turned at an angle to the ship's *course, the face of the rudder deflects the water in the direction in which it is turned, and the reaction of this force forces the ship's stern in the other direction, and thus the ship's head in the same direction as that in which the rudder is turned.

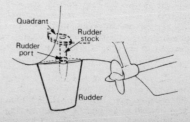

Balanced rudder

Rule of the Road, a set of thirty-one internationally agreed rules which govern the conduct of ships at sea in order to prevent collisions between them. They are compiled by the *International Convention for Safety of Life at Sea and are known officially as the International Regulations for Preventing Collisions at Sea, or colloquially as the Rule of the Road.

The thirty-one rules are divided into six parts, which cover definitions, lights and shapes to be carried by vessels at night or day by which they can be recognized, sound signals and conduct in restricted visibility, steering and sailing rules to keep vessels apart when they are approaching each other, sound signals for vessels in sight of one another, and miscellaneous signals, such as *distress signals, etc.

Of the definitions laid down, the most important are those which define a power-driven vessel and a sailing vessel. A vessel with any form of mechanical propulsion, including oars, counts as a power-driven vessel; a sailing vessel is one propelled by sails only; a yacht with her sails spread but also using her auxiliary engine is a power-driven vessel.

The lights laid down to be carried at night under the Rule of the Road serve two purposes. The navigation (or steaming) lights carried by a ship are so designed and placed that any other ship sighting them can tell reasonably accurately the *course of the vessel carrying them. Other lights laid down by the Rule of the Road are designed to indicate the type of vessel and her actual employment. See NAVIGATION LIGHTS.

During daylight signals are displayed by hoisting cones or black balls, and in fog or restricted visibility, day or night, sound signals are used to indicate a vessel's movements and sometimes her employment. The following are some of the more commonplace visual and sound signals, but this is not a complete list:

(a) A power-driven vessel in low visibility, when under way sounds one long blast at intervals of not more than two minutes; if stopped, two long blasts at intervals of not more than two minutes.

(b) A power-driven vessel towing another vessel, displays, if the length of tow exceeds 600 feet, a black diamond shape. In low visibility a vessel towing another sounds one long followed by two

short blasts on her siren or whistle at intervals of not more than one minute.

(c) All fishing vessels while engaged in fishing show a black shape consisting of two cones point to point. If outlying gear extends more than 500 feet, a black cone, point upwards, indicates the direction of the gear.

(d) A vessel under way but not under command and drifting, hoists two black balls. In low visibility, she sounds one long blast followed by two short blasts at intervals of not more than one minute.

(e) A sailing vessel under way in low visibility sounds the following signals at intervals of not more than one minute: one blast—vessel on the starboard tack; two blasts—vessel on port tack; three blasts—vessel running with the wind abaft the beam.

(f) A light-vessel when driven from her proper station shows two black balls, one forward and one aft, and the signal PC.

The most important group of rules are the steering and sailing rules, which lay down the procedure to be followed when ships approach each other and there is a danger of collision. Where this happens, the rules lay down which ship is to give way to the other. In a broad sense, vessels keep to the right when at sea. If, for example, two ships are approaching each other head on, both must alter course to starboard (or to the right) so that they pass each other port side to port side. Where a vessel is on the starboard hand of another, and steering a

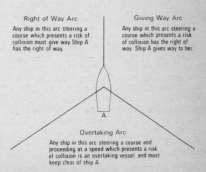

Rule of the road, powered vessels

course which may result in a collision, she has the right of way and should maintain her course and speed, the other vessel giving way to her. Where a vessel is on the port hand of another, and her course, if she maintains it, may result in a collision, she is the giving way vessel and must alter course to avoid the other. But any ship overtaking another, i.e., approaching at any angle from two *points abaft the beam on either side, must keep clear. Also, generally speaking, all power-driven vessels must keep clear of all vessels under sail, although there are always circumstances (e.g., a sailing vessel approaching a very large tanker in narrow waters) where the sailing vessel will keep clear. The only rule to which this does not apply is the overtaking rule; a sailing vessel overtaking a power-driven vessel must keep clear of her. When a vessel has the duty of giving way to another under the rules, she normally does so by altering course to pass astern of the other, and should make a clear and significant alteration of course in plenty of time to indicate to the other vessel that she is taking the appropriate action.

The rules which govern vessels under sail are clear and precise. They lay down that when two sailing vesels approach each other with the wind on a different side, the vessel with the wind on the port side must give way to the other. When both have the wind on the same side, the vessel to *windward keeps clear of the vessel to *leeward.

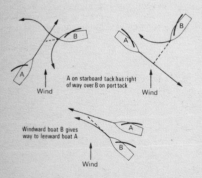

A on starboard tack has right of way over B on port tack

Windward boat B gives way to leeward boat A

Rule of the road, sailing vessels

When yachts are racing, however, they have additional rules which apply among themselves during a race, laid down by the International Yacht Racing Union. They fly a square racing flag at the masthead to indicate that they are racing and that these additional rules apply. For details of these racing rules, see YACHTING, Sail, Racing Rules. But the Rule of the Road overrides these special racing rules in cases where a racing yacht may be approaching another sailing vessel which is not herself engaged in a race and flies no racing flag.

The sailing and steering rules lay down that if a collision between two vessels appears possible, both vessels must take avoiding action even if such action involves a departure from the Rule of the Road on the part of one of them. This requirement is perhaps best summed up by the little verse which most seamen learn during the early years of their career:

'Here lies the body of Michael O'Day
Who died maintaining the right of way;
He was right, dead right, as he sailed along,
But he's just as dead as if he'd been wrong'.

run, the shape of the after part of the underbody of a ship in relation to the resistance it engenders as she goes through the water. A clean run, an underbody shape at the after end of the *hull of a ship which slips easily through the water without creating excessive turbulence. It could be said to be the complement of *entry, which describes the shape of the forward end of a ship's underbody.

run free, to, sail with the wind either well abaft the beam and within a point or two of blowing from directly astern or blowing directly from that direction. The term comes from the fact that with the wind from this direction, the *sheets of the sails are freed right away in order to present the maximum possible sail area as square as possible to the wind. See also BROACH-TO, and for illus. POINT OF SAILING.

runner, one of the two preventer *backstays, led from the masthead to each *quarter of a sailing yacht, which support the mast when the wind blows from abaft the beam. On each occasion of going *about, or *gybing, the *lee runner is *overhauled to allow the *boom of the mainsail to swing over without restriction, the *weather runner being set up taut to take the strain on the mast. In many modern yachts, in which the boom swings inside the *counter of the vessel, a single standing backstay takes the place of the two runners. See also RIGGING.

running bowline, see BOWLINE.

running rigging, see RIGGING.

run the easting down, to, sail the long easterly passage from the Cape of Good Hope to Australia between the *latitudes of 40° and 50° S., in the area known as the *Roaring Forties. It originally referred to the big square-rigged ships on the Australian run which used the prevailing westerly gales which blew in this area to help them on their way, but no doubt many of the modern yachts engaged in offshore cruising or round-the-world races continue to run their easting down in this area of the Indian Ocean.

S

saddle, a block of wood, or a wooden bracket, fixed to a *mast or *yard to support another spar attached to it. Thus, the *bowsprit of a sailing vessel has a saddle attached to it to support the heel of the *jib-boom, and a saddle on each lower yardarm supports the *studdingsail *boom in square-rigged ships.

sail, an assemblage of *cloths of canvas, Terylene, or other suitable material, cut to the necessary length and fashioned to a particular shape which is designed to catch the wind and use its force to give motion to a sailing vessel. The cloths are *seamed together with a double seam (see also PRICK) and the *leech of the sail shaped with *gores to give it the required aerodynamic curve.

Sails generally can be divided into two distinct types, those used in square-rigged ships which are set on horizontal *yards crossing the masts and those used in fore-and-aft rigged ships which are set from their *luffs on masts or *stays. There are areas where these two types of sail are used together, as with the *jibs, *staysails, and *spanker of a square-rigged ship or the occasional square sail set from a yard when running before the wind in a fore-and-aft rigged ship. The two exceptions to this general rule are *lateen sails and *lugsails which, though set on a yard, are generally accepted as fore-and-aft sails.

Square-rigged ships, setting all plain sail, have five square sails on each mast, though sometimes a sixth on the mainmast is included in this definition. Named in ascending order they are the *course, lower

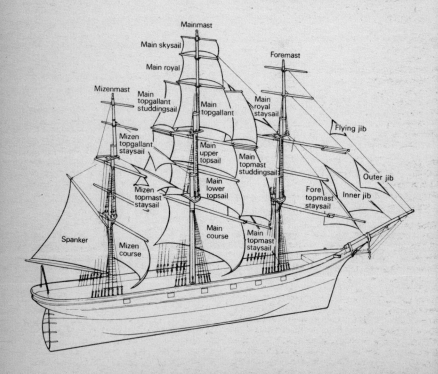

topsail, upper topsail, *topgallant, and *royal, the sixth sail on the mainmast being the *skysail. In fine settled weather, with the ship running with a wind abaft the beam, additional fine weather sails, known collectively as *kites, can be set to make the most of the wind. A short royal mast is fixed to the tops of the topgallant masts to set the *moonrakers above the royals and skysails, and *studdingsails (pron. stunsails) are set from booms rigged out from both yardarms of the topsail and topgallant yards of the fore- and mainmasts to extend temporarily the area of the topsails and topgallants. In older sailing days, the courses could also be enlarged by lacing a strip of canvas, known as a *bonnet, to the foot, but this went out of fashion at about the beginning of the 19th century. Only courses and topsails have *reef-points, and a reef is taken in on the head of the sail, not on the foot as in fore-and-aft sails. Square sails take their name from the mast on which they are set, as, for example, fore course, main lower topsail, mizen topgallant, etc.

Square sails are always cut from canvas, the working sails being of heavy duty material and the kites of lighter canvas. All square-rigged ships used to number a sailmaker among the essential crew since, with passages lasting on occasions for four months or more continuously at sea and out of reach of shore support, it was important to be self-sufficient in the making and repairing of all working sails. The four sides of a square sail are the *head (top), *foot (bottom), and two *leeches (sides), which are differentiated by the terms *weather and *lee, according to the *bracing of the yards, or port and starboard. The two top corners are the earing cringles, the bottom corners are the clews, or clues, again differentiated by weather and lee or by port and starboard. The central part of a square sail, usually cut with a full belly to hold the wind, is known as the *bunt.

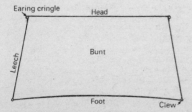

Parts of a square sail

Fore-and-aft sails are either triangular in shape, such as a jib, staysail, *spinnaker, 'leg-o'-mutton', or *Bermuda mainsail, or four-sided, such as a *gaff mainsail or a lugsail. As in the case of square sails, they take their names from the mast or stay on which they are set.

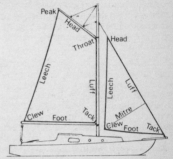

Parts of triangular and four-sided fore-and-aft sails

The four sides of a gaff sail are the head (top), foot (bottom), luff (leading edge), and leech (trailing edge), the corners are the *throat (top, leading edge), *peak (top, trailing edge), tack (bottom leading edge), and clew (bottom, trailing edge). Triangular sails have as their sides luff, leech, and foot, and as their corners tack, head, and clew. Only mainsails are reefed, either by being rolled round the boom or with rows (up to three) of reef points sewn on to the sails with *crow's feet. On occasions a reefing jib was set in fore-and-aft rig, the luff of the sail being attached to a cylindrical spar so that the jib could be reduced in size by being rolled up round the spar. But this is a comparatively rare type of sail, and the usual practice, if a vessel is carrying too much canvas forward, is to replace the jib set with a smaller one.

A gaff mainsail is frequently extended by setting a topsail above it to fill the area between the mast and the gaff. Two types of topsail can be set, a jib-headed topsail which extends from the *jaws of the gaff to the masthead, or a jackyard topsail which extends above the top of the mast to provide a greater area of sail in winds of light or moderate strength.

Until about 1950, all fore-and-aft sails were made of canvas, light or heavy according to the use of the sail in light or heavy winds. Since that date, man-made materials, such as Terylene, Dacron, etc., are much more widely used, particularly in yachts. The number of types of sail carried is also much greater so that the best use can be made of all the variations in wind strength likely to be encountered. Light winds naturally enable larger sails, such as *genoa jibs, *ghosters, and, when running with the wind abaft the beam, spinnakers to be set. These are invariably made of lightweight material, heavy canvas being used only for small storm sails such as jibs and staysails. The outfit of sails carried by a yacht is known collectively as her *wardrobe.

To set sail, strictly to hoist or loose the sails to give a vessel motion, but the term is frequently used of any ship when she departs on a voyage. **To make sail**, to spread additional sails to increase the speed of a sailing ship. **To shorten sail**, to take in or reef sails to reduce the speed of a ship. **To strike sail**, to lower it suddenly. Striking a topsail was in the old days a form of salute.

sail burton, the *purchase which extends from the heads of the topmasts to the deck in square-rigged ships and is used for hoisting sails aloft when it is required to *bend them on to the *yards. These sails are far too heavy, and the distance they have to be hoisted far too great, for them to be manhandled up the masts, hence the need for these purchases.

Sailing Directions, publications of the British Hydrographic Department of the Navy, were first produced in 1828. They are usually known as 'Pilots' and are a source of original, worldwide information, almost entirely coastal, to supplement that included on *charts. Each covers a particular area of coast, such as the Channel Pilot (southern England and northern France), China Sea Pilot, Mediterranean Pilot, etc. A main source of original information was the 'Remark' Books which masters, and later navigating officers, of HM ships were strictly enjoined to keep, and these remarks were co-ordinated and compiled in book form to cover various areas of seas and oceans. Modern additions come from a variety of sources, such as local announcements of new developments, etc. After the issue of each *Sailing Directions*, periodical corrections were made by hydrographical notices issued to all ships until, in 1884, printed supplements to the *Sailing Directions* were issued at intervals of from one to three years. The content of the *Sailing Directions*, at one time full of historical and other details of general interest, is now more restricted to their particular navigational purpose. The British series of *Sailing Directions* is completed by the volume *Ocean Passages of the World*, the only one of the Pilots which is non-coastal. Similar publications are produced of course by the authorities of other nations which produce navigational charts.

sailing thwart, a fore-and-aft *thwart running down the centre of some sailing/rowing boats to give support to the masts.

sailmaker's stitching, the types of stitching used when making sails, awnings, and other canvas articles. Most modern sails are stitched by machine, which has advantages not only of speed but also of a closer stitch with a more even tension than can be achieved with hand sewing. There are some tasks, however, that cannot be done by machine, either because of the shape of the seam to be sewn or because a machine cannot be used, for example, to draw together the edges of a tear in a sail or awning. Man-made materials, now widely used for sails in yachts, are always best stitched by machine as hand sewing tends to tear the fabric.

A sailmaker uses three types of stitch in his work, flat sewing, round sewing, and darning.

Flat sewing is used to join two pieces of cloth or canvas where strength is not of paramount importance. The selvedge edge of one piece of material is placed along the seam line of the other, both are hooked on to a sailmaker's hook to keep them taut, and the needle passed down through the single cloth close to the selvedge and then up through both cloths, and so on until the whole seam is completed, with a back stitch to terminate the line of sewing. The normal spacing is three stitches to an inch. When the first seam is completed, the work is reversed and the selvedge of the other piece of cloth sewn to the seam line in the same way. The direction of sewing in flat sewing is always away from the hook.

Round sewing is used where greater strength is required, the stitches passing through four thicknesses of the cloth instead of two. There are two forms of round sewing, known as single last and double last. In single last, each cloth to be joined has its edge turned in about half an inch, the two are then placed together, held taut with a sailmaker's hook, and joined at the edge by passing the needle through all four parts about $\frac{1}{8}$ inch from the edge and

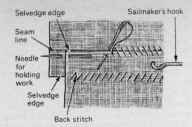

Flat sewing

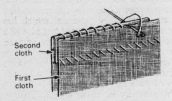

Round sewing

Sailmaker's darn

back over the top, making four stitches to the inch. In double last, the selvedge edge of one piece of cloth is placed level with the doubled edge of the other and the seam sewn as in the single last. The work is then reversed and the selvedge edge of the other piece is similarly stitched to the other, which is doubled at the seam line. In round sewing, the direction of sewing is always towards the hook.

Darning is used for the repair of small tears. The first stitch is made by bringing the needle up through the canvas about one inch from the side of the tear, down through the canvas a similar distance on the other side, then up through the tear and through the bight formed by the twine. Subsequent stitches are made by passing the needle through the tear, up through the

canvas on one side, down on the other side leaving a small bight, and then up through the tear and the bight. This forms a locked stitch, each one being drawn taut as it is finished. The stitches are made close together to give greater strength. See also TABLE, MONK'S SEAM.

sailmaker's whipping, a whipping used in cases where it is essential that it should not slip or come adrift, as in the ends of the *reef-points of a sail. It is made by unlaying the rope to be whipped for two or three inches and passing a bight of the whipping twine over the middle strand, leaving the two ends of the twine, one short and one long, and the bight hanging downwards. The rope is then laid up again and the turns of the whipping passed round the rope using the long end of the twine and working against the *lay of the rope and towards the end. When the whipping is long enough to take the bight, it is passed up outside the whipping, following the lay of the strand over which it was originally placed, and finally over the top of the same strand. The short end of the twine is now hauled taut, so that the bight is tightened, and is itself then brought up outside the whipping, again following the lay of the rope. The whipping is completed by joining the two ends of the twine with a reef knot concealed in the middle of the rope. See also COMMON WHIPPING, WEST COUNTRY WHIPPING.

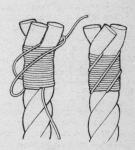

Sailmaker's whipping

St. Elmo's fire, the brush-like electric discharge which, under certain atmospheric conditions, takes place at the mastheads and yardarms of a ship. It is known by over fifty different names. It is also occasionally seen on aircraft flying among thunder clouds and sometimes on prominent points like church spires ashore.

salvage, a proportion of the value of ship or cargo paid by the owner or his insurance company to those by whose means they have been saved when in danger. The proportion is based on the labour and danger of saving the ship or cargo and the state of the prevailing weather. No salvage can however be claimed by the crew of a ship for their efforts in saving their own ship or its cargo.

sampan, the typical small light boats of oriental waters and rivers. There are two types, the harbour sampan which usually has an awning over the centre and after part and is normally propelled by a single *scull over the stern, and the coastal sampan fitted with a single mast and *junk-type sail. The origin of the name is said to come from the Chinese *san*, thin, and *ban*, board, but some hold it to have a Malaysian origin.

samson post. In the old days when *anchors were catted before being let go and on weighing, a samson post was a post erected temporarily on deck to take a *tackle with a sufficiently long lead for the whole crew to man the *fall. When all anchors had to be handled entirely by manpower, a large number of men were required on the tackles used in lifting and stowing.

sandbagger, a type of broad, shallow, open or partly decked sailing boat which originated about 1850 in America, and in which movable ballast in the form of sandbags was used while racing. The vogue lasted, mainly around New York harbour and at New Orleans, only some thirty years, when the boats, generally of the *cat-boat type, were divided into four classes: 26–30ft, 23–26 ft, 20–23 ft, and under 20 ft. They carried immense sail plans of mainsail and *jib, and agile crews of eight or more who shifted the sandbags on to the weather deck every time the boat *tacked. This type of spectacular racing, which usually carried wagers on results, disappeared during the 1880s with the advent of finer designs of yachts for racing, but it became a popular sport in Sydney harbour, New South Wales, where it lasted as a class until the 1960s.

Sargasso Sea, an area of the North Atlantic east of the Bahama Islands and stretching approximately between 25° and 30° N. and 40° and 60° W. where a powerful eddy in the water causes the Sargasso weed (*Fucus natans*, originally named *sargaço* by the Portuguese) to collect in vast quantities and float on the surface. It is mentioned by Christopher Columbus in his accounts of his voyages to the New World. This area of weed has given rise to many stories of ships trapped in it and unable to make their way out, a belief prevalent among many seamen of older days but finally disproved by Sir John Murray in the expedition of the *Michael Sars* in 1910 which proved that the surface was covered only in patches. It is said also to be the main breeding place of eels, the elvers swimming to Europe in the Gulf Stream.

save-all, a slang name given by seamen to a small additional sail or *bonnet which was sometimes set under a *studdingsail in a square-rigged ship in very fine weather with the wind *abaft the beam. It was also sometimes used to describe the bonnets proper, laced to the *courses, and also occasionally called by the slang term 'puff-ball'. There have been some references to this sail under the name *water sail, but this is an obviously wrong use of the term.

scandalize, to, reduce sail in *fore-and-aft rig by hauling up the *tack and lowering the *peak of a sail. It was used by the older sailing trawlers to reduce speed through the water when operating a trawl. Also the *yards in a square-rigged ship are said to be scandalized when they are not set square to the masts after the ship has anchored. Scandalizing the yards of a ship was a sign of mourning for a death on board.

scantlings, originally the dimensions of a *timber after it has been reduced to its standard size. It is now extended to cover the dimensions of all parts which go into the contruction of a ship's hull, including her *frames, *stringers, etc. Rules governing these sizes, based on long experience and study, are published by *Lloyd's Register of Shipping, and most ships of any size built throughout the world are constructed to these Lloyd's rules.

scarf or **scarph,** the joining of two timbers by bevelling off the edges so that the same thickness is maintained throughout the length of the joint. In the construction of a wooden ship, the *stem and *sternposts are scarfed to the *keel. A scarf which embodies a step in the middle of the joint, so preventing the two parts from drawing apart, is called a lock scarf. It is a joint of great antiquity, having been used by the early Egyptian and Phoenician shipbuilders.

A scarfed spar

scend (pron. send), the quick upward motion when a ship is *pitching in a heavy sea. In its old meaning it was the opposite of pitching, the quick roll when a sea knocks a vessel off her *course, but this meaning has now died out. Scend of the sea, the surge of the sea as it runs into a harbour.

schokker, a Dutch fishing vessel of the middle part of the Zuider Zee, usually from Enkhuisen, with a flat bottom, curved sides, a straight *stem raking at about 45°, and narrow *leeboards. They are similar to *hengsts but are generally larger. Dating from the early part of the 18th century, the schokker was normally built of oak in sizes varying between 45 and 52 feet in length and 16 to 19 feet in beam. They were originally rigged with a *sprit mainsail and a *gaff mizen in addition to a forestaysail and a jib set flying on a *bowsprit. Later schokkers were built of steel and some have been converted or built as yachts.

schooner, (Du. *schooner,* Ger. *schoner,* Dan. *skonnert,* Sp. and Port. *escaña*) all possibly deriving from the Scottish verb 'to scon or scoon', to skip over water like a flat stone. An alternative source for the name is said to have been a chance remark 'there she scoons' from a spectator at the launch of the first vessel of the type at Gloucester, Mass., in 1713, and there is some evidence that the type originated in North America and probably at Gloucester.

Whatever the origin of the name, a schooner is a vessel rigged with *fore-and-aft sails on her two or more masts, which originally carried square topsails on the foremast, though later, with the advance in rig designs, these were changed to jib-headed or *jackyard-topsails. Today, small schooner yachts normally set *Bermuda sails and thus have no topsails. Properly speaking, a schooner has two masts only,

with the mainmast taller than the fore, but three-masted, four-masted, and five-masted schooners have been built, and one, the *Thomas W. Lawson,* had as many as seven. They were largely used in the coasting trade and also for fishing on the Grand Banks off Newfoundland, their attraction to owners being that they required a smaller crew than a square-rigged vessel of comparable size.

sirocco, an alternative spelling of the Mediterranean wind *sirocco.

scope, the amount of *cable run out when a ship lies to a single *anchor. The minimum amount of cable to which a ship should lie is generally taken as three times the depth of water in which she is anchored, but conditions of wind and tide and the nature of the holding ground may call for up to double this amount. The scope of a ship's cable is approximately the radius of the circle through which she swings under the influence of the tide; approximate only because her cable is unlikely to lie in a straight line stretched taut between anchor and ship.

score, (1) the name given to the groove cut in the shell of a wooden *block in which the *strop is passed. Blocks are stropped with an *eye or hook at the top so that they can be used wherever necessary, and the score prevents the strop from slipping off the shell of the block. Similarly it is the groove cut round the body of a *deadeye for the same reason. **(2)** The space vacated in a rope when unlaying a strand in the course of making a *long splice is also known as a score.

scotchman, a piece of hide, or a wooden batten, secured to the *backstays or *shrouds of a sailing vessel so that any running rigging coming into contact with them should not be chafed. The name comes from the scotch, or notch, cut in the hide or batten along which is passed the line securing the scotchman to the backstays or shrouds so that it does not slip.

scow, a large boat, very full in the *bilges and with a flat bottom, used as a lighter or as a ferry to transport men a short distance at sea. Scows were either towed or pulled with oars. The term is used in the USA today to describe a small flat-bottomed racing yacht fitted with bilge boards or retractable *bilge keels.

screw, see PROPELLER.

scud, to, (of a sailing ship) to run before a gale with reduced canvas, or under bare poles in the case of gales so strong that no sails can be left spread. It is apt to be a dangerous practice, with the risk of the vessel being *pooped.

scull, the name given to a light oar as used in a *dinghy, particularly of a size which can be pulled by a single rower with one in each hand.

scull, to, in its original meaning, give a small boat headway by working a single oar to and fro over the stern of the boat, but this definition has now been extended to embrace one man working a pair of *sculls in a *dinghy or other light boat. See also YULOH.

scupper, one of the draining holes cut through the *bulwarks of a ship on the *waterways to allow any water on deck to drain away down the ship's side. Scupper shutters are flaps fitted over the outboard side of the scuppers and hinged on the top so that the pressure of water inboard will swing them open while water pressure outside the ship will keep them firmly closed.

scupper, to, a word with the same meaning as to *scuttle, deliberately to sink a ship by opening the seacocks in her hull or by blowing a hole in her side below the waterline. It presumably arises in the same general way as scuttle, from the idea of making a ship sink until the sea comes in through her scuppers to finish her off.

scuttle, a circular *port cut in the side of a ship to admit light and air, consisting of a circular metal frame with a thick disc of glass which is hinged on one side and which can be tightly secured to the ship's side by butterfly nuts. A deadlight, which is a metal plate hinged on the top and also secured by a butterfly nut at the bottom, is also fitted to a scuttle to prevent any light from inboard showing to seaward at night when a ship has to be darkened, as in time of war. Although many people call them portholes, the proper and more seamanlike name is scuttle.

scuttle, to, deliberately to sink a ship by opening her seacocks or by blowing holes in her bottom. The word may arise (as with the synonymous verb to *scupper) from the idea of making a ship sink to the level of her *scuttles when the sea will pour in through them and finish her off.

sea anchor, anything that will hold a vessel's bow to the sea in heavy weather. Oars, casks, or loose sails lashed together and veered from the bow on as long a line as possible will act as a satisfactory sea anchor to which a vessel can ride out a storm. Various forms of *drogue are often offered as sea anchors, but usually the vessel's own gear will prove as efficient a sea anchor as any. In very severe gales, such as typhoons, a ship's *anchor lowered to some depth on its cable has often been used to hold the ship's head to sea.

seam, the narrow gap between the planks forming the sides and decks of vessels constructed of wood which is *caulked with *oakum and pitch to keep out the water. As wood swells when it is in contact with water, a narrow seam between the planks must be left to accommodate the expansion, and as the planks 'take up' when immersed, they compress the oakum and add to the watertightness.

seam, to, the work of the sailmaker when joins together the *cloths from which a sail is made with a double seam. See also PRICK, SAIL, TABLE.

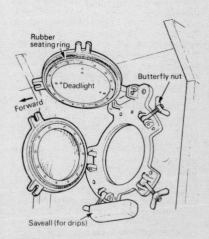

Scuttle

seamanship, in its widest sense, the whole art of taking a ship from one place to another at sea. It is an amalgam of all the arts of designing a ship and her motive power, whether sail, steam, or other means, of working her when at sea and in harbour, and the science of navigation by which the way is found from her point of departure to her point of arrival. It thus embraces every aspect of a ship's life in port and her progress at sea.

Seamanship, however, has also a narrower meaning, divorced from a ship's design and engines, from her navigation, and from the other specialist skills which have their part in the smooth running of a ship. It is that department of a ship's being which is concerned with the rest of the daily management of the ship, her gear, boats, anchors and cables, rigging; her sails if she is a sailing vessel; and the watch kept at sea and in harbour. It embodies a knowledge of knotting and splicing, of handling ropes and *hawsers, *blocks and *tackles, and it also embraces a knowledge of the weather and the means of competing with storms, of the *Rule of the Road, and of lights and their meanings. In fact, every aspect of the day-to-day work of the ship, apart from the specialized skills of the navigator, the engineer, the radar operator and telegraphist, are considered to be within this narrower meaning of the word.

sea-mark, the seaman's name for any floating navigational mark, such as a *buoy or *lightship, as opposed to a *landmark, which is a prominent mark on shore from which a navigational *compass *bearing can be obtained or which can be used as a *leading mark to indicate a safe channel. Because a sea-mark has to be *moored to the seabed and can drag its mooring, good navigators usually treat them with some caution when using them to *fix a ship's position. In olden days, marks set up ashore were known as sea-marks, not landmarks, and in its original charter *Trinity House was empowered to set up sea-marks ashore whenever necessary as an aid to navigation. Any person found destroying them was subject to a fine of $100, and if unable to pay, was to be outlawed. See also LEADING MARK.

section, a drawing made during the design stages of a ship showing the positions of the *frames and their exact curvature in relation to the hull shape of the vessel.

seize, to, bind with small stuff as, for instance, one rope to another, or the end of a rope to its own part to form an eye. There are many varieties of *seizing according to the method of binding and the function which is to be served, such as flat or round

seizing where the binding twine is passed in continuous turns, racking seizing where each turn is crossed between the two parts being seized, throat seizing where the seizing is passed with the turns crossing each other diagonally, etc. A seizing is always 'clapped on'.

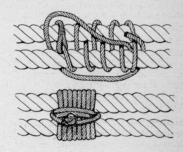

Racking seizing

seizing, (1) the cord or twine, generally known as small stuff, by which ropes are *seized to each other. **(2)** The name given to the finished product when the two parts have been seized together.

self-steering gear, an arrangement by which a ship can be left to steer herself on a desired course for long periods. In sailing vessels, particularly in ocean-going yachts, self-steering arrangements are usually based on a *vane mounted on the yacht's *counter. See, e.g., VANE SELF-STEERING GEAR.

selvagee, an untwisted skein of rope yarn *marled together to form a *strop. Selvagee strops are used for a variety of purposes on board ship, such as slings for heavy weights required to be hoisted by a *purchase or for securing masts and oars in ships' boats to prevent them rolling about in a seaway, etc.

semaphore, from the Greek *sema*, a sign and *phoros*, bearing, a telegraph which conveys signs by a machine with movable arms. The word was first introduced into Britain in 1816 when Admiral Sir Home Popham's new signalling system was installed to replace the older telegraph invented by the Revd. Lord George Murray and first set up in 1796. The days of Popham's semaphore as a long-distance signalling system began to be numbered in 1838 when Wheatstone's experiments in

electric signalling had their first major
success with signals made in London being
read in Birmingham. Thenceforward the
spread of the electric telegraph was rapid,
and the last of Popham's naval signal
stations, that at Portsmouth Dockyard, was
closed in April 1849.

Popham's semaphore poles, however,
did not die out with the closing of his long-
distance system, for it was quickly recognized as an admirable method of short-
distance communication for shore station-
to-ship, and ship-to-ship messages. It
became a universal code, widely used at sea
by ships of all nations, either by means of a
miniature Popham machine in which the
arms were worked by chain and sprocket
gear or by hand flags used as an extension
of a signalman's arms. It still remains a
simple, rapid, and reliable means of communication within visual range. See INTER-
NATIONAL CODE OF SIGNALS.

semi-diameter, a correction which has
to be applied to an *altitude observation of
the sun or moon when measured with a
*sextant. When a navigator takes a sun or
moon sight, he normally brings the lower
edge of it down to the horizon with his
sextant and reads off the angle on the
sextant scale. But the true altitude should
be measured with the centre of the sun or
moon brought to the horizon, and so a
correction must be made to the angle read
off the sextant to allow for half the
diameter. In comparison with stars, which
are so far distant from the earth that semi-
diameter can be ignored, the sun and moon
are relatively close, and there is an appreciable difference in the sextant angles
measured from the lower edge and the
centre. A table of semi-diameters is included in all editions of nautical tables.

serve, orig. **sarve, to,** wind *spunyarn
close round a rope which has been
*wormed and *parcelled, the serving being
wound on with a *serving mallet or board
to obtain maximum tension, with the turns
made against the *lay of the rope. The
purpose of worming, parcelling, and serving a rope is to make it impervious to water
and thus to preserve it against rot. The
expression was also used in the case of ships
which, through age or weakness, had their
hulls served round with *cables to hold
them together. See also MARL, POINT.

serving mallet, a wooden hand mallet
used on board ships for passing a serving
round a rope. The bottom of the mallet has

a semicircular groove which fits round the
rope, and marline or tarred hemp, with
which a serving is made, is led from the
rope and a turn with it taken round the
handle of the mallet. As the mallet is turned
round the rope, the spunyarn renders
round the mallet handle, by which means it
can be kept taut and the serving applied
with the maximum tightness. A board,
with a similar groove at the bottom, is
sometimes used instead of a mallet. See
SERVE.

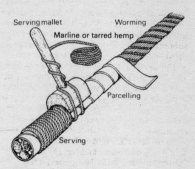

Worming, parcelling, and serving

set, (1) the word used as a noun and a verb
to denote the direction in which a current
flows and also the direction of the tide, e.g.,
'the tide is setting to the southward', and
the distance and direction in which a vessel
is moved by the tide in relation to its
desired *course and distance run. **(2)** It is
also applied to sails in relation to their angle
with the wind as, for example, in the set of a
*jib or the set of a mainsail. It has many
other maritime uses as a verb: a ship sets a
*course when she is steadied down on it, a
sail is set when it is hoisted and sheeted
home to the wind. But to set sail, said of a
ship when she departs on a voyage regard-
less of whether she uses sails or not. To set
an *anchor watch, to detail a member of
the crew of a ship to see that she does not
drag her anchor when lying at anchor or
*moored.

settee, a two-masted ship of the Mediterranean, *lateen-rigged on both masts.
Settees were single-decked with a long
sharp bow, and belonged more to the
eastern Mediterranean than to the western.
Their dates are from the 16th to about the
mid-19th century. Occasionally they were
called balancelles, from the double lateen
rig.

settle, to, after a sail has been hoisted, to ease a *halyard away slightly, usually a *peak halyard when a *gaff sail has been hoisted to such an extent that there are wrinkles in the canvas at the *throat of the sail. Where these occur, they are the result of the peak of the sail having been hoisted too high, and the halyard is then settled until the wrinkles have disappeared.

sextant, the modern navigational instrument for the measurement of vertical and horizontal angles at sea. It is an instrument of double reflection by means of two mirrors, and thus although its actual arc subtends an angle of 60° at the centre, it is capable of measuring angles up to 120°.

The sextant was developed in 1757 from an old nautical astronomical instrument called a quadrant, which could measure angles only up to 90°, following a suggestion of Captain John Campbell of the British Navy. The requirements for the additional 30° arose from the need to make lunar observations in order to discover a ship's *longitude, and even after the *chronometer had been perfected, by which longitude could be easily obtained and lunar observations made unnecessary, it was retained in use in preference to the quadrant as its additional measurement capability was still found to be of value in the measurement of horizontal angles.

rant, with a fixed mirror mounted on an arm of the sextant in line with the observer's telescope and parallel to the index bar when it is set at 0° on the sextant scale. This mirror is only half silvered, so that the horizon can be seen through the plain half and the reflected object seen in the silvered half. A second mirror is mounted on the index bar, which is pivoted at the centre of the sextant, and as the index bar is swung, so this mirror swings with it. When a navigator takes an *altitude of a heavenly body, he holds the sextant perpendicular and swings the index bar along the arc of the sextant until he can see the object of his sight (sun, moon, or star) reflected from the mirror on the index bar, which has of course swung with the bar, on to the silvered half of the mirror on the sextant arm, and he can also see simultaneously through the plain half of the mirror. Once it is there, he reads off the altitude indicated by the position of the index bar on the arc of the sextant, which is graduated in degrees and minutes. A vernier on the index bar gives an accurate interpolation between the minutes.

A modern sextant in perfect adjustment is capable of an accuracy of better than half a minute of arc.

shackle, a U-shaped iron closed with a pin across the jaws and used for securing such things as *halyards or sails, other parts of standing or running rigging where required, *anchors to their *cables, and joining lengths of chain cable, etc. Shackles

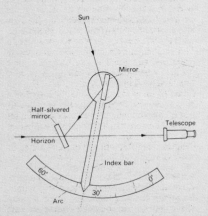

Path of light through sextant

The modern sextant employs the same optical principles as John Hadley's quad-

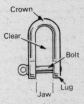

Shackle

used in the rigging normally have a threaded pin which is screwed into one of the jaws; those used to join lengths of cable are of two kinds. The older type of joining shackle is closed by a bolt flush with the lugs of the jaws which is kept in place by a tapered pin. This is driven into place with a hammer and punch and secured by means of a leaden pellet or ring which, when hammered in, expands into a socket cut round the inside of the hole. A more modern type of joining shackle is made in two parts with a fitted stud, the stud being kept in place by a steel pin which runs diagonally through the stud and both parts of the shackle. The advantage of this type of shackle is that it is the same size and shape as an ordinary link of the cable and so fits better into the snugs of the *cable-holder when veering or weighing.

A shackle is also the name given to a length of chain cable measuring 12½ fathoms, which is the amount of cable between each joining shackle. The length of a cable is eight shackles, 100 fathoms.

shake, (1) a longitudinal crack in a mast or spar. **(2)** The shivers of a sail when a sailing vessel is steered too close to the wind, a meaning which has given rise to the expression 'a brace of shakes' as very quickly or immediately, literally the time taken for a sail to shiver twice when too close to the wind.

shake out a reef, to, enlarge a sail by casting off the *reef-points and rehoisting it to spread a larger area to the wind.

shallop, (1) a light, small vessel of about 25 tons, originally usually *schooner-rigged but later more frequently rigged with *lug sails. **(2)** A large, heavy, undecked boat with a single mast, *fore-and-aft rigged. In many cases in the 17th and 18th centuries when ships were driven ashore in storms, contemporary accounts mention the ship's carpenters building a shallop from the timber of the wrecked ship. **(3)** The term was also frequently used also of a *skiff rowed by one or two men.

shamal, the name given to the prevailing wind from the north-west in the Persian Gulf.

shank, that part of an *anchor which connects the arms to the anchor ring.

shape, to, a verb frequently used in relation to the *course selected by the navigator for a ship to sail: e.g., 'a course was shaped to avoid some danger'; 'we will shape a course to reach such-and-such a destination'.

sharpie, a type of oyster dredger which originated among the oystermen of New Haven, Connecticut, USA, about 1830. Having a flat bottom with single *chines and a large wooden *centreboard, sharpies were built in sizes from 30 to 60 feet in length as oyster dredgers in Chesapeake Bay. They were developed later as flat-bottomed cruising yachts. The traditional colonial rig was a *ketch rig with jib-headed (*Bermuda) sails and no *headsails. The name came to be used during the decade preceding the Second World War to describe a class of small, hard-chine racing boat with a Bermudian *sloop rig which became very popular for racing in coastal waters at local regattas.

sharp up, of a square-rigged ship with her sails trimmed up as near as possible to the wind and with her *yards *braced up as far fore-and-aft as the lee rigging will allow.

sheave, the revolving wheel in a **block**. They are mostly made of *lignum vitae or brass, sometimes a combination of the two, in which case the brass forms the bush of the sheave. The older name for a sheave is *shiver, and many seamen today spell sheave as shiv, using the same pronunciation.

sheepshank, a hitch made in a rope temporarily to shorten it. It consists of two long *bights in the rope and a half hitch over the end of each bight made in the standing part of the rope. A knotted sheepshank is formed by passing the two ends of the rope through the *eyes of the bights.

Sheepshank

sheer, (1) the upward curve of the deck of a ship towards the bows and stern, with the lowest point of the upper deck level in the *waist. **Reverse sheer,** a downward curve of the deck level towards the bows and stern, the highest deck level amidships. Some cruising and ocean-racing yachts have been built to this principle chiefly in order to provide more head-room below the deck. **(2)** The angle which a ship takes to her *cable when lying to an *anchor, caused by the effects of wind and/or tide.

sheer draught, a drawing made during the design stages of a ship showing her outline in elevation, together with the spacing of her *frames.

sheer pole, a horizontal steel rod fitted at the base of the *shrouds supporting a mast. It is attached (seized) to each shroud just above its rigging screw (see BOTTLESCREW) and serves to keep any turns out of the shrouds when they are being set up.

sheer strake, the top *strake, or plank, of a wooden vessel next below the *gunwale. It runs from *stem to *stern, level with the upper deck of the vessel. See also GARBOARD STRAKE, which is the bottom strake of such a vessel, next to the *keel.

sheet, a *purchase or single line used for trimming a sail to the wind. A square sail set on a *yard has two sheets, one to each *clew; fore-and-aft sails have only a single sheet to the clew.

sheet anchor, an additional anchor carried on the largest ships for security should the *bower anchors fail to hold the ship. Originally two additional anchors were carried, one at either *chesstree abaft the fore rigging, one anchor termed the sheet, the other the spare. The present practice in ships of any size is to carry the sheet anchor in its own *hawsepipe abaft the *starboard bower anchor, complete with its own cable and cable-holder and ready to let go at any moment. The term sheet anchor is also used as a synonym for security generally.

sheet bend, also sometimes known as a swab hitch, a hitch used to secure a rope's end through a small *eye. It is a simple knot in which the end of the rope is threaded through the eye and the end led round the eye and underneath its own standing part so that it is jammed, or nipped, in the eye. The greater the pull on the rope, the tighter the nip. A double sheet bend is a similar knot but with the end of the rope led twice underneath the eye instead of once. A sheet bend is also sometimes used temporarily to join two ropes of approximately the same size, the end of one being passed through a bight in the other, round both parts of the other rope, and back underneath its own part.

The origin of the name presumably came from its original use as the means of bending a *sheet to the *clew of a small sail such as a *lugsail.

Sheet bend

shell, the outer part or body of a *block inside which the sheave revolves. The shells of wooden blocks are *scored to hold the *strop with which they are bound (stropped) and which embraces the *eye or hook at the top or bottom of the block.

shift, a term used at sea to denote a change in the direction of the wind. It is less positive than the terms *veer and *back, which indicate which way the wind is shifting.

ship, from the Old English *scip,* the generic name for a sea-going vessel, as opposed to a *boat, originally personified as masculine but by the 16th century almost universally expressed as feminine. In strict maritime usage the word also signifies a particular type of vessel, one with a *bowsprit and three masts, each with topmast and *top-gallant mast, and square-rigged on all three masts, but this narrow definition did not, even in the days of sail, invalidate the generic use of the term to encompass all types of sea-going vessels.

The genesis of the ship is lost in the mists of antiquity, beginning when man first thought to use a river or the sea as a means of conveying himself and his goods from one place to another, initially by means probably of a raft loosely constructed of tree trunks, branches, or bundles of reeds. The need to acquire additional buoyancy and stowage space was first met by means of a hollowed-out tree trunk, and so by natural evolution this water-borne means of conveyance developed to the planked craft on an essential framework of *stem and *stern pieces fixed to a *keel, and with *ribs to support the two sides. This is, in its essentials, the basis on which ships are still constructed today.

By around the year AD 1000 sail was beginning to oust the oar as the prime means of ship propulsion in all but Mediterranean waters. The single square sail carried by some of the Mediterranean galleys to provide a period of rest to the rowers when the wind was fair, and also for the same reason by the Scandinavian longships, although in their case the yard could be braced for sailing to windward, was developed from one mast to two, and then to three, and from one sail per mast to two, three, or more. The invention during the 12th century of the *rudder, hung from the *sternpost, in the place of the steering oar which projected from the *starboard quarter of the ship (later developed into two steering oars, one on each quarter), gave a greater manoeuvrability to ships and, in conjunction with such modifications as longer keels, a greater length/beam ratio, and flatter sails, provided a great impetus in the development of more efficient sail plans.

(a) **The sailing warship** was relatively slow to develop as an exclusive type of ship, the general practice in the early days of sail being to hire merchant ships for this purpose in time of war. The introduction of gunpowder, which provided the warship with its own means of battle instead of being, as previously, a means of carrying fighting men who fought at sea with basically land weapons, led directly to the various seafaring nations developing ships purely for war purposes and with no role in times of peace. The first such ships were low-freeboard, wall-sided ships with guns mounted on poop and *forecastle, but as guns developed in size and numbers, it became necessary for reasons of stability to mount them as low as possible in the ship, leading to a change in hull form to give an increase of *freeboard with a pronounced *tumble-home. High castles were erected at bow and stern to give a better field of fire for small anti-personnel guns and muskets, and also to provide a defence against boarders entering the ship by the waist between the two castles. These ships,

however, were poor performers when sailing on a wind, as the high forecastle resulted in their bows being blown down to *leeward.

In general, the largest warships built during these early years of their development were of about 500 tons, but in the early years of the 15th century some English shipwrights produced ships of twice this size. During the second half of the 16th century, again in England, the high forecastle was abandoned as a feature of warship building, resulting in a faster and more weatherly ship. The English pattern was followed by the shipbuilders of other European nations, and the general design of sailing warships became universally similar, differing only in size and number of guns mounted.

During the 17th and 18th centuries, and the first few years of the 19th, there was virtually no significant advance in design in the sailing warship, ships merely increasing in overall size up to a final tonnage, by the mid-19th century, of about 3,000, such ships carrying up to about 130 guns on three gundecks.

(b) **Merchant shipping.** In the field of merchant shipping, design during the years of sail changed more rapidly than with warships. Originally, when time spent on a voyage was of little economic importance, the average sailing merchant ship had a length/beam ratio of about three to one, chiefly to provide the maximum carrying space available. The usual rig was simpler than in the warship, with often no more than two sails on each of two masts. The reason for this simplicity was that owners could not afford the size of crew carried in a warship and, with fewer working men on board, had need to simplify the essential daily tasks in working the ship.

Until about 1500, the average merchant ship was small, the *cog of up to about 250 tons being a typical example. With the great discoveries in the 15th century of an all-sea route to the east and a new world to the west, and the consequent leap in trade which followed the opening of these new markets, the merchant ship made a substantial advance both in size and design, typified perhaps by the Spanish *carrack, of which the largest reached as much as 1,600 tons. It was the new trade to the east, where the immense profits of the early voyages attracted the attention of all European maritime nations, that was responsible for a further surge in development. East India Companies were formed in all the principal seafaring nations to develop this trade, endowed in the main with peculiar powers of expansion and self-government by their sponsoring countries, and the promise of great profits led to a surge of ship development to take advantage of the vast opportunities which were offered by the East. East Indiamen, as these ships were called, grew in size and design eventually to outstrip even the conventional warship, and they carried guns to an extent where they were able, with some degree of confidence, to defend themselves from the attacks of foreign warships.

With the continuing growth in trade during the 17th, 18th, and 19th centuries, and the consequent importance of time on voyage in relation to profits, the sailing merchant ship once again changed her design to improve her speed, mainly by increasing her length/beam ratio to five or six to one and by improving her rig through an increase in the number of sails carried on each mast. It was during the latter part of this period of increased competition that some owners increased the number of masts in their ships to four or five.

Even after the introduction of steam propulsion in ships, there remained for many years a profitable existence for merchant ships under sail. At first, the limitations of sufficient bunker space for long trans-ocean voyages made the steamship an uneconomic medium of transport except for relatively short voyages, and even after this disability had been overcome, certain trades and trade routes still offered advantages to the sailing merchant ship. The China tea trade and the Australian wool trade were examples in which the sailing ship not only held distinct advantages over the steamer but also stimulated the building of numerous magnificent ships like the *Cutty Sark*. The trade continued until, in 1869, the Suez Canal was opened, which so shortened the voyage to those places that the steam-driven merchant ship was able to capture the existing trade. The nitrate trade from South American nations on the Pacific coast remained in the hands of sailing ships until 1914 when, similarly, the opening of the Panama Canal made it more profitable to use steamships. It was this South American trade which lifted the design of

the sailing merchant ship to its highest peak of perfection. It was protected for so long a period by the inability of the steam-driven ship to use the Cape Horn route, and the competitive aspect of the trade encouraged the development of the great four-masted *barques and five-masted *schooners which were the epitome of grace and power. Except in schooners, the fore-and-aft rig was never adopted in the larger sailing-ships except as a half-and-half measure in *barquentines and *brigantines. See also SAIL, RIG, RIGGING.

Today steam and diesel engine propulsion have, with one or two minor exceptions, completely ousted the use of sail. However, a number of great sailing vessels remain in commission as sail training ships, while small sailing vessels of different types are still actively retained in trade in various parts of the world.

Only one area remains where the use of sail is still predominant, that of pleasure sailing (see YACHTING, Sail), where the variety of rig and hull design can still present a stimulus to the art of the marine architect.

Steam power became something in the nature of a status symbol in yachts in the mid-19th century, and continued to flourish for about seventy years until the diesel engine took over. The steam yacht was an expression of an owner's wealth and importance, not quite rivalling in size the official royal yachts of reigning monarchs but often surpassing them in the luxury and magnificence of their internal decoration and fittings. See also YACHTING, Power.

The use of the petrol engine in yachts began during the first decade of the 20th century, almost entirely as small auxiliary engines in sailing yachts. Some small motor yachts were also built, particularly between the two world wars when several races were organized for powered yachts. The improvement during this same period of diesel engines led to their substitution in the larger powered yachts for steam propulsion, being more economical both in the space they occupied and in the engine-room complement required to run and maintain them. They are used either in direct drive to the propellers or in conjunction with electric drive. Since the end of the Second World War, power boat racing has been developed into a considerable sport, with a big increase in the number of craft now powered by petrol engines and, in some cases, by large outboard engines.

ship's number, see SIGNAL LETTERS.

shiver, the word that used to be used for the *sheave of a *block. Today, many seamen still write sheave as shiv, using the same pronunciation.

shiver, to, shake of the sails of a vessel when she is brought so close to the wind that it lifts the *luffs and makes them shiver.

shoal, a derivative of the word 'shallow', indicating a patch of water in the sea with a depth less than that of the surrounding water. Shoals are the results of banks of sand, mud, or rock on the sea bed, and are usually marked, in pilotage waters, by buoys or other sea-marks.

shoe, (1) one of a pair of triangular wooden boards which were occasionally fixed to the *palm of an *anchor to increase its holding power on the bottom. An anchor thus treated was said to be shod. **(2)** A block of wood with a hole in it which fitted the sharp bill of the anchor *flukes to protect the ship's side when the anchor was being *fished. **(3)** A term occasionally used for a false keel. **(4)** The projection of the *keel abaft the stern frame on which the spindle of the *rudder rests.

shoot, to, a verb with more than one nautical meaning. A navigator is said to shoot the sun when he takes an *altitude of it with a *sextant. A sailing vessel shoots, or *fore-reaches, when she is *luffed into the wind and makes a distance to windward.

short, an adjective with several uses at sea. An *anchor cable hove in short is one on which the anchor is nearly *up and down in preparation for the vessel's weighing it and getting under way. A short sea is one in which the distance between the wave crests is less than normal.

shorten in, to, heave in the *anchor *cable *short until the anchor is nearly *up and down.

short splice, a method of *splicing two ropes together where the joined rope is not required to be rove through a *block. The ends of the two ropes are unlayed and then married together with the *strands of one rope alternating with the strands of the other. Each strand is then tucked over its adjacent strand and under the next, and the splice is completed when each strand has

been tucked twice. If the joined rope is intended for heavy use a third tuck is often made to provide an extra strong join. A short splice increases the diameter of the rope along the length of the splice, which is the reason why it is never employed when the joined rope is required to be used through a block. See also LONG SPLICE.

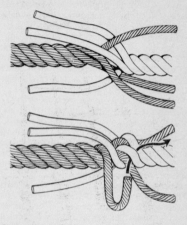

Short splice

short stay, see STAY.

shroud-laid rope, rope laid up with four *strands instead of the more usual three. In this case, the strands are laid up round a heart, or central strand, as the four strands would not bind close enough together and without a heart would leave a central hollow. Size for size, shroud-laid rope is not as strong as *hawser-laid rope having only three strands. Its advantage, however, is that it is less liable to stretch, and was therefore more suitable for use in the standing *rigging in sailing vessels.

shrouds, the standing *rigging of a sailing vessel which give a mast its lateral support, in the same way as *stays give it fore-and-aft support. In larger ships they were usually divided into pairs, or doubles, with an *eye spliced at the half-way point that slipped over the masthead and was supported by the *hounds. The ends were brought down to deck level and secured to the *chain-plates on each side of the vessel abreast the mast, either through pairs of *deadeyes or with a turnbuckle, enabling them to be set up taut. Each mast had its

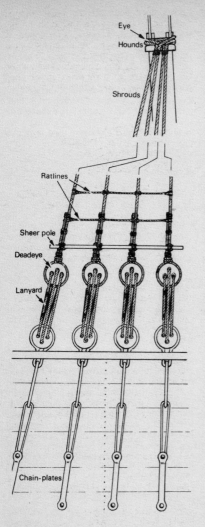

Eye
Hounds
Shrouds
Ratlines
Sheer pole
Deadeye
Lanyard
Chain-plates

Shrouds

*futtock staves of the lower rigging and extending to the opposite chain-plates, and futtock shrouds, which are those parts of the standing rigging between the futtock plates above the tops and the catharpings below.

Originally the rope used for shrouds was a finer quality of *hawser-laid rope, usually four-stranded and laid up from left to right. It was later replaced by wire rope, and in modern yacht design many mast shrouds are now made of solid bar mild steel, where its greater strength allows for a thinner shroud and consequently less windage when sailing. For illus. see RIGGING.

shutter, a detachable portion of the *gunwale or *washstrake of a wooden boat fitted with *rowlocks for rowing. When removed, the shutter provides space for an oar to be dropped into the rowlock. They were originally known as *poppets. For illus. see ROWLOCK.

sidelight, one of the red and green navigation lights which a vessel must display on either side when under way at night as a part of her *steaming lights.

sight, a nautical astronomical *altitude observation of sun, moon, or star by means of which a ship's *position line can be worked out and drawn on a *chart when out of sight of land. A sight entails the simultaneous measurement of altitude, obtained with a *sextant, and of *Greenwich Mean Time (GMT), obtained from a *chronometer. Many navigators when taking sights observe a rapid succession of altitudes of the observed heavenly body and the corresponding times. Each observation in this case is referred to as a shot (see SHOOT). The purpose of this practice is to reduce or eliminate random errors of observation by taking as the sight the altitude and Greenwich Mean Time which correspond to the mean averages of the shots. See NAVIGATION, SEXTANT.

signal letters, the four letters assigned to every ship as a means of identification, known for some reason as a ship's *number.

simoon, the name given to the hot wind coming in off the desert, frequently laden with dust, which blows in the Red Sea. It is the Arabian name for the *sirocco, a similar

shrouds, and in the larger sailing ships many pairs were used for each mast. Topmasts and *topgallant masts had their shrouds running to the edges of the *tops.

In addition to these shrouds running from hounds or masthead to the deck, large sailing vessels had two other types of shroud, Bentinck shrouds fixed on the hot southerly wind which blows in the Mediterranean.

sinnet, written sometimes as synet, sennet, sennit, or sinnit, a flat woven cordage formed by plaiting an odd number, usually five or seven, rope yarns together to form a decorative pattern. Its original maritime uses were for chafing gear (see also BAGGY-WRINKLE), *reef-points, *gaskets, *earings, etc., but as such fancy work fell out of fashion at sea, its later uses were purely decorative. Various forms of sinnet were developed, of which the major ones were square plat, chain, and crown sinnet.

sirocco, sometimes spelled as **scirocco,** the name of a hot southerly wind which blows across the Mediterranean after crossing the Sahara Desert. On occasions it can blow for days or weeks on end, usually during the summer months, bringing sand and acute discomfort with it. It is also often a precursor of a cyclonic storm. See also KHAMSIN, SIMOON.

sisal, a fibre used in rope-making, obtained from the leaves of *Agave sisalana.* It is a hard fibre, grown mainly in East Africa, Indonesia, and Cuba.

sister block, a block with two *sheaves in a single plane, one below the other. They were used for the running rigging of square-rigged ships and were fitted between the first pair of topmast *shrouds on each side and secured below the catharpings. The topsail *lift was rove through the lower sheave and the *reef-tackle pendant through the upper. See RIGGING.

skeg or **skegg,** the short length of *keel, normally tapered or cut to a step, which used to project aft beyond the *sternpost in early sailing vessels. Its purpose was to serve as a protection to the *rudder if the ship went aground and started to beat aft. The skeg did not last long as a shipbuilding practice as it was soon discovered that it was liable to snap off if the ship was beating aft when aground, that the cables of other ships were easily trapped between the skeg and the rudder as the ship swung to the tide, and that it held so much *dead water between skeg and rudder that ships fitted with them became sluggish under sail. They had gone completely out of shipbuilding fashion by about 1630. With the introduction of steam propulsion, however, the skeg came back as an extension of

the *deadwood to prevent a ship's *propellers digging into the ground if she went ashore on a bank. In many modern racing yachts a skeg, in conjunction with a separate fin keel, is commonly fitted to protect the rudder.

skiff, in its maritime sense, i.e., as a ship's working boat, a small *clinker-built boat pulling one or two pairs of oars and used for small errands around a ship when she is in harbour. It is not to be confused with the light pleasure boats used on inland waters and known generally as skiffs.

skipjack, a work-boat of the east coast of the USA, *sloop-rigged with a jib-headed mainsail and a foresail set on a *bowsprit. They were hard-*chined boats with a large wooden *centreboard. A feature of the rig was the mast *raked some 25° aft to enable cargo to be hoisted on board by means of the main *halyards. Skipjacks were introduced in Chesapeake Bay in about 1860 and largely superseded the *sharpie.

skipper, the captain or master of a ship, but particularly applicable to smaller vessels. The word was introduced in Britain in the late 14th century, probably from the Dutch *schipper,* captain, itself based on *schip,* ship.

skirt, an additional strip of material sewn on to the *foot of a racing yacht's *spinnaker and/or large *genoa jib to increase their pulling power. Its form and function is similar to that of the older *bonnet, except that the skirt is a permanent addition and the bonnet was only temporary, being laced and not sewn.

skylight, a glazed window frame, usually in pairs, set at an angle in the deck of a vessel to give light and ventilation to a compartment below. The glass is usually protected with brass rods.

Although once very common in yachts, skylights are difficult to keep watertight in bad weather and have been largely superseded by plastic hatches or transparent panels.

skysail, the name of the sail set next above the *royal in a square-rigged ship, the sixth sail in ascending order from the deck, its two tacks secured to the ends of the *yard on which the royal is set. Like the royal, it is a light-weather sail, set only when the wind is steady and favourable. See also KITES, and for illus. SAIL.

skyscraper, or **raffee,** the name given to a small triangular sail set above the *skysail in square-rigged ships in very fine weather in order to get the utmost advantage of every breath of wind. If it were square it would be called a *moonsail.

slab line, a small rope attached by two spans, or a *bridle, to the *foot of the main or fore *course of a square-rigged ship and rove through a *block on the lower *yard. Its purpose was to truss up the foot of the sail to allow the helmsman an uninterrupted view forward when navigating in waters congested with other shipping.

slack water, the periods in the tidal curve at the change of the tide when little or no stream runs. When a tide flows, its maximum rate of flow occurs during the two hours of mid-flow; as it approaches high water the rate of flow slackens until there is virtually no appreciable movement. The same pattern occurs on the ebb. The period of slack water is perhaps some 20 minutes or so each side of high and low water. During this period, at both high and low waters, the wind frequently drops or changes direction, and it is noticeable that bird life in and around estuaries becomes quiet.

slatch, the slack parts of any rope or *cable lying outside a ship, such as an anchor cable lying on the bottom in a loose *bight, or the lee running rigging slacked away too much, so that it hangs loose. Slatch of the cable is *roused- in; slatch of the rigging is hauled up.

sling, in general, the rope or chain attached to any heavy article to hoist it. Boat slings are made of strong rope or wire with hooks and thimbles in the ends to hook into the stem, keel, and stern bolts so that boats may be hoisted into or out of a ship. **Yard slings** are the ropes or chains which support a *yard on the mast. For illus. see YARD.

slippery hitch, a *bend or hitch used on board ship to attach a rope to a ring or spar so that, by a pull on the rope, the hitch comes free. This is achieved by passing a *bight of the rope under the other part so that when the strain is taken the bight is jammed. A pull on the end of the bight will clear it, and the bend is then dissolved. Hitches most often

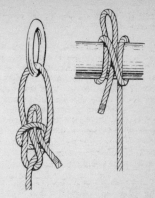

Slippery bowline and slippery clove hitch

used in slippery form are *sheet bends, *clove hitches, and *bowlines.

slipway, a sloping foreshore in front of a shipyard on which ships are built. A patent slipway is an inclined plane on the shore extending into the water, usually gravelled or made of concrete, and fitted with rails up which a small vessel, secured in a cradle, can be hauled for cleaning or repair.

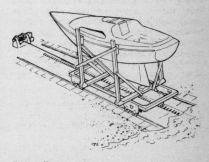

Patent slipway

sloop, a sailing vessel with a single mast, fore-and-aft rigged, setting, in western Europe, a single headsail. Its development, in respect of dates, etc., was parallel with that of the *cutter. In the USA the term sloop also embraces vessels setting two headsails, which in other parts of the world would be termed cutters. The US cutter is the old-fashioned vessel of that designation which set its *jib, which was capable of being reefed, on a long *bowsprit.

smack, originally a *cutter or *ketch-rigged sailing vessel, normally from about 15 to 50 tons, used for inshore fishing. In older days it was often known as, and rigged as, a *hoy, and during the 18th and early 19th centuries in Britain they were sometimes used as tenders in the King's service, particularly in the preventive (customs) service. Today, the word is frequently used as a generic term for all small fishing craft irrespective of whether they use sail or a small diesel engine for propulsion.

smiting line, a small rope made fast to the under side of the *mizen yardarm at its lower end during the period when the normal rig of sailing ships was a *lateen mizen. When the mizen sail was furled, or farthelled, this rope was led along the yard to the mizen peak with the sail and then down to the poop. The sail being stopped to the yard with ropeyarns, with the smiting line inside them, it could be set, or loosed, without striking down the yard simply by pulling on the smiting line and thus breaking the ropeyarns. **'Smite the mizen'**, the order to haul down on the smiting line.

snatch block, a *block with a single *sheave which has a hinged opening above the sheave to allow the *bight of a rope to be dropped in, thus saving the necessity of reeving the whole length of the rope through the block. It is also sometimes known as a notch-block.

Snatch block

snotter, the name given to the fitting which holds the *heel of a *sprit close to the

mast in a *spritsail-rigged barge. For illus. see SPRIT.

snub, to, bring a ship to a stop suddenly by letting go an *anchor with too much way on the ship. It is also the word used of a ship when she pitches while at anchor and the *cable tautens to such an extent that it holds the bows down at the top of the pitch. It is apt to occur when there is insufficient *scope to the cable, and is easily corrected by *veering some more. A *hawser is also said to be snubbed when it is *checked suddenly while running out by taking a quick turn round a pair of *bollards.

'soldier's wind', a name given to the wind when it blows on the *beam of a vessel under sail and therefore calls for no *tacking or *trimming of the sails. It is one which will take a sailing vessel there and back again without requiring much nautical ability.

sole, in some ships, and especially in yachts, the decks of the *cabin and *forecastle.

sole-piece, a name sometimes used for the *A-bracket which extends from the *sternpost of a steam or motor vessel and provides outboard support for the *propeller shaft where it extends beyond the hull.

'SOS', the internationally agreed wireless distress call made by a ship requiring assistance. It came into force on 1 July 1908. The three letters were chosen because they were easy to read and make in *Morse code (three dots, three dashes, three dots) and they did not stand for 'Save Our Souls', as many people thought. The first occasion on which it was used at sea was in August 1909 when the American steamer *Azaoahoe* was disabled with a broken propeller shaft.

sound, to, ascertain the depth of the sea in the vicinity of a ship. Until the wide adoption of *echo sounding in most vessels of any size, the main method of finding the depth of water, for moderate depths up to about 15 fathoms (27.4 m), was the *lead line, the lead being *armed with tallow in order to provide information about the nature of the bottom.

For greater depths, the deep sea lead line could measure depths of up to about 120 fathoms (220 m) with the ship either stopped or proceeding very slowly.

sounding, the name given to a depth of water obtained by a *lead line, *echo sounder, or other means. The figures on a maritime chart which indicate the depth of water are also known as soundings, and unless stated to the contrary are, in British charts, in *fathoms measured below the *chart datum. Eventually, all soundings on all charts will be indicated in metres. A ship in such a depth of water that the bottom can be reached with a deep sea lead is said to be *in soundings; where the bottom cannot be so reached, she is said to be *off soundings, or out of soundings. As a general rule, the 100-fathom (183 m) line on the chart is taken as the dividing line between in and off soundings.

Southern Cross, a constellation in the form of a cross visible in the southern hemisphere. It is of no particular navigational significance, as is for example the northern constellation of Ursa Minor which contains the Pole Star (see POLARIS), but it has acquired a sentimental interest among seamen since the first sight of it at sea is, to natives of the southern hemisphere, the sign that they are homeward bound, and similarly the last sight of the constellation by natives of the northern hemisphere indicates that they, too, are on the way home.

span, (1) a rope or wire with each end secured between fixed points, which is used for hooking on the standing *block of a *tackle where no other convenient point is available. (2) The distance between the *port and *starboard *turnbuckles or *deadeyes of the *chain-plates measured over the masthead of a sailing vessel is also known as the span of the rigging.

Spanish burton, a *purchase in which two single *blocks are used, the upper block being fitted with a hook, *eye, or tail and its standing part forming the *strop of the lower block. The power gained is four times, but the lift is very limited in comparison with a normal purchase. A double Spanish burton has the same arrangement but employs a double block in addition to the two singles, increasing the power gained to six times.

Spanish reef, a method of reefing the topsails or *topgallant sails of a square-rigged ship by lowering the yard on to the *cap of the mast. It was, in British eyes in the days of sailing navies, thought to be a slovenly method of shortening sail in a ship.

Another form of Spanish reef, considered equally slovenly, was to shorten sail by tying a knot in the head of the *jibs.

Spanish windlass, a means of increasing the tautness of a *seizing by taking a couple of turns with the seizing round a short bar and then turning the bar with a *marline spike, held to it by a bight of the seizing and used as a lever. A Spanish windlass is used where maximum tautness is required, as in seizing together a couple of hawsers or binding a *strop tightly round a large *block and holding it taut while the neck is seized.

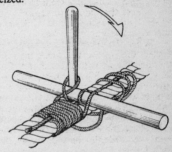

Spanish windlass

spanker, an additional sail hoisted on the *mizen-mast of sailing ships to take advantage of a following wind, the name used for the final form of the *driver. It was originally regarded as a fair weather sail set in place of the mizen *course, but after about 1840 it became a standard sail set on the mizen, taking the place entirely of the mizen course.

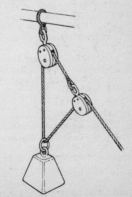

Single Spanish burton

spar, a general term for any wooden support used in the rigging of a ship; it embraces all masts, *yards, *booms, *gaffs, etc.

spar buoy, a *spar painted in a distinctive colour and moored from the bottom so as to float more or less upright as a navigational mark.

spar deck, in its strict maritime meaning a temporary *deck laid in any part of a ship, the *beams across which it is laid being known as skid beams. In modern usage, the term is sometimes employed to describe the upper deck of a flush- decked ship.

spectacle iron, two or three thimbles cast in a single mould so that two or three ropes may be hooked into it to lead in different directions.

spencer, the name given to a *trysail, laced to a *gaff and set on the after side of the fore- or mainmasts of a square-rigged ship, much as a *spanker is set on a mizen-mast. They were introduced to take the place of the maintopmast and mizen staysails.

spend, to. A mast or yard, broken during bad weather, is said to be spent.

spider, a metal outrigger to hold a *block clear of a mast or of a ship's side.

spider band, a metal band with many *eyes welded to it, fitted around the mast of a square-rigged ship to which, in the later sailing ships, the *futtock shrouds are *shackled. It was also known as a futtock band. Also a metal band near the bottom of the mast in a fore-and-aft sailing vessel to which the *gooseneck of the main *boom is attached and which in a *gaff-rigged vessel usually carries a number of *belaying pins to which the *halyards of the sails are *belayed.

spile, to, shape the forward and after *timbers of a wooden vessel to take account of any *sheer in the design, and similarly shape the *ribs of a steel vessel for the same purpose.

spill, to, take the wind out of a sail by bringing the vessel head to wind or by easing away the *sheet to an extent where the sail can hold no wind.

spilling lines, ropes rove round the square sails in a square-rigged ship to keep them from blowing away when the tacks are eased off for the sails to be *clewed up, and to assist in *reefing and *furling. They are secured to the after side of the *yard and are led under the sail and up to a *block on the forward side of the yard through which they are rove.

spinnaker, a three-cornered lightweight sail which is normally set forward of a yacht's mast with or without a boom to increase sail area with the wind abaft the beam. Its name is said to be derived from the 'spinxer', a word coined by yacht hands to describe the sail when it was first introduced aboard the yacht *Sphinx* during a race in the Solent in the 1870s. Since then many variations of the spinnaker have been tried out. At first the sail was shaped like a foresail, with only a moderate amount of flow or bulge in the belly of the canvas, but with the introduction of synthetic fibres for sail materials (e.g. Terylene, nylon, Dacron, etc.) more recent developments have produced spinnakers cut with a deep curve or *roach in the foot, and a great deal of flow in the belly of the sail. So full is this amount of flow in some sails that they quickly earned the name of parachute spinnakers. Designers and sailmakers have experimented with the effect of single or multiple large holes in the sail, following early parachute practice, which were designed to create a steady flow of air and prevent the wild gyrations that some spinnakers were prone to make when running before a freshening breeze.

Experiments continue in the handicap and off-shore racing fleets to improve the effectiveness and handling qualities of spinnakers, some of which have appeared with cloths laid radially from the head with integral airfoil sections, or with multi-cell sections which are claimed to give the sail increased 'lift' without extra weight. Racing spinnakers are noted for the variety and ingenuity of their coloured panels, making a colourful spectacle of any massed racing class.

Spinnaker was also the term bargees were wont to use to describe the jib topsail (usually of white canvas) which Thames *spritsail *barges set on their topmast forestays.

spitfire jib, a small storm *jib made of very heavy canvas, used when the strength of the wind is such that the normal foresails in a small sailing vessel cannot be carried. It is almost entirely applicable to yachts, the larger sailing ships with several jibs being able to reduce their fore canvas in heavy weather by lowering one or more of their jibs.

splice, to, join two ropes or wires together by unlaying the strands at the two ends and tucking or relaying them according to the nature of the splice required. Ropes and wires are spliced together to join them permanently, but knotted when the join is temporary. Ropes can be joined by a *long splice when required to *reeve through a *block, a *short splice, or a *cut splice if it is required to incorporate an *eye at the point of junction. An eye required at the end of a rope or wire is produced by an *eye splice.

spoil ground, an area of the seabed, marked by *buoys, on which sewage, spoil from dredging, and other rubbish may be deposited by vessels specially equipped for the task.

spoke, in any wheel a rod or bar extending outwards from the hub to support the rim, but in a ship's steering wheel the extension beyond the rim which forms a handle by which the wheel is turned to angle the *rudder.

spoon, to, an old maritime term meaning to *scud, or run before a gale with reduced canvas or under bare poles.

spreaders, (1) metal or wooden struts placed in pairs *athwartships on a yacht's mast to spread the angle of the upper or masthead *shrouds, or side *stays. In the older *gaff rig, such spreaders were commonly known as *crosstrees. (2) Metal bars fitted to the *bow of a square-rigged ship to give more spread to the *tacks of the fore *course.

spring, a rope or wire hawser led aft from the *bow or forward from the *stern of a ship and made fast to a *bollard ashore. They are known as a fore spring and a back spring respectively. In addition to preventing a ship from surging backwards or forwards when secured alongside, they enable a ship's bow or stern to be swung clear when leaving. By going ahead against a fore spring with the helm over, the stern swings outwards while the ship is held from moving ahead by the spring. Similarly, by going astern against a back spring with the helm over, the bow can be swung clear.

spring, to, break loose, used of a plank in the hull structure of a wooden vessel when one of its ends, or butts, breaks loose of the copper nails or *treenails which secure it to the *timbers of a ship and, because of its shape bent to the curve of the hull, springs outwards and projects beyond the curve of the hull. Such a plank is said to be sprung. Similarly, the verb is used of a wooden mast or spar when a crack develops by which the fibres are damaged, such a mast or spar then being sprung and needing to be *fished or, if very badly sprung, replaced.

spring a leak, to, develop a break in the hull of a vessel through which seawater can enter. The term originated from the occasional tendency of the hull planking of a wooden vessel to *spring, or to break free of its fastenings to the vessel's *timbers at the butts (ends) of the plank, but now applies to any hole or break in a ship's hull, however made, by which the sea comes in.

spring tides, those *tides which rise highest and fall lowest from the mean tide level, as compared with *neap tides, which are those which rise lowest and fall highest. Spring tides occur when the pull of the moon and of the sun act in conjunction whether 0° or 180° apart; neaps when they act in opposition, either 90° or 270° apart. These conditions occur twice in each lunar month, so that there are two spring tides and two neap tides every twenty-nine days.

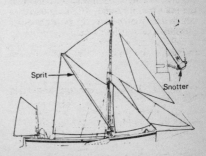

Sprit

Snotter

Thames barge with sprit

sprit, a long spar which stretches diagonally across a four-sided fore-and-aft sail to support the *peak, as in the typical *barge rig. Its heel or inboard end is held in a *snotter near the base of the mast. Although reliefs found at Thasos and dating from the 2nd century BC show that the sprit was known to the Greeks and Romans for small boats, it was not introduced into western Europe for seagoing ships until the early 15th century, almost certainly by the Dutch, as a rig for smaller coastal craft, proving much more weatherly than square-rig in the shoal and tidal waters off the Dutch coast. See SPRITSAIL.

spritsail, a fore-and-aft four-sided sail set on a *sprit, as in the typical *barge rig. The top of the sprit supports the *peak of the sail, the bottom is held close to the mast in a *snotter just above deck level at the *tack of the sail. This type of spritsail is always loose-footed, i.e., it is not *laced to a *boom. For a short period a spritsail was set on the *mizen of a three-masted square-rigged ship, replacing the *lateen sail in about 1550 and itself being replaced by a *gaff sail about 100 years later.

spunyarn, a small line made of two, three, or four yarns, not laid but loosely twisted. It has a variety of uses on board ship, particularly for such purposes as *seizing, *serving, etc. It is also used in sailing vessels for stopping sails, enabling them to be hoisted in stops (i.e., lightly secured with turns of spunyarn) and able to be broken out when required by a sharp pull on the *sheet.

squall, a sudden gust of wind of considerable strength. Squalls usually follow the passage of a *depression, when the barometer begins to rise from its lowest point. This is because the barometer gradient is almost always steeper in the wake of a depression than ahead of its centre. See METEOROLOGY.

square, the position of the *yards when a square-rigged ship is at anchor and set up in harbour trim. The yards are square by the *braces when they are at right-angles to the fore-and-aft line of the ship. They are square by the *lifts when they are horizontal.

square-butted. The *yardarms of smaller square-rigged ships are said to be square-butted when they are cut to a thickness where they can have a sheave-hole cut in

their ends without weakening them. These are used for *reeving the *braces.

square-rig, see RIG.

stanchion, one of the upright supports set along the side of the upper *deck of a ship which carry the guardrail, or, in the case of smaller vessels, the wires which act as a guardrail.

standing lug, a sailing rig in which the forward end of the *yard carrying a *lugsail lies close along the mast so that the sail does not have to be lowered and dipped round the mast when the vessel goes *about. It includes the *gunter rig.

Typical standing lug

standing part, that part of the rope used in a *purchase of which the end is secured to the eye of the *block which does not move, known as the standing block. The part of the rope which is between the standing and the moving blocks is the running part, and the remainder, as it comes out of the purchase, is the hauling part. The whole of the rope is known as the *fall.

standing rigging, the fixed and permanent rigging of a ship. See RIGGING.

starboard, the right-hand side of a vessel as seen from aft. It is generally accepted to be a corruption of steer-board, the board or oar which projected into the sea from the starboard quarter of old vessels and by which they were steered before the invention of the hanging *rudder. See also LARBOARD, PORT. At night a vessel under way at sea indicates her starboard side by carrying a green light on that side, visible from right ahead to two *points abaft the beam.

starboard gybe. A *fore-and-aft rigged sailing vessel is sometimes said to be on the *starboard *gybe, instead of on the *starboard tack, when the wind comes from abaft the beam on the starboard side.

starboard tack, with sails trimmed for a wind which comes over the *starboard side of the vessel. Although the verb 'to tack' postulates sailing *close-hauled, a vessel on any point of sailing is on the starboard tack if the wind comes over her starboard side. But see also STARBOARD GYBE.

stargazer, the name given to a small supplementary sail occasionally set in a square-rigged ship in very light weather to get the utmost out of a breeze. It was set above the *moonsail, which was set above the *skysail.

start, to, (1) ease away, as the *sheet of a sail, or a *hawser, by *rendering it round a *bollard. **(2)** A plank in the side of a wood ship has started when it works loose.

station pointer, a navigational instrument by which a ship's position on a *chart can be fixed in coastal waters by means of *horizontal sextant angles. In its simplest form a station pointer consists of a circular protractor of perspex about six inches in diameter which is fitted with three radial arms, each having a bevelled edge. The central arm is fixed at zero degrees on the protractor; the other two are pivoted at the axis of the protractor and each can be set to any angle relative to the fixed central arm. To use the station pointer, a navigator takes the horizontal sextant angles between three fixed points marked on the chart and sets these angles on the station pointer with the movable arms. When the station pointer thus set is laid on the chart so that the bevelled edges of the three arms correspond with the three fixed points marked on the chart, the ship's position is at the axis of the station pointer.

An alternative means of solving the station pointer fix is by means of a piece of tracing paper on which the observed angles have been constructed from a common point. By laying the tracing paper on the navigation chart and setting it so that the arms of the angles are coincident with the positions on the chart of the three observed marks, the ship's position is pricked through the tracing paper on to the chart at the intersection of the arms of the angle.

stave, to, break in the planking of a boat or vessel in order to sink her. The past tense of the verb is stove.

stave off, to, hold off a boat or small vessel with a spar to prevent her coming alongside too heavily, or hold off another vessel when she is approaching so as to risk a collision. See also FEND OFF.

stay, a part of the standing *rigging of a sailing vessel which supports a mast in the fore-and-aft line, forestays supporting it from forward and backstays from aft. They take their names from the masts they support, as forestay, fore topmast stay, fore topgallant-mast stay, etc.

stay, a word used of the position of the anchor and cable in relation to the ship. A cable is said to be at short stay when it is taut and leads down to the anchor at a steep angle; it is at long stay when it is taut and leads out to the anchor well away from the ship's bow, entering the water at and acute angle. See CATENARY.

stay, to, bring the head of a sailing vessel up to the wind in order to *tack, or go *about. The word is also used of the inclination of a mast in relation to the perpendicular: a mast is stayed forward or *raked aft according to whether it inclines forward or aft.

stayband, a metal ring fitted near the top of a mast, with projecting lugs to which are secured the *shrouds and *stays supporting the mast. It is the modern equivalent of the *hounds, which used to provide the support on which the top of the shrouds rested. See also RIGGING.

stays, the moment when, during the operation of *tacking, a sailing vessel is head to wind. If she hangs there, with her head not paying off on the opposite tack, she is said to be 'in stays'. If her head fails to pay off on the opposite tack but falls back on the original tack, she is said to have 'missed stays'.

staysail, a triangular fore-and-aft sail which is set by being *hanked to a *stay. They are set in both square-rigged and *fore-and-aft rigged ships, and take their names from the stay on which they are set, as fore staysail, fore topmast staysail, etc.

steaming lights, the compulsory white navigation lights carried on the masts of all vessels under way at sea by night by which their presence, and an indication of their *course, is made known to other vessels in the vicinity. See NAVIGATION LIGHTS.

steer, to, direct a vessel by means of a *tiller or steering-wheel connected to a *rudder so that she proceeds in the desired direction. **To steer small**, to keep a ship on her desired course with only small movements of the tiller or wheel. **To steer large**, the opposite of to steer small; or, in the case of a sailing vessel, to steer her so that she has the wind *free.

steerage way. A vessel has steerage way when she has sufficient headway for her *rudder to grip the water so that she will answer her *helm. A sailing vessel becalmed loses steerage way when it becomes impossible to hold her on *course.

steeve, the angle of the *bowsprit in relation to the horizontal. A high-steeved bowsprit, or one with a high steeve, is a bowsprit well cocked-up towards the vertical. In ancient single-masted sailing ships the bowsprit was always very high-steeved and in fact became the forerunner of the foremast when the two- and three-masted rig was adopted for ships.

stem, the foremost *timber or steel member forming the *bow of a vessel, joined at the bottom to the *keel either by *scarfing (wood) or riveting (steel). In wooden vessels all the timber *strakes are *rabbeted to the stem, in steel ones the fore plates are riveted to it.

stem, to, (of a vessel) to hold her own, or make only slight headway, against a contrary tidal stream or current.

stemhead, the top of the foremost *timber or steel member forming the bow of a ship.

step, a square framework of timber or steel built up and fixed to the *keelson of a ship to take the *heel of a mast. Masts are normally squared off at the heel, to fit securely into the square step so that they cannot twist or revolve. In some smaller craft, masts are stepped on the deck and not taken down through the deck to the keelson, and in such cases the deck is normally strengthened with an additional deck *beam to provide extra support. But see also TABERNACLE.

step a mast, to, erect a mast by fitting the *heel into the *step on the *keelson of a vessel and setting up all its standing rigging.

stern, the after end of a vessel, generally accepted as that part of the vessel built round the *sternpost, from the *counter up to the *taffrail.

sternboard, a manoeuvre by a ship when she wishes to turn in narrow waters where there is insufficient room for her to turn normally while going ahead. If she goes astern with reversed *helm, her bows will continue to swing in the required direction of her original turn. It is the equivalent of backing and filling until the vessel is heading on her new *course. It was also a manoeuvre, though usually involuntary, in sailing ships when they were taken *aback while *tacking. But see also CLUBHAUL.

stern light, a navigation light carried by ships, also known as an overtaking light.

sternpost, the aftermost *timber, in a wooden vessel, or steel member in one built of steel, forming the stern of a ship and joined to the *keel either by *scarfing (wood) or riveting (steel).

Originally the *rudder was hung on the after end of the sternpost, though today most ships of any size have a separate rudder post projecting vertically through the ship's *counter.

sternsheets, that part of an open boat between the *stern and the after *thwart, usually fitted with seats to accommodate passengers. It is occasionally written as stern-sheets but the single word is the more correct usage. No doubt it was so named because the sheet was handled from this position when the boat was under sail.

sternway, the movement of a ship when she is going backwards in relation to the ground. In its most usual form the term is used to mean motion backwards through the water, either by the use of engines running astern or, in the case of a sailing vessel, by laying a sail *aback. But a ship lying stopped in the water and carried backwards by an adverse tide is also said to be carrying sternway even though she may not be making any movement through the water.

stiff, an adjective which, when applied to a ship, indicates that she returns quickly to the vertical when rolling in a heavy seaway and, when applied to a vessel under sail, is one that stands up well to her canvas. This is a function of the *metacentric height which has been built into the ship. It is also applied to the strength of the wind, a stiff breeze being one in which a sailing ship is just able to carry her full canvas; a little more and she would need to tie down a *reef.

stirrup, one of the short ropes which hang from the *yards of square-rigged sailing ships and support at intervals the *foot-ropes on which the *topmen stand when working on the sails aloft. The footropes themselves are known as *horses, hence the name stirrups.

stock, the horizontal crosspiece of an Admiralty pattern or fisherman's *anchor, set at right-angles to the arms of the anchor so that when hitting the bottom it will turn the anchor to bring the arms vertical, thus enabling the *flukes to bite into the ground. Originally the anchor stock was fixed permanently in position, but later, for ease of stowage on board, it was made to slide through a ring in the *shank of the anchor so that it would lie parallel to the shank when not in use. Most modern anchors no longer have stocks—instead the flukes are fitted with a tripping palm to force them into the ground; but the Danforth and Meon anchors have stocks at the base of the shank in addition to tripping palms. For illus. see ANCHOR.

stocks, another name for keel blocks, the line of blocks in a building berth on which the *keel of a ship is laid when being built. Thus, a vessel that is on the stocks is one in the course of construction.

stopper, a short length of rope secured at one end to hold temporarily parts of the running rigging of sailing ships with a stopper *hitch while the *fall is being

*belayed. A stopper hitch is a *rolling hitch in which the second turn rides over the first.

stopper knot, a name generally used for any knot in which the strands are tucked back, such as in a *turk's head or *Matthew Walker knot, to form a knob at the end of the rope as a stop where, for example, the rope is threaded through an *eye or a ringbolt, perhaps for use as a handrope. Strictly speaking, a stopper knot is another name for a single or double *wall knot.

storm, a wind whose average speed lies between 48 and 63 knots, i.e., force 10 and 11 on the *Beaufort scale. The two types of storm recognized depend on the wind speed, from 48 to 55 knots being known as a storm, and from 56 to 63 knots as a violent storm. Winds blowing above 63 knots are classed as hurricanes. As with gales, the state of the sea gives an indication of the strength of the storm. When the waves are very high, with long overhanging crests, and the sea takes on a white appearance from the foam blown from them, a storm is in progress. In a violent storm the waves are so high that small and medium-sized ships are for a long time lost to view behind the waves, the sea is covered with long white patches of foam, the wave crests are blown into froth, and visibility is seriously affected by blown spray. See also TROPICAL STORM.

storm signal, a distant signal in the form of a black canvas cone or cones hoisted at coastguard stations and other prominent places along the coast when a gale is forecast; when the point of the cone is up, a northerly gale is forecast; with the point downwards, the gale is expected from the south. These are known as north and south cones respectively. When an easterly gale is forecast a south cone is hoisted above a north; a north cone above a south warns of a westerly gale.

strake, a line of planking in a wooden vessel, or plating in a vessel built of steel, which runs the length of the ship's hull. The hull form therefore consists of rows of strakes from the *keel up to the top edge of the vessel's hull.

strand, a number of ropeyarns twisted together, ready to be laid up into a rope with other strands. Almost all rope used at

sea is three-stranded, though where particular strength is required four-stranded
rope is occasionally used.

strand, to. A ship is stranded when she is
driven ashore, or on to a shoal, by force of
weather. A rope is stranded when one of its
strands is broken by too great a strain or
worn too thin by chafing.

stratus, a type of cloud formation. See
METEOROLOGY.

stretcher, a piece of wood fixed *athwartships in the bottom of a pulling boat against
which the rowers may brace their feet.

strike, to. A vessel strikes *soundings
when she can reach the bottom with a
deep-sea *lead when coming in from sea.
This is today generally accepted as the 100-
*fathom contour, and a ship is *in sound-
ings when she is inside this line.

strike down, to, lower a mast or *yard to
the deck in a square-rigged ship. Thus
*topgallant masts, topmasts, and yards are
struck down when they are lowered to the
deck (but see also HOUSE in the case of
masts where they are lowered only sufficiently to lie alongside the mast next below
them).

stringer, the modern name for the older
shelf-pieces, which were the fore-and-aft
members of the structure of a ship's hull.

stripped to the girt-line, of a sailing
vessel when all the standing *rigging,
*yards, topmasts, etc., have been stripped
off the masts in the course of dismantling,
so that the lower masts are mere poles
standing upright without support.

strop, a rope spliced into a circle for use
round the shell of a *block so as to form an
*eye at the bottom, or to form a sling for
heavy articles which need to be hoisted
with the aid of a *purchase, or parbuckled
to lift them up a slope. Strops are also
frequently used to double round a rope or
*hawser to form an eye into which a *tackle
can be hooked in order to give a greater
purchase.

studdingsail, pron. stunsail, an additional
sail, set only in fine weather, with the wind
abaft the beam, outside the square sails of a

ship. They are set by extending the *yards
with *booms, which are run out through a
ring at the yardarm, to which the studdingsails are *laced. Studdingsails were
normally set on the *topgallant and topmast yards, the topmast studdingsail extending across the depth of two sails, the
upper and lower topsails. Studdingsails
were first introduced during the first half
of the 16th century. For illus. see SAIL.

S-twist, used by ropemakers of *rope
which is laid up left-handed.

'S-twist' and 'Z-twist'

surge, to, stop the pull on a line or *hawser
when it is being brought in round a
*capstan or *winch by walking back on the
hauling part so that the capstan or winch
still revolves with the line or hawser
rendering round it without coming in. It is
a means of regulating the rate of pull with a
capstan or winch turning at a constant
speed. The word is also occasionally used as
a noun to indicate the tapered part of the
whelps of a capstan where the *messenger
was served when an *anchor was weighed
by hand. A more common use of the word
as a noun is to describe a *scend or
exceptional run of the sea into a harbour.

swallow, the space between the two sides
of the shell of a *block in which the sheave
is fitted.

'swallow the anchor, to,' a maritime
term meaning to give up, or retire from, a
life at sea and settle down to live ashore.

sway, to, hoist the topmasts and *yards of
a square-rigged sailing ship. They are

swayed up by means of the *jeers. It is also the term used for taking the strain on a mast rope and lifting it sufficiently for the *fid to be removed before the mast is *struck down or *housed.

'**sway away on all topropes, to,**' a nautical expression meaning to go to great lengths to get something done.

sweat, to, get the last bit of hoist, particularly in relation to *halyards, in order to get rid of any sign of slackness in the setting of a sail when it is hoisted by hand. A halyard is sweated up by taking a single turn round a *cleat, hauling the *standing part out from the mast horizontally while keeping tension on the end to prevent it slipping on the cleat. This raises the sail fractionally. The slack is then taken up round the cleat as the halyard is released so that the extra hoist gained is not lost. Today most of this hard labour in yachts is performed by hand winches.

sweep, a long, heavy oar carried in sailing vessels for use when the wind failed. Until the general use of auxiliary engines, *smacks, *barges, and sailing yachts used to carry at least one sweep on board.

swell, a condition of the sea resulting from storms or high winds. It is the vertical movement of surface water in the form of waves or undulations retaining the motion imparted to it by the wind for a period after the wind has dropped, eventually dying out as the resistance of the surrounding water takes effect and slows the motion down. The length of a swell is proportional to the *fetch.

swifter, a $1\frac{1}{2}$-inch or 2-inch rope with a *cut splice in the centre, a *thimble at one end, and *pointed at the other. Its purpose was to swift, or lash, together the ends of the *capstan bars when weighing an anchor by hand. The central cut splice was placed in the slot at the end of a capstan bar and the swifter passed from bar to bar, being secured to the end of each bar by means of

two turns through the slot, the first inside and the second outside the standing part of the swifter. The purpose of the swifter was to provide extra accommodation for the men weighing the anchor, as the swifter could be manned as well as the bars. The foremost shrouds of each lower mast were also known as swifters.

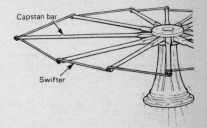

Capstan and bars, with a swifter fleeted

swing a ship, to, steady a ship on a succession of *courses, usually on *cardinal and half-cardinal *compass headings, in order to ascertain the *deviations of the compass on those headings as a preliminary to compensating the effects on a magnetic compass of a ship's magnetic condition. It is not the compass that is adjusted in this operation; it is the ship's magnetic field at the compass position which is neutralized by placing correctors.

synoptic chart, a weather map on which the *isobars derived from a large number of weather station reports are drawn to provide a full picture of the position, shape, size, and depth of the various weather systems in the area covered by the chart. These charts are normally kept up to date in meteorological offices round the world and, by a comparison with previous charts of the same area, meteorologists can see the directions in which movements are taking place and thus predict the weather patterns in the immediate and near future. The distance apart of the isobars gives a basis for the prediction of wind strengths: the closer they are together, the stronger the wind is likely to be. Weather forecasts broadcast from meteorological offices are based on the information obtained from synoptic charts. See METEOROLOGY.

T

tabernacle, a wooden or metal trunk fixed to the deck of a sailing vessel to support a mast which has its heel at deck level and is not *stepped below decks. It is used in cases where it is necessary occasionally to lower the mast to deck level, as in inland waters for passing under bridges, etc. The mast is pivoted on a steel pin which passes through the top of the tabernacle, the forward side of the tabernacle being left open to allow the heel of the mast to swing forward as the mast is lowered aft. A slightly different fitting, known as a *lutchet but serving the same purpose, is used in *spritsail *barges and *wherries.

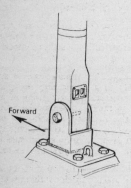

Forward

table, to, sew *reef-bands and *buntline bands on to sails to add additional strength where the reef points are fixed and to prevent chafe in a square sail where the buntline lies along the canvas. It is only the larger sails, particularly in square-rigged ships, that have these bands tabled on to them.

tabling, an extra strip of canvas sewn round the edges of sails to reinforce them where the *bolt-rope is sewn on.

tack, (1) a *board or *reach sailed with the wind kept on one side of the vessel. See also LEG, PORT TACK, STARBOARD TACK. **(2)** The lower forward corner of a fore-and-aft sail. For illus. see SAIL. **(3)** In square-rigged ships, the name of the rope used to hold in the *weather lower corners of *courses and *staysails when sailing *close-hauled. Also, when *studdingsails were set, it was the name given to the rope employed to haul out the lower outer *clew of the sail to the boom-end.

tack, to, bring a sailing vessel head to wind and across it so as to bring the wind on to the opposite side. During this manoeuvre the vessel is said to be in *stays, or staying, or coming about. When a sailing vessel wishes to make up to windward, she can only do so by tacking, crossing the wind continuously to make a series of *legs, of which the net distance gained is to windward.

tackle, (pron. tayckle), a *purchase in which two or more *blocks are used in order to multiply the power exerted on a rope. The gain in power is equivalent to the number of parts which enter and leave the moving block of the tackle, depending on whether the tackle is rigged to *advantage or disadvantage. Tackles are employed for most lifting or moving jobs, including *trimming the sails in a sailing vessel. They are of many varieties, depending partly on their particular purpose, e.g., a *luff tackle, and partly on the number and nature of the blocks used.

tackline, a six-foot length of signal line with signal clips at each end. It is used for inserting in a flag signal hoist to indicate a break in the signal. All flags used in signals at sea have a clip at each end of the *hoist so that they can be clipped quickly to each other to form a particular signal; the clips on the tackline are of the same pattern and can be clipped equally quickly to signal flags when it is required to insert a break in the hoist.

taffrail, strictly speaking, the after rail at the *stern of a ship, but formerly the curved wooden top of the stern of a sailing man-of-war or East Indiaman, usually carved or otherwise decorated. It is a contraction of taffarel, the original name for this adornment. In its modern meaning it is often used to indicate the deck area right at the stern of a vessel.

tail on to, to, in yachting, to haul in as rapidly as possible on that part of the *sheet of a sail that remains after it has been wound round a *winch.

talurit splicing, a modern method of splicing wire rope when a *thimble or eye is required in the end. The end of the wire is threaded through a non-corrosive alloy ferrule of a size convenient for the wire and then threaded back to form a loop round the thimble. The ferrule is then gripped lightly in a hydraulic press while the wire is pulled through to make the loop the required size or to lie closely round the thimble. Further pressure is then exerted to make the metal of the ferrule flow round the strands of the wire, thus holding each firmly in position, and the splice is complete.

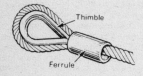

Talurit splicing

tan, to, preserve the life of canvas sails by dressing them with *cutch. The sails are immersed in a cutch solution for two or three hours, then hung over a spar to dry. The resultant colour is a rich deep red. When the sail is dry the cutch is fixed in the canvas by brushing into the sail, or immersing it in, a solution of one lb (0.453 kg) of bichromate to four gallons (18.18 l) of fresh water. This fixing process changes the colour of the sails from deep red to mahogany.

tarpaulin, orig. **tarpawling,** in the old days canvas treated with tar and cut up into clothing on board ship, but from about 1750 the painted canvas used for the covering and protection of hatches and gear on board.

tartan, sometimes written as **tartane,** a small coasting vessel of the Mediterranean, possibly a development of the medieval tarette, which originated with the Arabs for use as a cargo-carrying vessel. Tartans were single-masted with a *lateen mainsail and a small foresail set on a *bowsprit. They carried a crew of about thirty men. Simultaneously there were fishing vessels

in the Mediterranean known as tartanas; unlike the true tartan they had a flat bottom.

taut, the maritime word meaning tight, usually in relation to a sailing vessel's rigging or the hauling of ropes. Thus, a ship's rigging is taut when it is set up as hard as it will go; a rope is hauled taut when it is bar tight. A square-rigged ship sailing on a taut *bowline means that she is sailing as close to the wind as she will go, the bowlines on the weather *clews of the sails being hauled up taut as far forward as possible in order to *brace the yards round on the masts to form an acute angle in relation to the fore-and-aft line of the ship. The word is used for many similar meanings, as 'He's a taut hand', meaning 'he's a stern disciplinarian'; 'the ship is run on a taut string', meaning that she is a smart ship and well disciplined.

telltale, the name used in yachts for the five-inch lengths of wool sewn at intervals just abaft the *luff of a sail to indicate the airflow.

tender, originally a small vessel attached temporarily to a larger ship for general harbour duties such as collection of mail, etc. It is now the term used for the *dinghy kept on the deck of a yacht, or other pleasure vessel, or hung from *davits at the stern, and used for going ashore when the vessel is at anchor or lying to a mooring.

territorial waters, that area of sea adjacent to the coasts of nations which is under the full control of the nation concerned. A compromise between the claims of certain nations to exercise dominion over seas and oceans, and those of other nations which claimed that all areas of sea should be free to all ships, which was a point of argument, and even war, during the 16th and 17th centuries, was found in a suggestion made in 1702 by Bynkershoek, in his book *De dominio maris*. He proposed that a nation should exercise dominion over the adjacent seas only to the extent that she could defend them from the shore, which was taken as the range of a cannon, and agreed to be three miles. This universally agreed limit remained in force until the mid-20th century, when certain nations unilaterally declared an extension to their territorial waters, mainly to protect their inshore fisheries. The generally accepted figure in recent years, though as yet without international agreement, is 12 miles, but with certain reservations for fishing rights within that limit where such fishing has been historically exercised. More recently still, some nations have claimed a big extension of territorial waters of up to 200 miles, either to protect prolific fishing grounds, as for example the cod fishing off Iceland, or for other reasons, such as the existence of oilfields under the seabed. At the time of writing (1986) Libya's claim to the Gulf of Sirte as being part of her territorial waters has brought her into open conflict with the USA which insists that the Gulf's waters are international and anyone has a right to sail in them unmolested.

Terylene, see POLYESTER.

Thames Measurement, generally abbreviated to T.M., a formula for the measurement of the tonnage of yachts, introduced in 1855 by the Royal Thames Yacht Club to produce a fairer method of handicapping yachts for racing. Until that year the tonnage of yachts had been calculated by the *Builders Old Measurement formula, but some astute yacht designers had found a means of reducing a yacht's tonnage measurement, and thus increasing its handicap allowance, by shortening the keel as much as practicable. To prevent freak and unseaworthy yachts being built for the purpose of beating the race rules, and to introduce at the same time a more equitable means of handicapping yachts of widely differing sizes so that they could race against each other, the Thames Measurement rule was introduced. The new formula, still based on the Builders Old Measurement, was

$$\frac{(L - B) \times B \times \frac{1}{2}B}{94}$$

where L equals the length in feet taken from the forward side of the stem under the bowsprit and measured at deck level to the after side of the sternpost, and B equals the beam in feet measured to the outside of the hull planking.

This unit of Thames Measurement became adopted generally by British yachtsmen and is still used to indicate the tonnage of yachts. It is also used by some yacht builders in quoting approximately the cost of building a traditional cruising type of yacht—at so much per ton T.M.

thimble, a circular or heart-shaped ring, usually of iron or aluminium, grooved on the outside to receive a rope which is spliced round it to form an *eye. A thimble spliced into the *bolt-rope of a sail forms a *cringle.

thole pin, a wooden pin fixed in the *gunwale of a boat to which, by means of a *grommet, an oar is held when rowing. A more usual method is to use two thole pins close together, with the oar between them when rowing. They form a substitute for a *crutch or *rowlock.

thorough foot, to, (1) take out a large number of turns in a rope after it has been unduly twisted. If the turns are left-handed, the rope is coiled down left-handed and the end dipped through the coil; if the coil is then hauled out, the turns will be taken out. If the turns are right-handed the rope is coiled down right-handed, and the same process will remove the turns. (2) A method of joining two ropes when they have an *eye spliced into their ends. The eye of rope A is passed through the eye of rope B and the bight of rope B passed through the eye.

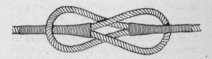

Thorough footing

three figure method, a method of graduating the card of a magnetic compass in degrees from 0° to 359°. The graduation starts at North, and continues in single degrees clockwise round the card until it again reaches North. In those cases where the number of degrees is less than 100, i.e., those with only one or two figures, the figure 0 is used as a prefix to bring them up to three figures. Thus, in this method, North would be read off the card as 000°, East as 090°, South as 180°, and West as 270°. This is the most usual method of compass graduation used in ships today, the other methods of division into *points or into *quadrants being now largely obsolescent.

'three sheets in the wind,' a phrase, with a nautical derivation, meaning unsteadiness through drink. It implies that even if a man who has had too much to drink had three sheets with which to trim his sails, he would still be too incapacitated to steer a steady course.

throat, the upper foremost corner of a four-sided fore-and-aft sail, and sometimes also the jaws of a *gaff. For illus. see SAIL.

throat halyards, the halyards used to hoist the *throat of a sail or the jaws of a *gaff.

throat seizing, the *seizing, put on with twine or spunyarn, to hold the hook and/or *thimble in the *strop which binds a block, and similarly the seizing with which two parts of a rope are bound together to form an *eye in the *bight.

thrum, to. A sail or piece of canvas is thrummed by sewing short lengths of rope yarn to it by their *bights for use as a *collision mat. Smaller thrummed mats are sometimes used in the standing rigging of the larger sailing vessels to prevent chafe in those places where sails or parts of the running rigging may come in contact with it. See also BAGGYWRINKLE.

thumb cleat, a small *cleat with a single arm, fixed near the end of a yardarm of a square-rigged ship to hold the topsail reef-*earings from slipping, or sometimes *seized to parts of the standing rigging to form a hook from which to suspend the *bight of a rope, for example, the *truss pendants on the lower masts. By looping them over a thumb cleat in the rigging, they are held secure and out of the way of other running rigging. Thumb cleats are also often fitted to the booms of sailing vessels as a means of securing the outhaul when the foot of the sail has been hauled out taut.

thumb knot, another name for an overhand knot, which is no more than laying the end of a rope over its own part and bringing the end under and through the loop thus made. It is sometimes used in place of a figure-of-eight knot to prevent the end of a rope or *fall unreeving through a block, but most good seamen advise against its use because of its liability to jam.

thwart, the transverse wooden seat in a rowing boat on which the oarsman sits. Thwarts are normally supported by grown wooden *knees (i.e., grown so that the grain of the wood follows the curve of the knee), fitted to the *ribs of the two sides.

They are additionally often supported by hanging knees, fixed to the ribs above the level of the thwarts so that the thwart is held securely between a knee above it and one below it.

tidal atlas, a collection of twelve charts covering the same area, each chart showing the direction of the tidal streams in the area for each hour while the tide rises or falls at a standard port, which in Great Britain is usually Dover. The directions are shown by arrows, figures against the arrows indicating the speed in knots. Where only one figure is given, it indicates the rate at *springs; where two figures are given, the higher is the spring rate, the lower is the rate at *neaps. Tidal atlases are included in some *nautical almanacs, and many are published separately.

'tiddley', the seaman's word for smart or neat. *Cheeses on deck are tiddley, *sinnet work is tiddley, and so on.

tide, the rise and fall of the sea as a result of the attraction of the sun and moon. The largest rise and fall of tide, known as *spring tides, occur when the sun and moon are in line and act together; the smallest rise and fall, known as *neap tides, when the sun and moon are in positions at right angles to each other, thus exerting less combined attraction. In each case the influence of the moon upon the tides is two and half times greater than that of the sun. The average level of the surface of the sea between high and low tide is known as the Mean Sea Level (M.S.L.).

Tides operate on a time period of 6 hours 20 minutes from high to low water or vice versa, and the total movement of the sea level between one high water and its succeeding one, a period of 12 hours 40 minutes, is known as the tidal oscillation. It follows that the true definition of high water is the highest level reached by the sea in one tidal oscillation, and of low water, the lowest level reached in one tidal oscillation. The direction of the tide is entirely vertical, the horizontal movement of the water as tides rise and fall being known as a tidal stream.

Inland seas, such as the Mediterranean and Baltic, are virtually tideless, the reason being that the entrances (Straits of Gibraltar for the Mediterranean and the Sound and Great Belt for the Baltic) are too narrow to allow the influx and outflow of sufficient tidal water within the duration of a tide to affect the level of the water within those seas by more than a few inches.

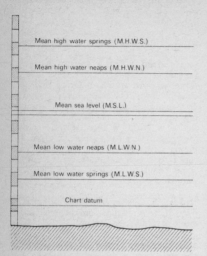

Mean high water springs (M.H.W.S.)

Mean high water neaps (M.H.W.N.)

Mean sea level (M.S.L.)

Mean low water neaps (M.L.W.N.)

Mean low water springs (M.L.W.S.)

Chart datum

Tidal ranges

The heights of the tide at high and low water are measured above *chart datum, and their daily times and heights are predicted for selected ports around the world, known as standard ports, and published annually in *Tide Tables*, produced by most national hydrographic authorities. These publications also include tables of tidal constants whereby the times of high and low water, with the height of the rise, can be easily ascertained for all intermediate ports. *Tide Tables* also enable a navigator to discover the actual height of the tide at any port at any time between high and low water.

tide-race, a sharp acceleration in the speed of flow of a tide by reason of a break or fault in the bottom formation, where the depth of water rises or falls suddenly, as over rocky ledges below water.

tide-rip, short waves or ripples caused by eddies made by a tide as it flows or ebbs over an uneven bottom, or at sea where two currents meet. Waves in a tide-rip do not break whereas in an *overfall they do, this being the principal difference between the two.

tide-rode, of a vessel lying at anchor when she is swung to her anchor by the force of

the tide. It contrasts with wind-rode, when it is the force of the wind, irrespective of the tide, which swings her to her anchor.

Tide Tables, a publication, in three main parts, of the British Hydrographic Department of the Navy, giving predictions for the time and height of high and low water for every standard port in the world and tables of tidal constants for intermediate ports. *Tide Tables* was first produced in 1833, and since 1938 tidal predictions have been based on harmonic analysis of tidal flows. *Tide Tables* is published annually.

tideway, a main *fairway in tidal waters, where the direction of ebb and flow of the tide is straight up and down the fairway.

tier, or **tyer,** see GASKET.

tiller, a wooden or metal bar which fits into or round the head of the *rudder and by which the rudder is moved as required. Until the introduction of the steering-wheel in the late 17th century, all ships, no matter how large, were steered by a tiller, which grew in length and size so that it needed many men to control it when sailing in a large ship in a high wind. Today, tillers are used only in small craft, wheel steering having been adopted for all vessels of any size. See also HELM.

tiller head, that part of a *tiller which is farthest away from the *rudder head and is thus the point of maximum moment.

tiller ropes, the lines which lead from the *rudder head, or an extension fitted to it, to the barrel of the steering-wheel, whereby the rudder is moved as the wheel is put over.

timber, one of the *frames or *ribs of a ship, connected to the *keel, which give a ship's hull both its shape and its strength. In wooden ships of any size, the timbers are made of several pieces of wood *scarfed together to the required shape. In steel ships the frames are of steel angle iron, bent to the desired shape by heat treatment.

timber heads, the prolongation of some of the *timbers in the hull of a wooden ship above the deck level so that they project above the *gunwale to serve as *bitts.

timber hitch, a method of securing a rope round a spar by taking the standing part of the rope round the spar with a *half hitch round itself and the end tucked three or four times round its own part. This forms a running, but self-jamming, eye.

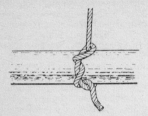

Timber hitch

tjalk, a Dutch *barge-type vessel for the carriage of cargo, dating from the 17th century. It originally had the normal barge rig of *jib and *spritsail, but today is built of steel and fitted with a diesel engine. The design has been adapted for yachting purposes and a tjalk yacht (*pavilijoen tjalk*) closely resembles an enlarged *boeier.

tjotter, the smallest of the traditional Dutch types of small craft, much like a *boeier in rig but only 15 to 20 feet (4.6–6.1 m) in overall length. They are normally half-decked, and are popular for racing in inland waters.

toggle, a strong wooden pin, in older days usually made of *lignum vitae*, occasionally still used through the *bight of a rope to hold it in position and for similar purposes. The typical duffle-coat, widely worn at sea, is buttoned by small toggles threaded through *beckets.

ton, a measure of weight ashore, a measure of capacity at sea. The origin of the word in its maritime sense was the tun, a large cask in which wine was transported, equivalent to two pipes, or four hogsheads, or 252 old wine gallons. The measurement of a ship in older days was by tunnage, or the number of tuns of wine she could carry in her holds. In ship measurement, a ton of oil fuel is 6.7 barrels, a ton of timber is 40 cubic feet in the rough and 50 when sawn. When calculating the gross *tonnage of a ship, one ton measurement is taken as 100 cubic feet capacity.

tonnage, originally the charge for the hire of a ship at so much a ton of her burthen, or cargo-carrying capacity, and also a tax, first levied in 1303 by Edward I of England

on all imports brought by ship into England, and a second tax, known as tunnage, levied in 1347 by Edward III, of three shillings on each tun (see TON) of wine imported.

It was from the first of these original meanings, the cost of the hire of a ship, that the word tonnage came into use as an alternative to burthen. Although tonnage or burthen was still theoretically based on the number of tuns of wine that a ship could carry in her holds, it became necessary, both for taxation purposes and for calculating the harbour dues payable by a ship, to devise a rough and ready formula by which the tonnage or burthen could be quickly calculated. It was found, in the general design of ships of those early days, that the vessel's length in feet, multiplied by her maximum beam in feet, multiplied by the depth of her hold below the main deck in feet, with the product divided by 100, gave a reasonably accurate measurement of her tonnage, and this was the formula used for the measurement of warships as well as of merchant ships.

In 1694, when a law was introduced in Britain requiring the marking of a waterline on merchant ships, when both light (in *ballast) and fully laden, this tonnage formula was officially adopted, though marginally amended to make the product of length, beam, and depth divisible by 94 instead of 100. This remained the standard of ship measurement until 1773, when more accurate limits of measurement were established. By an Act of Parliament passed in that year the length, for measurement purposes, was laid down to be along the *rabbet of the *keel from the fore side of the *stem beneath the *bowsprit to the afterside of the *sternpost, and the formula became

$$\frac{(L - \tfrac{3}{5}B) \times B \times \tfrac{1}{2}B}{94}$$

the result giving the tonnage, L being the length and B being the maximum beam. This formula was known as the *Builders Old Measurement (B.O.M.) and remained in force until the advent of iron for shipbuilding and steam for propulsion revolutionized the design and shape of ships.

The B.O.M. served its purpose well for the typical bluff-bowed, full-bodied ship of the timber and sail era but had no relevance to the longer, finer hulls of the iron ship in which the ratio of length to beam increased from the average three to one to four, five, and even six to one. In place of the old B.O.M., a system was adopted of calculating the actual capacity of the ship's hull below the upper deck in cubic feet, and dividing the total capacity by 100, the resulting figure being taken as the ship's gross tonnage. But this figure did not, of course, bear very much resemblance to her cargo-carrying capacity, since it was calculated on the total hull space below her upper deck and made no allowance for spaces inside her hull set aside for such necessities as crew's quarters, ship's stores, fuel bunkers, machinery spaces, etc. So a second calculation was made of the capacity in cubic feet of these necessary spaces and, still taking 100 cubic feet as equivalent to one ton, was deducted from the figure of her gross tonnage to give a net tonnage. Both these tonnages are known as register tonnages as they are entered on her certificate of registration. It is on the figure of a ship's net register tonnage that such charges as port and harbour dues, light and buoyage system dues, towage charges and salvage assessments, are normally levied.

Another tonnage measurement of merchant vessels is deadweight tonnage, which is a measurement of the number of tons of cargo she can carry to trim her hull down to her allotted Plimsoll marks. These tonnages should not be confused with the *displacement, or actual weight in tons, of the ship herself, measured by the volume of water she displaces when afloat. Merchant ships are normally quoted by their gross or their deadweight tonnage, warships by their displacement tonnage. The tonnage of yachts is calculated by the *Thames Measurement rule.

tonne, the metric ton of 1,000 kilograms, a measurement which, as a result of so many nations now adopting the metric system, is increasingly being used as the unit in the *displacement tonnage of ships. The metric ton (2,205 lb) varies from the avoirdupois ton (2,240 lb) by only 1.6 per cent, sufficiently close to the ton to be acceptable to shipowners and builders without large-scale re-registration, etc.

top, a platform at the masthead of a ship which, in the case of square-rigged ships, rests on the *trestle-trees and *crosstrees and of which the main purpose is to extend the topmast *shrouds to give additional support to the topmast.

topgallant mast, the *mast in a square-rigged ship stepped next above the *topmast to form the third division of a complete mast, the uppermost of the three until the days when yet more sails, known as *kites, were piled upon the masts, when an additional temporary mast was rigged above the topgallant mast. The name is believed to be derived from the *garland round the original pole masts used as an additional support for the *yards. That part of the mast above the circular *top was naturally named topmast, and when the third yard was added, the part of the mast above the garland was named top-garland, which in time became topgallant. Topgallant masts were always pole masts, in distinction to the made-up lower masts. For illus. see RIGGING.

topgallant sail, the sail on the topgallant *yard in square-rigged ships, next above the *topsail, and normally the third sail in ascending order from the deck, except in those vessels which set two topsails, when of course it became fourth in ascending order. For illus. see SAIL.

topman, or **yardman,** one of the seamen whose station, in the days of square-rigged sailing vessels, was on the *masts and *yards. They were the picked men of a ship's company, with the upper yardmen, those who worked on the *topsail and *topgallant sail yard, the aristocrats of the lower deck.

topmast, in sailing vessels, the *mast next above the lower mast, the second division of a complete mast. (See also TOPGALLANT MAST.) For illus. see RIGGING.

topping-lift, a rope or flexible wire tackle by which the end of a spar is hoisted or lowered. In yachts a topping-lift is usually attached at or near the after end of the *boom, and takes the weight of the boom while the sail is being hoisted or stowed. Twin topping-lifts may sometimes be rigged so that when the sail is being set the lift on the lee side can be slacked away clear of the sail, while the weather lift takes the weight of the boom. It has been common practice in the USA for twin topping-lifts to be joined by one or two loops of light line which pass loosely beneath the boom. Known as lazyjacks, these lines prevent the sail from bellying out to leeward as it is being hoisted or lowered, a convenience for a short-handed crew.

topsail, the sail set, in square-rigged ships, on the topsail yard, next above the *course and the second in ascending order from the deck. In many square-rigged ships, two topsails were often set, a lower and an upper topsail. In larger *fore-and-aft *gaff-rigged sailing vessels, a topsail was set above the mainsail, either in the form of a *jib-headed topsail, or set on a *jackyard. For illus. see SAIL.

topsides, (1) that part of the side of a ship which is above the main *wales. In its modern meaning it usually refers to the portion of the ship's side which rises above the upper deck, though the term is often loosely used to refer to the upper deck itself; 'I'm going topsides': 'I'm going on the upper deck.' **(2)** The sides of yachts, above the boot-topping, are also known as the topsides.

tow, to, haul another vessel through the water by means of a towing *hawser made fast astern of the towing vessel and in the bows of the vessel towed. When used as a noun, it signifies the vessel or vessels being towed.

track, a strip of metal on a yacht's mast or boom to take slides fixed to the *luff or *foot of a sail. They were introduced to take the place of the mast hoops and lacing of the old-fashioned *gaff sails. With the introduction of the Bermudian form of mainsail for racing yachts during the 1920s, the luff was at first set on a taut stay running from masthead to deck. This was soon found unsatisfactory and a track composed of a strong strip of metal was screwed to a hardwood batten on the after side of the mast. The luff of the sail was attached to metal clips or slides which fitted over the track and slid up and down as the sail was hoisted or lowered. In strong wind conditions, however, this type of track proved inadequate to stand the strain on the luff, the clips tore away from the track or jammed and caused difficulty in lowering the sail. A stronger type of track of C-section, with more robust slides running inside the track, was introduced, and variations of this pattern in brass, bronze, light alloy, and nylon are used in Bermuda-rigged yachts throughout the world. In modern yachts the luff- rope without slides often feeds directly into the C-section track, which becomes known as the groove. Similar tracks and slides are often fitted to the boom to take the foot of the sail in place of lacing, while much heavier section

tracks are employed on deck in many yachts for the sliding sheet leads.

trade wind, one of the steady regular winds which blow in a belt between approximately 30° N. and 30° S. of the equator. They are caused by the action of the sun on and near the equator in heating the atmosphere and causing it to rise, the heavier air to north and south coming in to fill the vacuum thus caused. If the earth did not revolve, these winds would come directly from the south in the southern hemisphere and the north in the northern, but as the speed of revolution is greater at the equator than in higher latitudes these winds coming in are diverted towards the west. As a result, the trade winds in the southern hemisphere blow from the south-east, and in the northern from the north-east. They are known as trade winds from the great regularity with which they blow, thus assisting the ships which used to carry the trade around the world in the days before steam propulsion.

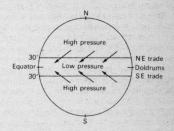

Trade winds

training ship, a vessel used specifically for giving young aspirants to the sea an initial training to fit them for such a career. A majority of training ships are run for this purpose by national, or in some cases naval, authorities and many nations have adopted training in sail, rather than in power-driven ships, to produce the most efficient type of seaman. In some countries similar training schemes on a non-national basis, such as, for example, the Sail Training Association in Great Britain, exist to provide experience for leisure purposes, such as yacht racing or cruising.

Sail training ships vary from large four-masted *barques, such as those used by the USSR for the training of seamen, to small *brigs, such as that used in Great Britain for the training of sea cadets. A majority of such sail training authorities have adopted the square rig as most likely to produce self-confidence and efficiency in the budding seaman.

tramontana, the cold northerly wind of the Mediterranean, particularly round the coasts of Italy. It is the same wind that in other localities is called the *bora.

transom, the *athwartship *timbers bolted to the *sternpost of a ship to give her a flat stern.

traveller, (1) the ring of a lower *sheet *block, when *shackled to a *horse on the deck or *counter of a sailing vessel, and thus free to travel from side to side of the horse according to the direction in which the sail is trimmed. **(2)** A metal ring fitted to slide up and down a *spar or to run in and out on a *boom or *gaff to extend or draw in the tack or clew of a sail. Thus, a traveller is normally fitted to a long *bowsprit so that the tack of the jib can be hauled out when being set. **(3)** A metal ring, to which a hook is welded, by which a *lugsail is hoisted with a *halyard, a *strop round the *yard to which the sail is laced being attached to the hook and the ring sliding up the mast. **(4)** Another name for a *parrel, by which the yards in square-rigged ships are held close to the mast. **(5)** A rope about three feet in length with a *thimble spliced in one end, used to control the swing of a *topgallant yard during hoisting or lowering in a square-rigged ship. Two of these travellers were fixed on each *backstay, the thimbles travelling up and down them, and the rope tails being secured to the ends of the topgallant yard to stop it swinging backwards and forwards while being *swayed up or *struck down at sea.

traverse table, a table, included in all books of navigational tables, which gives the measurement of the two sides of any right-angled triangle subtended by the hypotenuse. In navigational terms, it provides the navigator with the difference of *latitude and the *departure (from which he can find the change in his longitude) for any distance along a *rhumb-line *course steered by a ship, the course and distance forming the hypotenuse. This is essential information for the navigator when he needs to calculate his *dead reckoning position. Conversely, the navigator can discover from the traverse table, and without recourse to a chart, the distance

and the rhumb-line course he would have to steer between two points of known latitude and longitude. The table gives difference of latitude and departure for each degree between 0° and 90°, and for a hypoteneuse length from 0 to 600.

The table would appear to have taken its name from the traverse table of older days by which the mean course steered by a ship during a four-hour *watch could be ascertained.

treenails, pron. trennels, long cylindrical pins of oak which were used to secure the planks of a wooden ship's sides and bottom to her *timbers. Holes were bored with an auger through the planks and into the timbers, and the treenails driven home with a mallet. After the ends were cut flush with the planking and frame face, hardwood wedges were driven in at each end, the wedges lying at right angles to the run of the grain of planking and frame to prevent them splitting. They were of a diameter of one inch for every 100 feet of a ship's length; thus a ship with an overall length of 150 feet would use treenails 1½ inches in diameter.

trestle-trees, sometimes written tressel-trees, two short pieces of timber fixed horizontally fore-and-aft one on each side of the lower masthead of a square-rigged vessel and used to support the topmast, the lower *crosstrees, and the *top. Smaller trestle-trees are similarly fitted to the topmast-head to support the topmast cross-trees and the *topgallant mast. For illus. see RIGGING.

triatic stay, in square-rigged ships, a *stay secured at each head of the fore- and main masts with *thimbles spliced into the *bight to which the stay *tackles were hooked. In its modern meaning it is a stay between the two masts of a ship to which the signal *halyards are bent.

trice up, to, haul up, generally in order to make something more secure, or secure in a more convenient position. In square-rigged ships, the order to trice up was to lift the *studdingsail boom-ends so that the *topmen could move out on the *yards in order to *reef or *furl the sail.

trick, the usual name given to the spell of duty allotted to a helmsman at the wheel. In general, the degree of concentration required to steer a ship on a steady *course in large ships limits the time of each trick to half an hour, though in smaller vessels this may vary according to the size of the crew, and a regular trick at the wheel may be as much as an hour.

trim, the way in which a ship floats on the water, in relation to her fore-and-aft line, whether on an even *keel or down *by the head or by the *stern.

trim, to, set the sails of a sailing vessel by means of the *sheets in fore-and-aft rig, or the *yards by means of the *braces in square-rigged vessels, so that they lie at the best angle to the fore-and-aft line to take the fullest advantage of the wind.

trimaran, a type of vessel with a central hull and twin floats one on each side, propelled normally by sails or mechanical power. The form is a development of the *catamaran, a twin-hulled vessel. Trimarans have been largely developed during the 20th century as yachts for ocean racing and cruising. Being of light construction and with remarkable stability, they are faster than the single-hulled yacht for any given sail area. See also MULTI-HULL.

Trinity House, originally a guild of 'shipmen and mariners' of England set up by Henry VIII in 1517, 'to the praise and honour of the most glorious and undividable Trinity...in the parish church of Deptford-Strond in our county of Kent'. Its original purpose was to do all things necessary for the 'relief, increase and augmentation of the shipping of this our realm of England'. Henry's daughter, Elizabeth I, extended the duties of the guild to the erection of *sea-marks and since then the Corporation of Trinity House has been the body responsible in England for the erection and maintenance of *lighthouses, *lightships, *buoys, and other aids to navigation within the waters surrounding English shores, and is also the licensing authority for *pilots.

In 1604 the members of Trinity House were divided into Elder and Younger Brethren, of whom the former are responsible for the discharge of the Corporation's practical duties and also act as nautical assessors in the High Court, Admiralty Division. They number thirteen, of whom eleven are elected from the merchant service and two are appointed from the

Royal Navy. From time to time, persons of distinction are admitted as honorary Elder Brethren. Younger Brethren have no responsibility in the discharge of the practical duties of Trinity House, but have a vote in the election of a master and wardens.

trip an anchor, to, break out the *flukes of a ship's *anchor if they are caught in any obstruction on the bottom which prevents the anchor being weighed in the normal way. When this happens, the anchor can be tripped by being hauled up clear of the obstruction by the anchor *buoy-rope, which is always made fast to the *crown of the anchor. This buoy-rope is by some erroneously called a *tripping line.

tripping line, a small rope made fast to the *yardarm of a *topgallant *yard in a square-rigged sailing ship when it is being unrigged off the *lifts and *braces before being *struck down on deck. Its purpose was to hold one end of the yard so that it could be canted to the perpendicular before being lowered to the deck. Similarly, a tripping line was employed when lowering (striking) a topmast, being used to hoist the mast sufficiently to take its weight off the *fid to allow it to be withdrawn before lowering.

tropical storm, an intense storm of the kind which occur in tropical and subtropical *latitudes in all oceans except the South Atlantic. They never occur on the equator itself, and very rarely within about eight degrees of the equator. They consist of fairly small but intense *depressions around which the wind circulates anticlockwise in the northern hemisphere and clockwise in the southern, the normal directions for depressions in the two hemispheres, frequently at hurricane strength (64 knots and over on the *Beaufort scale). This wind always causes very heavy seas, with torrential rain and driven spray reducing the visibility almost to nothing. Like all other depressions their rate of advance can be anything up to about 25 knots and in the same way there is an area of calm in the centre or eye of the storm. Because of their extreme intensity, with the area of storm concentrated in a small area, they can be immensely destructive. Their position can be estimated, as with all other depressions, by the application of *Buys Ballot Law.

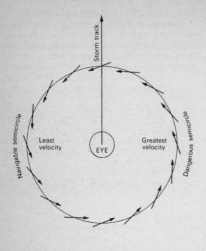

Tropical storm, northern hemisphere

The season for tropical storms in the northern hemisphere is June to November, with maximum frequency in August and September; in the southern hemisphere the normal season is from December to May, with February and March being the months of maximum frequency. An exception to this general rule is the Arabian Sea, where tropical storms normally occur at the times of change of the *monsoon, May and June, and October and November.

Tropical storms have different names in different oceans. They are known as hurricanes in the western North Atlantic, eastern North Pacific, and western South Pacific; as cyclones in the Arabian Sea, Bay of Bengal, south Indian Ocean, and in the vicinity of North-West Australia; and as typhoons in the western North Pacific. See also METEOROLOGY.

truck, (1) a circular wooden cap fitted to the top of a vessel's mast and often furnished with one or two small sheaves through which are rove signal *halyards for the hoisting of distinguishing flags, etc. (2) One of the spherical pieces of wood with a hole drilled through the centre through which was rove the rope of the *parrel in the days when parrels were used in square-rigged ships to hold the yards close to the mast. Their purpose was to give more ease of movement to the yards when they were

*braced to the wind. Similarly, the wooden balls which are threaded on the jaw-rope of a *gaff, and which serve to ease the gaff up and down the mast when the sail is hoisted or lowered, are known as trucks.

true, the direction of the North pole from any place on the earth's surface, or of any *course or *bearing in its relation to the North pole. The true direction of the North pole is an important function of all navigation, since all marine charts are drawn with their meridians of longitude passing through this pole, and as a result all courses and bearings laid down on the chart for navigational purposes must also relate to this pole.

There is, however, another North pole, known as the North magnetic pole, and it is to this pole, which is constantly changing its position, that a magnetic *compass points. Therefore, when using a magnetic compass for navigation, a correction must always be applied to any reading of the compass, whether it be a course or bearing, to relate it to the true North pole before it can be laid down on a chart. This difference is known as *variation, and since the position of the magnetic pole is constantly changing, so also does the amount of variation to be applied as a correction. See also DEVIATION.

truss, originally the *parrel of a *yard which bound it to its mast in a square-rigged ship, but the introduction of a metal goose-neck which centred and secured the yard well free of the mast made the original truss obsolete and itself took on the name of truss. It is hinged to allow both vertical and horizontal movement of the yard.

trysail, (1) a small sail, normally triangular, which is set in a sailing vessel when heaving-to in a gale of wind. In smaller single-masted sailing vessels it is set on the main *halyards; when used for this purpose in square-rigged ships, it was usually set in place of the *mizen *topsail. (2) Fore-and-aft sails set with a *boom and *gaff on the fore- and mainmasts of a three-masted square-rigged ship. They are the same sails as the *spencers of a *brig, and although they are correctly called trysails in a three-masted ship, they are more often known as spencers in sailing vessels with two masts to bring them in line with the brig rig. (3) By some, the sails better known as *spankers are called trysails.

tumble-home or **tumbling-home**, the amount by which the two sides of a ship are brought in towards the centreline after reaching their maximum beam. It is the opposite of *flare, in which the sides curve outwards.

turk's head, an ornamental knot to provide a *stopper on the end of a rope. It is a continuation of a simple manrope knot by tucking the strands of the rope a second time. A running turk's head is formed by making the knot around the other part of the rope.

turnbuckle, see BOTTLESCREW.

twice laid, rope made from a selection of the best yarns from old rope which has been unlaid.

'two blocks', a maritime term for a *purchase in which there is no more travel by reason of the moving *block having been hauled up to the standing block. By extension it has also come to mean a rope or wire which has been hauled to its maximum tautness. A similar term with the same meaning is 'chock-a-block'.

tye, a single rope attached to the centre of the lower *yard, led through a *block on the masthead and secured to the *jeers, to transmit the pull of the jeers to the yard when it was being *swayed up to its position on the mast.

typhoon, see TROPICAL STORM.

Turk's head

U

umiak, the Eskimo name for a *kayak when it is paddled by a woman. It is a kayak only when it has a male occupying the driving seat.

una rig, a small sailing boat's rig consisting of a relatively large *gaff and *boom mainsail or *lugsail, set on a mast stepped very close to the boat's *stem, and carrying no headsails. This rig was common enough in lightly built up-river racing boats in the 19th century, and obtained its name in the United Kingdom from the 16½-ft racing boat *Una* on which it was first tried in 1852. For generations it was the regular rig of the Cape Cod *cat-boats in the USA.

under bare poles, see BARE POLES.

under-run, to, haul a *hawser or *warp over a skiff or boat in order to clear it from an underwater obstruction. To under-run a *tackle is to separate all the moving parts so that none are crossing and the tackle is clear for use.

Under-running

under way, the description of a ship which has movement through the water. The term is frequently written as **under weigh.** Theoretically, a ship is considered to be under weigh only when her anchor has been broken out of the bottom and she herself is still stationary in the water; she is under way as soon as she begins to move under her own power. However, the two terms have become virtually synonymous today, under weigh being a modern spelling distortion of an older term. As the *rudder of a ship is effective only when she is moving through the water, the importance of being under way is that the ship will then answer her *helm and thus becomes subject to the *Rule of the Road and at night must burn the correct *navigation lights.

Universal Rule, the rating rule developed by the great American yacht designer Nat Herreshoff in the early 1890s. It was used by many American yacht clubs, including the New York Yacht Club which adopted it in December 1902 to take the place of the Seawanhaka Rule. Many changes were made to this rule, which governed all *America*'s Cup challenges between 1920 and 1937, but it never varied much from the original formula. Unlike the International Rule (see YACHTING) which governed *International Metre Class Yachts the waterline length of a yacht built to the Universal Rule could be increased with hardly any penalty for sail area provided the displacement was also increased. The rule's most famous products were the *J-class racing yachts built in the 1930s, all but one being constructed for the purpose of defending or challenging for the *America*'s Cup.

up and down, the situation of the *cable when it has been hove in sufficiently to bring the bows of the ship directly over her *anchor.

V

vail, to, an old seafaring word meaning to lower sails as a salute.

vane, a narrow *pendant or strip of bunting mounted on a spindle and flown at the masthead of a sailing vessel to indicate to the helmsman the direction of the wind. In modern yachts the place of a vane is usually taken by the club *burgee or a racing flag, one of which is normally hoisted at the masthead when the yacht is under way. In square-rigged ships, where the helmsman was unable to see the mastheads because of the canvas spread, a small vane, known as a dog-vane, was attached to a pike and placed on the *weather side of the *quarterdeck so that he could judge the direction of the wind. The dog-vane usually consisted of thin strips of cork strung on a piece of twine and sometimes stuck round with feathers.

vane self-steering gear, a method by which the wind, acting on a rotatable *vane connected by linkage to a *rudder, can be set to steer a small sailing yacht on a given course. This principle of wind-vane operated gear was introduced about 1924 to enable model racing yachts to be controllable while running down wind. Known as the Braine gear, after the name of its inventor, it proved highly effective, and in the model-yacht-racing world quickly superseded the older hit-and-miss contrivances of weights and springs then in use.

When applied first to full-sized yachts about 1948, the gear comprised an upright metal or hardboard vane, like a small sail, mounted on a freely turning swivel plate. With the vane adjusted like a weathercock to the wind relative to the desired course, and connected by means of rods and linkage to a servo-tab on the yacht's rudder, or to a separate small rudder mounted right aft, the yacht is made to keep her course whether *close-hauled, or with wind abeam, or with a following wind.

These self-steering gears, which are manufactured in a variety of types and sizes, have been widely used in the long voyages offshore, the circumnavigations with minimal crews, and the solo voyages and ocean races of recent years.

vang, one of the ropes leading from the outer end of a *gaff of a *fore-and-aft sail to the rail of sailing vessels, one on each side, to steady the gaff and prevent the sail from sagging away to *leeward when sailing *close-hauled or *off the wind. Vangs were used in square-rigged ships on the gaff of the *mizen, from which mast a gaff sail, known as a *spanker, was normally spread. The *sprit mainsails of *barges are also fitted with vangs. The *kicking-strap on the boom of a yacht is also often known as a vang.

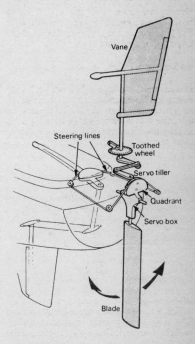

Vane self-steering gear of pendulum-servo type

variation, sometimes known as magnetic *declination, the angle between the *bearing of the magnetic North pole and that of the true North pole at the position of the observer. It is named east or west according to whether the direction of the magnetic pole lies to the right or left respectively of the true pole, and is applied, together with *deviation, to any *course steered or bearing obtained with a magnetic *compass in order to obtain the true course or bearing. The amount of variation may increase or decrease slightly from year to year according to the movement of the magnetic pole, but on all *charts the amount of variation is given for the year of publication together with the annual rate of increase or decrease. The first nautical chart on which lines of equal variation, known as *isogonic lines, were drawn was produced by the astronomer Edmund Halley in 1701.

veer, to, (1) pay out a rope or *cable in a ship. The word is most usually applied to a vessel's *anchor cable, as there are many occasions when it is necessary to veer the cable, as for example when *mooring or unmooring, one of the two cables being veered while the other is shortened in. If a ship is lying to a single anchor and the weather deteriorates seriously, veering more cable frequently adds to her safety as, generally speaking, the greater the *scope of the cable, the greater the security. *Hawsers used in securing a ship to a *buoy or alongside a *quay are veered when they are paid out, but a *sheet is *eased or *checked when it is paid out, never veered. **(2)** Another form of the verb to *wear, when a sailing vessel brings her stern instead of her bows across the wind in order to sail on the other tack. It is not quite so old a term as wear, and is hardly ever used in this sense today. **(3)** Of the wind, to change direction in a clockwise direction. A wind which veers is frequently a sign of settled weather in the northern hemisphere, of unsettled weather in the southern.

veer and haul, a means of obtaining an extra pull on a rope by alternately slackening it and hauling on it three or four times in preparation for a heavy haul by giving the men hauling on it a sense of timing that will concentrate their force. In a full-rigged ship, when hauling the *bowlines on the *tacks of the sails, the order was normally 'veer and haul'. This expression in sailing ship days was also used to describe a change in direction of the wind in relation to the ship; it veered when it swung aft and

hauled when it came forward. But see also VEER (3).

vertex, the two points on a *great circle which have the maximum *latitude north and south, each being antipodal to the other. The only great circle without vertices is the equator.

vertical sextant angle, the angle in the vertical plane between the top of a *lighthouse, a hill-top, mountain peak, or other prominent feature, and the sea level below it read off on a *sextant. If the height of the top of the observed object is known, it is possible for the navigator of a ship to discover his distance off the object, either by trigonometry, or more easily by reference to the table included in most almanacs for this purpose. Vertical sextant angles are useful to the navigator who wants to keep a definite distance off a particular point. If the angle corresponding to the required distance is pre-set on the sextant, an occasional glance through the sextant at a suitable vertical object will indicate at once whether the ship is inside or outside the required distance.

Very (pron. veery) **light,** a coloured pyrotechnic light fired from a pistol on board ship or from aircraft to indicate certain messages as from ship to ship, ship to aircraft, or aircraft to ship. They are in general confined to naval use for particular signals. Ocean-going yachts used at one time often to carry Very lights as distress signals when they did not carry *rockets or flares on board for this purpose, but they are very rarely used in yachts today as most offshore yachts have on board a distress 'pack' containing all necessary rockets or flares for immediate use in any emergency.

vigia, a hydrographic term meaning a rock or shoal marked on a chart, but whose actual existence has not yet been proved by a hydrographic survey.

voyage, a journey made at sea by a ship, generally held to include both the outward and homeward passages.

W

waist, that part of the upper deck of a ship between the *forecastle and the *quarter-deck. In sailing ships, the part of the upper deck between the fore- and the mainmasts.

wale, an extra thickness of wood bolted to the sides of a ship in positions where protection is needed. A wale running the full length of both sides of a ship just below the *gunwale is more often known as a *rubbing strake and it protects the hull from being damaged when a ship lies alongside a quay where the rise and fall of the tide may cause her to rub against the piers. It is a similar protection if another vessel bumps her while coming alongside.

wall knot, a *stopper knot on a rope to prevent anything passing beyond it. The rope is unlayed to a distance of four or five times the circumference of the rope and the individual strands tucked over the strand behind and under the strand in front. They are then each tucked again under the two strands in front and brought up to the centre. After each strand is hauled taut they are *whipped together close to the knot and the ends cut off.

Start of a wall knot

wardrobe, the name generally used to denote all the various sails carried on board a racing or cruising yacht. It ranges from the heavy weather sails, such as storm *jibs, storm staysails, etc., made of heavy duty canvas, to the light weather sails, such as *genoa and *yankee jibs, *spinnakers,

*ghosters, etc., usually made of nylon, Terylene, or Dacron.

warm front, the line, in a typical depression, where the cold air coming in to fill the low pressure area pushes the warm air up in a bulge. The front edge of the bulge, where the warm air has not yet been displaced by the cold, is the warm front. See DEPRESSION, METEOROLOGY.

warp, (1) a light *hawser used in the movement of a ship from one place to another by means of a *kedge anchor, a *capstan, or of men hauling on it. It is not a tow-rope, which involves the power of another ship. **(2)** One of the ropes used for securing a ship alongside a quay, jetty, etc., or another ship. See also SPRING.

washboard or **washstrake,** a movable upper *strake which can be attached to the *gunwales of some open boats when under sail to keep out the spray. The *coamings of the *cockpits of yachts are sometimes also known as washboards.

washstrake, see WASHBOARD.

watch, (1) the division of the 24 hours of the seaman's day into periods of duty of 4 hours. Thus there should be six 4-hour watches in a day, but as this would entail the crew of a ship, organized into two or three watches, keeping the same watches every day, the evening watch from 1600 to 2000 is divided into two 2-hour watches, known as the first and last dog watches. Starting at midnight, the names of the watches are Middle, Morning, Forenoon, Afternoon, First Dog, Last Dog, and First. **(2)** The basis of the internal organization of a ship's crew whereby individuals can obtain regular periods of rest although the work of the ship must go on day and night. The crew is divided either into two watches (*port and *starboard), with each watch alternating their periods of duty, or into three watches (usually red, white, and blue), so that every person gets two periods of rest to every one period of duty. The periods of duty correspond to the watches into which the seaman's day is divided.

watch, to. A navigational *buoy is said to be watching when it is floating in the correct position as marked on a *chart, and its light or other signal, if it has one, is in efficient working order. Other buoys are watching when they are carrying out the purpose for which they are intended, e.g., an *anchor buoy.

watch buoy, a *buoy moored in the vicinity of a *lightship from which she can check her position to make sure that she has not shifted by *dragging. Since the positions of all lightships are marked on *charts and are widely used by navigators for *fixing the position of their ships by visual *bearings, it is of vital importance that the lightship should be exactly in the position indicated on the chart.

water sail, a small sail spread in square-rigged ships in calm weather and a following wind to increase the area of canvas spread to the wind. There were two places where such sails could be spread, below the lower *studdingsail or below the boom of the *driver.

waterway, the outboard planks of a ship's deck, often hollowed to provide a shallow channel to carry off water on deck through the scuppers. Larger ships often have a channel-iron along the outboard sides of the deck to serve the same purpose. See also DEVIL.

wave, the oscillations of the sea caused by wind blowing along the surface and moving in the direction in which the wind blows. The water in a wave does not move forward in a horizontal direction but rises and falls below the surface, unless the force of the wind is enough to cause the crest of the wave to overbalance and break, when the water in the crest does move forward. The height of waves depends on the wind strength and the length of the *fetch, the distance that the wind has been blowing over the open sea; and the speed of waves depends on the wind strength, up to a maximum speed of about 25 knots. The maximum height of a wave from trough to crest is about 45 feet (14 m), except perhaps in the centre of a hurricane, where greater heights have occasionally been recorded. A code of the sea state, in the same form as the *Beaufort scale for winds, is:

Code	Description	Mean max. height of waves (feet)
0	glassy calm	0
1	calm (ripples)	0–1
2	smooth (wavelets)	1–2
3	slight	2–4
4	moderate	4–8
5	rough	8–13
6	very rough	13–20
7	high	20–30
8	very high	30–45
9	phenomenal	over 45

wave line theory, a theory explaining the pattern of waves caused by floating bodies when moving along the surface of the water. It was formulated by William Froude after a series of experiments he carried out from 1868 onwards with models of ships in his private test tank near Torquay. Froude propounded the theory, later substantiated by Scott Russell and other investigators in naval architecture, that when a floating body, such as a ship, moves through the water it creates a wave system around itself which is the complex result of varying pressures below the surface of the water. At the entrance of the body—in the case of a ship the bow—underwater pressures are set up which cause a heaping up of the water immediately ahead of and to each side of the vessel's bow. These bow waves are followed by alternate troughs and crests along the vessel's sides until this wave system meets round the stern, where reduced pressures—a partial suction, which can be intensified when the ship is propeller-driven—break up the waves, leaving a confused area of eddies and subsidiary waves in the wake of the vessel. From Froude's and Russell's observations was developed this theory of wave formation and pattern which has been used by naval architects and others connected with ship design ever since.

Boat of 40 ft at maximum of $(1 \cdot 4 \sqrt{L}) = 8 \cdot 5$ knots

Froude's experiments led to his discovery of the relative quantities of resistance to vessels of various forms when moving through water caused (a) by friction, or drag, as a film of water is drawn along by the surface of the hull and forms eddies or local areas of disturbance in the water adjacent, and (b) at higher speeds by the formation of a pattern of waves which varies with the design of the hull and with the speed, and is called the vessel's wash. At very low speeds, a *knot or two, when no surface waves and only eddies are formed, almost the whole of the resistance to the ship's progress (some 90–95 per cent) is due to the drag on the hull, or skin friction. As the speed rises, however, and a wave at the bow begins to form, the relation of skin friction to wave-making resistance changes. At normal service speed for a conventional ship, expressed by the formula 0.8√ knots (where L is the ship's waterline length in feet), which gives, for example, a 400-ft ship a speed of 16 knots, the wave-making or wash accounts for some 40–50 per cent of the total resistance, according to the design of the hull and the state of the ship's bottom, whether clean and smooth or rusty and coated with weed and barnacles.

With an increase of speed to a value of, say, 1.0√ (or 20 knots for a 400-ft waterline ship) the waves formed along the hull are considerably higher and their crests correspondingly further apart, with one at the bow, a second roughly amidships, and a third abreast the stern. Such a wave pattern accounts for some 55–60 per cent of the total resistance, again according to the design and state of the hull. If speed is made to increase still further, both wave-forming resistance and surface drag begin to increase so dramatically that it is conceded to be impracticable to attain anything of the order of a powered ship's theoretical maximum speed, expressed as 1.4√ knots, with a conventionally designed hull. If such speeds are demanded an entirely different design of hull is needed, with the fine entrance at the bow and broad flat stern of a conventional speed boat, which reduces the tendency to squat and enables the vessel to run as level in a fore-and-aft line as is practicable.

Sailing yachts of good racing design, when given the right conditions of a strong wind and a smooth sea, occasionally achieve this 1.4√ relative speed, when the lee bow wave will rise almost to the rail, the lee deck amidships will be close to the bow wave's hollow or trough, and the stern will be awash on the lee quarter

wave. This is the maximum theoretical speed of which the conventional single-hulled yacht is capable under sail power alone, the effective waterline length of the yacht, however, being increased by any overhang at the bow and stern. Beyond this speed in any normal yacht, more sail area or a strengthening wind will only cause her to heel further over, presenting a curious shape of hull in the water and burying her lee deck, so that resistance rises sharply and her speed at once drops. The diagram shows the wave formation of a conventional racing yacht with an effective waterline length of 40 feet (12.2 m) sailing at her maximum speed (1.4√) of approximately 8.5 knots. These ratios, however, do not apply to multihull yachts (*catamarans, *trimarans, etc.), speedboats, or racing *dinghies designed for *planing. See also LAMINAR FLOW.

way, the movement of a ship through the water by means of her own power, or the force of the wind on her sails. But see also UNDER WAY.

way, one of the two parallel platforms of timber which incline gradually towards the water, one on each side of the *keel of a ship being built, and down which the cradle in which she is held slides when she is *launched. The fixed platforms are known as the ground ways, the sliding part as the sliding or launching ways, and the two together as a slipway.

wear, to, bring a sailing vessel on to the other *tack by bringing the wind round the *stern, as opposed to tacking, when the wind is brought round the *bow. It has been suggested that the word originated from *veer, which has a similar meaning, but wear is the earlier of the two. In the past tense, a ship is wore, not worn.

weather, in addition to its normal meteorological meaning (for which see METEOROLOGY), weather is also used by seamen as an adjective applied to anything which lies to windward. Thus a ship is said to have the weather *gage of another when she lies to windward; a ship under way has a weather side, which is that side which faces the wind; a vessel under sail has weather shrouds on her windward side; a coastline that lies to windward of a ship is a weather shore. **Weather helm**: a ship under sail carries weather *helm when the *tiller has to be held to windward, or the wheel put down to leeward, to make her keep a steady course. See also GRIPE. A ship is said to be **weatherly** when she can steer closer to the wind than the average, thus gaining an advantage in manoeuvring or in making a passage when the destination is to windward.

weather lore, the ability of a seaman to foretell the weather by the appearance of the sky, change of direction of winds, cloud formations, variation of atmospheric pressure, etc. It is often expressed in terms of jingles, of which perhaps the best known are:

Mackerel skies and mares' tails,
Make tall ships carry short sails.

When the wind shifts against the sun,
Trust it not for back it will run.
When the wind follows the sun,
Fine weather will never be done.

Although this is often true of the northern hemisphere, the reverse holds good in the southern.

If the wind is north-east three days
    without rain,
Eight days will go by before south
    again.

If woolly fleeces deck the heavenly
    way
Be sure no rain will mar a summer's
    day.

With the rain before the wind
Stays and topsails you must mind,
But with the wind before the rain
Your topsails you may set again.

When the sea-hog (porpoise) jumps,
Stand by at your pumps.

First rise after low
Foretells a stronger blow.

Seagull, seagull, sit on the sand,
It's never good weather when you're
    on the land.

weigh, to, break out and lift an *anchor off the seabed to bring it on board. See also UNDER WAY.

well found, the description of a vessel which is adequately and fully equipped with all gear required for her efficient operation.

West Country whipping, a method of *whipping the end of a rope by centring the whipping twine round the part of the rope to be whipped and half knotting it with an overhand knot at every half turn so that each consecutive knot is on the opposite side of the rope. The whipping is finished off with a *reef knot. See SAILMAKER'S WHIPPING, COMMON WHIPPING.

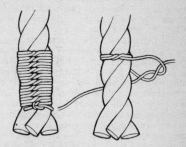

West country whipping

wetted surface, the part of the hull of a vessel below the water level when she is upright in the water. It varies, of course, with the loading of the vessel. The wetted surface is an element of the calculations of a vessel's speed; the greater the wetted surface, the less the speed. In yachts and other sailing vessels, the wetted surface decreases momentarily as they *heel to the wind, thus allowing them to go faster. A further increase in speed derives from the large overhangs forward and aft, which become immersed as the yacht heels, thus increasing her waterline length. For the relationship between speed and waterline length see HYDRODYNAMICS.

wheelhouse, the deckhouse of a vessel within which the steering-wheel is fitted. In smaller vessels it is a separate compartment raised above deck level to provide all-round visibility for the helmsman.

wherry, a decked sailing vessel of very shallow *draught used for the transport of small quantities of freight on the Norfolk Broads in England. They have a considerable *beam in relation to their length and are fitted with a single mast carrying a large loose-footed (i.e., without a *boom) *gaff mainsail and no headsails. The mast is normally *stepped with its heel on deck and supported in a *lutchet, similar to a *tabernacle, so that it can be lowered to the deck when passing under bridges, etc.

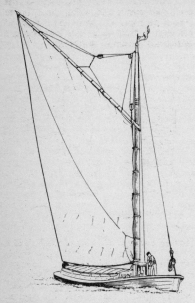

Norfolk wherry

whip, the name given to a single rope rove through a single block and used for hoisting articles. Where greater power is required, another single block can be introduced to make a double whip, or another single whip can be applied to the fall of the first to form what is known as a whip-upon-whip.

whip, to, bind twine or yarn round the strands at the end of a rope or wire rope to prevent them from unlaying or fraying. The final result is known as a whipping, of which the *common whipping, *sailmaker's whipping, and *West Country whipping are in the most general use at sea.

whisker pole, a short bearing-out spar used in yachts and sailing *dinghies to bear out the *clew of the jib on the opposite side of the mainsail when running before the wind, thus obtaining some of the advantage which would be gained in a larger vessel when she sets a *spinnaker. See also GOOSE-WINGS.

winch, a small horizontal *capstan, driven by either steam or electricity, around the drum of which the hauling part of a *purchase is passed to provide power for hoisting, etc. In yachts, smaller winches, turned by hand with a ratchet and pawl arrangement, are provided for *halyards, *sheets, etc.

windjammer, a non-nautical name by which square-rigged sailing ships are frequently known.

windlass, originally a small *capstan-like fitting, but on a horizontal shaft, in the fore part of a small vessel by which she rode to her *anchor. It was also used sometimes for weighing an anchor if this could be done without recourse to the capstan. Like the old-time capstan, windlasses were fitted with bars to be worked by hand, and had a pawl and ratchet gear to provide rotary motion to the spindle on which the windlass was mounted from an up and down motion of the bars.

wind-rode. A vessel is said to be wind-rode when she is riding head to wind in spite of the influence of a tidal current which may be running across the wind or even dead to windward.

windsurfing. This comparatively new sport has become so popular that it was chosen as an Olympic event for the first time in the 1984 Games. It was invented in 1969 by two Californian surfing enthusiasts who wanted to be able to take their boards beyond the breaking surf without having to paddle them. After a great deal of experiment they invented a wind-driven surfboard able to sail both off and on the wind, equipped with a small retractable *daggerboard, a mast that rotated on a universal joint, and a *wishbone boom on to which the surfer held while standing on the board. There was no *rudder, but the small *skeg fitted at the rear of the surfboard helped it to change direction. This is accomplished by altering the fore and aft angle of the rig. Moving the mast backwards makes the board move into the wind, while moving it forwards sends it away from the wind. To *tack the windsurfer sails into the wind, moves forward round the mast while retaining hold of the forward part of the boom, and then repositions himself on the opposite side of the board as the wind fills the other side of the sail.

From the early experiments of the two Californians has sprung the entirely new sport of windsurfing, or boardsailing, and it was not long before it had spread all over the world. Racing windsurfers soon became a popular pastime, and the sport is now practised by large numbers of enthusiasts, not only on the sea, but on rivers, inland lakes, and in sheltered bays and inlets. It first arrived in Europe in 1971, with the first European Championships taking place in 1973, and the first World Championships in 1974. Several classes of sailboards have now been granted International Class status by the International Yacht Racing Union, and it is generally acknowledged that windsurfing is one of the very few original ideas to appear in the world of sailing during the last hundred years or more.

windward, the weather side, or that from which the wind blows. It is the opposite side to *leeward. See also GAGE.

wishbone, a divided spar whose two arms are pivoted together at the fore end and arched on either side in a roughly parabolic curve. The wishbone spar extends the *clew of the sail which is hoisted between the two arms, and the curves in the arms allow the sail to take up its natural flow without *girt or chafe. Apart from its use in *windsurfing, where no sheets are used, and in the Freedom rig (see RIG), a wishbone can only be employed in two-masted sailing vessels, such as a *schooner or a *ketch, as it is set on the forward mast and sheeted to the top of the after mast. It came briefly into fashion during the period 1920–40 but is rarely seen today.

woolding, a binding of rope round a mast or spar to support it where it has been *fished. The rope used for this purpose is also called a woolding.

worm, to, pass a small rope spirally between the lays of a hemp cable, and similarly pass codline between the lays of a rope, as a preparation for *parcelling and *serving. Rope is wormed, parcelled, and served to protect it against the wet, which is liable to rot it. See also CONTLINE.

wreck, the hull of a ship which has become a total loss through stress of weather, stranding, collision, or any other cause, whether it lies on the bottom of the sea or on the shore. In maritime law, a vessel which is driven ashore is not a wreck if any man or domestic animal escaped death in her and is still alive on board when she *strands.

wreck buoy, a *buoy painted green with the letter W painted prominently on it in white, which is laid to mark the position of a wrecked ship and as a warning to navigators to keep clear. If the buoy is can shaped, it indicates that it is to be left to port when proceeding with the main flood stream, if conical to be left to starboard, and if spherical it may be left on either hand. If lit, it shows a green flashing light, one flash indicating that it may be left on either hand, two flashes on the port hand, and three flashes on the starboard hand.

wreck vessel, a dumb vessel (i.e., without means of self-propulsion) painted green, with the word 'WRECK' in white letters painted on each side, which is *moored head and stern to mark the position of a wreck which may be a danger to navigation. It carries by day two green balls below one yardarm if it is to be left on the port hand when proceeding with the main flood stream, three green balls if to be left on the starboard hand, and two green balls below each yardarm if it may be passed on either side. At night the balls are replaced by green lights. In a fog a bell is sounded every 30 seconds, two strokes if to be passed on the port hand, three if on the starboard hand, and four if it may be passed on either side.

Y

yacht, from the Dutch *jacht* (p.p. of *jachten*, to hurry, to hunt), originally 'a vessel of state, usually employed to convey princes, ambassadors or other great personages from one kingdom to another' (Falconer, *Marine Dictionary*, 1771); later any vessel propelled by either sail or power used for pleasure and not plying for hire. The word entered the English language in 1660, the year of the restoration of Charles II and the presentation to him by the States General of Holland of the *Mary* (100 tons, 8 guns) as a private pleasure vessel. There had been similar vessels long before this date, known as 'royal pleasure ships' or esneccas, but the word 'yacht' was then unknown in relation to them. See also YACHTING.

yacht design. Unlike merchant vessels whose sides for a long way amidships are usually straight and flat, the hulls of yachts usually follow a curve along their entire length. The art of the yacht designer, whether professional or amateur, has understandably therefore been likened to sculpture on paper. Faced with a client's requirements, or the need to meet exacting *rating rules, the yacht designer, like the naval architect, begins by submitting preliminary drawings, and goes on to estimate roughly the yacht's displacement or total weight in sailing trim, the weight of *ballast in the keel (in cast iron or lead) needed to give her the stability to stand up to the desired sail area, and the quantities of engine fuel and fresh water to be carried.

The completed plans which will be supplied to the yacht yard for building the vessel normally comprise the following:

(1) The lines plan. This is the equivalent of the merchant ship's sheer draught plan, and shows the yacht's hull form from three viewpoints at right angles to one another: the elevation, the half-breadth plan, and the body plan. Drawn usually to a scale from 1:24 to 1:12 (or 1:10 if metric) according to the size of the yacht, this plan shows accurately the curve of each cross-section (or frame station) in the body plan, and each of a series of level lines (or waterlines) spaced at regular intervals between the keel and the deck edge.

(2) Table of offsets. Often incorporated in the lines plan, this list of ordinates for all the curved lines and frame stations on the hull is used by the builder for shaping the moulds or patterns around which the hull will be built to the exact measurements on the drawing.

(3) General arrangement plan. This shows the layout of the accommodation below deck in both elevation and plan, together with a number of cross-sections (or half-sections) indicating how the interior arrangements are to be fitted in relation to the curved inside of the hull at various points.

(4) Construction plan. This gives details of all principal parts of the hull, ballast keel, decks, etc., with sizes and materials specified.

(5) Sail and rigging plan. An elevation view of the yacht afloat which gives positions and measurements of all the sails, the various sizes and types of standing rigging, and details of mast(s) and spars.

(6) Engine installation drawing. This may also include details of electrical installations, fuel and fresh water tanks, plumbing, deck winches and fittings, and individual ironwork for use by the yard engineers and foundry.

Traditional building methods. For many decades yachts were built by the methods which were traditional for contemporary wooden merchant vessels, *barges, and *smacks. The wooden keel, of oak, elm, pitch pine, or other local timber, was laid on the slipway or on building blocks, and the wooden stem, sternpost, and stern frame bolted into place. The various frames (or ribs) were sawn to shape and erected in their respective positions along both sides of the keel from stem to stern, the lower ends of each pair being fastened to floor frames which were commonly oak crooks laid athwart the top of the keel. An inner keel, or keelson, was sometimes bolted on to the tops of the floor frames, running from the inside of the stem to the sternpost. Beam shelves, running from bow to stern and fastened to the inside of the head of every frame, carried the outboard ends of the deck beams which in turn were fastened to the shelves, often with

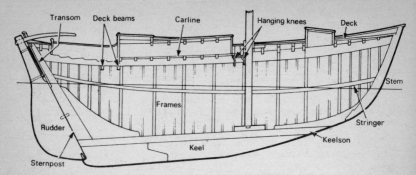

Profile construction of a typical wooden yacht

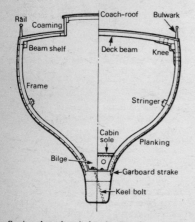

Sections through typical yacht of wooden construction

a half-dovetail joint. Openings in the deck beams for hatches or skylights were joined by *carlines, square-sectioned lengths of timber to which the upright *coamings were fastened. At all junctions beneath the deck where the racking strains of hard sailing in heavy seas were greatest, oak crook *knees or wrought iron angle plates were bolted to give rigid strength.

The planking of the hull was fastened to the frames and floors with galvanized iron spikes, bronze bolts, or in the smaller yachts with copper square-sectioned nails riveted over copper collars (or rooves) on the inside of every frame. The work of planking the vessels was started at the plank next to the keel (the *garboard strake) on each side, and continued in sequence up to

the turn of the *bilge, while other planks were fastened on from the deck edge (the *sheer strake) downwards, until the final gap between the two sets of planks could be filled in with an exactly fitting shutter strake. Deck planks, traditionally of white pine or teak, were laid fore and aft usually following the curve of the wide *covering board at the yacht's side. The seams between the planks, cut in the form of a deep V, were caulked with cotton and payed with hot pitch. The seams of the hull planking were likewise caulked with cotton (teased rope or *oakum for the merchant vessels) and finished smooth and flush with a patent stopping mixture which never set hard enough to crack when the seams worked in a seaway.

Towards the end of the 19th century sawn frames were replaced in the smaller yachts by steam-bent timbers, and this has remained standard boatbuilding practice for wood-built yachts under about 14 m (45 ft) to today. In building a hull for steam-bent framing, after the keel is laid and stem and sternpost erected, moulds, or patterns, cut to the shape and measurements on the designer's plan to fit inside the planking and spaced at their appropriate stations throughout the vessel, are erected and on each side thin lengths of wood (called splines) are temporarily screwed to the edges of the moulds, running from bow to stern and spaced roughly 15 to 23 cm (6 to 9 in.) apart. Each frame-timber is then made pliable by heating in a steam box, and while still boiling hot is smartly bent into shape on the inside of the splines, with its lower end fitting into a check slot already cut in the side of the keel. When all the timbers are thus in place and temporarily fastened to the splines, the splines are removed one

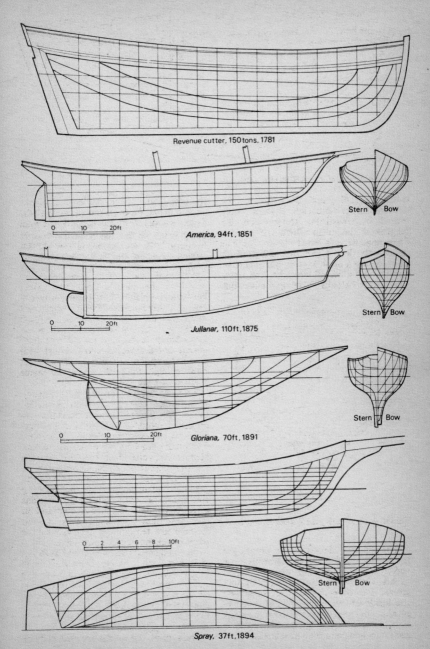

Revenue cutter, 150 tons, 1781

0   10   20 ft

Stern   Bow

America, 94 ft, 1851

0   10   20 ft

Stern   Bow

Jullanar, 110 ft, 1875

0   10   20 ft

Stern   Bow

Gloriana, 70 ft, 1891

0   2   4   6   8   10 ft

Stern   Bow

Spray, 37 ft, 1894

Evolution of yacht hulls

by one as the planks of the hull are laid in place, being fastened to the timbers by copper nails and rooves. Steam-bent timbering is suitable for either *carvel or *clinker (lapstrake) planking.

Modern developments. Developments in design and building techniques, together with the introduction of many new materials, have revolutionized yacht building since the Second World War. Water-resistant marine plywood, introduced during the war, opened up the possibilities for amateur builders to construct their own craft in back gardens, and numerous new designs were made available to yachtsmen to plank in plywood from small dinghies up to 12-m (40 ft) cruising yachts. Glass reinforced polyester (GRP) resins (see FIBRE GLASS) enabled all kinds of small vessels, from dinghies to 18-m (60 ft) yachts and even larger fishing boats and harbour craft, to be produced from a mould, identical in size and form and in large numbers. GRP production yachts in the United Kingdom, USA, France, Denmark, Sweden, and other yacht-building countries far outnumber boats built of wood, while other methods of construction such as cold-moulded laminates fixed with resin glue over a mould have produced many lightweight dinghies and yachts for racing. Other successful racing yachts have been constructed on the foam sandwich principle, the hull being formed over a mould from two GRP skins enclosing a centre core of polystyrene, balsa wood, or other very light material, the total weight being appreciably less than a similar hull of GRP or wood.

Added to other amateur home-building techniques is the *ferrocement or ferroconcrete boat, in which a closely knit framework of small-diameter steel pipes and 8-mm ($\frac{1}{4}$ in.) diameter reinforcing rods, criss-crossed at close spacing and wired at every joint to several layers of small size steel welded mesh, forms a strong and resilient hull of any size from about 8 m (25 ft) in length to 32 m (100 ft) or more, which is rendered homogeneous and water-tight by impregnation throughout with a fine mortar. Large numbers of yachts, fishing boats, and harbour launches have been built in ferrocement in many parts of the world, and in China sampans are made of it. Aluminium alloy is sometimes used for the hulls of racing yachts where speed is more important than cost. The principles of construction are the same as for a similar vessel in steel, but the considerably lower density of light alloy enables more ballast weight to be carried in the keel, so that the yacht can meet one of the racing designer's most important objectives—a favourable ballast-to-weight ratio. Like ship designers and builders, yachtsmen would welcome with open arms a light alloy which could be produced as cheaply as steel.

Recently wood has again become popular for the building of yacht hulls as a result of the Wood Epoxy Saturation Technique (WEST), a method of sealing wood to prevent the entry of water vapour. This has always been a drawback to the use of wood as a shipbuilding material as the entry of vapour can change the wood's shape and size and start to rot it. The sealing is done with a special self-levelling resin mixed with a hardener. The greatest strength of wood is tensile but the resin has greater strength in compression and it adds this quality to wood which has been treated with it.

yachting, the sport of racing or cruising in yachts under sail or power.

SAIL

Inshore racing. Although there are records of sailing races, or matches between two yachts, dating back to 1661, the sport of yacht racing did not begin to develop in a large way until the beginning of the 19th century. John Evelyn (Diary, 1 October 1661) was on board Charles II's yacht *Katherine* when the 1661 race was sailed on the Thames against the Duke of York's *Anne* over a course from Greenwich to Gravesend and back, and records that the King steered his yacht himself. Some records also exist of races in the 18th century organized by some of the clubs formed by members interested in sailing, particularly the Cork Harbour Water Club, later the Royal Cork Yacht Club, founded in 1720, and the Cumberland Society, later the Royal Thames Yacht Club, founded in 1775. Races were also sailed at Cowes, Isle of Wight, from 1780, but no yacht club was founded there until 1815.

The majority of yachts concerned in these early races were large vessels, mostly square-rigged, and sailed by professional crews. The usual practice was for an owner to issue a challenge, backing his yacht against any others with a substantial stake, which was rarely less than $100 and often very much more. Other owners would match his stake, and so the race would be sailed, the first yacht home taking the stake money. There was no form of handicap on size or sail area, and this was an encouragement to owners to build very large racing yachts, speed being closely related to size.

The first three decades of the 19th century saw the formation of many new yacht clubs round the coast of Britain, and most of them organized races for their members. Interest in the sport of yacht racing was slower to grow in other countries, with the possible exception of Holland; in the USA, for example, the New York Yacht Club was formed by nine local owners of yachts as late as 1844.

These early years of the 19th century saw racing yachts based very largely on the design of the revenue *cutters which, engaged in anti-smuggling duties, were in general the fastest vessels afloat. In addition to the hull design of the revenue cutters, racing owners also accepted their cutter *rig as being the most efficient. The rig consisted of a *jib set at the end of a long *bowsprit, a staysail, a *gaff mainsail laced to a *boom that extended several feet beyond the *counter, and upper and lower square topsails. Owners quickly discovered, however, that for their purpose it was unnecessary to build to the heavy *scantlings of the revenue cutters, and from about 1830 their yachts were built much lighter, though they still retained the typical revenue cutter design of a full forebody and a fine run aft. Since, in those years, there was still no proper system of handicapping, owners continued to build larger and larger in order to be able to spread a greater sail area. In 1830, for example, Joseph Weld's racing cutter Alarm, built at Lymington, had a measurement tonnage of 193. Other large yachts of the period were Lord Belfast's *brig Waterwitch of 331 tons and G. H. Ackers's *schooner Brilliant of 393 tons.

The naval architect J. Scott Russell drew attention in 1848 to the inefficiency of the standard yacht design of full forebody and fine run aft, known colloquially as the 'cod's head and mackerel tail' design, and produced an iron yacht, the Mosquito, with a long hollow bow and the maximum *beam well aft. She was a cutter of 50 tons, but the novelty of her design, in spite of her many successes in racing, aroused such acrimony and prejudice that only one other yacht was built to a similar design. It took

the visit of the yacht America to Cowes in 1851 to convince English owners that the old hull design needed changing. The America was a *schooner of 170 tons built in New York specially to race in English waters during the year of the great exhibition. She came in first in a race round the Isle of Wight to win a cup presented by the Royal Yacht Squadron, known ever since as the *America's Cup, and to father what is, perhaps, the best known series of races in the whole history of yachting. The novelty of her hull design was enhanced by the cut of her sails, which were of cotton and cut much flatter than the English sails of flax cut to produce a greater bagginess. For a time the America's success brought schooners into fashion, but it did not last for many years and the cutter soon came back into favour in Britain, and the *yawl rig also became popular. In the USA, however, the schooner remained the foremost racing rig right into the 1930s, and is still popular today as a yacht rig.

A large number of yachts were built all over the world during the latter half of the 19th century, more particularly in Britain, where both racing and cruising increased vastly in popularity. Many notable yachts were built, perhaps the most important from the point of view of racing design being the Jullanar, designed to his own ideas by E. H. Bentall, an agricultural engineer of Maldon, Essex. He built her himself on the Blackwater River in 1875 to have, in his own words, 'the longest waterline, the smallest frictional surface, and the shortest keel'. She proved phenomenally fast and during her racing life won more races than any other yacht. Her design was the direct forerunner of such famous yachts as King Edward VII's Britannia, built in 1893, Lord Dunraven's two Valkyries, and the magnificent Satanita, built for A. D. Clarke. In 1896 the Emperor of Germany had the huge cutter Meteor II, larger than the Britannia, built on the Clyde to designs by G. L. Watson, who in 1900 also produced the racing yawl Sybarita, the same size as Meteor II.

At almost exactly the same time Nathaniel Herreshoff was experimenting in the USA with hull forms for racing yachts. In 1891 he produced the Gloriana, which took America by storm. She was a small boat with a waterline length of 46 feet (14 m) but was completely different in hull form to anything yet seen in those waters. Built with very long overhangs at bow and stern, her forefoot was cut away to produce an entry that was almost a straight line from the stem to the bottom of the keel. It was a revolutionary design: and in every race in which she sailed that season there was never another yacht within striking distance of her. Herreshoff followed the *Gloriana* with the *Wasp* of an even more extreme design; a fin-keel type of boat with hard *bilges and a long narrow keel. Her racing successes stamped the Herreshoff design as an outstanding one for a purely racing yacht. He was commissioned to design and build racing boats for the big class, including a defender for the *America*'s Cup race of 1893, and of the two yachts he designed for that purpose, *Colonia* and *Vigilant*, the latter successfully defended the Cup against the challenge from Lord Dunraven's *Valkyrie II*.

By this time various *rating rules had been introduced on both sides of the Atlantic, systems of yacht measurement which enabled individual yachts to be given time allowances so that they could compete on more even terms with larger competitors. These formulae, based on certain measurements of a yacht such as her sail area and length, worked with varying degrees of success but often produced extreme types of yachts as designers strove to outwit the Rule then governing their designs. In America they produced the wide-beamed, lightly built 'skimming dish' which was to prove so unseaworthy. In Britain the narrow 'plank on edge' racing cutter, produced for an early Rule, was deemed equally undesirable, while later Rules encouraged yachts of inadequate draught, huge overhangs, and overlight construction. The *Universal Rule, developed by Nathaniel Herreshoff, helped counter the more extreme type of yacht in the USA and was adopted by most American yacht clubs around the turn of the century; while in Europe an international conference of thirteen European nations in London in 1906 adopted what has become known as the International Rule which produced the *International Metre Class Yachts. This taxed overhangs, eased the penalty on draught, and insisted that a yacht have adequate scantlings by being classed at Lloyds. To gain the maximum racing allowance under this new rule, new yachts were built that were not only habitable but were also excellent seaboats. This first International Rule, which, it was agreed, was to run for seven years, sparked off a new big racing class, which included such famous yachts as Sir Thomas Lipton's

Shamrock (not to be confused with any of his *America*'s Cup challengers), Myles Kennedy's *White Heather II*, and Sir James Pender's *Brynhild*, all constructed as 23-metres. Other classes constructed to this rule included 15-metre, 12-metre, 8-metre, and 6-metre yachts.

By 1911 the *Bermuda rig was beginning to be adopted for a few of the smaller racing and cruising yachts, particularly in the USA where research in *aerodynamics was demonstrating its improved efficiency over the gaff rig, but as yet the great majority of yachts, and all the big yachts, still retained the gaff rig. In Britain the cutter *Nyria* was the first of the big yachts to use the Bermudian rig—or Marconi rig as it was at first called—when the big class was resuscitated in 1920 by King George V announcing his intention of launching *Britannia* for that summer's regatta season. *Nyria* proved easily the most successful yacht that year against stiff opposition which included the new cutter *Terpsichore* and the schooner *Westward*.

The first International Rule had expired in 1914 and in 1920 a second one was introduced. The most important change it made was in the measurement of sail area, and it proved to be a watershed between the enormous spread of sail set pre-war and the more sparsely canvased yachts of the 1920s. The second International Rule was aimed at yachts that rated under 14½ metres, but a slightly modified one was also introduced for the bigger yachts. However, it was to the American Universal Rule that Lipton built his fourth challenger for the *America*'s Cup, the races taking place in 1920 instead of in 1914 as originally planned. *Shamrock IV* lost by three races to two and Lipton held out against making a fifth challenge until he felt that the challenging yacht could compete on more equal terms with the defender. One of the main stumbling blocks was that while the challenger had to be built sufficiently strongly to cross the Atlantic on her own bottom, at the time one of the conditions for challenging, the defender could be, and was, extremely lightly constructed as the Universal Rule did not require Lloyds scantlings. Change came slowly but in 1925 the North American Yacht Racing Union (N.A.Y.R.U.)was founded, the first national body the sport had had in the USA. This led to the Americans agreeing that large yachts had to conform to Lloyds scantlings and to their adopting the third International Rule, which came into force in 1928, for all yachts under 14½ metres, while the Europeans agreed to a number of changes to the International Rule to bring it more into line with American practices. However, for large yachts, like those which raced for the *America*'s Cup, each nation remained tied to its own rule until after the 1930 *America*'s Cup challenge, in which both sides raced in *J-class yachts, when Britain accepted a moderated form of the Universal Rule for all big class yachts.

While it was the big racing yachts which naturally attracted most public attention, the sport grew amazingly in popularity in the years which preceded and followed the First World War. A large number of yacht clubs produced their own classes of small racing yachts designed to the 1896 Linear Rating Rule which was modified in 1901. Known colloquially as 'raters', probably a hangover from the name by which the previous Rule rated a yacht, they were officially measured in feet, like the '30-footers' which raced very successfully for many years on the Clyde. France, Holland, Germany, the Scandinavian countries, and the USA also produced several classes of racing yachts, while on the other side of the world Australians and New Zealanders took to the sport in increasing numbers. International competition was provided at the big regattas, such as Cowes Week, Kiel Week, the Clyde fortnight, and many others, and also, from 1908, in the Olympic Games. From 1907 most of these international races were sailed in metre-class yachts, in which the existing rating rules had been accepted by the nations competing.

Many yacht clubs also introduced one-design classes, in which each boat in the class was built to exactly the same measurement and specification, including sails. They were introduced mainly as a test of a helmsman's skill, in which hull design had no place, but also partly to cater for the less wealthy yachtsmen who wanted to experience the excitement of racing. Most one-design classes were of small boats, some no larger than dinghies, but they filled a useful gap between the international metre classes and the other yachts which raced on handicap.

Racing yachts since the Second World War have seen the introduction of new materials and improved designs. Where mahogany or teak was, until about 1960, the prime material of which a yacht's hull was constructed, the introduction of materials such as marine plywood, glued laminates, and *fibre glass has subsequently revolutionized yacht building. *Ferro-cement, aluminium, and steel are also used for the hulls of racing yachts. As a result of aerodynamic research the traditional racing sail plan has similarly changed, with the main driving power being transferred from the mainsail to the fore triangle. Another postwar introduction into the racing scene has been the *catamaran and *trimaran, both of which are considerably faster than the conventional design of racing yacht, being capable of over 20 knots in favourable conditions.

It is not only in new materials for the hull that recent advances have been made; sails and running rigging are today almost universally made from man-made materials, such as *nylon or Terylene (see POLYESTER), instead of the traditional canvas and hemp, while mild-steel bars have replaced wire rope for the standing rigging in many racing and cruising yachts.

Offshore racing. Offshore racing and ocean racing have a long history. The first organized long-distance race was sailed in December 1866 from Sandy Hook, USA, to Cowes, England, and was contested by three schooners, *Henrietta*, *Fleetwing*, and *Vesta*. It was held under New York Yacht Club rules for a stake of 30,000 dollars for each yacht, winner take all. The winner was *Henrietta*. A second race across the Atlantic was held the following year from Queenstown, County Cork, to New York for the schooners *Dauntless* and *Cambria*, the *America*'s Cup challenger of that year. Several offshore races also took place in this era, including one from Dover to Liverpool in 1871, while the first Round Britain race was staged in 1887 by the Royal Thames Yacht Club to celebrate Queen Victoria's jubilee.

In 1897, in an attempt to lure British yachts to Kiel Week to make it a comparable attraction to Cowes Week, and also in honour of Queen Victoria's diamond jubilee, the German Emperor presented a trophy for a passage race from Dover to Heligoland, an event which became an annual competition up to 1908. The early organization of offshore racing, in fact, owes much to the German Kaiser who, at that time, and in the circumstances of the big programme of naval building which he was encouraging, was at pains to convince other countries that Germany was a truly maritime nation. During Kiel Week there were always a few offshore races for cruising yachts, and in 1905 he presented a trophy for a race across the Atlantic which attracted 11 starters.

Following this race, from Sandy Hook to the Lizard, which was won by the schooner *Atlantic* in 12 days, 4 hours, and 1 minute (a record which remained unbroken until 1980) the first of the Bermuda races, from New York to Bermuda, was held in 1906. The same year the first Transpac race, from Los Angeles to Honolulu, was also organized. Both remain major events in the ocean racing calendar, even though the former lapsed in 1910 and the latter in 1912 and they were not revived until 1923. The Cruising Club of America was formed in 1922 and it was the founding members of this organization who resuscitated the Bermuda race in 1923, and their example inspired a group of British yachtsmen to organize an ocean race of their own. A course from Cowes, round the Fastnet rock off south-west Ireland, and back to Plymouth, a distance of 605 miles, was decided upon and the first of what has become one of the most famous ocean races in the world was run in August 1925 with seven starters. At the end of that historic first race the Ocean Racing Club was founded, which six years later became the Royal Ocean Racing Club (R.O.R.C.), now the governing authority of offshore racing in Britain. The Bermuda race was held again in 1924 and then became biennial; the Fastnet was held annually until 1931 and then it, too, was raced every other year.

During the first few years of the Ocean Racing Club's existence competitors were mainly of a sturdy traditional cruising type, gaff cutter or yawl rigged with bowsprits, represented by such yachts as *Ilex*, a 20-ton yawl, *Altair*, a 14-ton cutter, *Penboch*, a 12-ton Breton-built cutter, and *Jolie Brise*, Commander E. G. Martin's 44-ton ex-French pilot cutter, which won the first Fastnet. For the second Fastnet race in 1926 William Fife designed and built a 50-ton racing Bermudian cutter, *Hallowe'en*, but almost without exception the entries for the early offshore races were cruising yachts which varied in both age and design. Then in 1931 the young American designer Olin Stephens brought over his 58-ft (18 m) yawl *Dorade*, and her resounding win in the Fastnet race that year, and in other events, brought about a new look in British yachts, and a faster, more sophisticated type of deep water racing yacht began to be developed during the 1930s.

Following the end of the Second World War, ocean racing started to become a major part of the yachting scene, and it largely took the place of the defunct big class racers of pre-war years, and from the late 1940s long-distance races were being organized in many parts of the world. Among the principal events which took place then, and which are still run today, were:

Newport–Bermuda, 660 miles, alternate years
Transpac, Los Angeles to Honolulu, 2,500 miles, alternate years
Sydney to Hobart, 690 miles, annually
Buenos Aires to Rio de Janeiro, 1,200 miles, every third year

But the best known and most prestigious ocean race is the Fastnet. It is sailed biennially, alternating with the Bermuda race. As well as the Fastnet the R.O.R.C. programme each year now includes a variety of offshore events in which several hundreds of yachts take part. In addition, through the efforts of the late Captain J. H. Illingworth RN, the Junior Offshore Group was formed in 1950 for less costly yachts, which are limited to between 16 and 24 feet (5–7 m) in waterline length and compete in races up to 250 miles. In the USA, the Midget Ocean Racing Club meets a similar demand.

Of major importance in ocean racing today is the series of races which form the competition for the *Admiral's Cup. It was instituted in 1957 by the R.O.R.C. to foster the sport of ocean racing in countries other than Britain and the USA, which had been the two most enthusiastic followers of the sport. It is sailed biennially between national teams of three yachts selected by the participating countries and consists of three short inshore races, the R.O.R.C.'s Channel race of 215 miles, and the Fastnet race. Other important ocean racing competitions include the One Ton Cup, an international challenge trophy put up by the Cercle de la Voile de Paris in 1965, and the success of this series has encouraged championships for Quarter Ton, Half Ton, Three-Quarter Ton, and Mini-Ton classes.

In order to provide a fair handicapping system to embrace offshore racing yachts of different size competing in the same race, a time correction factor is given to each yacht and applied to the elapsed time of completion of the course to produce a corrected time. This factor is based on measurements of the hulls, sail area, spars, and other features taken by officials of each national racing authority. See also RATING.

Besides the conventional offshore fixtures, a variety of other types of ocean racing have developed postwar. In the late 1950s Francis Chichester and 'Blondie' Hasler had a wager as to who could win in a single-handed race across the Atlantic east to west. The race, with three other competitors taking part, took place in 1960 and developed into a quadrennial race called simply the OSTAR (*Observer* Single-handed Trans Atlantic Race), sponsored by the *Observer* newspaper. This in turn spawned a huge number of single- and double-handed events, which includes regular events like the double-handed Round Britain race, the single-handed *Route du Rhum* from St. Malo to Guadaloupe, and the 'Around Alone' round-the-world race, fixtures which are almost entirely dominated by the *multi-hull racing yacht. The 'Around Alone' race is now run in stages, but the first single-handed round-the-world race, sponsored in 1969 by the *Sunday Times*, was non-stop and was won by Robin Knox-Johnston in his ketch *Suhaili* in a time of ten months and three days.

A third type of ocean racing far removed from the conventional offshore fixture is the inter-ocean crewed event like the Whitbread round-the-world race, which takes place every four years, and the one-off long distance crewed race organized and sponsored by a commercial organization to mark a centenary or something similar, but also to gain publicity for its products.

Racing rules. All yachts race under a set of rules drawn up by the International Yacht Racing Union (I.Y.R.U.), in which each country is represented by its national authority. These racing rules, last revised in 1989 and remaining in force until 1993, are based largely on the *International Regulations for Preventing Collisions at Sea (see RULE OF THE ROAD) internationally agreed to prevent the risk of collisions at sea, but differ from them in one or two respects applicable particularly in racing conditions. In cases where a strict application of the racing rules might present a risk of collision with another vessel which is, perhaps, proceeding through the area of the race, the Rule of the Road always takes precedence. When yachts are racing, they fly a square racing flag at the mainmast

head to indicate to other vessels that they are engaged in the race and are sailing under the I.Y.R.U. rules.

There are seventy-eight racing rules and they cover every aspect of yacht racing, including organization, starting signals, rights of way during the race, and adjudication of *protests. A yacht engaged in a race is bound by the racing rules from the time of the preparatory gun or signal before the start of her race until she crosses the finishing line at the end of the race. To be eligible to race in any event under I.Y.R.U. rules a yacht must have on board, as the owner or his representative, a member of a yacht club recognized by the national authority. The rules also govern the provision of lifebelts, signal flares, dinghy, *dan buoy, and other safety gear for yachts engaged in offshore races.

The actual sailing rules embody in general the Rule of the Road as it affects sailing vessels. Thus a yacht on the starboard tack has the right of way over a yacht on the port tack, a yacht to windward keeps clear of a yacht to leeward, and an overtaking yacht keeps clear of the yacht being overtaken. When two yachts approach each other on the same tack, the yacht with the wind free gives way to the yacht close-hauled.

Where the I.Y.R.U. rules differ from the Rule of the Road is in their application to yachts in close company. The main object of the Rule of the Road is to keep vessels well apart so that there is no risk of collision, but this is often not possible in highly competitive races where all the boats are set to sail the same course. So the I.Y.R.U. rules are designed not to keep the yachts apart but to govern their behaviour when in close company, indicating what additional duties or rights a yacht may have when in close competition with another.

If, during a race, one yacht is being overtaken to windward by another, she has the right under the racing rules to *luff up to windward to try to prevent the overtaking yacht getting past, and she may luff right up until she is head to wind if she likes. The overtaking yacht may not continue her course if to do so would entail any risk of collision, but must also luff to keep clear. If, however, the overtaking yacht has established an overlap by having her mast abeam of her opponent, which the helmsman signifies by a hail of 'mast abeam', then the yacht being overtaken must allow a free passage, and if her helmsman attempts to luff, a protest may be lodged.

a free passage, and if her helmsman attempts to luff, a protest may be lodged. And if during a race a yacht is being overtaken to leeward, the overtaking yacht must allow the yacht being overtaken plenty of room to keep clear. She may not luff up and crowd her opponent, and if she does so she will be disqualified if a protest is upheld by the race committee.

The I.Y.R.U. rules lay down procedures for rounding a mark of the course, where racing is likely to be at its closest with several yachts trying to round the the mark more or less simultaneously. Here the overlap rule is brought into play to prevent yachts being 'squeezed' between the mark and the yacht or yachts rounding it. If a yacht approaching a mark has established an overlap on the yacht ahead of her, that yacht must give her room to round the mark and may not alter course towards the mark to force the yacht with the overlap to give way. Similarly, if the overlapped yacht has herself an overlap on the yacht next ahead, she too can claim room to round the mark. This is a rule which is on occasions difficult to interpret and enforce as an overtaking yacht may not claim room between the yacht ahead of her and the mark if the yacht ahead obviously cannot give her room because she herself is rounding it inside other yachts in the race.

Another rule governs the occasions when two yachts on the same tack are approaching an obstruction or a shallow patch with insufficient depth of water for the yachts to pass safely over it. If the helmsman of the yacht nearer the dangers has insufficient room to *tack or *gybe without risk of a collision, he can oblige the other yacht to tack or gybe by calling 'water', but he must give the other y ht time to do so before he himself alters course away from the danger. But if the obstruction is a mark of the course, a yacht which has to tack to avoid it has no rights over a following yacht which is laying the mark correctly and she must keep clear.

Another I.Y.R.U. rule governs the rights of yachts at the start of a race. If a yacht is over the line when the starting gun is fired, she must return and recross the line before she can be considered as taking part in the race. And while she is doing so she loses all her rights under the I.Y.R.U. racing rules. She must keep clear of all the other yachts in the race, no matter what tack she may be on. Only when she has recovered the line and started correctly may she enjoy the rights under the racing rules.

A yacht which touches a mark of the course during a race must return and re-round the mark correctly (usually by going a full circle round it). Failure to do so results in automatic disqualification. During the manoeuvre she forfeits her usual rights of way with regard to others in the race.

The final section of the I.Y.R.U. rules covers the procedures for judging protests. A yacht which protests against another during a race must fly a *burgee or some similar piece of material in her *shrouds, and after the race must deliver a written protest to the race committee setting out the grounds of the protest. The protest is heard and judgement given as soon as possible after the end of the day's racing.

Cruising. The non-competitive side of yachting, where an owner sails a yacht designed to accommodate himself and his crew in tolerable comfort for a voyage which may last overnight or extend over several months or years, is generally known as cruising. In the years before the First World War (1914-18) some of the more popular types of cruising yacht were conversions from pilot cutters and fishing trawlers, well tried and strong vessels able to sail anywhere in the world, while several notable voyages, such as Captain Joshua Slocum's single-handed voyage round the world in the Spray in 1895-8, and Captain J. C. Voss's similar voyage in the Tilikum, 1901-4, gave a great impetus to the sport. Both these voyages were made in relatively small boats, the Spray having an overall length of 36 ft 9 in. (11 m) and a gross tonnage of nine tons, the Tilikum being even smaller, a dug-out canoe of red cedar with a tonnage less than a quarter of that of the Spray. Perhaps even more remarkable was the fact that both these voyages were achieved without any of the modern aids available to the cruising enthusiast today. Self-steering gear, radio direction finders and time signals, simplified navigational tables, purpose-built yachts, financial sponsorship, and modern food preservation techniques were all in the future when these voyages were made. Equally important in the birth of cruising as a sport were the writings of E. F. Knight, who cruised to the Baltic in a 29 ft (9 m) converted ship's lifeboat, and R. T. McMullen, whose cruises in British waters in small yachts opened the door for thousands of enthusiastic followers. All these had shown the possibilities of sailing very small yachts in safety over very long distances, and their examples inspired others to follow in their footsteps.

Before these pioneers had demonstrated what could be achieved in a small yacht, most owners who wanted to make extended cruises in their yachts had built big; some very big indeed. Lord Brassey's *Sunbeam*, which sailed round the world in 1876-7, was a three-masted auxiliary topsail schooner of 531 tons, and Lord Crawford's *Valhalla*, ship-rigged on three masts, had a tonnage of 1,490 and carried a professional crew of 100 men. These, however, were exceptions to the general rule, and few sailing cruisers were built above about 150 tons. As costs increased during the 20th century, the average size of cruising yachts became drastically smaller, and hulls were built in series to common designs. There was still latitude in the successful series design, however, for the individual owner to incorporate his own ideas of rig and accommodation below decks. A great advantage of series building was that production runs of the same design reduced the initial cost of purchase.

Traditional methods and materials of yacht building were largely superseded during the 1960s by new techniques, and the age-old shipwright's craft of building a vessel with selected woods became more of a rarity. Nowhere was this more in evidence than in yachts designed for cruising, and by 1972 more than 80 per cent of all new yachts and dinghies built in Britain, France, Holland, and the USA were of GRP moulded construction (see FIBRE GLASS).

The unprecedented growth of yachting as a sport since the Second World War has created many new conditions and new problems. Anchorages have become congested and rivers overcrowded as huge numbers of people have taken to boating in every form, and organized yacht harbours, or *marinas, have been, and are still being, built in America, Britain, and other countries where yachting is a popular sport.

One of the most notable aspects of yachting in the postwar years was the immense growth in long-distance voyaging made practicable with the well-designed and properly equipped modern cruising yacht with her *self-steering gear. *Sopranino*, a lightly constructed 20-foot (6 m) sloop and forerunner of the Junior Offshore Group class, crossed the Atlantic with a crew of two in 1952, while *Borer Bee*, a 24-foot (7 m) plywood *chine sloop with

*bilge keels, was sailed from Singapore, where her owner had built her, to England, via the Red Sea and the Mediterranean, in 1958. In recent decades yachtsmen have achieved even more remarkable voyages. In 1966 Francis Chichester set out alone in his 53-ft (16.3 m) ketch, *Gipsy Moth IV*, to beat the average passage time of the fully manned *clipper ships which in the previous century plied between England and Australia, reaching Sydney from Plymouth in 107 days. He then went on to complete the circumnavigation in the remarkable time of 274 days, 48 of which had been spent in Sydney, an achievement for which he was knighted on his return home. Perhaps even more remarkable was the fact that during the passage to Australia he had celebrated his 65th birthday. Other yachtsmen like David Lewis and Tristan Jones have striven to set new records or break old ones by attempting to circumnavigate Antarctica, sail to the source of the Amazon, or penetrate to northern latitudes never previously reached under sail. Women, too, have achieved some outstanding voyages with Nicolette Milne-Walker crossing the Atlantic single-handed nonstop in 1970 and Naomi James circumnavigating the world alone non-stop in 1978, a feat for which she was created a Dame of the British Empire. Nowadays, with such individuals to inspire them, many yachtsmen and yachtswomen of all ages, from teenagers to grandmothers, set off alone or as a family on voyages which not so long ago would have been astounding if not unthinkable.

POWER

With the adaptation of the steam engine as a means of ship propulsion during the first quarter of the 19th century, it was only to be expected that some yachtsmen should look to this new means of propulsion as an expression of their individuality. A steam yacht, as well as being more popular with the ladies, who in general preferred the stately progression available with the steam engine to the hurly-burly of sail, and also being far more conducive to the lavish entertaining of the period, was an outward expression of wealth and leisure that appealed greatly to the rich owner of the 19th century. Most of the large steam yachts of that century were fitted out with extreme luxury, with heavy carving and panelling, thick carpeting, and large staterooms equipped with every conceivable convenience.

Like most innovations, the introduction of power in yachts had a difficult birth, and in May 1827 the Royal Yacht Club (it became the Royal Yacht Squadron in 1833) passed a resolution that the 'object of this club is to promote seamanship to which the application of steam is inimical, and any member applying steam to his yacht shall be disqualified hereby and shall cease to be a member'. Two years later, angry at what he considered an unreasonable ban on individual freedom, Thomas Assheton-Smith resigned from the club and built the 400-ton *Menai*, in which he installed a steam engine and paddle-wheels. She was the first steam yacht to be built in Britain. The first steam yacht built in the USA was the *North Star*, a large paddle yacht of 1,876 gross tons built for Commodore Cornelius Vanderbilt in 1853.

Early steam yachts were all paddlers, usually fitted with one or two oscillating or walking beam engines and fire-tube boilers. With the introduction of the *propeller in the decade 1840–50, the power plant changed to the single-stage reciprocating engine, being replaced by the compound engine in the 1860–70 period, and by the triple expansion engine about ten years later. Water-tube boilers began to be installed in some yachts around 1865, but it was not until Sir Alfred Yarrow invented the three-drum type of water-tube boiler in 1889 that the older fire-tube boiler was finally discarded.

The first yacht to have turbines fitted in her was the *Turbinia*, built by Sir Charles Parsons in 1897 to demonstrate his new invention at the Naval Review held at Spithead to celebrate the diamond jubilee of Queen Victoria. She had three turbines giving direct drive to three propeller shafts, which each had three propellers mounted on them, and the three turbines developed a combined horsepower of 2,000. On the occasion of the Naval Review she achieved the remarkable speed, for that period, of over 30 *knots. But in general, except in the very largest yachts, the turbine proved unsuitable as a power plant, since to reach its maximum efficiency it needed to revolve at a rate too great to be used for direct drive to the propellers. Reduction gear was costly and noisy, and geared turbines, equally costly, gave poor manoeuvrability in small vessels. As a result, very few yachts, and those only the largest, adopted turbines in place of the triple expansion steam engine.

Steam had no rival as a reliable power in pleasure craft until about 1885, when launches fitted with an engine using naphtha gas in place of coal and water in the boiler appeared in numbers in British waters as well as in the USA. Fires, however, were a frequent occurrence, and when a few years later the more compact, if noisy, internal combustion petrol (gasoline) engine was introduced for boat propulsion, the naphtha launch disappeared.

Impromptu racing had long taken place between privately owned steam launches and yachts, and while in Britain Thornycroft and Yarrow were building fast launches, whose design later developed into these firms' naval torpedoboats and destroyers, in America the Herreshoff Company had introduced for wealthy businessmen living on Long Island Sound a series of lightly constructed steam yachts with small high-speed power plants capable of speeds up to 20 knots. As the petrol engine grew in power and reliability from the turn of the century, motor-boat racing became more popular and in 1905 there was held the first of the London-to-Cowes races which were to become an annual event until the outbreak of the First World War in 1914. The competing boats were still of the slender traditional round-*bilge type, but after the introduction of the Thornycroft torpedo-carrying coastal motor boats during the war, a faster design of boat was evolved, and some phenomenal speeds were attained.

Steady improvement in the power-to-weight ratio of high speed marine oil engines also enabled diesel-powered craft to compete in the principal racing events at sea, including the offshore races from Cowes to Torquay held annually from 1961. Reliability of modern power boats has made even longer courses practicable, and in the London to Monaco fourteen-stage race in 1972, eleven boats completed the 2,700-mile course out of twenty starters.

Outboard motors, compact portable power units which are clamped to the boat's stern, began to revolutionize the yachting scene with the sudden growth of boating from 1950. Ranging from easily carried units rated at 3 horsepower up to monster four-cylinder engines giving over 80 horsepower for racing boats, the outboard motor is found on all types of fun boat, small cabin cruiser, and mobile houseboat.

In some cases where boats are to be used in very shallow or weed- infested rivers a

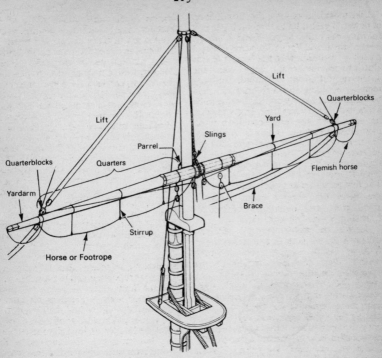

Yard

water jet propulsion unit is installed. In this an engine-driven impeller draws water through the bottom forward and ejects it in a powerful stream out at the stern. Gas turbine jets, introduced by a British company for fast naval motor gunboats, have also been a subject for experiment in private craft designed for water-speed record breaking.

yankee, a light-weather foresail used in yachts, set on the topmast stay with its *luff extending almost the whole length of the stay. It is similar to a *genoa but cut narrower, with its *leech not overlapping the *mainsail as does that of a genoa, and with its *clew higher than is normally the case with genoas. A yankee can be used in winds of up to about force 4 on the *Beaufort scale. See also GHOSTER.

yard, (1) a large wooden or metal spar crossing the *masts of a ship horizontally or

diagonally, from which a sail is set. Yards crossing the masts of a square-rigged ship horizontally are supported from the mastheads by *slings and *lifts and are held to the mast by a *truss or *parrel. Square sails are laced by their *heads to a jackstay on the top of the yards. By means of *braces, the yards can be turned at an angle to the fore-and-aft line of the vessel in order to take the greatest advantage of the wind direction in relation to the required *course. When a yard crosses a mast diagonally, it is known as a *lateen yard and is not supported by braces but hoisted by a *halyard attached to a point on the yard about one-third of its length from the forward end. **(2)** A shortened form of the word dockyard, in which vessels are built or repaired.

yardarm, the outer quarters of a *yard, that part which lies outboard of the *lifts, on either side of the ship, i.e., the port and starboard yardarms. They were the positions in a square-rigged ship where most of

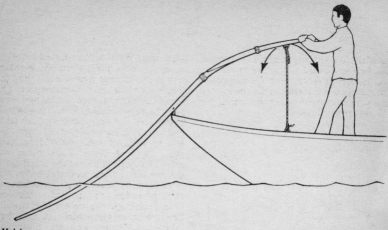

Yuloh

the flag signals were hoisted, and in the older days of sail, when the disciplinary code on board included punishments of death by hanging, were the traditional points from which men were hanged on board.

yardman, see TOPMAN.

yaw, to, fail to hold a straight *course, the effect on a ship's course produced by a following wind or sea. With the vessel travelling through the water in the same direction as the sea is running or the wind blowing, the effect of the *rudder is diminished and the vessel yaws away from the desired course. A good helmsman can often anticipate the moment when a vessel is most likely to yaw, and correct the tendency to do so by applying the requisite *helm to counteract it. The word is also used as a noun to denote the involuntary movement caused by wind or sea by which a ship deviates from her chosen course. A yaw can also be caused by unintelligent steering.

yawl, a type of rig of a small sailing boat or yacht, apparently an adaptation of the Dutch word *jol*, skiff. The true yawl rig consists of two masts, *cutter-rigged (in the English meaning of the term) on the foremast, with a small *mizen-mast *stepped abaft the *rudder-head carrying a *spanker or driving sail. The term, however, refers more to the positions of the masts than the particular rig they carry, and thus a sailing boat with masts stepped

as above but *sloop-rigged on the foremast would also be termed a yawl. The rig is very similar to that of a *ketch, the difference being the position in which the mizen is stepped. In a ketch, the mizen is stepped forward of the rudder-head; in a yawl it is stepped abaft it.

yoke, a transverse board fitted to the top of a *rudder in a small boat instead of a *tiller, the rudder being moved by yoke lines attached to the ends of the yoke and operated by the helmsman. Yokes are mainly to be found in small boats which are pulled by oars; and very occasionally in small, open sailing craft where the position of a mizen or *jigger-mast makes the operation of a tiller impossible.

yuloh, a form of long *oar or *sweep used by Chinese boatmen over the stern to propel *sampans and the smaller *junks. It is usually made in two parts, either *scarfed and pegged or lashed together, giving the yuloh a distinct bow which causes the blade to be very whippy or flexible. It is mounted loosely over a peg on the boat's stern, and the forward or inboard end is attached to the deck by a length of line, allowing the end to be roughly waist high, while the outboard end with the blade enters the water at an angle of about 30 degrees. By alternately pushing and pulling the inboard end of the yuloh athwartships the sampan man or girl causes the blade to flex from side to side in the water with a fish's tail or *sculling action, and so drives the sampan forward.

Z

zenith, in nautical astronomy the point in the heavens immediately above an observer on the surface of the earth. A line through the centre of the earth and the observer on its surface points directly to his zenith. See NAVIGATION, Celestial.

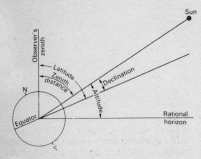

Zenith distance

zenith distance, the angle between an observer's *zenith and an observed celestial body subtended at the earth's centre. It is the complement of the true *altitude of a celestial body, and forms one side of the astronomical triangle, the basis of astronomical navigation at sea.

zone times, the division of the world by meridians of *longitude into zones and sectors where the same time is kept, particularly in ships at sea. The sun crosses each meridian of longitude at its local noon; four minutes later it reaches the next degree of longitude and crosses it also at its local noon. Without some agreed system of time, all clocks in the world would therefore show different times according to the longitude of the place where they are. The world therefore has been divided into zones of 15 degrees of longitude within which all clocks keep the same time. The sun takes one hour to cross 15 degrees of longitude, and so adjacent zones differ from each other by one hour. Zone times are measured east and west of the longitude of Greenwich (0°), and are designated as plus or minus as to whether the zone difference must be added or subtracted to the local time to indicate the time at Greenwich. Zones east of Greenwich are therefore minus, and zones west are plus. The longitude of 180°, where Zones + 12 and − 12 meet, is known as the *international dateline. Zone times were introduced in 1918.

Z-twist, see S-TWIST.

zulu, a type of fishing vessel peculiar to the north-east coastal ports of Scotland. It had a broad-beamed *carvel hull with a straight stem and a pointed stern with a pronounced rake, at times as much as 45°. These boats were rigged with a dipping *lug foresail and a standing lug mizen. they were introduced by a boat-bulder named Cameron as an improvement on local types of fishing craft and were first produced during the Zulu War (1878–9), hence their name. The introduction of the internal combustion engine has rendered the type obsolete.